Henry R. Hellier

E.M. Cross and Co.'s Baltimore City Business Directory

1863-1864

Henry R. Hellier

E.M. Cross and Co.'s Baltimore City Business Directory
1863-1864

ISBN/EAN: 9783337257064

Printed in Europe, USA, Canada, Australia, Japan

Cover: Foto ©Suzi / pixelio.de

More available books at **www.hansebooks.com**

E. M. CROSS & CO.'S

ALTIMORE CITY

BUSINESS DIRECTORY,

1863–64.

COMPILED BY

HENRY R. HELLIER.

PUBLISHED ANNUALLY.

E. M. CROSS & CO.—PUBLISHERS,
110 W. BALTIMORE ST., BALTIMORE, MD.

BRANCH OFFICES:

337 CHESTNUT STREET, PHILADELPHIA, PA.

335 BROADWAY, NEW YORK.

13 TREMONT ROW, BOSTON, MASSACHUSETTS.

PRICE, ONE DOLLAR AND FIFTY CENTS.

CAUTION.

. ALL persons authorized to collect moneys, receive subscriptions, or act as our agents in any way or manner for this work, are furnished with a PRINTED AUTHORITY, setting forth the nature and extent of such power. Any persons not so provided are NOT our agents.

E. M. CROSS & CO., PUBLISHERS,

110 W. *Baltimore Street.*

PREFACE.

THE publishers, on presenting to the Public the present volume of the "Baltimore City Business Directory" (being the first edition published by them), beg to thank the business men of Baltimore for the liberal support bestowed thereon, and trust that the work will meet with their approval. The labor and expense which have been bestowed in obtaining the names of our business men have been very great through the influence of Mr. Woods, the publisher of the City Directory, who took upon himself the *personal* trouble of going amongst our business men and informing them that this was an outside arrangement, and requesting them not to subscribe thereto; notwithstanding the drawbacks, we believe that this Directory is the best ever published in Baltimore, at all events, from the number of our subscribers we feel proud to say that a great need has been felt by the business men of Baltimore for a reliable Business Directory.

We shall continue the work annually, *and publish it annually*, and with acquaintance hope that we shall receive your cordial support. We will here take occasion to say that all persons authorized to act as agents for this work are furnished with a PRINTED certificate of authority, signed by the publishers, a reference to which will, at all times, protect the public from fraud.

Our experience in the Directory business is second to none, and we hope by strict attention to the wants of the public to always receive their patronage.

Respectfully,

E. M. CROSS & CO., *Publishers.*

August 25, 1863.

INDEX TO ADVERTISEMENTS.

1*

INDEX.

2

E. M. CROSS & CO.'S
BALTIMORE CITY
BUSINESS DIRECTORY,
1863–64.

ABBREVIATIONS.

N north; S south; E east; W west; ct court; av avenue; al alley; la lane; c corner; mkt market; wbf wharf; bet between; L little.

Academies, Dancing.
Buckingham P. G., 123 Mulberry
Lehmann Edward G., St. Paul c Centre
Russell H. J., 29 N Gay
Spies Chas. L., 1 S Charles

Accountants.
GLOCKER & NORRIS, 63 W Fayette

Agencies, Commercial and Mercantile.
Blick T. H., 36 Second
Pratt J. D. & Co., c Baltimore and S Charles

Agents, Advertising.
CROSS E. M. & CO., 110 W Baltimore; Wilmington, Del.; 337 Chestnut, Philad'a; 335 Broadway, New York, and 13 Tremont Row, Boston, Mass.; advertisements inserted in any paper in the U. S. and Canada at publisher's prices.

Agents, Book.
Sheehy James, 15 St. Paul

Agents, General.
Davis John W., 41 St. Paul
Demuth G. O. & Co., 55 W Fayette
Lipscomb Philip D., 18 S Calhoun, Colonization Agent
Pittman Edward, 9 North

Agents, Insurance.
(*See* INSURANCE AGENTS.)

Agents, Land.
(*See* LAND Co's.)

Agents, Property and Collecting.
(*See also* COLLECTORS.)
Bride John H., 129 W Madison
Davis G. W., 61 W Fayette

Garritee Wm. L., 61 W Fayette

GLOCKER & NORRIS, 63 W Fayette

GRIFFIN THOMAS W., 170 S Broadway

Scharfe Wm., 67 W Fayette

Weil A., 236 Canton av

Agents, Pension and Claim.

Baudel M. L. & Co., 30 Second

COLTON GEO & CO., 28 Second. AGENTS AND ATTORNEYS for SOLDIERS, THEIR WIDOWS, and ORPHANS; PENSION BOUNTY, and all other claims, collected promptly, and for a small commission. (REGULARLY LICENSED by the GOVERNMENT.)

Forrester Allen E., 28 St. Paul

Lotridge S. C. A., 20 Second

Murray & Jones, 22 Second

PFERDNER PAUL & CO.,

OFFICE

28 SECOND STREET,

(UP STAIRS.)

ARMY AND NAVY

AGENTS

For GOVERNMENT CLAIMS, PENSIONS, BOUNTY, BOUNTY LAND, BACK PAY, CLOTHING, &c. &c. (*Authorized by the U S. Government*). Orders from abroad promptly attended to. Particular attention paid to German orders.

Ringrose Col. J. W., 29 N Howard

Willie J. & Co., Sun Iron Building, Baltimore c South

Agents, Real Estate.

(*See also* BROKERS, REAL ESTATE, *also* CONVEYANCERS.)

COLTON GEO. & CO., PROPERTY AGENTS and GENERAL COL-

LECTORS, *office* 28 Second, nearly opposite the Post-office. We collect House rents, Ground rents, and individual claims generally. *Our motto* is, speedy collections, prompt returns, and moderate charges. Please give us a call.

Colton Wm., 51 W Fayette

GORSUCH PEREGRINE, 32 St. Paul

Gross John I., 17 St. Paul

HARVEY J. W., 22 Second, REAL ESTATE and GROUND RENT BROKER

HILL THOMAS, S W c St Paul and Fayette. (See card under CONVEYANCERS.)

LIVEZEY E., 48 W Lexington

Reid T. N., 71 W Fayette

ROGERS HENRY W., c Charles & Fayette. REAL ESTATE PURCHASED, SOLD, OR EXCHANGED. FARMS, MILLS, COUNTRY SEATS, COTTAGES, CITY HOUSES, BUILDING LOTS, AND GROUND RENTS FOR SALE OR EXCHANGE.

SNOWDEN P. M., 83 W Fayette

Snowden Samuel, 83 W Fayette

Tinges Geo. W, St. Paul c Bank la

WALKER JOHN M., AGENT FOR THE PURCHASE AND SALE OF REAL ESTATE, GROUND RENTS, &c. &c., has now for sale, Farms, Country Seats, Dwelling Houses, Ground Rents, &c.

Young John, 17 St. Paul

Agricultural Implement Manufacturers and Warehouses.

(*See also* SEEDSMEN.)

BRUSTER & GRIFFITH, 49 N Paca. MANUFACTURERS OF THE BUCKEYE MOWER & REAPER.

CHAPMAN N. P.

MARYLAND

AGRICULTURAL

Implement House,

145 W. PRATT, OPPOSITE MALTBY HOUSE.

CROMWELL RICHARD, 46 & 48 Light. (*See advertisement.*)
Edwards E. G., 90 S Charles
HARDING WILLIAM H., 33 Grant and 11 Hollingsworth, op Light. MANUFACTURER OF PLOUGHS, AGRICULTURAL IMPLE-MENTS, &c.
HEATH F. W., 2 Gillingham al, r 44 S Howard. (Ploughs.)
MONTGOMERY J. & BRO., 155 N High, Inventors and Manufacturers of their Double Screened Rockaway Wheat Fan. Manufactured and for sale at 155 N High.
Mott A. G., 40 Ensor
NORRIS THOMAS, 141 W Pratt
Ray Francis, 505 W Pratt
Sinclair R. J. & Co., 62 Light

Whiteman E. & Sons,

22 & 24 S. CALVERT,

Manufacturers and Dealers in all kinds of

AGRICULTURAL IMPLEMENTS, SEEDS, FERTILIZERS, &c.

Alcohol Works.

(*See also* CAMPHENE ; *also* DISTIL-LERS.)
Baily James, 97 W Lombard

McNEAL & JONES, 34 S Calvert, DEALERS IN COAL OIL, GREASING & LUBRICATING OILS, ALCOHOL, &c.

Ale and Porter.

(*See also* BOTTLERS.)
PIER G. W. & CO., Hanover c Baltimore
COUGHLAN WILLIAM, 169 and 171 Central av
WALSH EDMOND, 29 S Frederick

Amusements, Places of.

Baltimore Museum, Geo. Lea, Proprietor, S Calvert and Baltimore
Front St. Theatre. Front, bet Gay and Low, Geo. Kunkel, Lessee
Holiday St. Theatre, Holiday bet Fayette and Lexington, J. T. Ford, Lessee
Maryland Institute, Centre Market Space and Baltimore
Melodeon Concert Saloon, I E Baltimore

Appraisers, Local.

Meredith J. F., Lombard c Gay
Nicholls Wm. S , Lombard c Gay
Wagner J. F., Lombard c Gay

Architects.

(*See also* ENGINEERS CIVIL ; *also* SURVEYORS; *also* CARPENTERS & BUILDERS.)
Andrews R. S. N., 147 W Baltimore
Beldin James, 13 North
Caldwell Wm. Q , 85 W Fayette
Dixon Thomas, 117 Baltimore
Harris Samuel, 141 W Fayette
Husband J. J., 9 North
LIND F. G., ARCHITECT AND SUPERINTENDENT, c Charles and Fayette sts., entrance on Fayette
Neilson J. Crawford, 39 N Charles
Reasin W. H., Sun Building, Baltimore c South

*Army and Navy Pension Offices.

COLTON GEO. & CO., 28 Second
PFERDNER PAUL & CO., 28 Second

Artificial Flowers.

BELL, JOHN,

MANUFACTURER OF

ARTIFICIAL FLOWERS,

130 W Lexington, bet Howard and Park.

BROWN M. & S., 243 W Baltimore, up stairs
Marcusi M., 146 W Lexington
Shaffner Mrs. S., 74 W Baltimore
Toldridge Mrs. E., 191 W Baltimore

Artificial Limb Maker.

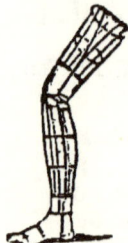

REINHARDT H. D.,

206 W. Pratt.

Artists.
(*See also* PHOTOGRAPHERS.)

Dreyer E., 152 W Fayette
Harley James K., cor Charles and Fayette
Johnson John R., 147 W Baltimore
RUDOLPH E., 125 W Baltimore, begs leave to inform the Public and Profession that he is still prepared to retouch Photographs in Oil, Water Colors, or in Pastel and India Ink

Artists' Materials.

DODGE GEORGE R. & CO., 42 W Baltimore
RODENMAYER JOHN, 51 N Paca
Depot of Artists, Grainers, Paint-

ers, Drawing Materials, and every variety of Pictures for Studies or Framing
Scobell Mrs. H., 79 Lexington

Auctioneers.
(*See also* MERCHANTS, COMMISSION.)

Adreon & Co., 22 S Charles
Bennett F. W. & Co., 28 and 30 S Charles
CLARK LEWIS & CO. (Marble Building), 184 W Baltimore. op Light, AUCTIONEERS AND COMMISSION MERCHANTS, and dealers in Cutlery, Plated-Ware, Watches, Jewelry, Stationery, Sutler's Goods, &c.
Gibson & Co., 7 N Charles
GOVER SAMUEL H., AUCTION-EER AND COMMISSION MER-CHANT, 84 W Baltimore
Hamilton William, 64 and 66 S Charles

RICHARDS JOHN P. & CO.,

AUCTIONEERS,

For the sale of

HORSES, CARRIAGES, HARNESS, &c.,

No. 55 GERMAN STREET,
Between Howard and Eutaw Sts.,
BALTIMORE.

Regular Sales by Auction every Wednesday and Saturday Morning, at 10 o'clock.
Cash advances made on Carriages, &c., consigned for Auction.
Storage for Carriages, and Horses taken at Livery.
JOHN PFISTER.   J. P. RICHARDS.

SOPER SAM'L J. & CO., 42 and 44 S Charles c Lombard, General Auctioneers and Commission Merchants.
TAYLOR & GARDNER, 8 German

Awning Makers.

HAMBLETON THOMAS B., 6 Bowly's whf

LOANE J. W., 67 W Pratt, AWNING MAKER. SAILS FOR BOATS, AMERICAN AND BUSINESS FLAGS OF ALL NATIONS, AWNINGS, TENTS, WAGON AND CANAL BOAT COVERS

MULLER LOUIS, 110 W Baltimore. (See advertisement opposite Upholsterers.)

Axle Grease.

AMMIDON & CROMBIE, 337 W Baltimore and 52 German. (See advertisement interleaved opposite Oil.)

CRESCENT COAL OIL CO. OF BALTIMORE, 62 S Gay. (See advertisement interleaved opposite Oil.)

GARDNER WM. G. & CO., 1 S Liberty. (See advertisement opposite Oil.)

HAMILL R. W. & CO., 64 Hanover

HARDESTER & BOKEE, 321 W Baltimore n Howard. (See advertisement opposite Oil.)

RICHARDSON & CO., 26 S Calvert c Mercer. (See advertisement interleaved opposite Oil.)

Bags and Bagging.

Baltimore Bag Factory,

JOHN C. GRAFFLIN,

Nos. 75 and 77 South.

Bags, Bagging. Sail Ducks, Russia Bolt Rope, Manilla Cordage, &c.

LOANE J. W., 67 W Pratt, MANUFACTURER OF ALL KINDS OF BAGS, AWNINGS, &c.

MARYLAND BAG FACTORY. S. H. DUNGAN, Proprietor, c South and Pratt Sts, Baltimore. MANUFACTURER AND DEALER IN BAGS AND BAGGING OF ALL KINDS. SECOND HAND BAGS BOUGHT AND SOLD

Bakers.

Ahlers Henry, 180 Centre mkt

Alice Mary E., Bell Air mkt

Arnold G. W., 120 W Fayette and 94 N Howard

Arthur H., 53 N Eutaw and Lexington mkt

Babbe John D., 68 S Charles and Lexington mkt

Baepler Henry, Lexington mkt

Bast John, 98 E Lombard

Bechtold John, 185 E Pratt

Bensel K., 139 S Wolf

Berder T., Lexington mkt

Berger George, 493 W Lombard

Beste Hammond, 46 Gough

Black Daniel, 413 Light

Black Jacob, 74 Columbia

Bohne H., 3 Leadenhall

Bossle Chas., 5 E Pratt

Brende J. G., 83 Warner

Brill John, 157 Centre mkt

Brown George, Lexington mkt

Brown Jacob, 178 Columbia

Bruehl Justus, Bank c Bond

Bucking Francis, 31 Hollis mkt

Bunn John, Barre c Warner

Burkamp F., 149 N Eutaw

Caulk Susanna, 278 S Ann

Clasz John George, 239 Light

Connolly John, 22 S Fremont

Corcoran Jos., 3 S Paca

Craft Henry, 81 Harrison

Dailey James, 751 W Baltimore

Deibel Peter, 724 W Baltimore

Deists Martin, 225 W Fayette

Deist Wm., 34 S Poppleton

Deitz George, Gough c Ann

Dexter C., 136 W Lexington

Dickerson M. J., 19 Aisquith

4*

Dietrich Wm., 82 Fell's Point mkt
Dietrich Wm., 279 Canton av
Dippell Mrs. E., 102 N Fremont
Doyle Mrs. Jane, 32 Camden
Eckert F., 36 S Republican
Eldridge Robert, 106 E Pratt
Elwich Joseph, 314 W Pratt
Emmel August, 86 Pearl
England Mrs. M., 228 N Gay
Finley Thomas, 230 W Saratoga
Fink Henry, 77 Fell's Point mkt
Frances S., Ann c Gough
Frank Jacob, 248 Hanover
Franz Ferdinand, 35 N Register
Fredericks Henry, 8 S Ann
Frine Chas., 51 Hollins' mkt
Garver W., 238 Columbia
Gebhart John, 9 L Paca
German Chas. F., 33 N Frederick
Getteman Louis, Bell Air mkt
Gillen William, 90 Holiday
Gilmour, A. M., 239 W Pratt
Glass Geo., Lexington mkt
Glasser Frederick, 113 S Dallas
Gossman J., 63 Ensor
Greenabaum E., 193 Eager
Greenhood Adam, 80 Harrison
Griegett Wm. G., 72 Leadenhall
Gromester John, 63 Fell's Point mkt
Grossman George, 23 Penn av
Hainke August, 51 President
Haln Frederic, 39 Fell's Point mkt
Horners Ernest, 298 Canton av
Hawkins Mrs. Sarah, 274 Light
Heath Ann, Bell Air mkt
Hebbells G., Orleans c Spring
Helig William. Lexington mkt
Helptz Mr., Fell's Point mkt
Herbst H., 193 Gough
Hess Mrs. C., 58 Union
Hessenauer John, 153 Eastern av
Higgins Ellen, 81 Second
Hoffmeister Philip, 29 Bank
Horst Conrad, 191 S Caroline and
   Fell's Point mkt
Jackseh T., Canton av c Washington
Jacobi Wm., 3 N High
JEANNERET L. P. & CO., 163 N
   Eutaw, FRENCH BAKERY.

ALL ORDERS PROMPTLY ATTEND-
ED TO.
Jockel Martin, 204 S Sharp and
   Lexington mkt
John Charles, 235 Alice Anna
Jolck John, Fell's Point mkt
Jones Paul, 75 Fell's Point mkt
Kaffman Frederick, Bell Air mkt
Kammer William, 324 S Sharp
Kaufman Jas., Lexington mkt
Kaufmann G., 408 N Gay
Kelley H., 104 Richmond
Kemp Ann, 81 Fell's Point mkt and
   106 Centre mkt
Kindewater Christ'n, 192 S Charles
Klingelhefer John E. 266 S Eutaw
Knarr M., 400 Canton av
Kotchler Lewis, Bell Air mkt
Kratry John, Carlton c Vine
Kratz John, Lexington mkt
Krupf Frederick, 329 S Bond
Kuhl Fred., 652 Light
Kullmann Adolph, 54 President
Lamotte Louis, 148 Centre mkt
Lange F. C., 88 Fell's Point mkt
Lauster John D., 96 N Caroline
Lehman Henry, 401 Light
Leman Louis, 138 Henrietta
Lembach Jacob, 166 Ensor
Lemster E., 138 Centre mkt
Limberger Jacob, Bell Air mkt
Lourmann M., 239 S Sharp
McCoulray Geo., 193 E. Lombard
McGuire Mrs. Jane, 56½ N Howard
Mechanical Bakery Co., King c.
   Howard
Medinger S. M., 164 Forrest
Melcher C., 58 Johnston
Mellis Martin, 102 Fell's Point mkt
Messersmith Jacob, 137 S Fremont
Messner George, N E c Gay & Chew
Miller Jacob, 230 N Caroline
Mueller John, 234 Alice Anna
Muhr John Henry, 65 Fell's Point
   mkt
Mull John H., 2 Gist
Muller Anna, Lexington mkt
Neiling P., Ramsey c Poppleton
Nichols John, 188 Centre mkt

Ossa Sophia, 33 Hollins mkt
Paff Fred., 145 Centre mkt
Pepersack Joseph, 305 Aisquith
Peters H., 275 Eastern av
Peters L. M., 91 Thames
Peters Wm. G., S Eden c Pratt
Plitt Charles, 246 S Charles
Plumhoff Henry, 262 Alice Anna
Polley Charles, 72 S Charles
Protzman S., 11 New
Rapp Henry, Lexington mkt
Reis David, 68 N Schroeder
Renwer D., 274 S Sharp
Requa & Co., 452 & 454 W Baltimore
Reus Ph., 44 S Republican
Rice John, 14 Warner
Roach J., 124 N Gay
Ropp Henry, 223 Centre mkt
Roth Peter, Lexington mkt
Rubert D , Lexington mkt
Rudolph A., 338 Canton av
Rudolp Francis, 31 N Frederick
Rullman Charles, Jefferson N E c
    Spring
Saffen C. F., Lexington mkt
Schaffer M., 21 S Wolf
Schaible C. F.. 535 W Baltimore
Scherlf M., 315 S Charles
Schillinge George, 280 Light
Schmidt Wm. J., 669 W Baltimore
Schneider M., 234 Franklin
Schwartz D., Lexington mkt
Seeback Mrs. Catharine, 439 W
    Pratt
Sehibeferling George, 171 Chesnut
Seward A. R., 66 Fell's Point mkt
Shipferling G., Bell av mkt
Shoop Lewis, Lexington mkt
Shummeyer T., 661 W Baltimore
Sick Henry, 238 S Sharp
Sieck Henry, Lexington mkt
Sickel Edward, 188 E Baltimore
Sikes George, Fell's Point mkt
Sinclair John, 772 W Baltimore
Sloan John, 146 N Front
Smith M. C., 118 Centre mkt
Smith P., 5 Warner
Smoke Geo., 60 Fell's Point mkt
Snyder Christian, Fell's Point mkt

Snyder Mrs. H., 232 N Gay
Sorg Charles, 435 W Pratt
Sorgeier Francis, 73 Aisquith
Spitzniel Philip, 17 Pine
Stoedzer Charles, 94 Jefferson
Struck Bernard, 68 Mulberry
Swartzs Daniel, 123 Centre mkt and
    120 Columbia
Swarzts Ellen. 69 Fell's Point mkt
Swartzs Louisa, 166 Centre mkt
Sweckendrick George, Lexington
    mkt and 21 N Paca
Sykes Mrs.. Fell's Point mkt
Thompson Peter, 3 Bethel
Trier P., 334 S Charles
Underwood H., 136 Centre mkt
UNKLEBACH ANDREW, 211
    Chesnut
Wagner G. W., 502 N Gay
Wambaoh E., 86 Ensor
Webers J., Ann c Pratt
White G. T., 157 E Baltimore
White Welcome, 4 N High
Wilber Dietrich, Hollins mkt
Will John, 104 S Caroline
Wilson Mrs. Agnes, Lexington mkt
WILSON J. A., 139 N High
Wise Elizabeth, Bell Air mkt
Wiseman Geo., 74 Fell's Point mkt
    and 144 Centre mkt
Wolf George, Fell's Point mkt
Wolf John, Centre mkt
Wood George, Fell's Point mkt
Young Michael, 261 S Broadway
Zink Ph. Fr., 223 S Charles

Bakers, Cracker and Ship Biscuit.

BALTIMORE COMPANY
BISCUIT AND CRACKER
MANUFACTORY.

JAMES BEATTY,
SHIP BISCUIT, CRACKER, and
    CAKE BAKER.
Nos. 92, 94, and 96 Dugan's Wharf,
    near Pratt Street.
Vessels supplied with stores.

GILMOUR A. M., 239 W Pratt
McCoubray Thomas, 158 W Pratt

MASON JAMES D. & CO.

PATENT BAKERY.

SHIP BREAD
and
CRACKER BAKERY,

114 W Pratt Street,

(bet. South and Commerce)

BALTIMORE.

MASON R. & SON, 128 W Pratt, Pilot, Navy, Ship Bread, and Biscuit Bakers
Tyler & Brothers, S E c Pratt and Patterson

Bankers.

(*See also* BROKERS, STOCK AND EXCHANGE.)

Bayne & Co., 208 W Baltimore
BENNER. DENISON & CO.. Walker's Building, 263 W Baltimore

BROTHERS McKIM,
BANKERS,
150 W Baltimore.

BROWN ALEXANDER & SONS, 153 W Baltimore
BROWN BROS. & CO., 153 W Baltimore. BANKERS and STERLING EXCHANGE DEALERS.
Carson Thomas, 204 W Baltimore

COX JAMES H.,

N. E. c. North and Baltimore.

Agent for the sale of

GOVERNMENT REVENUE STAMPS,

Dealer in COIN,

All kinds of

UNCURRENT MONEY

and EXCHANGE.

Collections made at all accessible points in the country.

Evans Isaac J., 162 W Baltimore
Garrett R. & Sons, 34 N Howard
GITTINGS JOHN S. & CO., 29 South
Gorer Philip & Co., 22 W Baltimore
Harris Samuel & Sons, 196 W Baltimore
JOHNSTON BROTHERS & CO., 198 W Baltimore. LAND WARRANTS BOUGHT AND SOLD.
McKIM BROTHERS, 150 W Baltimore
McKim & Co., 186 W Baltimore
Nicholson Isaac L. & Co., 28 W Baltimore
Nicholson J. J. & Sons, 284 W Baltimore
PURVIS & CO., 192 W Baltimore, Bankers and Stock Exchange Brokers. Jas. F. Purvis, Jas. P. Thomas.
STONE JAMES H., DEALER IN STOCKS, BONDS, COMMERCIAL PAPER, GOLD COIN, AND ALL DESIRABLE SECURITIES. OFFICES N E C BALTIMORE AND CHARLES
TORMEY LEONARD J., 22 South

WAINWRIGHT, CLOUD & CO.

167 *W. Baltimore,*

BANKERS, STOCK

AND

EXCHANGE BROKERS.

H. H. Wainwright, Daniel Cloud, Edwin F. Reese.

REFERENCES.

R. H. Lowry, Esq., Pres. Bank of Republic, New York.
Jas. Mott, Esq., Cash. of Duncan, Sherman & Co., New York.
Messrs. Dibble & Camblos, Stock Brokers, New York.
Messrs. Jay Cooke & Co., Bankers, Phila. and Washington.
Messrs. Chas. Camblos & Co., Bankers, Phila.
Chas. B. Wainwright, Esq., Phila.
J. Reese, Esq., Cash. Far. & Mech. Bank, Westminster.
Johns Hopkins, Esq., Baltimore.
Geo. R. Gaither, Esq., Baltimore.
Messrs. Woodward, Baldwin & Co., Baltimore.
R. Mickle, Esq., Cash. Union Bank of Md., Balto.
Trueman Cross, Esq., Cash. Com. & Far. Bank, Balto.
P. Gibson, Esq., Cash. Bk. of Balto.
J. J. Clark, Esq., Pres. Citizens Bk. Balto.
Messrs. Wm. Fisher & Sons, Stock Brokers, Balto.
Messrs. Daniel Miller & Co., Balto.
"   Devries, Stephens & Co. "
"   J. S. Barry & Co.   "

Banks.

Bank of Baltimore, N E c St Paul and Baltimore
BANK OF COMMERCE, 26 South
Chesapeake, North c Fayette

CITIZENS', Hanover c Pratt, John Clark, *Pres't,* J. Wesley Guest, *Cashier.*
Commercial & Farmers' Bank, German c Howard
FARMERS' & MERCHANTS', c South and Lombard
Farmers' & Planters', 17 South
Fell's Point, Broadway n Canton av
FRANKLIN. 15 South
Howard, N W c Howard & Fayette
MARINE, N E c Gay and Second
MECHANICS', Michael Warner, *President,* Chas. R. Coleman, *Cashier,* N E c Calvert & Fayette
Merchants', Second c Gay
Peoples', Baltimore c Paca
Union. Charles c Fayette
WESTERN. Chauncy Brooks, *President,* Wm. H. Norris, *Cash.* 12 N Eutaw

Bank for Saving.

Baltimore, Gay c Second
Dime Saving Bank, 9 N Calvert
Eutaw, Eutaw c Fayette

Bark Mills.

Appold A., Caroline c McEllDerry

Basket Makers.

Acomb William, 121 Franklin
Dwyer John, 97 N Eutaw
Gado M., 26 S Eutaw
Pope Jacob, 11 N Pearl
Rentz M. J., 40 N Paca

Bedding and Mattresses.
(*See also* UPHOLSTERERS.)

ANDERSON W E., 10 & 12 Second (See advertisement.)
Frey J J., 41 N Gay
Frey & Co. C., 7 Greenmount av
GODEY THOMAS, 54 Hanover
HODES JOHN, 474 W Baltimore, Manufacturer of Mattresses and Bedding. Constantly on hand a large assortment of all kinds of Mattresses and Bedding. Orders will be punctually attended to.

MULLER LOUIS, 110 W Baltimore. (See advertisement opposite Upholsterers.)
POLLACK A., 96 N Howard
Wheatfield A., 6 Second

Bill Poster.

Harper J. W., 12 North

Billiard Saloons.

Dickinson David, Franklin Hall,
North
Hall L. J., Baltimore c Light
McElroy P., 5½ North

Billiard Table Manufacturer.

Petersen Louis G., 1 Low

Bitters, Manufacturer of.

Kuhlman Christian, 274 N Gay

Blacksmiths.

(*See also* WHEELWRIGHTS.)
Anderson Charles, 4 S'Eutaw
Baker Christian, 173 Hardford av
Baltimore City Railroad Co., 942 W
Baltimore
Burnham J. T., 48 N Paca
Chester William, 9 Pleasant
Clautier Peter, 375 Portland
Cook George, Columbia c Scott
Cunningham Thomas, 42 Ellicott
Devalin Hugh, 89 Harrison
Dooley Charles, 140 Hardford av
Doyle James, Central av c Bank
Eilbacher John V., 16 Lee
Einwaechter Alex., 116 Columbia
Fairvall W. H., 133 S Fremont
Fisher William, York
Gesell T., 588 W Baltimore
Hall Nelson M., 111 N Paca
Hays & Sellman, 94 Central av
Heagerty M., 761 W Baltimore
Hitchcock Josiah, 273 S Ann
Lally M., 126 Franklin
Lee Charles, 412 W Baltimore
Leonard C. M., 113 W Lombard
Lestrange Patrick, Centre c Davis
McClelland George, John al

McCurley James, 17 L Sharp
Meyd F., 167 Henrietta
Mueller J. P., 68 Greenmount av
Ottelein P., 267 S Bond
Rau John, 95 Low
Richwine Henry, 600 W Pratt
ROBERTS OWEN G., 292½ S Caro-
line
Schaffer David, 20 W Fayette
Schlutter Aug't, Holiday c Sara-
toga
SCHMITT V. J., 346 Light
Sindall P., 117 Hillen
Snyder John, 498 N Gay
Steck Charles, 94 Central av
Steck Louis, 108 Greenmount av
STEPHENS HENRY, 397 S Charles
Strange L., Davis c Centre
Talbot Benjamin, 118 N Calvert
Towner J., Ridgly
Vath A., Hanover
Watkins Evan, 37 Light
Winters Conrad, 87 Central av
Yorghert Casper, 260 Washington
Zinkhan A., 763 W Baltimore

Blank Book Manufacturers.

(*See also* STATIONERS ; *also*, BOOK
BINDERS.)
Hetzler Francis D., 95 W Baltimore
Peters Wm. H., 151 W Pratt

Bleachers—Bonnets, Hats.

Hill Mark, 40 German
Hill Richard, Sharp and German
Naeder Mad. T., 77 N Howard

Block and Pump Makers.

(*See also* PUMP MAKERS.)
Bandel L. J., 97 McElderry's whf
Cathcart R. & W. H., 113 Thames
CHURCH & BROWN, 4 Dugan.—
Dealers in New and Second-Hand
Standing and Running Rigging,
Blocks, Hooks, Thimbles, &c.
DELANO W. H., 72 W Pratt
Lewis Levi, South side of Basin
Mallon John, 61 W Pratt

Moore John F., 5 Fell
Peregoy Wm., Thames c Bond
Powell Henry, 131 McElderry's whf
Rice Thos., 4 Covington
Wood Thos., 145 McElderry's whf

Boarding Houses.

Askew Thomas B., 119 N Eutaw
Beltz Mrs. N., 14 New Church
Chapman Mrs. C., 230 W Pratt
Collins Patrick, 53 President
Cordery Mrs. W., 137 W Lexington
Cox Mrs. A., 103 Hanover
Crockett R. H., 73 S Charles
Cullimore Mrs. John, 193 E Pratt
Dahle Mary, 94 N Gay
Elzey Mrs. L., 14 S Calvert
Guest Mrs. M. C., 42 W Lexington
Haurander Mrs. L., 64 N Gay
Herzog Louis, 161 W Lombard
Isaac R., 89 S Sharp
Jones T., 136 Cross
Kerr Eliza, 28 Hanover
Kenidy Mrs. Anna, 19 W Baltimore
McDonald Mrs., 61 N Howard
Murphy Jeanet, 1 James
Pennington, Mrs. S., 10 S Gay
Reckitt Mrs. A. M., 238 W Pratt
Slicer Mrs. Wm. C., 119 N Gay
Smith Ann, 69 S Schroder
Stevens Mrs. Martha M., 23 N Gay
Travers Mary Ann, 106 W Fayette
Wheeler Mrs. R. E., 23 S Gay

Boat Builders.

(See also SHIP BUILDERS.)

Bartlett & Bro., S side of Basin
James Levi, 158 Thames
Miles John S., York
Rennous E. G., 115 McElderry's whf

Boiler Makers.

(See also IRON FOUNDERS.)

MURRAY, CLARK, THORNTON & CO., 42 and 44 York. (See advertisement.)

Bolts, Nuts, Rivets, &c.

West William, 151 North

Bone Factory.

Horner Joshua, Stirling c Chew

Bonnet Frame Makers.

DONOHUE B., 253 N Gay
McCAFFERTY ARTHUR, 68 W Lexington
Todhunter Silas, 25 Chesnut

Bonnet Makers.

(See also MILLINERS.)

Hamburger J., 173 N Gay
Hart Mrs. M., 156½ W Lexington
Kessler & Co. M., 214 W Lexington
MULLER Mrs. LOUIS, 110 W Baltimore. (See advertisement op Newspapers.)

Book Binders.

(See also BLANK BOOK MANUFACTURERS.)

Heise Elias, 12 W Fayette
Hetzler F. D., r 95 W Baltimore
Lindsay Wm. R., 114 W Baltimore
Peters Wm. H., 151 W Pratt
Wright Joel, 160 and 162 W Baltimore

Booksellers and Publishers.

(Marked thus * *are Publishers.)*

American Farmer, 147 W Baltimore
Armstrong & Berry, 156 W Baltimore
Bennett Adolph, 100 N Fremont
Bond J. W. & Co., 86 W Baltimore
Brady John, 104 W Lexington
Brown Geo. W., 207 E Baltimore
*Carr & Co., 21 South (Merchant's Guide)
Caspari A. R., 129 N Howard
Cathers J. & Bro., 36 W Baltimore
Chickering E. C., 226 W Pratt
Cook Isaac P., 76 W Baltimore

*CROSS E. M. & CO., 110 W Baltimore, PUBLISHERS OF THE BALTIMORE CITY BUSINESS DIRECTORY, THE PHILADELPHIA CITY BUSINESS DIRECTORY. and the WILMINGTON, DELAWARE, CITY DIRECTORY. Branch office. 337 Chestnut St., Philadelphia, Pa.
Cushings & Bailey, 262 W Baltimore
Des Forges John P., 12 Light
Donnelly Martha, 60 S Howard
Doyle A. J., 11 Pennsylvania av
Doyle Thomas G., 297 N Gay
Dutton T. W., 162½ E Baltimore
ENTY & BOSH, 35 N Charles
Fisher and Bro., 64 W Baltimore
Graham John, 514 W Baltimore
GRATTON GEORGE, W Baltimore c Holiday. (See advertisement.)
Henninghausen L. & G., 28½ W Pratt
Hesselbacher August, 174 S Broadway
*Jerningham J. A. C., 123 E Baltimore
*Johnson, Fry, & Co., 81 Second
*KELLY, HEDIAN, & PIET, 174 W Baltimore
Kurtz T. Newton, 151 W Pratt
Lockwood Charles, 42 N Green
*Lucas Brothers, 170 W Baltimore
*Maryland State Bible Society, T. H. Quinan agt, 75 W Fayette
*Maryland Tract Sunday School and Book Depository, S. Guielau Sec'y, 73 W Fayette
Magers G. W., 175 W Lexington
*Methodist Protest't Church Book Concern. 12 N Gay, Thomas W. Ewing, Editor and Agent
METROPOLITAN Gift Book Store Holiday c Baltimore. (See advertisement.)
Metzger Mrs. S. A., 151 N Gay
Minifie Wm., 114 W Baltimore
Morrow James S., 103 N Gay
Ramesey J. A., 115 S Broadway
Reed Robert A., 76 N Eutaw
*SACHSE E. & CO., 104 S Charles

Schmidt W. R., 94 W Baltimore
Sheehy James, 15 St Paul
Smith Ellen, 51 N Gay
Tall Anthony, 265 N Gay
Taylor Henry, Sun Iron Bdg 111 W Baltimore
*Virtue, Yorston, & Co., 24 Second
*Waite M. H., 138 W Baltimore
WATERS JAMES S., 168 W Baltimore
WEISHAMPEL J. F., jr., BOOKSELLER and STATIONER, 8 Eutaw House, c Baltimore and Eutaw, also 484 Baltimore n Pine.
WHITNEY, CUSHING, & CO., LAW SCHOOL, and MISCELLANEOUS BOOKSELLERS and STATIONERS, 6 N Howard, op Howard House. Jos. C. Whitney, Jos. Cushing, J. H. Medairy
Woods John W., 202 W Baltimore, Publisher of the Baltimore City Directory

Boot and Shoe Findings.

(*See also* LEATHER and FINDINGS; *also* LEATHER DEALERS.)

Canox L., 177 Hanover
Desvarreux James. 164 N Gay
Grupy Jacob, 132 N Gay
Helmers John, 250 W Pratt
Mason William, 189 W Lexington
Maxwell John 5 Ensor
Rouque F., 19 Harrison
SCHMIDT JACOB, 312 W Pratt, Leather and Finding Store, Shoe Uppers and all other kinds of Uppers, Ladies' Uppers, and Philadelphia Lasts constantly on hand
STEHLI A., 27 Harrison

Boot and Shoe Commission Merchants.

(*See also* BOOTS and SHOES, WHOLESALE.)

BALDERSTON, WARD, & CO., 14 and 16 German, COMMISSION

MERCHANTS and MANUFAC-
TURERS, AGENTS for the sale of
BOOTS and SHOES. John C. Bal-
derston, J. Wheelwright, J.
Henry Ward
BROOKS ROBERT, 257 W Balti-
more

GRINNELL & JENKINS,

275 W. BALTIMORE,

WHOLESALE

COMMISSION DEALERS

IN

BOOTS, SHOES,

HATS, AND CAPS.

Pendexter, Alden & Co., 19 S
Charles

Boot and Shoe Makers.

(*See also* BOOTS AND SHOES, LA-
DIES'; *also*, BOOTS AND SHOES,
RETAIL.)

Abendschon Ambrose, 74 Leaden-
hall
Aidt L., 60 Ross
Aiken Henry, 103 S Dallas
Alschnee George, 107 W Lombard
Anzmann Joseph, 173 German
Anel A., 213 Montgomery
Awalt Ferdinand, 54 Mulberry
Bamberger John, 696 W Baltimore
Banks Henry, 181 S Caroline
Barth Christian, 30 N Paca
Baumann Wm., 131 S Fremont
Beausle John, 158 Columbia
Beck G., 70 S Fremont
Beck, Perry R., 259 Light
Becker Geo. W., 41 S Liberty
Becker L., 42 Tyson
Beeswagner J., 49 Douglass
Beitzler Daniel, 118 S Howard
5

Bertram William, 768 W Baltimore
Birkenwald S., 62 Thames
Bitner Leonard 248 S Ann
Bittenger J. D., 9 Penn av.
Blomeire E., 32 President
Blum Jacob, 142 Hollins
Blumenthal L., 239 Montgomery
Bode J., 184 Orleans
Bohrman Daniel, 269 S Charles
Bokel Mrs. J. H., 62 Park
Bonnet J., 303 Canton av
Bower John, 95 N Calvert
Brandford Henry, 369 S Eutaw
Brandmuller Geo., 27 Brown
Brazier Mrs. Robert, 263 W Lex-
ington
Brautigam M., 54 Park
Bromwell Geo., 107 S Wolf
Brooks John, 11 E Pratt
Bruns B., 281 N Gay
Brown Francis, 283 S Bond
Buchner Conrad, 246 S Eutaw
Burkamp F. C., 111 N Eutaw
Connoly James H., 496 W Baltimore
Carr James, 94 Franklin
Chaney A. W., 44 E Baltimore
Cook B. M., 803 W Baltimore
Cook C., 266 S Howard
Cook Leonard, 254 Alice Anna
Copper J. H., 57 Ensor
Corigan Daniel, 107 Britton
Cronhardt John, 29 Ensor
Curll Henry, 229 Hollins
Dalsheimer D., 178 W Lexington
Davis Noah, 6 Marion
Debring John G., 133 N Eutaw
Dietrich Adam, 205 W Fayette
Dietrich James, 747 W Baltimore
Dietrich Philip, 347 W Fayette
Dietrick Adam, 354 S Charles
Dobson Jno., 12 Central av
Dobson Robert, 90 Jefferson
Doud Simon, 85 N Fremont
Dreyer Wm., 166 S Broadway
Duffy Patrick, 77 Chestnut
Dundlack George, 107 W Lombard
Eaton W. C., 327 Aisquith
Ebner Martin, 196 Hollins
Eckelman Rudolph, 10 W Lombard

Eizer Michael, 14! Johnston
Eiseman Moses, 90 Harrison
Ele Conrad, 70 N Caroline
Elgert John, 37 Bank
Ellis & Lockwood, 754 W Baltimore
EMMERICH C., 18 South
Emerick Philip, 4 Harrison
Engelhardt Henry, 222 Light
Epron Peter, 45 Gay
Euler Ernest, 184 E Baltimore
Fach Jacob, 5 Penn av
Fette Henry, 11 Warner
Fick C. A., 104 Cross
Fickinschere Henry, 91 Harrison
Firnstein Valentine, 40 N Eutaw
Fisher George, 65 North
Fisher H., 131 Franklin
Fleischman G., 22 Douglas
Flynn Jacob, 33 Central av
Fox John, 226 S Eutaw
Frederick C. F., 307 Canton av
Freede A., 58 Mulberry
Freund H , 97 Schroeder
Frese J. Henry, 32 E Fayette
Gallagher Allen R., 95 N Eutaw
Gardner James F., 58 W Lexington
Gaydeke F., 122 Greenmount av
Gebhart F., 7 N High
Geier Aug., 394 Hanover
Geisz N., 96 Hillen
Glaese Jacob, 638 Light
Glaeszer Wm., 68 McElderry
Gluckstein A., N E cor Eutaw and
  Mulberry
Goldsmith Charles, 30 E Baltimore
Goodwin T., 48 Beuren
Greuzebart Henry, 240 S Sharp
Gruelih Louis, 35 S Caroline
Gunclach Chas., 145 Columbia
HAENFTLING G., 152 Henrietta
Hagedorn H., 28 Ross
Hall James B.,.Caroline c McEll-
  derry
Harle L., 342 W Pratt
Harrison W. E., 84 S Charles
Hartman John & Son, 678 W Balti-
  more
Heer Henry J., 186 Cross
Heck Charles, 315 W Pratt

Heitmuller Henry, 346 Canton av
Heimerlinger John C., 14 Ross
Herman G., 60 N Register
Herman H., 84 Market Space
Hesse Henry, 523 W Baltimore
Herzog Adam H., 119 W Lexington
Hick Joseph, 234 Light
Honmkamp Joseph, 5 S Poppleton
Hull George, 168 E Baltimore
Hulshoff Gerhard, 24 Park
Hummel A., 935 W Baltimore
Jacob J., 61 S Fremont
Johnson Theodore R., 14 Mosher
Kahlert F., 284 S Ann
Keener Andrew, 287 Canton av
Keim H. W. A., 46 German
Kenny James, 13 Ensor
Keurner Henry, Howard c Henri-
  etta
Kiesling Andrew, 352 Canton av
Kinzer N., 67 Richmond
Kipp George, 217 Eastern av
Knell George A., 185 Biddle
Kniss Peter, 4 Second
Koch Gus., 21 Dover
Koch John, 92 Harrison
Koehler Henry, 536 W Baltimore
Koerner Henry, Howard c Henrietta
Kohl John A., 125 W Lombard
Kook F., 21 Pine
Kornman H., Exeter c Watson
Kraft H., 157 N Register
Krample Wolftang, 420 Canton av
Krope John, 27 Abbey pl
Kratzer A., 119 N Register
Krumholtz F., 241 S Eutaw
Kurtz Henry, 16 N Register
Lang George, Dallas c Pratt
Langa Henry, 232 Canton av
Laughlin Thomas, 2 St Paul
Lauterbach Jacob, 284 Canton av
Leddor Geo. M., 201 E. Baltimore
Lenbke A. & Co., 5 N Eutaw
Lenz August, 54 N Schroeder
Leutner Frank, 241 S Sharp
Lewis J. S., 137 S Broadway
Lind George, 26 S Oregon
Lindaw Abraham, 101 Harrison
List A. J., 123 Columbia

List Jacob, 213 W Lexington
Livingston Seth, 272 Light
Lohrmann Henry, 317 S Charles
Lohmuller Mrs. D., 116 E Lombard
Long Casper, 1 Castle al
LONG JOHN F, 1 N Calvert, opposite Barnum's. French Boot and Shoe Maker.
Long William, 249 S Broadway
Louis F., 242 Hanover
Lutz John, 17 Fish Market Space
McCadden T., 99 N Front
McCarthy J. J., 58½ N Howard
Maddux Thomas, 12 Light
Magee P., 175 Franklin
Marshall John, 119 E Pratt
Mason Richard, 6 North
Mather James, 92 W Lexington
Mechthold George, 197 S Charles
Meerdter J., 37 S Paca
Mehring P., 350 Light
Menner John, 194 Hollins
Merck A., 829 W Baltimore
Metchold Charles, 197 S Charles
Metzger, Frederick, 237 Canton av
Meyer Geo. H. L., 41 N Liberty
Mingo A., 254 S Broadway
Mitchell M., 54 S Howard
Miller B. H., 246 S Broadway
Miller Casper, 93 N Caroline
Miller Peter, 259 S Broadway
Miller F. T., 757 W Baltimore
Moszrer C. R., 16 New
Mullenberg J., 112 N Paca
Muller Frederick, 66 N Register
Murray Mrs. S., 30 Russell
Myers Andrew, 157 S Sharp
Naas J., 10 Park
Nash John W., 103 S Broadway
Nolte D., 27 Thames
Ohrenschall C., 56 S Charles
Olbaugh John W., 207 Light
Oppenmeyer H., 230 S Eutaw
Otterbeir J., 23 Ensor
Overbeck August, 19 Watson
Parr J. G., N Caroline c Fayette
Peck Louis, 16 E Baltimore
Pennig Casper, 61 Bank
Pfaff John, 71 Washington

Polleti J., 206 Hanover
Raos John, 350 S Charles
Rapp C., 5 Carlton
Reise F., 40 Douglass
Renner Jacob, 40 Greenmount av.
Renoff Fred., 55 Ensor
Rexroff A., 150 Central av
Reynolds G. L., 406 W Lombard
Richenberger J., 184 Light st whf
Ridgaway Joseph, Aisquith c Douglass
Rink J., 205 S Charles
Ritter Christian, 10 E Pratt
Ritter Frederick, 30 E Pratt
Roberts W., 69 W Fayette
Roeth Christian, 288 S Charles

ROSS DAVID J.,

BOOT AND SHOE

MAKER AND IMPORTER,

CALVERT STREET,

UNDER BARNUM'S HOTEL.

Roth John, 34 Central av
Rothhaupt Chas., 61 Britton
Rupple H., 6 L Paca
Schlien E., 75 Harrison
Schmidt Aug., 367 Light
Schmidt C., 685 W Baltimore
Schmit Harmon 9 W Fayette
Schorr Frederick, 47 President
Schminke W., 312 Alice Anna
Schroeder Henry, Low c Front
Schroeder John, 90 Hamburg
Schulmeyer Charles, 23 Harrison
Schrufer John, 94 Greenmount av
Schultzbach Peter, 690 W Baltimore
Schurer A., 19 Arch
Schultze M., 300 Alice Anna

Schultze Henry, 1 N Register
Schulz Mather, 113 Henrietta
Schuszler Adam, 23 S Wolf
Schwab S., Central av c Orleans
Schwaz G., 323 S Charles
SELLERS JESSE, 5 Holiday,
  NEW BOOT, SHOE, AND GAI-
  TER ESTABLISHMENT, is pre-
  pared to furnish the latest styles of
  Gentlemen's and Youth's Boots,
  Shoes, and Gaiters, made in the
  most durable and workmanlike
  manner, and of the best material.
Seller John, 250 Canton av
Shutze A. D., 15 Light
Siess J., 9 Carlton
Sielricht George, 11 S Dallas
Smidt John, 192 Columbia
Smith A., 151 N Eutaw
Smith C., 35 McElderry
Smith George H., 45 Thames
Smith John, 35 Britton
Staffort Lewis, 21 S Liberty
Stein John, 69 Thames
Stembler John V., 800 W Baltimore
Stembler N., 497 W Baltimore
Stenger C. H., 65 Bank
Stinson R., 4 Holiday
Stintz Wm. F., 158 E Lombard
Straupp Peter, 343 S Charles
Strauss F., 258 Montgomery
Strauss Fred, 195 Light
Strauss George, 226 S Charles
Suchbradle Geo., 197 Eager
Swope F. T., 18 Chestnut
Syms James, 146 S Fremont
Thomas P., 5 S Gay
Thompson James, 143 E Baltimore
Tindle Rob. W., 20 Camden
Tuhlman C., 833 W Baltimore
Ulrich Fred. W., 113 N Calvert
Veara Frances, 35 E Baltimore
Vogler Andrew, 299 Alice Anna
Vogt J., 253 Light
Voget Henry, 570 W Lombard
Volk Francis, 48 S Charles
Volk John R., 12 Russell
Volker J., 16 Ross
Volker Michael, 82 North

Vonderheide, J. H. G., 2 Saratoga
Waldeck Valentine, 271 S Bond
Wagner A., 55 S Poppleton
Wagner Philip, 35 S Schroder
Walker W. T., 139 W Lombard
Wardell J. A., 167 Columbia
Waring S. M., 44 S Howard
WAMBACK WM., 16 South
WATKINS WM. B., 80 W Lexing-
  ton
Weaver Andrew, 411 Light
Weckenmann E., 93 Green
Weigel Geo., 46 S Republican
Wengert Leonard, Bond c Thames
Wever A., 413 W Pratt
Wever H. D., 70 Camden
Wheatley T., 241 E Baltimore
Wheeler Samuel, 250 W Lexington
Willer John, 64 S Schroder
Williamson Wm. M., 18 Ensor
Wilson David, 54 Harrison
Wilson John T., 748 W Baltimore
Winkler F. J., 31 S Oregon
Winter Florence, 6 N Green
Wolf Henry, 20 Scott
Wright L. D., 208 S Broadway
Zehle C. & A. Koss, 550 W Balti-
  more
Zigler Fred., 50 Camden
Zimmerman John V., 280 Aisquith
Zimmisch Fred'k, 72 Camden

Boots and Shoes—Ladies'.

ARDIN D., 36 N Charles, MANU-
  FACTURER OF LADIES' FASH-
  IONABLE BOOTS AND SHOES.
Bangs John, S E c Pratt and Sharp
Berry Geo. W., 284 N Gay
Brady James, 472 W Baltimore
Bussmann Mrs. Anna, 240 S Charles
Caples W. M., 71 N Eutaw
Hall F. J., 306 N Gay
Hamer William H., 56 N Howard
Harper William, S E c Eutaw and
  Saratoga
Hults Robert, 22 Water
LYON H., 9 E Baltimore. Ladies',
  Misses' and Children's Shoes con-
  stantly on hand.

Moreland Wm. II., 56 N Gay
PERRY'S JOHN B., SHOE EMPO-
RIUM FOR LADIES, MISSES AND
CHILDREN. A great variety of
BOOTS, SHOES AND GAITERS kept
constantly on hand MEASURES
TAKEN FOR BOOTS and SHOES of
every and all kinds, and a perfect
fit guaranteed. 231 W Lexington.
PICKERING WM., 232 W Lexing-
ton market space
Reboul Mme. N., 87 N Howard
Whelan George, 158 N Eutaw
Williams J. S., 70 N Charles
WILLIAMS & SPENCER, LA-
DIES' BOOT & SHOE STORE,
c Hanover and Lombard

**Boots and Shoes, Ladies',
Manufacturers of.**

Ebaugh D. F., 220 N Eutaw
FAUST JOHN, 16 S Charles
Norris James, 222 N Eutaw

Boot & Shoe Manufactur'rs.

Buckley C. R., 89 Hanover
CLOGG GEO. S., 2 S Calvert, Manufacturer of Boots and Shoes

FAUST JOHN,

WHOLESALE MANUFACTURER OF

Gentlemen's Fine French Calf

BOOTS,

SHOES AND GAITERS.

ALSO,

LADIES'

SHOES AND GAITERS.

16 S. CHARLES.

Gallagher Thomas, S W c Paca and
Saratoga
Ireland David, 347½ W Baltimore
NEURATH E., 117 W Fayette
Perry Levi & Co., 179 W Baltimore
Phillips John T., agt., 11 S Sharp

Smith C., 31 W Baltimore
THATER PHILIP, 280 W Pratt

Boots and Shoes, Retail.

Addison Samuel S., 230 W Pratt
Andrews Wm., 272 W Pratt
Apt John, 199 S Broadway
Arnett Levi, 361 N Gay
Aul Michael, 312 N Gay
Bailey Wm., 108 W Lexington
Bangs John, S E c Pratt and Sharp
Bannenberg Frederick, 344 W Pratt
Bantz Theo. S. (agent), 320 W Bal-
timore
Baulch James, 213 Light
Berg Philip, 64 W Pratt
Berney B., 24 W Pratt and 18 Cen-
tre market space
Bertram & Son, 214 W Pratt
Betschler M., 244 S Charles
Better Wm., 249 S Broadway
Biggins Wm. H., 182 N Gay
Billmyer Joseph, 142 W Pratt
Blunnanar Lewis, 235 S Charles
Bodicker, 43 N Gay
Bowen J. L., 11 E Baltimore
Brown Jacob, 79 McElderry's whf
Bulack Joseph, 248 W Pratt
Bunting Wm. J., 70 N Howard
Burke Laurence, 62 Market space
Butter Thomas, 211 Hollins
Buzby Joseph, 175 Hanover
Carback E. & Son, 165 W Lexing-
ton
CASSIDY JAMES, 33 W Pratt
Chamberlain J. C., 285 W Pratt
CROOK G. W. M., 69 W Baltimore
Cross H. L., 234 W Lexington
Dalsheimers D., 192 W Lexington
Damme Sophia, 214 S Broadway
Davidson J. & Miss, 665 W Balti-
more
Davis S., 150 W Lexington
De Baufre S. E., 254 Washington
De Baufre W. H., 84 Broadway
Deuges Peter, 22 Park
Doenges Ernest, 514 W Baltimore
Dorsey Daniel W., 172 N Gay
Dryden Samuel, 334 W Baltimore

5*

Eisema Moses, 34 Centre Market Space
Eliel Solomon, 220 W Pratt
Ely M. S., N E c Gay and Exeter
Emerich A., 16 Harrison
Emerich W. H., 9 N Eutaw
Epstein & Co., 127 N Gay
Fensley Wm., 141 S Broadway
Field J., 80 W Pratt
Fillbert George, 388 N Gay
Fisher G. F., 64 N Gay
Fisher Henry, 42½ W Pratt
Fleming James, 121 N Gay
Fluharty James, 23 N Gay
Fox Stephen P., 510 W Baltimore
Frank Henry, 193 N Gay
Frank Solomon, 157 W Lexington
Fried Louis, 6 and 30 Centre mkt space
Friedel J. C., 73 N Gay
Friedeman Henry, 60 Market space
GAHAN P., BOOT MAKER, 88 W Baltimore, bet Gay and Holiday. Where may be obtained the latets French and English Styles.
Gareis G., 10 E Monument
Gawthrops Wm. H., 163 W Lexington
George Isaac S., 806 Market space
Hammacks Geo. M., 221 N Gay
Hand Alexander, 65 N Eutaw
Hecht & Putzels, 180 W Lexington
Heintz George, 86 S Front
Heinz Andrew, 86 N Gay
Hemmick Jacob, 39 N Liberty
Herdtman F., 66 N Gay
Herman C., 124 W Lexington
Herman L., 72 Market space
Hernsheim Mrs. B., 152½ S Broadway
Herrmann Aaron, 174 N Gay
Hessler Peter, 34½ W Pratt
Hill Geo. D. & Co., 53 N Gay
HIMMELREICH B., 647 W Baltimore
HURSELL J. C., 119 N Gay
Jandorf Reuben, 108 W Pratt
Johnson Wm., 110 N Gay
Junker Philip, 225 Light

Kange Lewis, 296 W Pratt
Kayton H. H., 70 Hanover
Kinner John, 397 W Baltimore
Kramer H., 85 N Gay
Kroeger Joseph, 128 W Lexington
Kruger D., 49 N Gay
Kuper, F. J., 251 N Gay
Levy Moses, 44 Centre mkt space
Lloyd F., 146 W Baltimore
Lubke A., 241 S Charles
McAllister Mrs. M., 340 Light
McLaughlin J., 236 N Gay
Manko R. H., 250 W Pratt
Markert A., 210 S Sharp
Martin Samuel, 516 W Baltimore
Maxwell Alex., 309 N Gay
Meeth John, S E c Light & Warren
Meseke Frederick, 322 W Pratt
MILLER H., 792 W Baltimore. Manufacturer of Boots, Shoes, and Gaiters for Gentlemen, Ladies', and Children
Minners Mrs. S., 98 Richmond
Mitchell J. W., 22 S Sharp
MOCKBEE W. T., 29 W Baltimore
Mouse John Henry, 63 Harrison
Mules Thomas, 176 W Lexington
Murray Wm., 68 Market space
Myer Philip, 316 W Pratt
Nicolai John C., 553 W Baltimore
Offner J. A., N E c Gay and Forrest
Oppenhiem Isaac, 280 S Charles
Peck Henry, 159 W Pratt
PICKERING WM., Manufacturer of LADIES' and GENTLEMEN'S BOOTS and SHOES, 232 W Lexington market space
Pistel George, 100 N Howard
Rauch Mrs. Sibald, 542 W Baltimore
Richards J. H., 120 Light st whf
Richards J. T., 76 N Pearl
Rityer H., 49½ N Eutaw
Roswald J., 177 N Gay
Rothauge K., 674 W Baltimore
Schloss Moses, 57 Harrison
Schott J. & Bro., 424 W Baltimore
Schwaze William F., 222 W Lexington

Sellers Jesse, 5 Holiday
Smith Nicholas, 489 N Gay
Spamer Henry, 272 N Gay and 92 S High
Spezzel A., 113 W Lexington
Stein John K., 19 Penn av
STOOPS WM. HENRY, 60 Hanover
Thomas Henry, 14 N. Liberty
Tucker Enoch G., 139 E Baltimore
Unger & Rumohr, 37 N Eutaw
Vantill S. J., 133 S Fremont
Volkert N. H., 641 W Baltimore
Vollmer L., 169 W Pratt
Weil E. P. & Sons, 113 N Gay
White Mathew, 64 Richmond
Whitmarsh George, 159 W Lexington
Wilcox J. H., 252 N Gay
Wilcox Thomas S., 134 N Gay
Wilcox William L., 150 N Gay
Winter Frederick, 283 N Gay
Zink John H., 277 W Pratt

Boots and Shoes—Wholesale.

(*See also* BOOT AND SHOE COMMISSION MERCHANTS.)

BROOKS ROBERT,

257 W. BALTIMORE,

one door E. of Hanover,

WHOLESALE DEALER AND COMMISSION MERCHANT

for the sale of

BOOTS, SHOES,

AND LEATHER.

Brooks, Fulton & Co., 346 W Baltimore
BURNS GEO. W., Wholesale Dealer in BOOTS, SHOES, HATS, AND CAPS, 338 W Baltimore n Howard. Particular attention paid to orders.
Carey, Bangs & Woodward, 266 Baltimore
Carroll, Adams & New, 286 Baltimore
Dalsheimer D., 269 W Baltimore
DIXON WM. T. & BRO., 306 W Baltimore. — Wholesale Dealers and Commission Merchants in Boots and Shoes, Hats and Caps. WM.T. DIXON, JAMES DIXON, JR.
Griffin R. B. & Sons, 17 S Charles
GRINNELL & JENKINS, 275 W Baltimore
Hecht & Putzel, 302 W Baltimore
Horner Frank F. & Co., 324 W Baltimore
Kimberly J. M., Baltimore c Howard
RUSSELL BENJAMIN, 293 W Baltimore, WHOLESALE BOOT AND SHOE MANUFACTURER. Every Description of ARMY AND CAVALRY BOOTS AND SHOES made to order.
Ruthrauff & Smith, 290 W Baltimore
Tucker & Smith, 250 W Baltimore
Warner & Bro., 254 W Baltimore
Wirt J. & Co., 3 N Howard

Boots and Shoes, Wholesale and Retail.

CROOK G. W. M.,

69 W Baltimore, four doors W. of Gay,

WHOLESALE AND RETAIL

Manufacturer of and Dealer in

BOOTS AND SHOES

Of every Description.

Mockbee, 29 E Baltimore
Wharton Wm., 106½ W Pratt

Bottlers.

(See also ALE AND PORTER ; *also,*
MINERAL WATERS.)

COUGHLAN WILLIAM,

Sole Agent for R. Smith's

PHILADELPHIA

XX ALE,

AND BOTTLER OF

PORTER, ALE, CIDER,

MINERAL WATER,

SCOTCH ALE,

LONDON BROWN STOUT,

&c.,

169 & 171 CENTRAL AVENUE,

BALTIMORE.

Ellis & Cairnes, City ct N Calvert
Gray Henry H., 2 N Stricker
Lubecker John, 21 Thames, F P
McKay James, 132 Franklin
Madden J., 16 President
Mitchell Edward, Barre c Warner
PIER G. W. & CO., Hanover c Bal-
timore, dealers in ALE, PORTER,
CIDER, LAGER BEER, &c., and
agents for the celebrated CHEST-
NUT GROVE BOURBON
Russell Wm., 5 Mercer

EDMOND WALSH'S

Old Established

BOTTLING VAULTS,

29 SOUTH FREDERICK ST.

near Lombard,

BALTIMORE, MD.

Who keeps constantly on hand
Foreign and Domestic

PORTER AND ALE,

Wholesale and Retail.

*Mineral and Sarsaparilla
Waters.*

Walsh Thomas, 45 N Frederick
Wisenauer Jacob, 407 W Pratt

Bowling Saloon.

(See also BILLIARD SALOONS ; *also*
HOTELS ; *also* TAVERNS.)
FOLTZ GEORGE & H. EHLEN, 5
Lovely lane

Box Makers.

(See also CARPENTERS AND BUILD-
ERS.)
ASHLEY W. H. & C. C., 216 W
Pratt
EHRMAN & BERSCH, 210 S How-
ard.   (See advertisement inter-
leaved.)
Klare & Winkleman, 15 L Sharp
KLINGMEYER & HEISE, 18 Mc-
Clellen's al.   (See advertisement
interleaved.)
RADECKE & CO., 22 McClellan's
al.   (See advertisement inter-
leaved.)
Schroeder R., 31 Albemarle
SCHULZE ERNEST, S E c Balti-
more and Charles and 2 Cedar al.
(See advertisement interleaved.)

SIEMERS HERMAN, 21 S Liberty.
BOX MAKER, ALL KINDS OF
BOXES MADE AT THE SHORT-
EST NOTICE AND ON THE
MOST REASONABLE TERMS.
Smith James, 69 S Dallas
Tiemeyer & Waltjen, 17 German
Winkalman John, 15 Grant

Brass Cock Manufacturers.

McSHANE HENRY & CO., 157
North. (See advertisement interleaved.)

**Brass Founders, Finishers
and Manufacturers.**

Aitcheson James, 67 North
Baker & Brown, 10 W Pratt
Hardesty George W., 44 Holiday
McSHANE HENRY & CO., 157
North. (See advertisement in-
terleaved.)
Regester Joshua, 58 Holiday
WAGNER AUGUST, 30 Harrison.
(See advertisement interleaved.)

Brewers.

BALTIMORE BREWERY, F.
DANDELET, Proprietor, Hano-
ver c Conway. (See advertise-
ment.)
Clagett William & Co., E Lombard
n the Bridge
DANDELET F., Hanover c Con-
way. (See advertisement.)
Frenie George, 146 Penna av
PIER G. W. & CO., Hanover c
Baltimore
Wissman A., 138 Hollins

Brewers—Lager Beer.

BAUR JOHN, 392 Canton av. (See
advertisement.)
Bauernschmidt G. & Co., 281 W
Pratt

HERZOG CONRAD,

LAGER BEER BREWERY,

corner of

Lancaster and Burk Sts.,

CANTON.

SEEGER JACOB, 23 German

Brick Dealers.

(*See also* FIRE BRICK.)

BURNS, RUSSELL & CO., 30
Columbia
Harman Samuel, Light
Merryman & Young, 64 W Fayette
Miller F. A., 116 Mulberry
SCHARF WM. JAMES, 825 W
Baltimore

*Bristles, Manufacturers of.

WILKENS WILLIAM & CO., Pratt
c Charles

**Britannia Ware Manufactu-
rers.**

Eisenhard A., 254 N Gay
FEICHMAN S., 80 N Eutaw
Sach Charles, 63 German

Brokers, Bill or Note.

(*See also* BANKERS ; *also* BROKERS,
GENERAL ; *also* BROKERS, STOCK
AND EXCHANGE.)

CARSON THOMAS J., 204 W Balti-
more
Evans Isaac jr., 162 W Baltimore
FISHER WM. & SONS, STOCK &
BILL BROKERS, 32 South

GOVER PHILIP & CO.,

BROKERS,

No. 22 Baltimore Street,

Opposite Maryland Institute,

BALTIMORE.

Buy and sell North Carolina, Virginia, & all uncurrent Bank Notes, Checks, Drafts, Gold and Silver Coin at best rates.

COLLECTIONS.—We collect, on all accessible points, on the most favorable terms.

HOUGH WILLIAM T., 208 W Baltimore

LAWRASON & SMITH, 6 South

Lewis Martin, 44 Second

Lownds James, 81 Second

Murdock & Pennington, 71 Second

NORMAN M. S. & SON, Stock and Bill Brokers. *Office*, 69 Second. *Dwelling*, 61 McCulloch.

RHODES J. M., 79 Second n South. NEGOTIATES TIME PAPER AND LOANS.

Robinson J. S., 11 North

Sprigg J. A., 32 Second

*Brokers, Coffee.

SMALL E. C. & CO., 1 Commerce

White & Elder, Exchange pl

Broker, Custom House.

NORRIS THOMAS M.,

NOTARIAL WRITER

AND

Custom House Broker,

NOTES AND EXTENDS MARINE PROTESTS; ADJUSTS AVERAGE ACCOUNTS; PROCURES PASSPORTS;

Draws Bills of Sale and Mortgages for Vessels; prepares Custom House

and all other papers appertaining to Commercial Business.

S. W. corner Gay & Lombard Sts.

BALTIMORE, MD.

MARINE SURVEYORS ALSO AT THIS OFFICE.—Joseph Clackner, Joshua Binney, Joseph B. Cole.

---

*Brokers, Foreign.

GRAF & ENGLER, 18 Second, Foreign Exchange & Bill Brokers.

Broker, Insurance.

(*See also* INSURANCE AGENTS.)

Conegys Benj'n, N E c Charles and Baltimore

Brokers, Merchandise.

BARRY & HOOGEWERFF, 4 Grocers' Exchange, Commerce

BRANNAN & PEARSON, MERCHANDISE BROKERS, 3 Commerce Street.

HYLAND & WOODS, 1 Exchange pl

KEYS ROBERT T. & CO., MERCHANDISE BROKERS, 79 Exchange pl, Baltimore, and 95 Wall Street, New York

---

SMALL E. C. & CO.,

1 *Commerce,*

COFFEE, SUGAR,

AND

General Merchandise Brokers.

Thompson S. P. & Co., 69 Exchange pl

Brokers, Produce.

Foard A. K., 69 Exchange pl

Brokers, Real Estate.

(*See also* AGENTS, REAL ESTATE; *also* CONVEYANCERS.)

Bayzand Wm. H., 34 St Paul
BUNTING SMITH K., 26 St Paul, buys and sells Ground Rents, Mortgages, Houses, Farms, &c.&c.
GORSUCH PEREGRINE, 32 St Paul
HAMMOND, BRO. & CO.,29 St Paul
HARVEY J. W., 22 Second
HILL THOMAS, S W c St Paul & Fayette. See card under Conveyancers.
Jackson John J., 38 St Paul
LIVEZEY E., 48 Lexington
MARRIOTT WM. H., 24 N Charles
Powles Henry, 26 St Paul
Stevenson Wesley, 34 St Paul
Tinges Geo. W., 3 St Paul
WILLIS HENRY M., Real Estate Broker, 67 W Fayette

Brokers, Ship.

Applegarth Wm. & Son, 37 W Pratt
Berry C. A., 62 S Gay
KELSEY & GRAY, c Buchanan's whf & Pratt, head of Frederick st Dock, Commission Merchants and Ship Brokers.
Maguire A. J., 79 Smith's whf
Mitchell M. A., 2 Spear's whf
RHOADS W. & SON, c Smith's whf and Pratt, Ship Brokers and Commission Merchants
Rose & Lyon, 1 O'Donnell's whf
Sullivan James, Gay c Pratt

Brokers, Stock and Exchange.

(*See also* BANKERS; *also* BROKERS, BILL, and NOTE; *also* BROKERS, GENERAL.)

Baltzell P. C., 24 South
Berg O. H., 16 South

BOULDEN J. E. P.,

Stock and Exchange Brokers,

79 Second.

Broadbent Brothers, 23 South
COHEN ISRAEL, Stock Broker, 7 South
Cox James H., N E c Baltimore and North
FISHER WM. & SONS, 32 South, Stock and Bill Brokers. Orders for sale of Stocks, Bonds, &c., executed at the Stock Board
GILDERSLEVE & WHITRIDGE, STOCK AND BILL BROKERS, 61 SECOND
GITTINGS JOHN S. & CO., 29 South
Hall Thomas W., 21 South
Harris Samuel, jr., 13 North
Hartzog George, 24 South
Hoffman Gillmore, 9 South
HOUGH WILLIAM T., 20S W Baltimore
JOHNSTON BROTHERS & CO., 198 W Baltimore

LAWRASON & SMITH,

Stock and Bill Brokers,

6 South Street, Baltimore.

WM. W. LAWRASON,

CHARLES F. SMITH.

LOWNDS JAMES,
STOCK BROKER,
. 91 SECOND.

Murdock & Pennington, 71 Second
Norman M. S. & Son, 69 Second

PATTERSON A. B., N E c South
and Exchange pl
Perine E. G., 24 South
PURVIS & CO., 192 W Baltimore
Rayner Wm. S., 5 St. Paul
SCOTT T. & SONS, STOCK BRO-
KERS, North c Fayette. Buy
and sell Stocks and Bonds on
Commission in the New York,
Philadelphia, and Baltimore mar-
kets
STONE JAMES H., N E c Balti-
more and Charles
Sullivan P. H., 34 Second

TORMEY LEONARD J.,
22 South,

Stock and Bill Broker.

STOCKS and SECURITIES of
this and other markets bought and
sold on Commission.

Prices and sales of New York
Stocks received daily by telegraph.

COMMERCIAL PAPER
AND LOANS
NEGOTIATED.

WAINWRIGHT, CLOUD & CO.,
176 W Baltimore
Wilkins Joseph, 85 Second
Winchester James, 16 South
Woodville Wm., 5 North
Zimmerson J. W., 24 South

Brokers, Tobacco.

BASS W. ALEX., TOBACCO BRO-
KER, 122 Water st, New York,
and 51 Exchange pl, Baltimore

Broom Makers.

Acomb William, 121 Franklin
CHIPMAN GEO., c Calvert and
' Lombard
Kahmer Philip, 28 Ensor
Reisenweber Frederick, 280 N Gay

Brush Makers.

ATWOOD B., 62 S Calvert
Daily T. H., Lombard and Charles

JONES WILLIAM H.,

Brush Manufacturer,

15 S. Sharp street, Baltimore.

All kinds of

FACTORY BRUSHES

made to order.

MEGRAW WILLIAM A., 210 W
Pratt
Orem & Albaugh, 278 W Pratt
POPPLEIN G. & N., jr., (Paint), 50
South.   (See advertisement.)
Slater Henry, 172 E Baltimore
Thompson James S., 712 W Balti-
more
Whitson John, 148 N Gay

Builders' Materials.
Stevens George O., 47 W Pratt
Turner Jonathan, 25 W Pratt

Butchers.
ABELL C., Lexington mkt and 48
Centre mkt
Abell J. & Bro., 24 Richmond mkt
Albach John, 26 Fell's Point mkt
Albert John, Lexington mkt, & 15
Hollins mkt
Albert Michael, Lexington mkt
Althaus Peter, 27 Bell Air mkt
Arbin Henry J., 25 Bell Air mkt
ATKINSON GEORGE, 27 Centre
market, Lexington mkt, and
32 Hanover mkt
Baker Geo., 23 Fell's Point mkt

Baker Jacob, 55 Hanover mkt and Lexington mkt
Bandell William, Hanover mkt
Bankard Jacob J., Lexington mkt and 29 Centre mkt
BARRANGER LEWIS L., jr., 74 Hanover mkt, Hollins st mkt, and Lexington mkt
Baum H., 17 Fell's Point mkt
Beck John, 16 Hollins st mkt and Lexington mkt
Bender William, 77 Centre mkt and Bell Air mkt
Benner Adam, 15 Richmond mkt
Bently H. D., 201 and 208 Hanover mkt
Berenger James, Bell Air mkt
Berenstecher Mrs. C., Lexington mkt
Bersch Christian, Lexington mkt
Bertram Wm., 58 Bell Air mkt and 102 Centre mkt
Beyer Christian, 13 Hollins st mkt
Blidd M., Lexington mkt
Bold Rhinhart, 17 Richmond mkt
Bower J. Jacob, 33 Hanover mkt
Bower Mrs. J. Jacob, 29 Hanover mkt, Lexington mkt, and 40 Centre mkt
Brandon P., 66 Bell Air mkt
Brauer Henry, 34 Bell Air mkt
BREDSTEIN AUGUST, 87 Bell Air mkt
Breitenstein A., 32 Centre mkt
Brewer John, 109 Centre mkt and 44 Fell's Point mkt
Briel Christian, 7 Hollins st mkt
BRIGGS THOMAS H., 5 Richmond mkt
Brixse George, Hanover mkt
Broseker Charles, 13 Cross mkt
Buckwald M., 5 Bell Air mkt
Bump J. L., Hanover mkt
Carmichael Wm., Lexington mkt and 30 Centre mkt
CARTER G., 51 Bell Air mkt
Christ John, 32 Bell Air mkt and 121 Centre mkt

Codorie John A., 48 Bell Air mkt and 123 Centre mkt
COLLINS WILLIAM R., 91 Bell Air mkt and 115 Centre mkt
Coleman Lemon, 46 Bell Air mkt
Contain Henry, 16 Centre mkt, Lexington mkt, and 16 Richmond mkt
Cooper & Seltzer, 20 Fell's Point mkt
Conway G., Centre mkt
Cook Frederick, 56 Hanover mkt and Lexington mkt
Cook John F., 36 Bell Air mkt
Craft J. Thomas, 21 Richmond mkt
Crawford Robert K., Hanover mkt
CRINER ISAAC, 19 Hollins st mkt
Crowl Andrew S., 119 Centre mkt
Curtin J., 14 Centre mkt
Deal George, Lexington mkt, 22 Hanover mkt, and 42 Centre mkt
Decker Chas., 35 Fell's Point mkt
Deichelbore Michael, 49 Fell's Point mkt
Deichelbohrer M. & Bro., 37 Fell's Point mkt
DERUFF FRED., 45 Bell Air mkt
DIDEMON J., 100 Bell Air mkt
Dickel Henry, 53 Bell Air mkt
Dimiling Conrad, 41 Hanover market and 25 Hollins st mkt
Dimling Chas F., Fell's Point mkt
Dittus J. Frederick, Lexington mkt
Dollinger Chas., 30 Bell Air mkt
Doughler Conrad, 12 Fell's Point market
East Caleb J., Lexington mkt and 12 Hollins st market
Egner L., Lexington market
EHMANN GOTTFRED, 21 Bell Air market
Eichberg Lewis, Lexington mkt
Eichner John, Lexington mkt and 27 Hollins st mkt
Eishel George, Lexington mkt
Eitchem Chs., Lexington mkt
Eitchner David, 114 Centre mkt
Ellender Geo. W., 103 Bell Air mkt

6

Elmore James, 14 Hanover mkt and 18 Centre mkt

Fisher G. H., 56 Bell Air mkt

Fleichman & Son, Fell's Point mkt

Fleigth Chas., 22 Fell's Point mkt

Foss John, 19 Fell's Point mkt

Fowner James, Lexington mkt

Fox Samuel, 2 Fell's Point mkt

Frank Samuel, 42 Fell's Point mkt

Frankestein S., 47 Fell's Point mkt

Franz Jacob, Centre mkt

Frederic George, 40 Bell Air mkt

French William, 62 Bell Air mkt

Freyby Ferdinand, 68 Hanover mkt and Lexington mkt

Fuchs Meyer, 50 Fell's Point mkt

Funk J. J., Lexington mkt

Fughs Moses, 55 Fell's Point mkt

Gaebele Paul, 85 Centre mkt and 14 Fell's Point mkt

Gallagher Hugh, 126 Centre mkt

Gardner A. M., Lexington mkt

Gebb George, 24 Bell Air mkt

GEBELEIN GEORGE, 93 Bell Air market

Gengagel Jacob, Fell's Point mkt

German Thos. E. J., Lexington mkt and 53 Bell Air mkt

Glenn Mrs. E., 31 Bell Air mkt

Godman John D., Lexington mkt

GODMAN THOMAS, 72 Hanover mkt, 21 Hollins st mkt and Lexington mkt

Goldman Laman, 95 Centre mkt

Goldsmith Harmon, 81 Centre mkt, 102 Bell Air mkt and 70 Hanover mkt

Goodrick George, Hanover mkt

Gottlieb Philip, 49 Bell Air mkt

Grane Jacob, Hanover mkt

Greasley Chas., 9 Richmond mkt and 10 Hanover mkt

Greasley Jacob F., 12 Richmond

Grimmel John, Bell Air mkt

GUERTTER F., 19 Bell Air mkt

Gutman John B., 8 Fell's Point mkt

Hahn D. J., Lexington mkt and 5 Hollins st mkt

HAHN HARRY G., 101 Bell Air mkt

Haines Alfred F., 243 Light

Harmer Wm., 33 Fell's Point mkt

Hanan F. W., 118 Centre mkt

Hanan G. F., 120 Centre mkt

Hartmaier Richard, Lexington mkt

Hass A., 52 Harrison

HAYS WILLIAM, 15 Centre mkt, and 110 Bell Air mkt

Hein G. F., 40 Fell's Point mkt

Hein George & D., Lexington mkt

Heldman Henry, 23 Hollins st mkt and Lexington mkt

Herman John, 140 Centre mkt

Hess John J., 51 Fell's Point mkt

Hildmann Henry, 65 Hanover mkt

Hoff Jacob & Son, Lexington mkt

Hoffert F., 138 Centre mkt

Hoffman Ann & Bro., Lexington mkt, 22 Richmond mkt, & 20 Hollins st mkt

Hoffman M., 26 Centre mkt

HOLLAND E., 71 Bell Air mkt

Holland George F. & Bro., 50 Centre mkt

Hoover Francis, 24 Hanover mkt, and Lexington mkt

Hoover George, Lexington mkt, and 103 Centre mkt

Hoover I. & G., 42 Hanover mkt

Howser Louis A., Hanover mkt

Huster Andrew, Lexington mkt

Ingling Frederick, 41 Fell's Point mkt

Johnson Lewis, 2 Centre mkt

Josenhaus Charles C., Lexington mkt, and 10 Centre mkt

Jungling Chas., 31 Fell's Point mkt

KAMPE JOHN F., 108 Centre mkt and Bell Air mkt

Kats Samuel, 54 Bell Air mkt

Kauffman H., Lexington mkt

Kell Peter, 23 Richmond mkt

Keller Edward B., Lexington mkt, and 24 Hollins st mkt

Kenzie Jacob, 82 Bell Air mkt

Keseling Franz, 57 Hanover mkt

Kimberly Harry, 19 Centre mkt

Kirk James, Lexington mkt
Kirk Wm. J., Lexington mkt
Kline Wm. II., 4 Cross mkt, and 13 Hanover st mkt
Knell Henry, Lexington mkt
Knell J. Henry, 14 Richmond mkt, and 8 Centre mkt
KNOBLOCK JOHN C., 112 Centre mkt, and 35 Hanover mkt
KOBER ADOLPH, 39 Bell Air mkt
KOEHLER GEO. L., 81 Bell Air mkt
Koenig David, 4 Fell's Point mkt
Kraft Christian, 67 Bell Air mkt, 38 Fell's Point mkt, and 127 Centre mkt
Kratz John N., Lexington mkt
Krebs David II., Fell's Point mkt
Kriel Jacob, Lexington mkt and 91 Centre mkt
Kriel Charles G., 21 Hanover mkt
KRUTMAN P., 65 Bell Air mkt
Lackey Thos., 159 Centre mkt
Laib Frederick, 17 Hanover mkt
Larkin Wm., Lexington mkt
LAUTERBACK ANDREW, 83 Bell Air mkt
Lawson James, 46 Hanover mkt, & Lexington mkt
Leonner William, Bell Air mkt
Leonard Terrence, Hanover mkt
Leppardt Peter, 42 Bell Air mkt
Lering Jacob, Lexington mkt
Link John, 28 Bell Air mkt
Loney Chas., Lexington mkt
Loran James, 44 Bell Air mkt
Lour Herman, Fell's Point mkt
Lucas Francis, Lexington mkt
Lutz Henry, 16 Bell Air mkt
Lydecker Philip, Lexington mkt
Lydecker Theodore, 3 Hanover mkt
Lydecker Thomas, Lexington mkt
McCoy James, 10 Hollins st mkt
McGill Charles, Lexington mkt
McGowan Henry, 63 Centre mkt
Maase T. E., 6 Fell's Point mkt
Maisel George, 6 Hollins st mkt
Magill Charles J., 3 Hollins st mkt
Manger Martin M., 2 Richmond mkt

Marks Henry, 44 Centre mkt and 69 Hanover mkt
Martin George, 95 Bell Air mkt
Maul John, 52 Fell's Point mkt
Mayford Martin, 13 Fell's Point mkt
Megary Alex'r, Lexington mkt
Meisel George, 10 Hanover mkt
Messensmith Chas., Lexington mkt
Meyers John, 1 Cross mkt
Miller D. S. K., Lexington mkt
Miller Mr., 18 Bell Air mkt
Moedinger G., 77 Bell Air mkt
Moojer George, Bell Air mkt
Moon Edward, Lexington mkt & 71 Hanover mkt
MULES THOS. H., Lexington mkt and 24 Centre mkt
MULLER JOS., 79 Bell Air mkt
MUMMA DAVID, 13 Bell Air mkt and 53 Fell's Point mkt
Mumma Jacob, 21 Centre mkt
Myers Timothy, 9 Hollins st mkt
Nicholson Jacob R., 61 Bell Air mkt
Nicholson Jas. A., Lexington mkt
Nicholson J., 37 Centre mkt, 1 & 28 Hollins st mkt, and Lexington mkt
Oler Samuel, 25 Hanover mkt and Lexington mkt
Olgart C. Philip, 68 Bell Air mkt
Ohlgant G. Ph., 130 Centre mkt
Pappler Jacob, 38 Centre mkt and 54 Fell's Point mkt
Pappler Washington, 16 & 18 Fell's Point mkt
Parrish W., 11 Bell Air mkt
Pentz E. McK., 89 Centre mkt and 64 Bell Air mkt
PENTZ HENEY S., 63 Bell Air mkt
Pentz Jacob H., 6 Richmond mkt
Pentz John W., 19 Richmond mkt and 43 Centre mkt
Pentz S. J., 28 Hanover mkt, Lexington mkt, and 52 Centre mkt
PEPPLER ALEXANDER, 99 Bell Air mkt and 8 Richmond mkt
Peppler George, 58 Hanover mkt and Lexington mkt
Perry Josiah, 287 N Gay

Pillman August, 23 Hanover mkt & Lexington mkt
Plitt Max'n, 62 Hanover mkt
Price Sarah, Centre mkt
Proseker Charles, 406 Light
Quanz Anton, 98 Bell Air mkt
Raine D. M., 49 Centre mkt
Reetinger John, 35 Bell Air mkt
Rehnhart George, Lexington mkt
Reifle Henry, Lexington mkt
REIGN DAVID M., 44 Hanover mkt and Lexington mkt
Reisinger Wm., 20 Bell Air mkt
Riberg Henry, 29 Fell's Point mkt
Rice Wm. & Lewis, Lexington mkt
Rickter R., 146 Columbia
Rine Jacob & F., Lexington mkt
Ritter George, 76 Bell Air mkt
Roth Henrich, 17 Bell Air mkt
ROSE GEORGE, jr., Lexington mkt and 11 Hanover mkt
Ruil Daniel, 18 Hollins st mkt
Rundle Jos., 262 Light
RUSK E. W., 116 Centre mkt and 47 Bell Air mkt
Rusk G. W., 56 Fell's Point mkt
Rusk T. J., 3, 5 & 7 Centre mkt
Rusk Jacob K., 10 Fell's Point mkt
Rusk Thomas, 2 Hanover mkt
Rusk Wm. L., 4 Hanover mkt, Lexington mkt, and 9 Centre mkt
Samuel Jacob, 12 Fell's Point mkt
Schaeffer John, 89 Bell Air mkt and Lexington mkt
Scheleiger Ernest, 13 Centre mkt
Scheuerman Herman, 53 Hanover mkt
Schillinberg Daniel, 7 Hanover mkt
SCHLEIGH E., 107 Bell Air mkt
Schlipper G., 14 Cross mkt
Schluderberg H., 60 Hanover mkt
Schnipp John, 43 Hanover mkt
SCHOTTE CHRISTOPHER, Lexington mkt
Schwanz C. M., 46 Fell's Point mkt
Schouthaler Philip, 2 Bell Air mkt
Seets George, Lexington mkt
Segil Joseph, 70 Bell Air mkt

Seltzer G. & Wm., 48 Hanover mkt and 11 Centre mkt
Seltzer W. H. D., Lexington mkt
Shaab John J., 56 Hanover mkt
Shauer George, Lexington mkt and 128 Centre mkt
Shenge Charles, 34 Hanover mkt
Siebert Ernest, 5 Fell's Point mkt
SINCLAIR JAMES E., Lexington mkt, 11 Richmond mkt, and 25 Centre mkt
Slessman Geo., Lexington mkt
Smith Charles, 107 Centre mkt
Smith Frederick H., 37 Hanover mkt and 11 Hollins st mkt
Smith George, 2 Hollins st mkt, 3 Richmond mkt, and Lexington mkt
SMITH G. H., 102 Bell Air mkt
Smith George W., 78 Bell Air mkt and 74 Centre mkt
Smith Hartman, 106 Bell Air mkt and 17 Centre mkt
Smith Henry, 1 Centre mkt, 5 Hanover mkt, and Lexington mkt
SMITH JOS. S., 45 Centre mkt and 59 Bell Air mkt
Snyder J., 51 Centre mkt
SNYDER JACOB, Lexington mkt and 46 Centre mkt
Snyder J. H. & Bro., 10 Centre mkt
Snyder Jos. F., Lexington mkt
Snyder Wm. & Son, 7 Richmond mkt
Springer Charles, 8 Hollins st mkt
Springer E. W., 17 Hollins st mkt
Staylor J., 50 Bell Air mkt and 22 Centre mkt
Staylor John, 8 and 41 Bell Air mkt and 73 Hanover mkt
STAYLOR PHILIP, 95 Bell Air mkt
Stein Casper, 72 Bell Air mkt
Stein Geo. D., 12 Hanover mkt and 20 Centre mkt
Stengel Frederick, 38 Bell Air mkt and 20 Richmond mkt
Sterling T., 41 Centre mkt.

STIEBRITZ GOTLEIB, 43 Bell Air mkt
Stier Wm., 25 Fell's Point mkt
STOLL JOHN, 97 Bell Air mkt
Stolzenbarch Harman H., 64 Hanover mkt and 3 Cross mkt
STRACKE JACOB J., 101 and 104 Bell Air mkt
Street J. C., Hanover mkt
Stump Geo. L., 4 Richmond
Super Wm. H., Lexington mkt and 6 Centre mkt
Swain Jacob, 7 Bell Air mkt
Swain John, 33 Bell air mkt
SWITZER GEO. F., 13 Richmond mkt, Lexington mkt, and 106 Centre mkt
Switzer William, Lexington mkt
TABELING J. H., 75 Bell Air mkt
Temperly John H., 18 Richmond mkt and Lexington mkt
Thomas S., Lexington mkt, 47 Hanover mkt, and 69 Bell Air mkt
TIGG HENRY, 47 Hanover mkt
Tilling Fred., 61 Hanover mkt
Toffling John H., 66 Hanover mkt and Lexington mkt
Tucker Chas. E., 40 Hanover mkt
Tucker John L., 52 Bell Air mkt
Turner F. S., 38 Hanover mkt, 31 Centre mkt, and Lexington mkt
Turner Lewis, 9 Hanover mkt and Lexington mkt
Turner William, 49 Hanover mkt
Vain Edward, 21 Fell's Point mkt
VITZHUM JOHN, 73 Bell Air mkt and 110 Centre mkt
Vogelman Chas., 6 Cross mkt
VOLKER ADAM J., 37 Bell Air mkt
Walber John, 6 Hanover mkt
Walter Edward H., 26 Hollins st mkt and Lexington mkt
Walleinstein A., 96 Bell Air mkt
Wannenwetsch Charles J., 30 Hanover mkt and Lexington mkt
Wannenwetsch Fred., 31 Hanover mkt and Lexington mkt

Weaver A. C., 13 Cross mkt
Weaver Chas. H., Willow c Cross, and 16 Cross mkt
Weaver Wm. H., 15 Cross mkt, and 75 Hanover mkt
Weigel George, 15 Fell's Point mkt
Weik Wm. L., Lexington mkt
Weis Lewis, 27 Hanover mkt
Wessersmith Wm., Lexington mkt
Wetzelberger M., 104 Centre mkt
Wetzerberger N., 60 Bell Air mkt
Wetzler Philip, 45 Fell's Point mkt
White A. D., 28 Centre mkt
Wienke John G., 93 Centre mkt
Wilcox John, 111 Centre mkt
Wilcox John F., 20 Hanover mkt
Wilcox Joseph, 1 Bell Air mkt
Wilson Geo. H., 15 Hanover mkt
Wise Lewis F., 36 Centre mkt and Lexington mkt
Wolf Alonzo, 74 Bell Air mkt
Wolf John G., 4 Centre mkt
Wolf Joseph, 48 Fell's Point mkt
Wolf M., 12 Centre mkt
Wright Luther, Centre mkt
Wust John P., 59 Hanover mkt
Yunger George, 50 Hanover mkt and Lexington mkt
Zell Jacob, 67 Hanover mkt, 28 Centre mkt, and Lexington mkt
Zerweck Daniel, 19 Hanover mkt
Zerweck John, 16 Hanover mkt
Ziegler John F., 39 Hanover mkt and Lexington mkt
Ziegler Martin, 23 Centre mkt and Lexington mkt

Butter Dealers.

Abbott George, 165 Centre mkt
Ahlsleger Mrs. C. A., Lexington mkt
Austin Mary, 124 Centre mkt
Baker Samuel, 42 N Pearl
Banting George, 6 Centre mkt
Baxter Mrs., 215 Hanover mkt
Bevans Margaret, Lexington mkt and Centre mkt
Bevans P., Lexington mkt
Boyd T., Bell Air mkt

Bromwell H. J., 242 W Lexington
Brandall Mrs. M., Lexington mkt
Brittan John, Hollins mkt
Cannon Ann, Bell Air mkt
Carnes Mgt., 22 & 24 Hollins st mkt
Cassidy Elizabeth, Lexington mkt
Clark Mrs. Ann, 87 W Lexington
Clayton Alfred S., 82 Hanover
Conse C., 155 Centre mkt
Cook Catharine, 46 Centre mkt
Cook D. F., Lexington mkt and 52
and 54 Centre mkt
Cook Geo., 160 Centre mkt
Cooper John, Bell Air mkt
Cross D., Centre mkt
Dannmer C., 47 Hollins st mkt
Dell E., 30 and 32 Centre mkt
Dentry Mrs. R. B., 40 N Pearl
Donnely Mary, Bell Air mkt and
152 Centre mkt
Dorsey W. H. G., 12 Centre mkt
Doyle Mrs. Ellen, 35 Market space
and 209 Centre mkt
Dryden C. H., N E c Eutaw and
Clay
Duwees John, 208 N Gay
Edel J., 86 Centre mkt
Edell & Son, Lexington mkt and 97
Hanover mkt
Eden Mark, Lexington mkt
Ehlers Mrs. S., 2 Centre mkt
Elshell Mrs. C., 207 and 209 Hano-
ver mkt
Essender James, 262 S Broadway
and Fell's Point mkt
FEIG GEORGE A., 15 Brown
Fillbert Michael, 384 N Gay
Fisher Charles, 245 Centre mkt
Fisher H., 225 Centre mkt
Fisher H. E., 72 Fell's Point mkt
Fishpole Rebecca, Lexington mkt
Gardner Thos., Lexington mkt
Hall John H., jr., 308 N Gay
Harp Celia, 43 Fell's Point mkt
Haycock Israel, Lexington mkt
Haycock John P., Hollins st mkt
Hoffman Mrs. Ann, 133 W Lexing-
ton
Hook Catherine, Lexington mkt

Hughs Robert, Lexington mkt
Jenkins William M., 313 S Bond
Kamba Meany, 58 Harrison
Kaylor Robert, 46 Camden
Kubert John, 23 E Pratt
Lang C., 82 Fell's Point mkt
Lapp Susan, 219 Centre mkt and
106 Fell's Point mkt
Lazenby D. L., 311 N Gay
McGowen Henry, Lexington mkt
Mager P. A., 212 N Gay
Manning H. S., 42 Camden
Marks Thomas, 3 Hollins st mkt
Marr John G., Lexington mkt
Mason Edward, Lexington mkt and
205 and 207 Hanover mkt
Mason Henry, 58 and 60 Centre
mkt
Millett J. F., 20 E Baltimore
Nagle Catherine, 79 Fell's Point
mkt
New Peter, 78 Fell's Point mkt
Newbell John E., 217 Bell Air mkt
Noble James, 183 Broadway and
Fell's Point mkt
Page C., Lexington mkt
Page Elizabeth, 49 and 50 Hollins
st mkt
Parrish Mrs., Fell's Point mkt
Philip John T., 510 N Gay
Price Miss Mary, 62 Centre mkt
Repka Lucy, 188 S Ann
Richards Randolph, 291 and 293
Hanover mkt and 11 Centre mkt
Robinson Mrs., Fell's Point mkt
Rouse Catherine, Fell's Point mkt
Salbachee C., 101 Centre mkt
Schmidt Mrs. Mary, 199 and 201
Hanover mkt
Smith Mrs. Mary, Lexington mkt
Smith Rose, 215 Centre mkt
Spellisfy Martin, Lexington mkt
Stansberry William E., Centre mkt
Sturdon Joseph, 13 Centre mkt
Sturgeon Frederick, N E c Gay and
Monument
Sunntroun R., 42 Centre mkt
Taylor B., 16 Centre mkt
Taylor Geo., 18 Centre mkt

Taylor Thomas H., Centre mkt
Teepe Henry, 191 Hanover mkt and Lexington mkt
Tnabbery Ann, Centre mkt
Vogell Mrs. Louise, 195 and 197 Hanover mkt, 129 Centre mkt, and Lexington mkt
White Margaret, Hollins st mkt
Wicker Ann, Lexington mkt
Willstayer Catherine, Fell's Point mkt

*Button Depot.

DIETZ L. D. & CO., 308 W Baltimore. (See advertisement inside back cover.)

Cabinet Makers.

(*See also* FURNITURE DEALERS; *also* CHAIR MAKERS.)
ANDERSON W. E., 10 & 12 Second. (See advertisement.)
Bein Henry, 137 Wolf
Berger Simon, 99 Harrison
Beyer Louis, 12 E Pratt
Biscoff Ch., 239 S Charles
Brenan P. E., 21 N Gay
BRICK WALTER, 34½ N Howard. (See advertisement.)
Briele H., 81 Hamilton
BYRNE JAMES P., 39 N Front
Cockserbich John, 71 N Fremont
Cramer F., 162 Broadway
Cramer Francis, 219 Canton av
Finknaure H., 106 N Calvert
Fitzgerald S. M., 242 E Lombard
Foss William W., 30 N Howard
Gibmeyer H. M., 383 Canton av
GODEY THOMAS, 58 Hanover
Graefe Edward, 16 Clay
Graff C. E., 9 Clay
Hall Richard, 196 E Baltimore
Heck J., 261 Eastern av
Heimiler & Millis, 49 N High
Herold Chas., 189 S Sharp
Hickman William H., 230 N Gay
Hoeck Henry, 412 N Gay
Hollander Charles, 22 W Pratt
Hughes John & Son, 65 S Broadway

Jordon James H., 74 Holiday
JORDAN JOHN C., 93 Mulberry
Kessler George C., 229 Eager
Kneipp Wm., 63 Chestnut
Krause Wm., 272 S Caroline
Kreuter J. J., 340 S Charles
Kuhst G. N., 83 W Lexington
Kunckel C., 58 Park
Lancaster J. D., 39 E Pratt
Langood M., 263 Canton av
Leitz Andrew, 49 Penna av
Mears E. A. F., 6 W Baltimore
Meyer Henry, 106 N Howard
Mount E., 31 N Gay
Muller Jacob, 21 Harrison
Nell Andrew, 206 Columbia
Numuth F. T., Fremont
Ohr Frederick, 211 Eastern av
Pender Geo. W., 522 W Baltimore
Priester Valentine, 268 W Pratt
RENWICK ROBERT, 92 N Howard
Rodenmayer George, 38 Ensor
Rohr Leonard, 68 Richmond
Sachse Charles, 16 Ensor
Scherer Christoph, 11 Harrison
Schorr John, 67 N Gay
Schuh John C., 253 Alice Anna
Schulthers John, 159 Mulberry
Scriven T. J., 145 N Eutaw
Sellers Andrew, 222 Hollins
Skottl Fetrl, 418 Canton av
Spahn Conrad, 44 Holiday
Spence Wm., 230 E Lombard
Teufel John, 283 W Pratt
Trego William, 5 Hughes
Waskey Benjamin, 3 N Gay
WEAVER JACOB, 21 Ross, Undertaker in General. Metallic Coffins and Zinc Cases always on hand. Ready made Coffins furnished at the shortest notice.
Weaver J. H., 22 W Fayette
WHEELER SAMUEL E., Aisquith c Monument
Wiegand John, 53 Ross
Zapf John, 33 S Caroline

Cabinet Makers' Materials.

BRENAN P. E., 21 N Gay
WILKENS WILLIAM & CO., Pratt
  c Charles
WILLIAMS J. & J. & CO., 130 S
  Charles

Camphene.

(*See also* ALCOHOL.)

BOLTON W. B. & CO., 26 Cheapside and 55 S Calvert

Cane Makers.

ROMBACH P., 61 N Eutaw .

Cap Makers.

(*See also* HAT AND CAP MANUFAC-
TURERS; *also* HATS AND CAPS.)

Danz Edward, 20 President
Goldstein Simon, 57 S Eutaw
Goldstrom M., 248 Alice Anna
Grim Joseph, 197 Light
Korach L. & Bro., 70 S Charles
LENZBERG J., 469 W Baltimore.
  Military and Navy Cap Manufac-
  turer, Wholesale. All orders
  promptly attended to.
Ruben Jacob, 246 W Baltimore

Carpenters and Builders.

(*Marked thus * are Builders. See
also SASH AND BLIND MAKERS.)

Adam Frederick, Wayne
*Balke Fred., 33 Clay
BEAN JOSEPH H., 1 L Sharp
*Belt Hickman, 48 Holiday
Belt Norwood & Bro., 14 Vine
Bennett B. F., 44 S Howard
Blessing Daniel, c High and Neces-
  sity al
BOWEN JOHN W., 54 Clay
Boyd F. H. B., Braidenbaugh al
Brady Edward, Centre c Calvert
*Briel & Burns, 14 McClellan's al
Brown E., 19 Pleasant
Brown James R., Exchange al
Brown Jasper, 27 Balderston
Clark B., 17 Pleasant

Clem Peter, 35 L Sharp
Colley J. W., S Stricker
Davis John F., 35 L Sharp
Delahany Jesse S., 74 Dover
Dieffenderfer J. P., 5 L Sharp
Ehrman Jacob, 11 L Sharp
Fenehagan John C., 22 S Eden
Folks Geo. F., 13 L Sharp
Fowble Wm., 219 W Fayette
Fowble & Miller, 18 Vine
Gardner & Mathews, 179 W Lombard
Gorsuch W. G., 3 Clay
*Gott J. C., 31 N Paca
Harding J., 25 McClellan's al
Hillman A., 163 Eager
Hogg J. H. & J. S., 8 & 10 Clay
Holland Jackson, Uhler's al, bet
  Charles and Hanover
Hopkins Wm. & G. P., 69 Hanover
Isaac, 93 N Green
Jacobs Jas. M., 1 E Lombard
Loo Ephraim, 31 Harrison
*McClain James, 694 W Baltimore
Markland & Bro., Portland
Miller Isaac, 1 N Exeter
Minnick U., 2 Lovely la
Morris L. F., Franklin pl
Mylander Henry, 52 Penn av
Paine John A., 7 L Sharp
Parsons Wm., 28 Boyd
*Porter George H., 148 S Charles
Potts David S., 74 N Fremont
PRICE GEO. R., 11 L Sharp
Quigley & Tucker, 27 Marion
Reindollar J. T., 16 Clay
Reynolds Josiah, 69 N Front
*ROCHE M. & SON, 158 N Calvert
Seccombe Thomas, 18 W Fayette
Sellers Jacob, 33 Arch
Shinecomb S., Portland
Shipley A. R., 14 Vine
Snyder John H., 130 Henrietta
Sorter & Sweeny, 396 W Pratt
*Stinchcomb George, 144 N Calvert
SUTTON & THEBAN, 16 N High
Warfield & James. 14 Dover
Wesner Henry, 21 Henrietta
Wingate & Lusby, 76 N Register
Yeisley Jacob, 89 Bank

*Zimmerman Geo. J., 142 N Howard

Carpet and Floor Oil Cloth Dealers.

(*See also* CARPET MANUFACTURER.)

Griffith G. S., 77 W Baltimore
McDOWELL, ROBINSON, & CO., 264 W Baltimore
Saylor John, 2 W Baltimore and Broadway c Eastern av
TURNBULL JOHN, JR., 248 W Baltimore
Victory Joseph, 245 W Lexington
WALSH & CONRADT, CARPET WAREHOUSE, 1 NORTH GAY

Carpet Manufacturer.

(*See also* CARPET WEAVERS.)

Gelston V. D., 5 E Baltimore

Carpet Shaker.

Marz Charles, 26 Albemarle

Carpet Weavers.

Abendshan C., 232 S Charles
John George, 233 Alice Ann
KISSNER BENEDICT, 93 Bank. (See advertisement op Upholsterers.)
Niebold John, 29 S Caroline
Rosemer John, 48 Harrison
Rosemer S., 57 Penn av
Snyder John, 33 S Paca
Stober Jacob, 19 N Schroeder
Waggoner F., 19 Pine

Carriage Trimmings.

Flynn, Emrich, & Murrill, 55 Holiday. Coach Lace.
PAINE ALLEN, 2 S Liberty
WILKENS WILLIAM & CO., Pratt c Charles
WILLIAMS J. & J. & CO., 130 S Charles

Carriage and Coach Makers.

(*See also* WAGON MAKERS; *also* WHEELWRIGHTS.)

Bishop R., 93 W Fayette
Bowers William & Sons, 406 W Baltimore
Brashear George, North
CHAMPAYNE HENRY R., CARRIAGE and EXPRESS WAGON MANUFACTURER, 84 German, bet Eutaw and Paca. SECOND HAND CARRIAGES FOR SALE OR EXCHANGE.
COLFLESH GEO. B., 101 German, COACH MAKERS, REPAIRING promptly attended to.
Cross Samuel B., 69 S Howard
Curlett John & Son, 33 North

DORSEY & HISSEY,

COACH MAKERS

AND

REPAIRERS,

96 N. Calvert St.

Baltimore, Md.

Egerton & Keys, N W c North and Saratoga
Green & Hoffman, 167 W Lombard
Hazenlip J. N., 8 Swan
Kurtz Geo. J., 97 N Paca
McCann Wm., 35 S Gay
McCurley James, 31 N Liberty
Massons J., 17 N Frederick

CHAS. E. MINNICK,

CARRIAGE MAKER,

Having bought out the interest of
JONES & WEBSTER,

in the Establishment formerly
occupied by
MINNICK, JONES, & WEBSTER,
No. 65 North Calvert Street,
(OPPOSITE CITY SPRING),

Is now prepared to build all kinds of
CARRIAGES
at the shortest notice, and on the
most reasonable terms.

Repairing in all its branches done
with neatness and dispatch.

MULLIN THOMAS, JR., 91 Holi-
day
MULLMYER & HUNTER. CAR-
RIAGE MANUFACTURERS, c
Howard and Franklin
O'Connell Henry O., 29 N Gay
O'Neill John F., 78 German
Oelmann F., 61 & 63 German
Peduezzi F., 51 North
Pennington S. E., 56 German
Renshaw Joseph, 145 Franklin
RICHARDS JOHN P. & CO., 55
German
Riddlemoser & Weatherley, 92 W
Fayette
Savage Joseph R.. 4 N Frederick
SCHAEFFER CONARD W., 149½
N High
SCHROEDER F. H., JR., 44 S Eu-
taw. (See advertisement.)
Slinkman H., 812 W Baltimore
Sommer Jacob & Sons, 39 S Howard
Stevens W. H., 51 North
Toner & Cheny, 131 N Calvert
White & Albaugh, 106 Penna av

Carriages for Children.

Stembach Geo. P., 79 W Baltimore

Carvers.

(See also LOOKING-GLASS & PIC-
TURE FRAME MAKERS.)

Byrne Joseph, 32 N Calvert
Eckhardt Wm., 58 N Gay
Hays & Morse, 41 Clay
Randolph James T., 280 S Ann
Rupprecht Wm., 3 Clay
Weildenforest Louis, 124 Henrietta
Wirts M., 52 N Pearl
Yager John P., 22 E Baltimore

Cement and Plaster.

(See also PLASTER OF PARIS.)

McALLISTER JAMES, Albemarle
c Fawn
SCHARF WM. JAMES, 825 W Baltimore
SMITH C. HART, agent for Geo.
S. Page & Brother, 111 Smith's
whf. (See advertisement.)

Cemeteries.

BALTIMORE CEMETERY CO., 6
South. Thos. Wilson, Prest. E.
G. Diggs, Secy.
Loudon Park Cemetery, office 56 W
Fayette
Mount Olive, 12 Light

Chair Makers.

(See also CABINET MAKERS; also
FURNITURE DEALERS.)

BRICK WALTER, 34½ N Howard.
(See advertisement.)
Michel Adam, 56 S Eutaw
Pfiffer N. A.. 26 N Howard
RENWICK ROBERT, 92 N Howard
Sprenkle Chas. jr., S Caroline c
Lombard
Stevenson Robert, 2 E Lombard
Timmons Chas., 263 Montgomery

Chair Painters.

Daily E., 66 Ensor
Hamilton John, 22 Carleton

*Chemical Apparatus.

SHARP & DOHME, Howard c Pratt

*Chemicals, Importers of.

PITT CHARLES F., 116 W Lombard. SODA ASH, CAUSTIC SODA, SAL SODA, BICARB. SODA, BLEACHING POWDER, INDIGO, CANDLES, PEARL STARCH, GROCERS' DRUGS, &c. &c.

Chemists, Manufacturing.

(*See also* DRUGGISTS.)

Atwell R. H., 71 South
BAKER R. J., 36 S Charles. (See advertisement.)
Stimpson & Neilson, 370 W Baltimore
TYSON JESSE & CO., 7 South
"OGELER A. & CO., 5 S Liberty

China, Glass, and Queensware.

(*Marked thus * are wholesale.*)

Ball David, 166 Franklin
*BANKS ROBERT T., 53 and 55 South. IMPORTER OF CHINA, GLASS AND QUEENSWARE, AND MANUFACTURER OF STONEWARE
Bartgis Mary C., 162 N Gay
Bayley R. P. & Co., 6 Hanover
*BOKEE GEO. M., 41 N Howard
BOKEE WM. F. & CO., 1 and 3 Harrison
Booden Wm., Lexington mkt
Bote Simon, 543 W Baltimore
*COOK & HERRING, 7 S Charles. (See advertisement interleaved.)
CORTLAN & CO., 216 and 218 W Baltimore
Cowles W. & Sons, 25 S Calvert
*Dobson John A., 2 and 4 N Charles

Farmer Mrs. P., 21 N Eutaw
Frohlinger Nicholas, 197 S Broadway
Golder G., Bell Air mkt
Goodman L. & Son, 68 Harrison
Harrington Ann, 60 S Calvert
Harteveld Adolph, 506 W Baltimore and Lexington mkt
Kirsch Chas. & Co., 146 N Gay
*Marston & Bros., 246 W Baltimore
Morton P. & Son, 137 N Howard ·
Munroe M. L., 41 N Eutaw
Murray E., 290 N Gay
Parr D. Preston, 210 W Baltimore
PARR HENRY, 243 N Gay opposite Mott
Pawley Finley, 18 S Calvert
Roth Amelia, Bell Air mkt
*Sharkey John & Co., 317 W Baltimore
*SHIRLEY WM., 5 S Calvert
Slacher Henry, Fell's Point mkt
Slanich E., 220 Alice Anna
Thater G., 328 Light
Towson W. O., 26 W Baltimore
*Valiant T. D. & Co., 46 N Howard
*Valiant Wm. Thomas & Co., 216 W Pratt
Wagner Mrs. Catharine, 97 Harrison
Wonderly Wm. S., 116 N Gay
*WONDERLY WM. S. & CO., 75 W Baltimore. Importers & Dealers in China, Glass and Queensware, and manufacturers of Stoneware

Chronometer Makers.

HAGGER & BROTHER, 72 W Pratt
WALTHER PETER, 70 W Pratt

Cigar Dealers.

(*See also* TOBACCONISTS.)

ALEXANDER M., 242 W Pratt
Barker W. K., 265 W Pratt
Baldwin John F., 98 N Gay
BIRD E. CARRERE, 28 W Pratt ⸗
Black Samuel, 188 W Pratt

BLOME & JACOBI, 445 W Baltimore
Bolenius G. H., N W c Pratt & Charles
Boon John, ½ Second
BRINGMANN WM., 18 S Sharp
Castine E. M., 10 S Gay
Dellevie Samuel, 20 W Pratt
DEMITZ H. F., 118½ Light st whf
Duering Chas. S., 39 N Eutaw
Forsyth J. M., 103 N Paca
FOX CHARLES, 302 W Pratt
FINLEY F. H. & BRO., South c Lombard
Gehrmann Julius & Co., 84 N Gay
Granger M., 109 N Howard
Granger W. H., 117 N Howard
Grauer Samuel, 170 W Pratt
GREGORY J. H. D., 201 Light
HAMILTON GEO. W., 112 W Pratt
Held Charles, 289 W Pratt
HILD JOHN C., 214 Light
Holste Arnold, 12 North
Hucht C., 93 N Eutaw
KLEMM C., 105 N Calvert
Kreis Peter, 127 N Eutaw
Kuhlman Christian, 274 N Gray
LENZBERG M., 56 S Howard
Liebman & Dellevie, N W c Gay & Fayette
LINDSEY C. D., 106 W Baltimore
McCARTY & BRO., 9 St Paul, dealers in VIRGINIA MANUFACTURED TOBACCO, IMPORTED & DOMESTIC CIGARS, SMOKING TOBACCO, & PIPES—keeps constantly on hand the most choice brands of Chewing Tobacco and imported Cigars.
Martin Edward, 121 S Sharp
May & Brother, 32 N Charles

WILLIAM MICHEL,

117 N. Calvert.

TOBACCO, CIGARS, & SNUFF,

Wholesale & Retail.

MUTHERT F. R., 76 S Eutaw
Neideliss Louisa, 63 S Sharp
NEWELL PETER, 176 W Pratt
PRIDGEON JOHNSON, 301 W Baltimore
Richardson John, 30 W Pratt
Robins James, 258 N Gay
ROSENFELD S. & CO., 20 S Gay
  (See advertisement interleaved.)
Rudolph Jacob, 55 Hanover
SCHEMBERG W. H. G., 146¼ Light st whf
Seenuck Conrad, 118 E Lombard
Seidenstricker John W., 302 N Gay
TAYLOR ELIAS, 50 W Pratt
WARTMAN J. C., under Eutaw House
WEBB SAMUEL M., 9 N Liberty
WEBB THOMAS N., S E c Madison & Garden
WEINGARTEN SOLOMON, 173 W Lexington

Cigar Importers.

BECKER & BROTHER, 94 W Lombard
BOLENIUS G. H., 202 W Pratt
DE FORD CHARLES D. & Co., 37 S Gay
DOLIVEYRA, PERIDO & CO., 6 Water
GARMENDID C. G. DE, 18 Commerce, Importer of Havana Cigars
Goldsmith E., 20 S Charles
Hanna John, 7 N Calvert
Hanna William, Baltimore c St Paul
Held Charles, 289 W Pratt
KEENE E. A. & CO., 59¼ S Charles
NODLINGER & CO., 102 W Lombard
PARLETT B. F. & CO., 92 Lombard and 5 Water
WELSH WM. & SONS, 27 S Gay
  (See advertisement interleaved.)
WILKENS H. & CO., 181 W Pratt

Cigar Manufacturers.

BECKER & BROTHER, 94 W Lombard, one door from Light st, MANUFACTURERS and IMPORTERS of HAVANA CIGARS
Cullington T., 15 W Lombard
Franklin Joshua D., 275 W Pratt

GEO. W. HAMILTON,

112 W. Pratt,

bet South and Commerce,

MANUFACTURER AND DEALER

IN

TOBACCO,

   CIGARS,

     PIPES, &c.

Best brands of CIGARS constantly on hand.

Harrison P. H , 41 Clay
HUNCKEL PH.,24 S Charles

C. KLEMM,

105 N. Calvert,

MANUFACTURER AND DEALER

IN

CIGARS AND TOBACCO.

KRAUS R. & Co., 63 S Calvert and 38 Cheapside
MUELLER F., Manufacturer of and Dealer in CIGARS, TOBACCO, SNUFF, &c. &c., S E c German and Liberty
MYERS W. H., 5 Water
Requart John J., 43 Albemarle
Van Witsen E. S., 38 N Eutaw
WATTS G. S. & CO., 21 S Calvert
7

Clergymen.

Alford James E., 132 S High
Amos J. Edwin, 73 E Pratt
Armstrong Hosea, Canton
Barnes William M., 319 N Eutaw
Bell Henry, Huntingdon av
Bell Richard P.. 309 S Eutaw
Blake Cato, 48 Rock
Blake Samuel V., 92 Columbia
Bowser Jos. P., 6 Elbow la
Brightman Henry, 48 Vine
Brown Benjamin, 282 S Howard
Brown J. Wesley, 26 Greenmount av
Carroll Nathan M., 133 Hill
Carter Jos., 836 W Baltimore
Coggins John, 37 Greenmount av
Coggins Thomas, 39 Greenmount av
Collins George, Canton
Collins Joseph S., 28 W Baltimore
Cook Isaac P., 76 W Baltimore
Cooper Geo. W., 101 N Bond
Cornelius Richard, 352 W Fayette
Creighton Samuel, 100 Chew
Cronin C. C., 92 Lee
Curns James, 95 S High
Dickson Samuel M., 51 German
Edwards William B., 296 W Fayette
Elbert Henry, 85 East
Evans David, 18 Jackson sq
Evans French S., 180 Garden
Evans William, 1 N Calhoun
Foreman William, 41 Douglas
Furlong Henry, 329 E Baltimore
Gere John A., 69 Broadway
Gibson Alexander E., 202 Eastern av
Goheen Mayberry, 99 Mulberry
Gray G. Tarring, Mt Vernon
Green John J., 119 Grundy
Hamilton William, 356 Franklin
Hand Thomas R., 38 Pennsylvania av
Harman Henry M., 54 S Sharp
Heffner Edward, Greenmount av
Henderson David, 146 Forrest
Higgins James, 48 Saratoga
Hinkle Richard, 174 Aisquith
Hobbs Caleb, 167 Hollins

Hulton Henry, 49 Moore's al
Jackson Tilghman, 11 Jordan al
Jameson Andrew, 234 W Biddle
Jones David P., 100 Raborg
Justice John, 315 Franklin
Kane G. K., 363 Penn'a av
Kennedy Alexander, 263 Hamburgh
Keyworth Charles B., Baltimore
County
Kirkley John W., 454 W Lexington
Kramer James, 164 Henrietta
Kramer Samuel, 656 W Lombard
Laney William H., 214 Montgomery
Langley J. W., 320 N Caroline
Lewis George W., 40 Orchard
Lipscomb Philip D., 18 S Calhoun
McCauley J. A., 69 Barre
McCord James H., Decker
McNemar H., 127 Sharp
Marine Fletcher E., 96 E Pratt
Mark John H , 203 Ross
Matthews Henry, 120 Cider al
Mathews Perry H., 25 Wayne
Maybury John, 169 York
Merritt George, 31 East
Monroe Dr. W. R., Charles st av
Morgan Lyttleton F., 20 N Eutaw
Morgan N. J. B., 56 Conway
Morgan Tillotson A., 84 William
Murphy R. R., Baltimore County
Murray Levin, 190 Henrietta
Musson John, 50 Ensor
Ockemy James, 303 S Eutaw
Peck James, 6 Raborg
Price S. Wesley, 83 Biddle
Randolph John W., 145 Broadway
Reese Aquila A., Fort McHenry
Reese John L., 174 Hanover
Reese Philip B., Fremont
Reese William, 156 S Sharp
Reid Charles A., 22 S Calhoun
Reiley J. McKendree, 99 N Exeter
Renick William H., 52 Biddle
Richards Joseph T., 44 Pearl
Roberts Dr. George C. M., 125 Hanover
Sewall Thomas, Light st Church
parsonage
Shreck George W., 62 S High

Slicer Henry, 332 E Baltimore
Smith Mager, 36 Greenwillow
Smith Nicholas M., 78 Gough
Smith Thomas F., 1 Ogden al
Snyder E. B., 122 N Exeter
Sparklin Samuel, 102 S Eden
Spriddle Martin, 187 Henrietta
Stansbury J. T., 857 W Baltimore
Stevens I. Collins, 345 E Pratt
Stevenson Wesley, 164 N Eutaw
Tarter Henry H., 29 Ross
Thomas Garretson, 261 Montgomery
Tippett Charles B., 7 S Caroline
Turner Jonathan, 132 N High
Valiant John, 295 E Pratt
Van Orsdell Hezekiah, 158 N Eutaw
Vinton R. Spencer, 343 N Gay
Vallentine John H., 185 Henrietta
Ward William F., 156 Hanover
Westwood Henry C., 134 Hoffman
Wilson Samuel A., 190 Pennsylva-
nia av
Wright James, 209 Chestnut
Young Jos., 27 Wayne
Young William G., 18 Hill

Clocks.

(See also JEWELERS; also WATCHES
AND JEWELRY.)

Fasbender Marion J., 255 W Pratt
MANN JOHN, N E c Charles and
Lombard
Morrill H. O., 23 N Liberty
Parr John H., 234 W Baltimore

Clothes Scourers.

(See SCOURERS.)

Clothiers.

Bar & Bro., 189 S Broadway
Bergen Michael, 113 N Howard
B nel S., 74 and 76 Market space
Blondheim H., 105 N Howard
BOPP L., 154 Light st whf, Whole-
sale and Retail dealer in Ready-
made Clothing and Gents' Fur-
nishing Goods. Constantly on
hand a large assortment of
CLOTHS, CASSIMERES and

VESTINGS, which he will make up to order in the best Fashionable Style, on the most reasonable terms.

Brafman Abraham, 32 Centre mkt space

Brafman & Hardesty, 160 W Pratt

Brenner M., 100 W Pratt

Brenner & Bro., Thames c Bond

Brestaner Abraham, 213 S Charles

Burgunder Joseph, 295 W Pratt

Burgunder Simon, 53 W Baltimore

Carr Henry, N E c Pratt and Gay

Coonan Daniel, 70 Market space and 119 W Baltimore

Coulter E. P., 113 N Eutaw

DIETZ JOHN B., 204 W Pratt

Dode Peter, 38 W Pratt

Englepaupt C., 46 and 48 W Pratt

Fletcher J. H., 140 W Pratt

Frank Kauffman, 243 S Broadway

Frank Nison, 110 W Pratt

FRANKEL & BRO., N E c W Pratt and Market space

Frayman S., 346 W Pratt

Fried Henry, 88 Harrison

Goldman B., 4 Market space

Goldman L., 80½ Market space

Goodman A., 75 N Howard

Goodman Joseph, 10 Centre mkt space

Goodman Josiah, 22 Centre mkt space

Greenbaum J., 146 W Pratt

Greenbaum Meyer, 168 Forrest

Greennove Anna, 72 S Eutaw

Greentree Jacob, agt., 84½ Market space

Greef Levi, 213 S Broadway

Grothous C., 14 W Pratt

Gutmann Moses & Co., 331 W Baltimore

Haar H., 115 N Howard

Hamburg M., 235 S Broadway

Hamburger Isaac, 181 S Broadway

HARZBERG & STIEFEL, 168 W Pratt

HECHT JACOB & CO., 88 Market space

Herzberg S., 28 Centre mkt space

Hess & Stern, 213 W Pratt

Hexter George, 182 S Broadway

Hirsh B. D., 106 W Pratt

Hofheimer Brothers, 72 W Pratt

HOYT WM. H., 41 N Charles

Jarrett Asbury, 12 E Baltimore

Jarrett L., 126 W Baltimore

Jordan Levi, N E c Market space & Lombard

KAHN & SCHLOSS, 305 W Baltimore

Kaufman Charles, 44 W Pratt

Keyser P L., 358 W Pratt

Kronhymer Simon, 122 W Pratt

Kuhn & Co., S E c Lexington & Green

Lamm & Brother, 96 W Pratt

Laugheimer M. H., 134 W Pratt

Laupheimer Jacob & Co., 184 W Pratt

Linderman L. Gustav, 314 W Pratt

Lipp & Co., S W c Baltimore & Paca

LONG & TANNEBAUM, 162 & 164 Light st whf, Wholesale & Retail Clothiers' & Gentlemen's Furnishing Goods; constantly on hand a large assortment of CLOTHS, CASSIMERES, & VESTINGS, which they make up to order in the best and most fashionable style on the most reasonable terms.

MANDLEBAUM G., 83 N Howard

Mandlebaum Mrs. J., 129 N Howard

Meyer E., 161 Franklin

Meyer L., 177½ Franklin

PATTERSON & FIELD, 81 Thames F P

Rea John H. & Co., N E c South & Pratt

Rose B., 252 W Pratt

Rosenthal Adolphus, 61 S Eutaw

Rosenthal Simon, 72 Harrison

Row & Landower, 62 W Pratt

Rudney John B., 209 W Baltimore

SANNEBORN HENRY, 315 W Baltimore
Schiff Levi, 127 N Howard
Schiff Meyer, 97 N Howard
Schloss Nathan, 229 S Broadway
Schloss Wm., 169 S Broadway
Schudle F., 257 Light
Seal Geo. McK., 50 W Baltimore
Seldner & Co., 105 & 107 N Gay
SHIPLEY, ROANE & CO., 303 W Baltimore
Siegel, Grunebaum & Schmidt, 323 W Baltimore
SMITH, BROS. & CO., 40 W Baltimore. (See advertisement outside front cover.)
Sonneborn L., 273 W Pratt
Sonnehill K. B., 125 N Howard
SPRINGER WOLF, 52 & 54 W Pratt
Springer & Freidenrich, 305 W Baltimore
Stang Henry, 320 W Pratt
STANSBURY JAS. E., 83 Thames F P, N Broadway, S side, Wholesale & Retail Fashionable Clothing, in all its varieties. *Clothing made to order.*
Starnglanz L., 318 W Pratt
Stein John, 209 Light
STEIN BROTHERS, 295 W Baltimore
Stine B., 73 W Baltimore bet South & Gay — Clothing House. Clothing of superior quality readymade, and made to order; also Gentlemen's Furnishing Goods.
Stine N. H., 55 N Howard
Stocksdale N., 78 Market space
STRASBURGER K., 97 and 99 N Gay
THANHOUSER JACOB, 124 W Pratt
THRASHER ROGERS & CO., 343 W Baltimore
WALKER NOAH & CO., Washington Bdgs, Baltimore bet Calvert and Light, op Adams' Express. (See advertisement.)

Weil Jacob, 205 Light
Weil Jonathan, 87 Thames
Weisgerber Henry, 173½ Franklin
Whitestone David, 103 Harrison
Wiesenfield & Co., Baltimore c Centre mkt space
Wise Jacob, 233 S Broadway
Wolf & Bergman, 244 W Pratt
Wornitz A., 12 Centre mkt space
Wurtzburger A., 169 Franklin
Wurtzburger S., 147 Franklin
Wurtzburger Sam'l, 108 Franklin
Wurtzburger Simon, 32 W Pratt
Zirckel Wm., 56 W Pratt

Clothiers, Wholesale.

Burgunder B., 276 W Pratt
Ellinger S., 297 W Baltimore
Frank L. & A., 287 W Baltimore
Friedman M., 241 W Pratt
HARTMAN & STRAUS, 326 W Baltimore
Hirshberg & Reinbard, 294 W Baltimore
KAHN & SCHLOSS, 305 W Baltimore, bet Liberty and Howard. MANUFACTURERS AND WHOLESALE DEALERS IN READY-MADE CLOTHING. HENRY KAHN.   WM. SCHLOSS.
SHIPLEY, ROANE & CO., 303 W Baltimore. WHOLESALE AND RETAIL CLOTHIERS. MILITARY CLOTHING OF EVERY DESCRIPTION ON HAND AND MADE TO ORDER AT SHORT NOTICE.

Sonneborn, Seligman & Marx, 310 W Baltimore

STEIN BROTHERS,

295 W. BALTIMORE.

Manufacturers and Wholesale Dealers in Clothing.

Walter R., 300 W Baltimore
Wiesenfeld & Co., 270 W Baltimore

Clothiers, Wholesale and Retail.

Brafman & Hardesty, 160 W Pratt
Brenner & Bro., Thames c Bond
FRANKEL & BROTHER, N E c W Pratt and Market space
HECHT JACOB & CO., 88 Market space N W c Pratt. Wholesale and Retail CLOTHIERS and dealers in GENTLEMEN'S FURNISHING GOODS, and a general assortment of India Rubber Clothing. Particular attention given to Customer Work.
Herzberg S., Centre mkt space

SMITH, BRO'S & CO.,

MARBLE HALL

CLOTHING HOUSE,

40 W. BALTIMORE.

Ready-made Clothing for MEN and BOYS' Wear,

, And the most Beautiful Styles of Cloths, Cassimeres and Vestings to be made to order.

PRICES VERY MODERATE.

MARBLE HALL,

No. 40 West Baltimore Street,
1 door ab. Raymond & Burton's.
(See advertisement outside front cover.)

Wiesenfeld & Co., Baltimore c Centre mkt space and 270 W Baltimore

Clothiers, Boys.

Finn Catharine. 111 St. Paul
Gardner S. S. & M. E., 62 W Lexington
HOYT WM. H., 41 N Charles
Ring Moses, 221½ and 223 W Pratt
SCHEER M. A., 65 W Lexington

Clothing, Second-hand.

Bergmann Moses, 230 S Charles
Bonhim B., 144 S Eutaw
Cline Mrs. Sarah, 700 W Baltimore
Cohen M., 21 Second
Deevie Solomon, 2 Harrison
Friedman Samuel. 5 Second
Hart Tobias, 11 Second
Levan Henry, 238 Light
Meyers Jacob, 15 Second
Poskrixky Israel, 1 Second
Reiden Adam, 274 S Eutaw
Rosenberg A., 7 Second
Smith J. C., 80 N Gay
Weil B., 110 S Eutaw

Cloths, Cassimeres & Vestings.

DAMMANN F. W. & E., IMPORTERS and COMMISSION MERCHANTS, 19 Hanover. FRENCH & GERMAN CLOTHS, DOESKINS, FANCY WOOLLENS, HOSIERY, &c. &c.
Frank Simon & Co., S E c German & Hanover
HESS, BLUM & CO., 271 W Baltimore, bet Hanover & Sharp, Jobers & Dealers in CLOTHS, CASSIMERES & VESTINGS
MOORE ROBERT & BRO., 233 W Baltimore, IMPORTERS and JOBBERS of CLOTHS, CASSIMERES & VESTINGS
OBERNDORF A., 10 S Charles, Importer & Jobber of Cloths, Cassimeres & Vestings

OREM, HOPKINS & CO., Importers and Wholesale Dealers in CLOTHS, CASSIMERES, VESTINGS, PIECE TRIMMINGS AND GOODS EXCLUSIVELY ADAPTED TO MEN'S WEAR. 238 W Baltimore

Schleunes & Hinrichs, 84½ W Baltimore

Sigel David, 7 Hanover

SPILLER & ALCOCK, 252 W Baltimore

STRAUS M. L. & CO., Importers and Jobbers of Cloths, Cassimeres Doeskins, Coatings, Vestings, &c. 256 W Baltimore. M. L. Straus, M. Rich

Coal Dealers.

(*See also* COAL MINERS & SHIPPERS.)

Adams Emelus, Back Basin c Caroline

Bennett G. R. & L. E., 169 Howard

BROWN, MITTAN & CO., North n Monument

CALLIS JAMES H., 226 E Baltimore

Campbell & Slack, 95 W Lombard

Carson & Spedden, 164 Hollins

Collins J. B., 88 North

Crothers David, 77 North .

CRUSSE JOHN, jr., Boston c Leakin, Canton

Cushing & Ehlen, 36 Second

Davis G., Bond c Lombard

Davis Geo. M., 200 E Lombard

Davis M. A., 16 Gough

Fenhagen James C., 214 N Gay

Ford C. W., 32 Light

Forman A. D. & H. C., 513 W Baltimore

Giese J. Henry, 9 South

Haines B. F., N W c Fayette and Fremont

High & Shanley, 123½ W Lombard

HOUSE WM. A., & CO.,

WHOLESALE AND RETAIL DEALERS

IN

ANTHRACITE & BITUMINOUS

COAL.

Office—S W c South and Lombard.

Yards—Head of Union Dock.
  Cathedral st n Bolton Depot.

Houck A. V., 61½ N Eutaw

Jameson & Brown, 253 W Lexington

JANNEY R. M, 19½ South

JENKINS JAMES W., 67 Second, WHITE AND RED ASH COAL, FROM BEST MINES. CUMBERLAND COAL. SAWED AND SPLIT WOOD.

KREBS C. W., 83 Second

LEISENRING G. W., dealer in ANTHRACITE AND CUMBERLAND COAL. *Office*, N E c Howard and Franklin.

McClymont Wm. & Co., Falls av bel Pratt

McCULLOUGH JOHN C., Fremont c Pratt. (See advertisement p. 4 back.)

McNeal James, jr., 58 Second

McPHERSON JOHN H. T., agent, 79 South

Miller J., jr., Paca c German

Miller J. H., 6 St Paul

Moore John A., 3 W Fayette

MYERS DANIEL E., North near Monument

Onion E. D., Forrest c Britton

Onion Wm. F., Central av c Lombard ,

RIEMAN R. G., *Office*, 12 South; *Yards*, Foot Albemarle and Back Basin, c Howard & Richmond mkt

ROBINS EDWARD, *Office*, No. 7 Sun Iron Building; *Yards*, Cathedral st and c York and Johnson. WHOLESALE & RETAIL DEALER IN ALL KINDS OF COAL.

Silverwood & Sheckells, 154 Central av

Storm Jeremiah, 78 North

Sullivan J. F., 102 Light st whf

SUTTON, PENNINGTON & CO.,

13 South Street,

DEALERS IN ALL KINDS

OF

COAL.

YARDS, cor. North and Madison, and south side of Basin.

Timanus John T., 65 N Green

WALKER G. W. & T. S., DEALERS IN ANTHRACITE AND BITUMINOUS COAL, 3 S Sharp

WASHBURN W. F., Lee c Light

Wright Isaac H. & Co., 26 N Gay

Coal Miners and Shippers.

AMERICAN COAL CO., 57 Exchange pl

AUDENRIED LEWIS & CO., 20 Second

BALTIMORE COAL CO., HOFFMAN & SON, sole Agents, 6 South

BOYCE JAMES,

36 Second St., Baltimore.

Miner and Shipper of Wyoming and Lorberry, Anthracite and George's Creek Bituminous Coals.

Shipping wharves, Locust Point, Baltimore; and Havre-de-Grace, Maryland.

DOBBIN & CO.,

24 Second St.

MINERS AND SHIPPERS OF THE BEST WHITE AND RED ASH COALS;

Also Cumberland Coals,

From the best GEORGE'S CREEK MINES.

GEMMELL THOMAS, MINER & SHIPPER of COAL, 44 Second

Hamilton S. M. & Co., Baltimore c South

Hern M. P. & Co., 24 Second

HOFFMAN & SON,

6 South st, opposite Sun Building.

SOLE AGENTS

OF THE

BALTIMORE COAL COMPANY;

Also offer *Cumberland Coal,*

From the best *George's Creek Mines.*

G. B. HOFFMAN,

HOWARD HOFFMAN.

HOUSE, WASHBURN & CO.,
Shippers and Dealers in

CUMBERLAND COAL,

FROM THE

GEORGE'S CREEK VALLEY.

Office—S W c South and Lombard.
Shipping Wharf—Locust Point,
Baltimore.

PIEDMONT COAL & IRON CO.,
57 Exchange pl

RIEMAN R. G.,

Wholesale and Retail Dealer in

BLACK DIAMOND,

LEE, LORBERRY, LAMBERT,

AND TREVORTON

C O A L S .

Office—No. 12 South.

Yards—Foot of Albemarle Street,
and Back Basin, cor Howard St.
and Richmond Market, Baltimore

SHORT (THE) MOUNTAIN COAL
COMPANY OF LYKEN'S VAL-
LEY, PENNA. *Office*—23 South
St, Baltimore. EDW. JESSOP,
PRESIDENT. E. STABLER, JR.,
SECR'Y and TREAS.

STABLER E., JR., & CO.

23 SOUTH STREET,

Shippers and Wholesale dealers in

ANTHRACITE

AND

BITUMINOUS

C O A L S .

Wilkesbarre, Pittston, Mount Car-

mel and Shamokin White Ash, Lyken's Valley and Pine Grove Red
Ash Coals.

George's Creek Bituminous Coal.

Lehigh Coal for Cupola Furnaces,
&c. &c.
Shipping Wharves—Havre-de-
Grace, Md., and Canton and Locust
Point, Baltimore.

STICKNEY & CO., 57 Exchange
pl. SHIPPERS OF THE AMERI-
CAN COMPANY, AND PIED-
MONT COMPANY'S COAL.

SUTTON, PENNINGTON & CO.,

13 SOUTH STREET,

Sole Shippers of Genuine

Lyken's Valley Coal,

ALSO

BALTIMORE COAL CO.,

AND SUNBURY

AND GEORGE'S CREEK COAL.

Shipping Wharves—South side
Basin, Locust Point, and Havre-
de-Grace, Md.

Wilson Thomas, 6 South

Coal and Wood Dealers.

CRUSSE JOHN, JR., dealer in
COAL AND WOOD, PURE LY-
KEN'S VALLEY AND WHITE
ASH COALS. HICKORY, OAK
AND PINE WOOD Constantly on
hand at lowest Cash Prices. AND
DEALER IN SAND OF ALL KINDS.
Yard—Cor Boston and Leakin,
Canton.
GIESE J. HENRY, 9 South
Houck A. V., 61½ N Eutaw

McCULLOUGH JOHN, *Yard and Office*—Pratt and Fremont, and Park and Fayette. *Wharf*—Eutaw. (See advertisement p. 4 back.)

Coffee Importer.

Bacon J. E., 476 W Baltimore

Coffee Roasters and Spice Factors.

Crawford Wm. H. & Co., 62 South
MARKELL CHARLES, S E c Calvert and Lombard
Ridgway S. C., 505 W Pratt
Siegmann C., 152 Hillen
Siegmann J. G., 68 Ensor

Coffin Trimmings.

GMINDER JACOB, 10½ S Calvert

MEYER L.,
216 W. PRATT STREET,
Manufacturer of
Coffin Screws and Tacks.
Britannia Work in all its Branches.

NORRIS C. SIDNEY, 36 Hanover
SAUTER P. & BRO., 20 S Sharp
SCHMIDT M. F., MANUFACTURER OF COFFIN TRIMMINGS, 8 W Water

Collar Makers (Horse).

Bullock Jos., 21 Mercer
HAMMOND JOHN D., 348 W Baltimore
Harvey Thomas & Sons, 33 N Green
LAWSON ROBERT, 277 W Baltimore
MERCER LUTHUR O., 334 W Baltimore

Collectors.

(*See also* AGENTS, PROPERTY AND COLLECTING.)
Boyd S. & S., 84 N Caroline
Elias Samuel, 65 Harrison

Ker Dashiell S., 32 St Paul
Lindsay G. W., 20 N Paca
Mackenheimer J. N., 28 St Paul (Constable)
Nally Richard, N W e St Paul and Fayette (Constable)
Patterson Wm. G., 32 St Paul
Ray John B., 28 St Paul
Reese Samuel, N W c St Paul and Fayette (Constable)
Ridgely James L., 26½ E Baltimore. Internal Revenue, 2d District.
Stevenson Henry, 67 Second
VALLEE JOSEPH A., 72 W Fayette
Whiteley J. H., 101 N Paca
Wilson James J., N W c St Paul & Fayette (Constable)
Woollen L. R., N W c St Paul and Fayette (Constable)

Colleges.

Carter J. P., 118 E Baltimore

F. H. GALLAGHER'S
Mercantile College,
207 & 209 Baltimore St., between Charles and Light,
BALTIMORE.

PRACTICAL INSTRUCTION IN
Practical Bookkeeping, Business Writing, and Practical Mercantile Affairs.

Ornamental Penmanship,
By A. McLAURIN,
Executed Beautifully, Tastefully, & Skilfully.
See advertisement outside back cover.

LOSIER E. K., PRINCIPAL BALTIMORE COMMERCIAL COLLEGE, over N E c Baltimore and Charles. Dwelling, Eutaw House.

*Colors, Importers of.

POPPLEIN G. & N. JR., 50 North.
(See advertisement op DRUGGISTS.)

Colonization Office.

Hall G. W. S. & Co., 65 Second

Commissioners of Deeds.

(*See also* LAWYERS.)

Atkinson Joseph T., 36 St Paul
Benzinger Frederick F., Law bdgs
Bryan Wm. S., 36 St Paul
Burgess Henry Howard, 4 Spurrier's
ct, Lexington
DANELS BOLIVAR D., 57 W
Fayette
LATIMER JAS. B., S W c Fayette
and St Paul
Pratt J. D., Baltimore c Charles
Root H R., 5 St Paul
Snyder John J., 53 Fayette
Sprague E. R., 5 St Paul
Whelan Thomas, jr., 16 St Paul
Williams Dalrymple, N W c Calvert
and Lexington

Confectioners, Wholesale.

BLOME & JACOBI, 445 W Balti-
more, STEAM CANDY MANU-
FACTORY, Wholesale and Retail
Dealers in CANDIES, FRUITS,
CIGARS, &c. All Candies war-
ranted to keep in any climate.
G. Blome.   G. Jacobi.

BRIDGES, WILLIAM & SON,
313 W. Baltimore,
WHOLESALE DEALERS IN

Foreign Fruits, Candies,

*Almonds, Raisins, Oranges,
Lemons,*

REFINED SUGARS,

&c. &c.

Country Merchants are solicited to

call and examine our stock before
purchasing elsewhere.
CLARK & JONES, 20 Light
GILMOUR'S A. M., NEW YORK
BAKERY AND CONFECTION-
ERY, 239 W Pratt, bet Howard
and Sharp. GOODS DELIVERED
FREE OF CHARGE. Weddings and
Parties supplied at all times with
despatch. All kinds of fine CAKES
& CONFECTIONERY on hand.
Hamilton John, N E c Howard and
Lexington
KIDD AMELIA, 35 W Baltimore,
Wholesale and Retail Confection-
ery, Fancy Goods, Foreign Fruits
and Nuts.
MARTIN JOHN & CO , 92 W Pratt
op Patterson, IMPORTERS and
DEALERS IN FOREIGN
FRUITS and CANDY MANU-
FACTURERS.
MERCHANT J. & SON, 174 W
Pratt. (See adver. p. 5 back.)
Munder C. F., 27 S Liberty
Ness G. W., 361 W Baltimore
PRACHT CHARLES & CO., 155
and 157 Franklin, steam candy
manufacturers. Wholesale deal-
ers in foreign fruits, confection-
ery of all kinds, oranges, lemons,
filberts, walnuts, palmnuts, pe-
cans, almonds, Havana and German cigars, sardines, fire crack-
ers, &c. &c.
SUMMERS & CO., 301 W Baltimore, confectioners and fruit
dealers
VIGHERI S., 57 N Charles
White & Bixler, 311 W Baltimore

Confectioners and Fruit-erers.

Abler Mrs. Catharaine, 409 Canton
av
Appell Christian, c Pearl and Fayette
Ashton John, N W c Pine and Fayette

Baccegaluppo Vincenzo, 60 N Gay
Baccigaluho J., 146 Light st whf
Baker Mrs. Caroline, 262 S Charles
Beckner Mrs. L., 10 N Green
Bedencopf Mary, 173 Hanover
Bergner George, Lexington mkt
BIRKMEYER JOHN F., 112 Franklin
Bittering John, 7 Penn av
Blair Mrs. A., Mulberry c Chatsworth
Blessing Mary, 14 Eden
BLOME & JACOBI, 445 W Baltimore
Bower George, Lexington mkt
Boyer John, Lexington mkt
Brand Mrs. H., 187 S Charles
Brandt Mrs. Kate, 550 W Pratt
Bregel Joseph H. T., 71 N Gay
BRIDGES WM. & SON, 313 W Baltimore
Brooks A. S., 57 N Calvert
Brown George, 31 Ross
Brown Mrs. Mary, 68 Thames
Brugel Joseph, 128 Centre mkt
Burman Ernest H., Lexington mkt
Burnett Mrs. J., 188 E Baltimore
Busky Miss Anna, 108 Thames
Butcher Alexander, 160 W Baltimore
Caddy J. N., 315 N Gay
Caldwell A. P., 149½ N Gay
Carroll E., 79 North
Clagett Mrs. E., 20 President
CLARKE & JONES, 20 Light
Clinton David, 73 Fell's Point mkt
Clinton David (col'd), 144 N Register.
Close Nicholas, 139 Gough
Coates James A., 54 W Baltimore
Cole Mrs. J., 86½ Hanover
Colton Frederick, 100 Hillen
Connell Mrs. M., L Sharp c Barnet
Conner Mrs. R., 644 W Baltimore
Conrad John F., 253 Franklin
Conroade John, Lexington mkt
Cook Elizabeth, 221 Alice Anna
Cox Mrs. M., 229 Biddle
Cullison J. M., 182 Madison av

Cunio A., Douglass c Forrest
Dankmeyer Mrs. W., 830 W Baltimore
Darling L., 137 N Eutaw
Derenberger Jacob, 67 Ross
Derringhugh G. & J., Lexington mkt
Drexell Henry, 57 N Gay
Eck Henry, 179 S Broadway
ECKHARDT CHARLES, 239 N Gay
Edwards Mrs. M., 195 E Pratt
Ehrardt Mrs. M., 252 S Eutaw
EMMEL JOHN, 283 Canton av
Engel Mrs. C., 12 Ensor
Engel Mrs. Elizabeth, 580 W Baltimore
Eshman Mrs. F., 176 Madison av
Everitt J. J., 357 N Gay
Evers Mrs. Ann, 249 Canton av
Falkenstein F., 257 Light
Farley Edward, 76 S Broadway
Feister Mrs. Susan, 213 Eastern av
Feite Mrs. A., 78 Park
Ferguson M., 224 N Eutaw
Fisher Mrs. E., 18 E Baltimore
FLAMM MRS. M., 88 W Lexington
Flecher Mrs. A., 165 Penn. av
Fritz Harriet, 266 Aisquith
Furguson Mrs. E., 458 W. Baltimore
Gafford Mrs. D., 466 W Baltimore
Gambrell James, 22 Greenmount av
Gardner Mrs. E., 311 W Pratt
George Mrs. H., 710 W Baltimore
Gebel Jacob, 501 W Pratt
Geiger John, 16 E Pratt
Getz F. W., 185 S Sharp
Getz George, 843 W Baltimore
Gibson W., 746 W Baltimore
GILMOUR A. M., 239 W Pratt
GILMOUR JAS. D., Madison av c Eutaw
Girty Mrs. B., 270 S Charles
Gisrehn Frederick, 120 Greemount av
Glenn Mrs. R., 20 Fell's Point mkt
Goty Mrs. Mary Ann, 123 Eastern av
Gray Mrs. E., 61 President

Gray Mrs. Mary, 83 N Front
Greaves Mrs. T., 252 Montgomery
Green Mrs. Cordelia, 140 Aisquith
Greenies Louis, Biddle c Ross
Grimm John A., 544 W Baltimore
Hagan Martin, Valley c Neighbor
HAMILTON JOHN, Manufacturer of New York Candies, Wholesale and Retail, N E c Howard and Lexington. N. B.—Country orders promptly attended to.
Hammersley D. L , 26 N Green
HARBAUGH MRS. A. M., 121 N Calvert, Ice Cream and Eating Saloon, meals at all hours, also a general assortment of Figs, Nuts, Fruits, &c.
Hardagon Mrs. Ellen, 365 W Pratt
Hatter Martin, 133 N Gay
Henderson Mrs. K., 31 S Caroline
Henson James (col.), 35 Douglas
Herghe M. E., Lexington mkt
HERMAN C. C., 73 N Charles
Hersch Mrs. L., 170 E Baltimore
Hershfeld John E., 171 S Broadway
Hickey Thomas, 152 S Broadway
HICKLEY G. T., 139½ N Gay
Hickson J. S., 77 W Lexington
Hines Mrs. P., 119 Thames
Hoffmeister George, 119 Eastern av
Hopkins Rebecca, 3 S Broadway
Howard Mrs. E., 40 Pine
Imwald Mrs. Mary A., 550 W Baltimore
Irvin John A., 95 N Charles
Jennings Mary, 18 Fell's Point mkt
Johnson S., 34 St Paul
Jones Levin, 115 E Pratt
Keglers John G., 246 Lexington
Kelley Mrs. Ellen, 42 Greenmount av
Kemp Mrs. Ann, 244 S Broadway
Kessler George, N E c Gay and Aisquith
Keyser E., 217 Montgomery
KIDD AMELIA, 35 W Baltimore
Kidd and White, 16 W Baltimore
Kierste M. M., 78 S Broadway

King James, Baltimore c Caroline
Kittering Peter, Lexington mkt
Kinckmann Mrs. Emma, 265 Montgomery
Knight Mrs. M. A., 19 Marion
Koestner Mrs. F., 187 E Pratt
Koss Charles, 54 N Eutaw
Kreamer John, 8 Greenmount av
Krite Mrs. Lucinda, 361 Canton av
Kugler Samuel 262 W Pratt
Lang Mrs. G., 181 E Pratt
LAUTERBACH F., S Poppleton c Hollins
Leistner Joseph, 294 Alice Anna
Lentz Mrs. Elizabeth, 174 S Broadway
Lewis P. B. A., 55 Pearl
Lloyd P., c Sharp and Fayette and 145 E Baltimore
Loman Mrs. M., Fell's Point mkt
Lyon Mrs. Kate, 248 Central av
McClayton John, 53 Centre
McNeil Hugh, 208 Light
McNeill Archibald, 332 N Gay
Mackel Mrs. Catharine, 319 W Pratt
McSweeney John, 258 Light
Marberger Mrs. E., Mulberry c State
Martin Charles & Co., 4 N Calvert
Martin H. A., 547 W Baltimore
MARTIN JOHN & CO., 92 W Pratt
Mathews Mrs. E., 7 Pine
Maurer E., 3 S Poppleton
Meazel Mrs. C., 20 Clay
Meekins Mrs. Nancy, 209 Cross
Mirtle Wm., 63 S Fremont
Michial Louis, 421 Gay
Monteverde J., 196 W Pratt
Moon Mrs. E., 11 Fish mkt space
Moylan Mrs. B., 360 W Pratt
Mukly E., 391 S Charles
Munder C. F., 27 S Liberty
Murr W. F., 139 Hanover
Musch Mrs. D., 122 Thames
Myer John H., 704 W Baltimore
Ness G. W., 361 W Baltimore
Neeke E., 125 S Broadway
O'Donald John, 86 S Charles
Ockermo A., 86 St. Paul

Parks Mrs. Mary E., 442 Light
Parsons Mrs. Silas E., 321 E Baltimore
Patenfeld Ann, 351 Canton av
Pels S., 109 N Howard
Phelan Mrs. E., Front c Fayette
Pool George T., 432 W Baltimore
PRACHT CHAS. & CO., 155 and 157 Franklin
Pryor Mrs. Mary, 820 W Baltimore
Pund J. C., 260 N Gay
Punt John C., Centre mkt
Reed Ann, 182 Centre mkt
Reed Hannah, 58 Fell's Point mkt
Reeves Mrs. E., 152 S Charles
Rull Henry, 92 S Caroline
Russell H. J., Baltimore c Bond
Schaer J. F., 52 E Baltimore
Schillinger Henry, 101 N Calvert
Schœnpflug Julius, 62 N Pearl
Schultz William, 30 N Pearl
Schulz E., 14 E Baltimore
Schulz Charles, 492 W Baltimore
Schupp Louis, 72 N Pearl
Seabright Mary, S Green c German
Seebode Louis, 313 Light
Senderling John, 50 Aisquith
Shermer Anna, 863 W Baltimore
Shoemaker R., 236 S Fremont
Siebold Conrad, 132 N Caroline
Smith Chr., 247 Eastern av
Smith John, 59 S Howard
Smith Mrs. Sarah E., 111 S Wolf
Staikler ——, 138 Centre mkt
Stalh Adam, Eden c Lombard
Stansbury John, 236 Franklin
Stolpp J. L., Lexington mkt
Striebel George, 51 Aisquith
Sudbrick Henry, 158½ Light st whf
SUMMERS & CO., 301 W Baltimore
Taylor Alfred G., 16 W Fayette
Theas Mrs. Mimi, 500 W Baltimore
Van Holland John P., Baltimore c Caroline
VELLINES B. H., WHOLESALE and RETAIL, 85 W Baltimore
VIGHERI S., 57 N Charles. Fine Confectionery, Fresh Fruits and

8

Preserves, & all kinds of Pickles, Sauces, &c. Families supplied.
Wagner Margaret B., 458 W Lombard
Walker Mrs. F., 48 Gough
Welde George, 13 Aisquith
Wenig Alfred, 182 Forrest
Whitner Mrs. C., 89 N Schroeder
Whistler Mrs. M. J., 878 W Baltimore
White & Bixler, 311 W Baltimore
Wick Simon, 102 Central av
Willfiend Mrs. C., 66 Ross
Wolf Chris., 154 E Lombard
Wolf Geo. W., 166 S Broadway
Wolford Mrs. C., 73 Penn. av
Woodward Mrs. M., 74 Penn. av
Yingling Henry, 43 Penn. av

Constables.

Mackenheimer J. N., 28 St Paul
Morrison F. L, 58 Camden
Nally Richard, N E c St Paul and Fayette
Reese Samuel, N W c St Paul and Fayette
Whiteley J. H., 101 N Paca
Whitson David, 58 Camden
Wilson James J., N W c St Paul and Fayette
Woolen L. R., N W c St Paul and Fayette
Zenn George, 58 Camden

Consuls, Foreign.

Agent for the Underwriters at Bremen—F. W. Brune & Sons
Agent for the Underwriters at Lloyds—James Carey Coale, Exchange bdg
Austria—J. D. Kremelberg, Vice Consul, 11 Cheapside
Baden—W. Dresel, 11 Cheapside
Bavaria—W. Dresel, 11 Cheapside
Belgium—G. O. Gorter, 52 S Gay
Brazil—C. O. O'Donnell, 52 Gay
British—Frederick K. Bernaul, Second adj Post office

Buenos Ayres—C. Morton Stewart, 52 S Gay
Chili—Richard B. Fitzgerald, 6 S Gay
Darmstadt—W. Dresel, 11 Cheapside
Denmark—F. B. Graf, Vice Consul, 18 Second
France—A. Louvan, 38 Mulberry
Great Britain—Frederick K. Bernaul, over Exchange Reading Room
Hamburg and Bremen—A. Schumacher, Consul General, 9 S Charles
Hanover — Edward Urhlaub, 54 Courtland
Hesse-Cassel—W. Dresel, 11 Cheapside
Lubec—H. von Kapff, 22 German
Mexico—J. A. Pizarro, 3 Barnet
Montevideo—P. Murguiondo, 67 S Gay
Netherlands—Class Vocke, 116 S Charles
New Grenada—R. A. Fisher, 54 S Gay
Nicaraugua—C. O. O'Donnell, 52 Gay
Norway—F. B. Graf, Vice Consul, 18 Second
Oldenburg—Charles Bulling, 143 W Lombard
Peru—Richard B. Fitzgerald, 6 S Gay
Peru and Equador—James I. Fisher, 54 S Gay
Portugal—C. O. O'Donnell, 52 Gay
Prussia—W. Dresel, 11 Cheapside
Russia—Aug. Kohler, acting Vice Consul, 63 Exchange pl
Sardinia—C. A. Williamson, Union Bank, c Charles & Fayette
Saxony—W. Dresel, 11 Cheapside
Spain—J. A. Pizarro, 3 Barnet
Sweden and Norway—F. B. Graf, 18 Second
Two Sicilies—A. C. Rhodes, 63 Exchange pl

Uruguay, Oriental Republic of— Pde Murguiondo, 59 S Gay, residence 57 N Fayette
Venezuela—Bolivar D. Danels, 57 W Fayette
Vice-Consul of the Pontifical States —T. P. Scott, 16 St Paul
Wurtemberg—W. Dresel, 11 Cheapside

Conveyancers.

CINNAMOND & BROWNING, 59 W Fayette
Gill D. D., N W c St Paul & Fayette
GLOCKER & NORRIS, 63 W Fayette
GORSUCH PEREGRINE, 32 St Paul
GRIFFIN THO'S W., 170 S Broadway
Grove Jacob F., 15 St Paul
HILL THOMAS, CONVEYANCER and REAL ESTATE AGENT, S W c St Paul and Fayette. DEEDS, WILLS, MORTGAGES, &c. carefully prepared. LANDS, HOUSES, GROUND RENTS, &c., bought and sold. Also GROUND RENTS, HOUSE RENTS, and other claims collected, and a general supervision given to property placed under his charge.
Israel F. & Son, 22 St. Paul
JONES & MYLES, 53 W Fayette
Pallitt Alfred H., 10 Law bdg, 36 St. Paul
Pennington A. H. & Son, 65 Hanover
Smith R. T., 61 W Fayette
Thompson A. W., 30 St. Paul
Warfield Wm., 13 St. Paul
Yearley Alex. & Son, 15 St. Paul

Coopers.

Barickmans Jacob, 200 E Baltimore
Black J. & S., 115 Smith's whf
BOTTFFESHOF GEORGE, 240 Cross

Carroll John K., 27 Commerce
COAK J. W., 25 McClellan's al.
All kinds of work made of old
and new stuff. Beer, Flour, and
Liquor Barrels, Vats, Tubs, &c.,
made to order.
COOK WM. W., 14 McClellan's al
Cousins John, Commerce c Cable
Culver Wm. T., 5 L Sharp
Curtain Samuel, Ellicott
Eppler Jacob, 9 Cypress al
Evans George & Co., 22 Patterson
EVERIST JOHN M., 108 Holiday
bet Pleasant and Bath. Keeps
constantly on hand and makes to
order, every description of Casks,
Hogsheads, Liquor Barrels, Flour
Barrels, and everything usually
manufactured in a first class
Coopering establishment. Repairs
done with promptness and at
moderate rates.
Felder John II., 144 Central av
Feller Charles, 139 S Caroline
Frederick Laurence, 110 Franklin
Gratler Frederick, 310 Montgomery
Green R. C., Patterson c Cable
GRUETTER FRED. L., shop 208 &
210 Montgomery. Residence 222
S Sharp
Gruver & Costolay, 120 and 148
Franklin
Hermann John, Ridley c Steritt
Kees Laurence, 111 Hillen
McCann Edward, Cross n Leaden-
hall
McDANIEL C. M., 112 Dugan's
whf. Dealer in all kinds of Old
and New Barrels. Merchants and
Contractors supplied at the short-
est notice.
Miller, Laurence, 60 N Schroeder
Placide H. S. & Son, 72 Buchanan's
whf
Pollett John F., 27 Commerce
Raynold Thomas, 216 S Eutaw
Reeger John C., 186 S Charles
Scham August, 141 S Caroline
Scheckels John, Ridgely

Sheiler Anthony, 112 N Gay
Streeper, Soltar & Marshall, Ex-
change al
Thurlow & Bonday, 111 Thames
WOOLLEN JAMES, 31 Commerce.
Oak Cooper in all its branches.
Iron bound work constantly on
hand, and trimming done at the
shortest notice.
Zane Peter, 70 Smith's whf
Zorn Thos., 590 N Gay

Coppersmiths.
Bruce John M., 94 N Calvert
McCleary & Connelly, 44 Holiday
Mahler C., 28 Concord
Reed Robert, 1 W Falls av

Cordage, Rope, and Twine.
Dukehart J. & Co., 130 W Baltimore
DURAND JOHN H., 132 W Pratt
Henderson John & Co., warehouse
S E c Pratt and Commerce; fac-
tory c Harford av and Point la
RAMSAY JAS.G.,13 Thames F. P.
Westcott Jas., 113 McElderry's whf

Cork, Importers of.
BLOCK AUGUSTUS, 96 W Lom-
bard.—Importer of Cork of every
description.
BLOCK EDWARD,114 W Lombard.
Corks in all varieties.
Chestnut S. & Co., 38 S Calvert

Corset Makers.
Carey Mrs. W. F., 45 N Gay
Donelly M., 172 W Lexington

Natali Mary, 49 S Liberty
Seibert Mrs., 103 E Baltimore

Cotton and Woollen Goods, Manufacturers of.

BANKS DANIEL B., President UNION MANUFACTURING CO. OF MARYLAND, 8 S Howard. Residence, 194 Franklin.
Dickey W. J., 21 German.

GARY JAMES S. & SON,
ALBERTON COTTON MILLS,
MANUFACTURERS OF

TWILLS,
  DUCKS,
    OSNABURGS,
      WARPS,
        SHEETINGS,
          COTTON YARN, &c.
24 GERMAN STREET.

Green, Amon & Co., Exeter c Hillen
Thistle Manufacturing Cotton Factory, 166 W Fayette, N. Shannon, Agent.
UNION MANUFACTURING CO. OF MARYLAND, Daniel B. Banks, President, 8 S Howard. Residence, 194 Franklin.

Cotton Duck.

Hooper Wm. E. & Co., S E c Pratt and South
MOUNT VERNON CO., MANUFACTURERS OF COTTON DUCK, TWINE, &c., c LOMBARD AND FRANKLIN LANE, BALTIMORE.

Cuppers and Leechers.

Jane Margaret, 73 S Sharp
Stodard Mrs. J. B., 36 S Bond
Wombel Mrs. Ann, 8 Castel al

Curriers.

(See also TANNERS ; also LEATHER DEALERS.)

ACHEY FREDERICK & SON, 22 S Liberty. (See advertisment op Leather Dealers.)
ANDERSON JAMES G., 5 Balderston n Light. (See advertisement opposite Leather Dealers.)
Favere Henry, 40 Harrison
Flinspach F. W., 122 Light st whf
Friese Charles, 213 Canton av
KLEES HENRY & SONS, 15, 17, and 19 Saratoga
Kuhn E. G., 160 Light st whf
Musgrave James, 101 N Front
Printz Hartman, 369 S Charles
SCHLARB P. & H., CURRIERS AND DEALERS IN ALL KINDS OF UPPER, SOLE, AND HARNESS LEATHER; also MOROCCOS, LININGS, &c., &c., 61 S Sharp n Pratt
SPARHAWK STERNS, 7 Mercer
Stalfort F., 326 W Pratt
Thomas N. & Co., 118 N Eutaw and East c Ensor.
Vey F. E., 62 Penn av

Curtain Materials.

CROOK WALTER, JR., 220 W Baltimore
MULLER LOUIS, 110 W Baltimore
(See advertisement opUpholsterers.)

Cutlers.

Carey W. F., 45 N Gay
Daffin Benjamin, 2 Holiday
DIETZ L. D. & CO., 308 W Baltimore. (See advertisement inside back cover.)
FEICHTMAN S., 80 N Eutaw
Friese John, 142 W Fayette
Halbach Charles, 94 N Gay
Jackson Samuel, 194 W Baltimore
Koch John, 4 E Pratt

REINHARDT CHARLES C., 7 N
  Gay
Reinhardt H. D., 206 W Pratt

Dentists.

Baldetston I. & Son, 23 W Lexington
Booth R. R., 49 W Baltimore
Brown A. J. & Son, Lexington c
  Charles
Burton C. A., 94 W Fayette
Cassell & Cherry, 1 S Liberty

CHANDLEE EDWIN,

DENTIST,

15 S. Howard, West side.

Cherry M. J., 45 Hanover
Church Samuel T., 87 N Charles
Cook G. W., 67 N Charles
Etheridge W. H.. 21 S Broadway
Evan Wm. W., 79 N Charles
Gibney Richard, 32 N Gay
Gill B. J., jr., 212 N Eutaw
Gill & Bro., N W c Hanover and
  Lombard
Gill & Corrie, 56 S Sharp
Gorgas Austin, 79 N Charles
Gunther C., 183 E Baltimore
Hooper James, 189 E Baltimore
Hoopes W. H., 84 and 86 N Eutaw
Hopkinson M. A., 87 N Eutaw
McDowell Wm., 39 W Lexington
Merryman George, 50 N Calvert
Morse Wm. L., 65 N Paca
Noyes James, 320 W Lombard
OULD PERRY, 19 N High
Postley A. M., 167 N Eutaw
Stinson Wm. F., 43 Hanover

H. W. TILYARD,

DENTAL SURGEON,

14 S. Eutaw.

Tucker W. Geo., 15 N Front
Volkman Aug., 210 S Eutaw
Wilson William W., 79 N Charles

Dentists' Findings.

Snowden H. & Co., 3 N Liberty

Dining Saloons.

(*See also* HOTELS; *also* RESTAU-
RANTS; *also* TAVERNS.)
GILMOUR'S SALOON, 125 W
  Baltimore. (See advertisement.)
RUTHEFORD JOSEPH, 125 W
  Baltimore. (See advertisement.)
Wilson & Ruskell, 87 W Baltimore

Dispensaries.

Baltimore, Liberty c Fayette
Eastern, Baltimore c Canal
North Eastern, E Monument n Gay
Southern, 48 Conway

Distillers.

Bailey James, 267 Cross
Clabaugh E. A., 38 South and Rus-
  sell c Orten
Hazlehurst & Phelan, 17 Spear's
  whf
MAITLAND B. & CO., 89 South
ULMAN & CO., 48 W Lombard and
  5 N Gay

Dress Makers.

(*See also* SEAMSTRESSES.)
Ayler Mrs., 76 Greenmount av
Baggott Mrs., 194 Madison av
Benteen Mrs. R., 116 Pearl
Black Catharine, 98 Chesnut
Black Mrs. Kate, 628 W Baltimore
Brice Mrs., 125 N Eutaw
Bride Mrs. E., 129 W Madison
Brun Mrs. F., 86 W Lexington
Button Francis, 81 Chesnut
Curvall Francis, 145 Central av
Dorman Ann, 176 N Front
Dorsey Mrs. R., 203 Mulberry
Dudley Mary, 289 Light
Flanary Miss H., 85 W Lexington
Frizell E., 551 W Baltimore
Gaines Mrs. Jane, 19 S Eutaw
Gaines Mrs. M., 19 S Eutaw
Glasser Mrs. Catharine, 111 S Dal-
  las

8*

Gould Mrs., 121 N Howard
Gormley Mrs. M. R., 122 Mulberry
Hanson Amelia, 301 S Bond
Hill Mrs. M. J. (col'd), 47 Raburg
Hunley Miss A., 7 S Green
James Mrs. Ann, 74 Park
Johnston S. E., 100 W Fayette
Knipe Mrs. E., 59 Centre
Lalor M. & C., 114 N Calvert
Litsinger M. J., 21 S Eutaw
Lloyd S., 138 N Eutaw
Lowders Misses, 20 S Paca
McCormick Mrs. L., 36 Ross
Molldy Mrs. A., 64 S Republican
Moxley Mrs. E. A., 187 Hanover
Mulligan Mrs. Martha, 258 Central av
Norman Mrs. A., 27 S Caroline
O'Brien Mrs. F., 44 Ross
O'Connor Mrs. S., 300 N Gay
Parr Mrs. R. W., 151 E Baltimore
Reid Miss, 182 Hanover
Rheim Mrs. E., 53 N Poplar
Rutledge Miss S., 16 N Liberty
Sharkey Mrs. M., 78 Mulberry
Sherwood M. A. W., 135 N Paca
Shumwalt Mrs. C. E., 66 S Sharp
Waggoner Mrs. Mary, 55 Albemarle
Wilhelm Elizabeth, 278 Canton av

Dress Patterns.

(*See* LADIES' DRESS PATTERNS.)

Drug Importers.

BAKER R. J., 36 S Charles. (See advertisement.)
Thomsen & Block, 26 Hanover

Druggists' Glassware.

BAKER BROTHERS & CO., 32 and 34 S Charles. (See advertisement.)
George Andrew J., 41 S Charles
JOHNSON W. R., 38 S Charles. (See advertisement.)

Druggists, Wholesale.

Bartlett John M., 70 S Calvert
Brown Wm. H. & Bro., 4 S Liberty
Burrough Bros., 52 Light
CANBY, GILPIN & CO., N W c Light and Lombard

CURLEY HENRY R. (Successor to ROGERS & CURLEY), 3 Howard. WHOLESALE DRUGGIST AND APOTHECARY. Keeps constantly on hand a full assortment of Drugs and Medicines. *Orders promptly filled.*
Davis & Miller, 12 N Howard
Frey E. & S., 314 W Baltimore
Janney Wm. J., c Bowly's whf and Pratt
JOHNSON W. R., 38 S Charles. (See advertisement.)
King Solomon, 1 S Calvert

LARRABEE EPHRAIM & SONS,

LABORATORY OF

THOMSONIAN · BOTANIC

MEDICINES,

20 S. CALVERT,

Proprietors of Larrabee's Pain Killer.

Ober & Co., 29 Hanover
SMITH J. IRWIN, 152 Pratt st whf. Manufacturer and Wholesale Dealer in Drugs, Medicines, Paints, Oils, Dye-stuffs, Glass, Putty, Varnishes, Perfumery, Patent Medicines, &c.
STABLER F. & COALE, Baltimore c Sharp
VOGELER A. & CO., 5 S Liberty
Walker, Richardson & Co., 39 S Charles

Druggists, Retail.

Andrews & Thompson, 5 W Baltimore
Ash & Russell, Caroline c Orleans
Balmer James, Baltimore N E c High
Baxey J. B., 138 N Howard
Benson Philander V., Hollins c Oregon
Biede A., Broadway c Alice Anna
Bode Wm., 120 S Front
Boewing Charles, 1 Boston
Boucsein L., 125 E Pratt
Bowers J. W., S W c Baltimore and Schroeder
Bowling J. Wm. & Bro., Madison av c Biddle
BRACK C. E., 17 Brown
Caspari Chas. & Wm., Pennsylvania av c Biddle and 44 N Gay
Caspari & Co., Baltimore c Calhoun

Coleman & Rogers, 173 W Baltimore
Coskery Henry J., Fayette c St. Paul
Cox E. Gover & Co., 511 W Baltimore
Creek J. W., 99 North
Cruikshank J. A., 173 Penn. av
Cunningham Wm. C., Central av c Monument
Duhurst C. H., 27 W Pratt
Duke A. W., Eager c Harford av
ELLIOTT H. A. & BRO'S., S E c Lexington and Pine
Ely William T., Saratoga c Calvert
Evans C. A., Ann c Alice Anna
Evans Chas. H., Mulberry c Chatsworth
EWING DR. JAMES H., APOTHECARY AND DRUGGIST, 280 W Baltimore
Fleming Dr. J. K., Fayette c Poppleton
Fleming W. S., 440 W Baltimore
Frames James P. & Brother, N W c Gay and Aisquith
Gosman Adam J., N E c Baltimore and Gay
Hancock John F., N W c Baltimore and Caroline
HARRIS & CO., N E c Eutaw and Saratoga, Dealers in Fancy Goods, Soaps, Perfumery, Tooth Brushes. &c.
Harrison & Co., Saratoga c Eutaw
Hasenbalg H., Broadway c Canton av
Hassencamp F., 73 Hanover
Healy James E., N W c Baltimore and Eden
Hillyard Dr. B. R., 538 W Baltimore
Horn Phillip, S E c Hanover and Lombard
Jennings N. Hynson & Co., 88 N Charles
Johnson J. G. & Bro., 657 W Baltimore
Keyser Moses, 231 W Pratt

Koechling H. M., 95 S Broadway
Laroque John M., 20 W Baltimore
Leibig G. A., 67 S Gay
Lemmon J. H., 659 W Baltimore
Macpherson Samuel, 56 N Charles
MEDINGER EDWARD G., formerly Medinger & Co., N E c Aisquith and Monument
Metzger F., N W c Gay and Exeter
Micheau T. J., 249 S Howard
Monsarrat Oscar, 113 S Broadway
Mone & Dieffenbach, Hanover c Hill
Nicholls W. J., Biddle c Ross
Noelle Chas. & Son, 118 S Broadway
Ohlendorf J. C., 84 N Howard
Orrick W. K., S W c Park and Fayette
Perkins Elisha H., S E c Baltimore and Green
Perkins James H. & Co., 136 N Howard
Perkins J. F. & Bro., Green c Franklin
Phillip L., 321 W Pratt
Pitt Thomas J., Pratt c High
Read John W., 96 S Broadway
Read W. H., 63 S Broadway
Robbins Amos, 245 Light
Roberts Joseph, Greenmount av
Robinson N. N., N W c Gay and Saratoga
ROSS JAMES F., S E c Baltimore and Republican
Russell Eugene J., Ann c Canton av
Sappington Richard, 132 N Gay
Seelbach W., 455 W Baltimore
Sharp D., S W c Pratt and Howard
Smith J. Jacob, N E c Eutaw and Lexington
Stehl August, N E c Gay and Mott
Stehl John, 31 N Eutaw
Sweetser & Co., N E c Charles and Pratt
TURNER J. H., 116 N Green
Wagner C. A., 310 N Gay
Webster William, Charles c Lee
Weineburg Wm., 229 Montgomery

Willis Richard, 353 W Lombard
Winter Jonas, S E c Baltimore and Caroline
WISEMAN MRS. CHARLES, apothecary and druggist, Baltimore c Fremont
Wolf G. W., 100 W Lexington
WOODS & RUSSELL, PHARMACEUTISTS and dealers in DRUGS, CHEMICALS, &c., 354 W Baltimore op Eutaw House
Wroth E. W., 108 Richmond

Drum Maker.

Sauer Francis, 98 W Baltimore

Dry Goods Commission Merchants.

Aldridge & Brewer, 5 German
BARRY JOHN S. & CO., 20 Hanover

BREHME O. & CO.,

DRY GOODS IMPORTERS

AND

Commission Merchants,

12 Hanover.

BROWN ROBT. D. & CO.,

COMMISSION MERCHANTS

AND

IMPORTERS OF IRISH LINENS,

2 German St., Baltimore.

CAMPBELL, ROSS & CO., 24 Hanover
Close & Brother, 4 German
Criss M., 1 Hanover

DALL AUSTIN & CO.,

DRY GOODS

COMMISSION MERCHANTS,

22 Hanover Street.

DRYDEN R. W. & SON,

DRY GOODS

COMMISSION MERCHANTS,

14 and 16 German

ROBERT W. DRYDEN.
J. MEREDITH DRYDEN.

Eaton Bros. & Co., 13 S Charles
Frank Simon & Co., German c Hanover
Frick George P., 2 German
GARY JAMES S. & SON, 24 German
Goodwin Thomas, 12 Hanover

LONEY B. S. & W. A. & CO.,

DRY GOODS

COMMISSION MERCHANTS,

11 and 13 German.

Makepeace & Co., 1 and 3 German

MIDDLETON & WARFIELD,

Commission Merchants.

FOREIGN AND DOMESTIC

DRY GOODS,

7 German Street, Baltimore.

MILNOR J. N. L.,

DRY GOODS

COMMISSION MERCHANT,

5 S Charles St., Baltimore.

Murdoch Alex. & Co., 14 S Charles
Norris & Baldwin, 19 German
Peirce Wm. H., 9 German
Peirson & Randall, 10 S Charles

RIACH & MURDOCH,

DRY GOODS

COMMISSION MERCHANTS,

15 S Charles Street.

RICE, CHASE & CO., DRY GOODS
COMMISSION MERCHANTS,
10 and 12 German St., Baltimore,
and 43 Park Place, New York.
Slothower, Mathews & Co., 17 German

TURNBULL, SLADE & CO.,

11 S Charles Street,

Baltimore, Md.,

and 38 Park Place,

New York.

WARTMAN M., 17 German
Woodward, Baldwin & Co., 9 and
11 Hanover
Wyman, Byrd & Co., 16 Hanover

Dry Goods, Importers and Jobbers.

BEVAN S. & CO.,

FOREIGN AND DOMESTIC

DRY GOODS,

279 W Baltimore Street.

SAMUEL BEVAN.   WM. A. WILLIAR.

EDGAR G. MILLER.

BREHME O. & CO., 12 Hanover
Brooks, Fahnestock & Co., 345 W
Baltimore, and 56 German

CAMPBELL ROSS & CO.,

IMPORTERS OF

DRY GOODS,

24 Hanover Street, Baltimore.

ROSS CAMPBELL.

FRANCIS L. REED.

COHEN MOSES,

IMPORTER AND JOBBER.

DOMESTIC GOODS,
SHAWLS, CLOAKS,
DRESS GOODS, &c. &c.

269 W Baltimore Street.

Dean William A., 236 W Baltimore

HOBLITZELL JAS. H.,

IMPORTER AND JOBBER OF

DRY GOODS, NOTIONS,

. AND

FANCY ARTICLES,

273 W Baltimore Street, between
Hanover and Sharp.

Holliday Daniel, 5 Hanover
Hopkins & Co., 258 W Baltimore
Howard Geo. W. & Co., 351 W Baltimore, and 64 German

HURST & CO.,

IMPORTERS AND JOBBERS

OF

DRY GOODS,

241 W Baltimore, bet Charles and
Hanover.

WM. R. HURST.   JOHN E. HURST.
L. B. PURNELL.

MILLER DANIEL & CO.,

IMPORTERS

AND WHOLESALE DEALERS IN
AMERICAN, ENGLISH,
SWISS, GERMAN, and
FRENCH DRY GOODS,

329 W Baltimore, and 44 German.

DANIEL MILLER.   JNO. M. MILLER.

Taylor Henry S., 243 W Baltimore

WHITELEY BROTHER & CO.,
IMPORTERS AND JOBBERS OF
DRY GOODS, 281 W Baltimore

Dry Goods, Refinishers.

Smith Thomas, 9 McClellan's al

Dry Goods, Retail.

(*See also* TRIMMINGS & DRY GOODS,
RETAIL.)

Adler Julius, 210 S Broadway
Adler M., 195 S Broadway

AKERS EDWIN,

Jobber and Retailer of

FOREIGN AND DOMESTIC

DRY GOODS,

138 W Lexington, and 23 Marion,
bet Liberty and Howard.

Akers Mrs. S. R., 216 Biddle
Bachsarach A., 77 Ensor
BAMBERGER BROTHERS, Deal-
ers in Staple & Domestic DRESS
TRIMMINGS, HOSIERY,
GLOVES, Mitts, Embroideries,
and Fancy Goods, 147 W Lexing-
ton.
BARRUS G. W., 211 W Baltimore
Bell Mrs. T., 43 N Fremont
Behrends C., 152 W Lexington
BENZINGER & RENEHAU, 61 N
Howard
Blumenthal B. P., 156 W Lexington
Bopp Lawrence, 413 Light
Brandes F. F., 27 E Pratt
Brannon Miss S., 6 Mosher
Broadbent A. G. & Co., 18 N Charles
Brown Jacob, 215 Hanover
Brown M. & S., 155 S Broadway
Brumwell A., 143 Columbia
BRYAN SAMUEL L. & CO., 221 W
Baltimore
Bucksbaum G., 194 S Broadway
Binswanger E., 756 W Baltimore

Byrn William, 163 N Gay
Chism Richard, 229 W Lexington
Christopher R. W., 164 W Lexing-
ton
COALE E. H., 67 W Lexington
Cohen Moses, 183 W Lexington
Collison T. W., Ann c Lombard
COWMAN M. & CO., 71 W Lexing-
ton
Curry Francis, 102 Bank
Darling Taylor F., 157 Forrest
Davies Wm., 81 N Howard
Deems Mrs. S., 193 Conway
Dixson Mrs. Jane E., 716 W Balti-
more
Dogged Martin, 141 Central av
Dorritee M. & D., 223 W Lexington
Dowling Elizabeth, 262 N Gay
Dugan Osborn J., Gay c High
Eachus E., S W c Pratt & Hanover
EICHELBERGER J., S W c Charles
and Hamburg. Dry Goods and
Notions always on hand.
Fay Henry, 48 & 50 Centre mkt space
Felber Louis, 217 S Broadway
Fenby T., 141 N Gay
Floss Sarah, 196 S Broadway
Frank David, 195 N Gay
Fuldo B. S., Ann c Pratt
Furlong M. A., 27 E Baltimore
Gaopple Henry, 168 S Eutaw
Garrett J. P., 212 Hanover
George Mrs. M. L., 92 Richmond
Getty James, S E c Gay and Front
Goldsmith Mrs. Rachel, N E c Gay
and Chew
Goldsmith Reuben, 208 Alice Anna
Grauer J., 159 N Gay
Greenbaum Isaac & Son, 200 S
Broadway
Greenbaum S., 204 S Broadway
Greenstein Simon, 190 S Broadway
Guy Robert J., 122 W Lexington
Guyton & Hyde, 62 Hanover
Hall Mrs. F., 226 E Lombard
Hamburger A., 181 N Gay
Hamburger Mrs. E., 123 E Pratt
Hammerslough John, S Eden c
Pratt

HAMMERSLOUGH LEWIS,Retail Dealer in STAPLE and FANCY DRY GOODS, LACES, FRINGES and GIMPS ; also CLOAKS, MANTILLAS, and FURS always kept on hand and made to order. Cloths, Cassimeres, Vestings, Domestics, Gloves, Merinos, French Worked Collars and Satins, Silks, Laces, Lawns, Bareges,Cashmeres, Mous. D'Laines,Alpacas, Handkerchiefs, Plain and Embroidered, Hosiery, &c. &c., 155 W Lexington.

Harper Mrs., 67 N Eutaw

Harris Beulah, 140 W Lexington

Hartz Sampson, 197 N Gay   .

Harvey Joshua, N W c Pratt and Hanover

Hayward Elizabeth, 47 S Liberty

Hecht Samuel, 148 S Broadway

Hess M., 39 N Howard

Herold Frederick, 183 S Sharp

Hineman Trueman, 106 S Caroline

HITZELBERGER MRS. F., 336 N Gay

Himmel L., 285 N Gay

Hines Julius, 153 and 155 N Gay

Holdefer Mrs.Margaret, 117 Eastern av

Horn John W., 111 S Broadway

Horner Wm., 79 N Howard

Hosbach F., 643 W Baltimore

Howell W. P., 37 E Baltimore

Hunckey Mrs. D., 134 Harford av

Hyde Miss E., 175 Montgomery

Johnson Mrs. M., 78 Pine

Kadz Henry, 228 S Broadway

Kann S., 156 S Broadway

KERNGOOD & BRO., 537 and 699 W Baltimore

KEYSER MOSES,231 Pratt c Sharp

Lamb Mrs. E., 75 N Fremont

Lauer Henry, 169 N Gay

Lawn Mrs. M. A., 238 N Gay

LETCHER DAVID, 78 Hanover

Lieblich M., 151 W Lexington

LINDEMAN JOHN, 173 E Baltimore

LIPSCHUETZ L., 349 N Gay c

Monument, Dealer in Dry Goods, Shawls, Hoop Skirts, Gents' Furnishing Goods, Hosiery, Notions, &c.

McCafferty M. C., 144 W Lexington

McNutt Mrs. R., 44 N Green

Macks Isaac, 165 N Gay

MAILHOUSE E., 149 S Broadway

Mailhouse Joseph J., 124 S Broadway

Malone E., 158 W Lexington

MARCH & McNEALLY, 76 Hanover

Marshall Mrs. J., 111 E Pratt

Meloney Mrs. M., 106 W Lexington

Merriken Wm. & George, 1 Water

Meyer M. D., 143 N Gay

Meyer Mrs. B., 215 E Pratt

Meyer Philip, 189 N Gay

MILLIKEN R. H., 195 W Baltimore

MOONEY MICHAEL E., 231 Light

Moore Mrs. M., 27 Douglass

Nachman Abraham, 161 N Gay

Nachman Adolph, 139 N Gay

NEAL GEORGE H. C., 97 W Baltimore. (See advertisement, p. 5, back of book.)

Negengerd Fred. A., 167 N Gay

Noah B., 188 S Broadway

Nusbaum Henry, 206 S Broadway

Oppenheim E., 250 S Charles

Oppenheim H., Canton c Chappel

Perkins & Co., 6 N Charles

Rider Moses, 235 W Lexington

Rider S., 25 N Eutaw

ROMM NICHOLAS, 433 W Baltimore

Rose Jacob, 170 W Lexington

Rosenblatt Samuel, Aisquith c Hull's la

Rosenbaum Elias, 154 W Lexington

Rothchild R., 745 W Baltimore

Royston Brothers, 81 W Baltimore

Salomon M., 653 W Baltimore

Seliger Joel, 13 E Baltimore

Seliger Joseph, 27 W Baltimore

Schaub Henry, 242 S Charles

Schoolhouse Daniel, 28 E Pratt

Scott John, 106 Richmond
Scherwood Mrs. R., 39 E Baltimore
Shumway Thomas S., 56 Hanover
Silbereisens Mrs. E., 18 E Pratt
Simon H., 149 W Lexington
Snettinger Samuel, 74 Camden
Snodheimer B., 20 Eden
Stern Henry Aisquith c Madison
Stern Simon, 192 S Broadway
Strautman John, 307 N Gay
Sultzbacher A. B., 176 W Lexington
Taylor Mrs. Jane, 208 Hanover
THOMAS BENJAMIN, 253 E Baltimore c Bond. Dealer in FANCY AND STAPLE DRY GOODS.
Uhler Geo. W., 170 Franklin
Volkmar Henry, 549 W Baltimore
Webster E., 233 W Lexington
Weisler Abraham, 260 Alice Anna
Weglein Louis, 67 W Baltimore
Wolff Mrs. U. S., 233 W Pratt
Wright Mrs. Sarah, 248 W Lexington
Zoellinger George, 100 S Broadway
Zorn Adam, 580 N Gay

Dry Goods, Wholesale.

BARRUS G. W., 211 W Baltimore.
CASH HOUSE, FANCY AND STAPLE DRY GOODS. ONE PRICE.
Bird J. Edward, Agt., 213 W Baltimore
Bird S. L & Co., 57 N Howard
Bruff John W. & Co., 245 W Baltimore
DEVRIES, STEPHENS & CO., 312 W Baltimore
Easter, Hamilton & Co., 199, 201, and 203 W Baltimore
Getty James, 67 N Howard
GUSDORFF ALEXANDER, 655 W Baltimore
HAMILTON BROS. & CO., 24 South
Heilbrun M., 52 Hanover
McGinniss C. G., 65 W Baltimore
Merrefield Joseph, 258 W Baltimore

9

NEAL GEORGE H. C., 97 W Baltimore. (See advertisement, p. 5, back of book.)
ROYSTON BROTHERS, 81 W Baltimore. Wholesale and Retail Dealers in French, British, and American Dry Goods, Carpetings, House and Ship Furnishing Goods.

SIMON CHARLES,

DRY GOODS.

63 N. HOWARD ST.

STRAUSS BROTHERS, 54 Hanover and 649 W Baltimore. Wholesale and Retail Dealers in FOREIGN AND DOMESTIC DRY GOODS, FASHIONABLE MILLINERY, AND FANCY GOODS.
Sutherland, Geo. A., 85 W Baltimore

Dyers.
(*See also* SCOURERS.)

Bandel Geo. M., 187 E Baltimore
Bineleweld Louis, 211 W Fayette
BONHEIM M., 150 S Eutaw
BURTON THOS. C., 121 W Lexington
Caldwell D., 6 N High
Cosar Nathan, 32 Hanover
Drexel & Co., 52 W Fayette
FEUILLAN & DANDELET (Successors to F. GUERAND). From Paris. French Steam Dyers and Scourers, 124 N Howard
Fisher Brothers, 139 W Fayette
FISHER THOMAS, 10 S Calvert. STEAM DYEING AND SCOURING ESTABLISHMENT.

Galloway Mrs. J., 123½ W Lexington
Haultsich John, 33 W Lombard
HULSE JAMES II., 453 W Baltimore, 269 W Pratt, and 70 N Eutaw
Hulse John, Holliday c Saratoga
Kernals Charles, 37 Harrison
MEINETSBERGER STEPHEN, 24 S Sharp six doors below German. FRENCH SCOURER AND TAILOR.
NEW YORK STEAM DYEING AND SCOURING ESTABLISHMENT. *Office* 121 W Lexington, two doors from Park. SILK AND WOOLLEN GOODS *Dyed and Refinished in the best manner.* THOS. C. BURTON, *Proprietor.*
Nolen M., 34 German
Polack M., 81 Gough
Seabrook T., 29 Balderston
Semrad A., 25 W Fayette
Wetter W., 9 Clay
Willax M., 288 N Gay
Wylies S. F. & J. H., 142 W Lexington

Dyestuffs and Chemicals.

(*See also* CHEMISTS, MANUFACTURING.)

BAKER R. J., 36 S Charles. (See advertisement op Druggists.)

Edge Tool Makers.

Baker & Brown, 10 W Pratt
Helmers John, 250 W Pratt. (Shoemaker's Tools.)
Hudgins John, 27 W Pratt. (Tool Dresser.)
Kidd Charles, 400 W Pratt
Miller G. W., 7 Camden
Monroe Henry, 13 Concord
Ross Joseph, 79 N Front. (Awl and Needle.)
Solze J. A., 312 W Pratt. (Shoemaker's Tools.)

Electrotypers.

Ryan & Rickets, 114 W Baltimore

Embroidery Stampers.

Bentley P., 48 E Baltimore
Gunthers Chas., 26 E Baltimore
Hedges Mrs. E., 180 Madison av
Moissonnier Mad., 49 E Baltimore
Scott James, 546 W Baltimore and 46 N Green

*Embroidering.

Wagner Mrs. A. & Schroeder, 113 W Lexington

Engineer.

Goodwin H. S., Northern Central R R, 47 N Calvert

Engineers, Civil.

Clarkson Jos. & Sons, 75 N Front
Lumley D. T., 63 Second
MARTENET S. J., 6 South
MURRAY. CLARK, THORNTON & CO., 42 and 44 York. (See advertisement inside back cover.)
POTTS R. C., 62½ W Baltimore
SHIPLEY WM. H., 48 Lexington
TEMPLEMAN R. W., 48 Lexington
TEMPLEMAN R. W. & WM. H. SHIPLEY, 48 Lexington
Wells J. & Sons, 136 Eastern av

Engineers, Mechanical.

POTTS R. C., Mechanical Engineer, 62½ W Baltimore. DAVISON, DICKINSON & CO., Civil, Mining and Mechanical Engineers, 229 Broadway, New York. Plans and Specifications furnished and Estimates procured for all kinds of Machinery, and Superintended during Construction. Gas Works erected on the most approved Plans. New and Second Hand Machinery constantly on hand. Steam Engines, Boilers, Locomotive and Car Builders' Supplies, &c. &c. HENRY J. DAVISON, *Mechanical Engineer.* P. P. DICKINSON, *Civil and Mining Engineer.*

Engineer, Mining.

POTTS R. C., 62½ W Baltimore

Engravers and Die Sinkers.

Koehler F. X., 11 W Liberty
Pilkinton James E., 83 Exchange pl

Engravers, General.

ANDERSON JAMES M. & SON,
148 W Baltimore. CARD EN-
GRAVER AND PLATE PRIN-
TER.
BROSS EDWARD, 149 W Lom-
bard. (See advertisement, p. 1,
back of book.)
Merriken Frank, 159 W Baltimore

Engravers, Wood.

Ehlers John D., Baltimore c South

Expresses.

ADAMS' EXPRESS CO., 164 W
Baltimore. (See advertisement
inside back cover.)
AMERICAN EUROPEAN EX-
PRESS, 293 W Baltimore c Sharp
HARDEN EXPRESS, 293 W Balti-
more. (See advertisement inside
back cover.)
REID & CO., 116 S Eutaw
Renshaw Joseph, 77 N Calvert
Southern Express Co., 50 S Howard

Fancy Goods, Importers and Jobbers.

ALBERTI H. F. & CO., IMPORTERS
OF GERMAN, FRENCH, and
ENGLISH FANCY GOODS, 6 and
8 S Liberty. Henry F. Alberti,
Chas. Deliuz, Henry A. D. Brink.
Bamberger David, 43 and 45 N
Howard
Bennett E., 326 W Baltimore
CANFIELD BROTHER & CO., 229
W Baltimore c Charles. (See
advertisement inside back cover.)
Chance Jas. R., 220 W Baltimore

Cacle, Sickel & Co., 285 W Balti-
more
DIETZ L. D. & CO., 308 W Balti-
more. (See advertisement inside
back cover.)
DIGGS JOHN R., 219 W. Balti-
more, Cutlery, Combs, Brushes,
Morocco Bags, Carpet Bags,
Portmonnaies, Work Boxes, Writ-
ing Desks, Jewelry, Chessmen,
Dominoes, Baskets, Vases, Mu-
sical Instruments, Bird Cages,
Fans, Toys, &c.
DROST & SUTRO, 253 W Balti-
more
HOBLITZELL JAS. II., 273 W
Baltimore
Horner E. R., 316 W Baltimore
Horner John A., 306 W Baltimore
JOHNSON W. R., 38 S Charles.
(See advertisement.)
JORDAN & ROSE, 1 N Howard
LORD CHARLES W., 88 and 90
W Lombard
McLaughlin James II., 138 W Pratt
MAYER & BROTHER, 4 N Howard,
op Howard House. Importers
and Jobbers of German, English,
and French Fancy goods and
notions
Mortimer & Mowbray, 240 W Balti-
more
OBERNDORF JULIUS, Jobber in
AUCTION GOODS, Hosiery,
Gloves, Handkerchiefs, Skirts,
&c., 228 W Baltimore
OHLENDORF WILLIAM G., 86
N Howard, two doors ab Saratoga,
Importer and Dealer in Fancy
and Variety Goods, Hosiery,
Gloves, Undershirts, Drawers,
Suspenders, Yarns, Worsteds,
Combs, Brushes, Buttons, Porte-
monnaies, Cutlery, Toys, &c.
Passano Leonard, 268 W Baltimore
POULSON A. W., 319 W Baltimore
Seim M. J., 111 N Howard
SCHWERDTMAN & CO., 7 and 9
N Howard and 133 W Baltimore

SCHWERDTMANN & CO.,
IMPORTERS
OF

TOYS AND FANCY GOODS,

STORES

7 and 9 N. Howard.

SPILKER CHARLES & CO., 10 Hanover
STEINBACH GEO. P., 79 W Baltimore, Importer, Wholesale and Retail Dealer in Fancy Goods, Toys, and Baskets, Musical instruments, Perfumery, Portemonnaies, Cutlery, Brushes, Combs, Work Boxes, Beads, Canes, China Ware, Children's Gigs, Hobby Horses, &c. &c.
Swayne B. B., 37 N Charles
Werdebaugh H. J. & Co., 292 W Baltimore

Fancy Goods, Retail.

(*See also* VARIETY STORES.)

Cappan C., 673 W Baltimore
Elliott Edward, 126 W Lexington
Gardner James, 64 Ensor
Gerns Mrs. Ellen R., 652 W Baltimore
Gutman J., 29 N Eutaw
Hartman Mrs. A., Lexington mkt
Hersberg & Co., 175 N Gay
KRESSE CHARLES, 201 S Broadway
Larupp Mrs. A., Lexington mkt
McComas Mrs. A., 190 Madison av
Moriarty Miss Ann, 66 W Lexington
OHLENDORF WILLIAM G., 86 N Howard
Passano Leonard, 52 Centre mkt space
Sarlous Mrs. E., Eutaw c Lexington
Sheehy Miss M., 190 W Lexington

Stern H., S Charles c Hill
White & Weishampel, 488 W Baltimore
Wilson M. A., 182 W Lexington
Young Mrs. R., 78 W Lexington

Fertilizers.

(*See also* GUANO.)

DUGDALE GEORGE, 105 Smith's whf, Phosphate of Lime
GRIFFITH ROMULUS R., Office—No 84 Exchange Place, S E c Lombard & South, WAREHOUSE No 3 O'Donnell's whf, Manufacturer and Dealer in all kinds of FERTILIZING MANURES, and General Agent of all such articles, and Sole Agent for the CELEBRATED FISH GUANO, prepared by the QUINNIPIAC CO., goods for all soils and all crops.
Reese John S. & Co., 71 South
RHODES B. M. & CO., MANUFACTURERS OF RHODES' STANDARD SUPER-PHOSPHATE, DEALERS IN GUANOS, GROUND BONE PLASTER, &c., OFFICE AND WAREHOUSE, 82 SOUTH St., BOWLY'S whf. (See advertisement outside front cover.)
Turner J. J. & F., 42 W Pratt
WHITELOCK W. & CO., 44 South, PROPRIETORS OF WHITELOCK'S SUPER-PHOSPHATE OF LIME, DEALERS IN FIELD SEEDS, GUANOS, AND ALL APPROVED FERTILIZERS, CEMENT, &c.
WHITMAN E. & SONS, 22 and 24 S Calvert

File Makers.

(*See also* EDGE TOOLS ; *also* SAW MAKERS.)

Jervis James, 70 Washington
Jervis William, 197 Montgomery, (Cutter)
Kesting P., 87 N Front
Rudolph Christian, 154 East

:icks.

: DEALERS.)

George, Sharp c

NS, 711 and 713

Builders.

ENGINE BUILD-
.)
& SON, 48 and

:s, Retail.

ON DEALERS.),
entre mkt
Lexington mkt,
kt
xington mkt
entre mkt
'ell's Point mkt
Fell's Point mkt
, 23 Centre mkt
ington mkt
Lexington mkt,
int mkt
19 Centre mkt
entre mkt
:, Lexington mkt
Iollins mkt
Centre mkt
'entre mkt
? Fell's Point mkt
xington mkt
Lexington mkt
, 27 Hollins mkt
211 and 213 Han-

Bellair mkt
re mkt
'ell's Point mkt
xington mkt
xington mkt
entre mkt
13 Centre mkt
, Lexington mkt
:ington mkt
igton mkt
:e mkt

9*

Seabold Michael, Lexington mkt
Sessions A. D'., 6 Fell's Point mkt
SESSIONS & CO., Hanover mkt,
  Centre mkt and Lexington mkt
Shangery Margaret, Lexington mkt
Sheneey Margaret, Centre mkt
Sheppard Ellen, Lexington mkt
Sheppard & Jones, Centre mkt
Smith Wm. J., Lexington mkt
Snider Hannah, Lexington mkt
Toundsand Edward A. & Co., Lex-
  ington mkt
Treeberger Jacob, Centre mkt
Turner & Cogginsons, Lexington
  mkt
Walker S., 15 and 17 Centre mkt
Wiley Wm., 12 Fell's Point mkt
Williams B. A., Centre mkt

Fish Dealers, Wholesale.

(*See also* PROVISION DEALERS.)

GRIFFITH R. R., Jr., 14 Commerce,
  wholesale dealer in MACKEREL,
  HERRING, HAKE, COD and
  SALMON, and RECEIVER of
  WESTERN PRODUCE ON CONSIGN-
  MENT.
Palmer, Edward L. & Co., 15 Bow-
  ly's whf
POPE F. F.. 85 South bel Pratt,
  COMMISSION MERCHANT &
  WHOLESALE AND RETAIL
  DEALER IN MACKEREL HER-
  RING, CODFISH AND OTHER
  FISH.
Post J. & W. W., 43 South
Purington Z. S., 39 and 41 W Pratt
Sellman Alexander, 156 W Pratt
  and 2 Ellicott
SHURTZ W. D. & CO., 11 Com-
  merce
VOSBURGH & CO., 72 South and
  8 Bowly's whf

Flag Makers.

LOANE J. W., 67 W Pratt, MARINE,
  NATIONAL AND FANCY FLAG
  MANUFACTURERS
MULLER LOUIS, 110 W Baltimore

THE NATIONAL
FLAG STORE,
UNITED STATES
SILK AND BUNTING

FLAGS,

OF ALL SIZES,

Constantly on hand.

Regimental and Company FLAGS
for presentation, made to order
at short notice.
FLAG SILK, BUNTING, GILT
AND SILK FLAG TASSELS,
GILT SPEARS, POLES, BELTS
AND'COVERS SUPPLIED. MIL-
ITARY GOODS &c.
SISCO BROTHERS,
95 W Baltimore street,
opposite Holiday street.

Flour Commission Merchants.

(*See also* MILLERS, MERCHANT.)
BERRY J. THOMAS, 28 S Howard
DARE, SPROSTON & CO., 95 S
Charles.
EHRMAN GEO. M., N W c How-
ard and Pratt
FOWLER, ZEIGLER & CO., 91 &
93 S Charles
Hinks C. D. & Co., 41 S Howard
KAHLER ADAM, 2 S Eutaw
Newcomer & Co., 26 & 43 S Howard
STONEBRAKER & CO., 53 and 55
S Howard

Flour Mills.

(*See also* MILLERS, MERCHANT.)
Abbott E. A. & Sons, City Block,
n Falls av
HOOPER JAMES & SONS, 15
Spear's whf
Huntington, V. V. Klinefelter &
Co., 202 W Falls av
MACTIER SAMUEL, 6 Spear's whf
Warden J. & H., ft Smith's whf
Warfield Daniel & Son, North

Flour and Feed.

Bach Adam, Lexington mkt, Ster-
ling c Aisquith, and 110 Centre
mkt
Bell John H., 530 W Baltimore
and 133 Centre mkt
Brown M. J. & W. A., 11 W Pratt
BROWNE & RONEY, 67 S Gay,
commission merchants and dea-
lers in FLOUR, GRAIN, GUA-
NO, SEEDS, CORN MEAL,
MILL FEED, BALED HAY &
STRAW, Split Peas, Beans,Lime,
Plaster, &c
Bowen Solomon, 855 W Baltimore,
Lexington mkt, and 38 and 40
Hollins mkt
Bubert John D., 101 S Charles
Classen, H. 145 S Sharp
Clemm J. E. & Co., 73 South
Com J., Frederick av
Corn and Flour Exchange, South
c Wood
Corner S., 11 Spear's whf
Cullum Nelson 13 W Lombard
Cunningham W. H., Ensor c East
Diggs R. H. & Son, 258 S Caroline
DORSEY WM. A., 68 South
Ehrman Geo. M., N W c Pratt and
Howard
Evans George, 802 W Baltimore
GIESE J. HENRY, 21 Spear's whf
GOVER & GARDNER, 13 Com-
merce
GROVE & NIELSON,132 N Howard
GROVERMAN A., JR., 374 W
Baltimore
GROVERMAN H., JR., 545 W
Baltimore. Flour and Feed.
Haines Ephraim, 110 N Howard
Haueman R., N E c Gay and Eden
Hausenwald John H., 3 Penn. av
Hestry S., Front c Hillen
Hobbs R., 167 Hollins
Hussey Martin, 38 E Pratt
JEBB HENRY, 52 S Charles,
Dealer in Flour, Corn Meal, and
all kinds of Mill Feed, Corn,
Oats, Bale Hay, Straw, &c. &c.

JOHNSTON JAMES, N E c Calvert and Centre
Khuller Martin, 188 Columbia
Klinefelter & Bro., 180 Light st whf
Leabold Margaret, 187 Centre mkt
Lee James F., 123 McElderry's whf
Logan James & Son, 77 McElderry's whf
LOGUE JAMES, 118 N Howard
McDonald P. M., c McElderry's whf and Pratt
McGill Patrick, 410 W Baltimore
Mabbett M., 146 Franklin
MACTIER SAMUEL,8 Spear's whf, Miller and Wholesale Dealer in Flour of all brands.
MARTIN ALLEN, 44 Tyson
Meehan Patrick, N E c Gay and Madison
Misch F., Lexington mkt
Murray John, 365 W Baltimore
Nixon John, 181 Centre mkt
Pabst Andrew, 139 N Howard
Pentland Robert F., 204 N Gay
Picker J. C., Agt., 4 Pennsylvania av
PLACK GEORGE, 376 Light
Plack Louis, 218 S Sharp
QUINEAN JOS.E.& CO.,39 Penn av
Quinlan John F. & Son, 149 N Gay
Quinn Joseph, Lexington mkt
RANDALL & FAIRBANK, Flour and Feed, 491 W Baltimore
Robinson & Brinkman, Penn av c Dolphin
Saumenig Jacob, 106 Columbia
Sauerwein Geo.& Co.,153 N Howard
Sayers Henry, 80 Fell's Point mkt
SCHARF WM. JAMES, 825 W Baltimore
Serft Henry, 311 S Bond
Sinsheimer Louis, 226 Alice Anna
Snyder Henry, 95 Franklin
Telegraph Mills, Welby & Co., President c Fawn
Turner Jonathan, 25 W Pratt
WALKER J. & E., WHOLESALE FEED DEALERS, 99 South
Warfield D. & Son, 9 Spear's whf

Weaver Francis,Lexington mkt and Hollins mkt
Welby & Co., President c Fawn
Wilks Jabez, 380 & 382 Canton av
Wooden John, Lexington mkt
Worman A., 525 W Baltimore
Wright J. & Son, 107 Hillen

Freight Lines.

Carlisle and Gettysburg Transportation Line, G. Small, 64 North
Cumberland Valley, Chambersburg and Greencastle Transportation Line, Kneller & Frick, 165 North
DRILL JAMES M., Northern Central R. R. Station, Calvert
Hanover, Gettysburg and Littlestown Transportation Line, George Young & Co., 199 North
Pennsylvania R. R. to Pittsburg & the West, 80 North
WESTERN FREIGHT DEPOT N. CENTRAL & PA. R. R., Wm. Brown, agent, 80 North

*Fruit Cans and Jars.

(See HERMETICALLY SEALED CANNED GOODS.)

Fruit Dealers, Retail.

(See also CONFECTIONERS & FRUITERERS.)
Casey Mrs. Ellen, 53 N Front
Crowl Mrs. E., 475 N Gay
Daa Richard, 66 Harrison
Hammond Charles, Lexington c Howard
McKeon Mrs. Mary, 15 Holiday
Martin Charles & Co , 4 N Calvert
Mathiot & Sons, 25 N Gay
Pisani A., 16 S Sharp

*Fruits, Preserved.

(See also HERMETICALLY SEALED CANNED GOODS.)
THOMAS S. W. & E. C., JR., 143 German. (See advertisement.)

Fruits, Wholesale.

BOND JAMES, Jr., 6 Hollingsworth
BRIDGES WILLIAM & SON, 313 W Baltimore
DARBY & CO., 296 W Baltimore
Dix & Steiner, 112 W Lombard
Friend, Ricketts & Co., 79 Smith's whf
KIDD AMELIA, 35 W Baltimore
Laws & Moore, N E c Light and Pratt
MARTIN JOHN & CO , 92 W Pratt. (See card under Confectioners, Wholesale.)
MERCHANT J. & SON, 174 W Pratt. (See advertisement.)
Moore John W., 39 South
Pracht Chas. & Co., 155 & 157 Franklin
Price Wm. C., 102 & 103 W Lombard
Sloan James, 91 W Lombard
SUMMERS & CO., 301 W Baltimore
WHITE WILLIAM, 311 W Baltimore. Wholesale dealer in Foreign and Domestic Fruits.

Fur Dealers and Furriers.

ARTHUR W. W., 1 W Baltimore
Gerke C., 60 W Lexington
Hindes S. & Son, 100 N Gay
Kleineibst, A., 213 N Gay
Quail G. K., 238 W Pratt
Sigmund A., 225 W Baltimore
Taylor R. Q., 5 N Calvert
TIRALLA J. F., 105 W Baltimore, fourth door below the Sun Iron Building, FURRIER AND IMPORTER OF STRAW GOODS & TRIMMINGS.

Furnaces, Hot Air.

(*See also* Stoves & Ranges ; *also* Heaters, Steam.)

Collins, Heath & Co , 22 Light
Hayward, Bartlett & Co., 24 Light

SEXTON S. B. & CO., 111 W Lombard
WEATHERBY J. & SONS, 40 and 42 Light, HOT AIR FURNACES and STOVE DEALERS.

Furniture Dealers, New.

(*See also* Cabinet Makers.)

Allen A. & Co., 27 Hanover and 4 E Lombard
ANDERSON W. E., 10 & 12 Second. (See advertisement p. 2 back.)
Armstrong & Denny, 263 Light
Banks D., 59 South
Beck George, 42 Harrison
BRICK WALTER, 34½ N Howard. (See advertisement p. 2 back.)
Clotworthy A., 76 N Howard
Collins Margaret, 49 Harrison
Collins Patrick, 83 Harrison
Cook J. H. & Son, 707 W Baltimore
Daiger M. A., 74 S Broadway
Freeman James, 507 W Baltimore

GODEY THOMAS,

Manufacturer of

CABINET FURNITURE,

No. 58 Hanover Street, Baltimore.

Hair and Husk Mattresses.

Good John B., 50 Harrison
Graham William, 138 Franklin
Guyton Wm. K., 78 N Howard
Hamilton & Jones, 240 W Pratt
Hanson Thomas H., 25 and 27 S Calvert
HEYWOOD R. W., 10½ N Charles on hand and constantly manufacturing Oak, Walnut and Enamelled COTTAGE CHAMBER SETTS and Dining-room Furniture of every variety.
Hinkler George, 715 and 717 W Baltimore

HISS & BROTHER,

FURNITURE,

128 W Fayette.

P. HANSON HISS.   WM. J. HISS.

Holtzman, Mrs. B., 278 Alice Anna
Hyde James, 251 Light
Ingram E. Peacock, 275 W Pratt
Jenkins Henry W., 16 Light
Kann Julius, 70 Harrison
Kinnard A., 32 N Liberty
Kraft G., 274 Alice Anna
Logan J. H. & Co., 41 N Paca
McGannan Thomas, 404 W Baltimore
McMullan John, 15 N Gay
Mandelberg Jacob, 61 Harrison

MARTIN & BEVANS,

Successors to

J. & J. WILLIAMS & CO.

FASHIONABLE FURNITURE,

AND CURTAINS,

BEDS AND MATTRESSES,

11 S Calvert.

Coffins Furnished
and
Undertaking promptly
attended to.

Mathiot & Sons, 25 and 27 N Gay
Miller Nicholas, 88 N Howard
Myer Abraham, 766 W Baltimore
Pfeiffer N. A., S E c Pratt and
Sharp, and 26 N Howard
Phillips J. E., N E c Charles and
Lombard
RENWICK ROBERT, 92 N Howard, Manufacturer of Cabinet
Furniture, Chairs, and Hair and
Stork Mattresses.
Russell John, 54 S Charles
Sander Henry, 252 Canton av
Shryock H. S. & Son, 6 S Calvert
Smith George, 38 N Howard
Stevens S. S. & Sons, 6 Low

TARR'S CABINET FURNITURE
FACTORY, 11 N Gay, where
will be found at all times a large
variety of the most beautiful patterns of furniture.
Watkins John T., 47 South
Wheatfield A., 6 Second

Furniture Dealers, Second Hand.

Abercrombie Thomas, 66 Camden
Arold John, 660 W Baltimore
Bluhenthal Abraham, 270 S Charles
Kahn Joseph, 473 W Baltimore
Kauffman Solomon, 170 Columbia
Klug John, 326 S Charles
Lunt M., 144 S Fremont
Morrow T. G , 63 N Eutaw
Myers Abraham, 206 S Charles
Packer David, 409 W Pratt
Pezetell John, 431 W Baltimore
Rose Myer, 116 S Howard
Staenberk Levi, 208 S Charles
Stein Julius, 290 S Charles

Gas Companies.

Baltimore Gas-Light Co., 19 South
Gas-Light Company of Baltimore,
19 South
MARYLAND GAS COMPANY,
Office—5 St Paul. E. R. Sprague,
President; L. Morrison, Secretary and Treasurer
MARYLAND GAS COMPANY'S
Works—N W c Ridgley and Ostend

Gas Fitters.

(*See also* PLUMBERS.)

Broderick D., 88 St Paul
Calaghan P. & Co., 30 N Calvert
Eggleston Edwin C., 121 N High
Grattan Thomas L. 78 North W. B c li
Hunter E. J., 28 E Baltimore
Jevens John W., St Paul c Bank la
Kaflinski Charles, 138 W Fayette
LYONS A. J. & CO., 8 and 10 Holliday

Gas Fixture Makers.

CORTLAN & CO., 216 and 218 W Baltimore
DAVIDSON C. Y. (Successor to John Davidson), 15 N Liberty bet Baltimore and Fayette. Gas Fitting and Fixtures and Plumbing
Merz Henry, 254 W Pratt
Shorey & Eigelberner, 9 Eutaw House
WAGNER AUGUST, 30 Hanover. (See advertisement opp. Brass.)

Gaugers.

(*See also* COOPERS.)
Ensor & Linaweaver, 61 W Pratt
Smith Wm. H., 69 Exchange pl

Gentlemen's Furnishing Stores.

(*See also* SHIRT MANUFACTURERS.)
Adler H. M., 37 W Baltimore
Coale Isaac, Jr. & Bro., 17 and 19 Hanover (wholesale)
Danskin & Co., 155 W Baltimore
DIETZ JOHN B., 204 W Pratt
FOCKE EDWARD L., Dealer in Gentlemen's Furnishing Goods and Tailors' Trimmings, 252 W Baltimore
FRANKEL & BROTHER, N E c Market space and Pratt
Hartman J. P., 197 W Baltimore
Hubbard Mrs. S. T., 4 W Baltimore
JOHNSTON ROBERT, Merchant Tailor, 357 W Baltimore n Eutaw. Constantly on hand, an assortment of GENTLEMEN'S FURNISHING GOODS, Fine Cloths, Cassimeres, and Vestings, for measured work
LAUER LEWIS & CO., 283 W Baltimore
LIPSCHUETZ L., 349 N Gay c Monument
McShane L., 202 S Broadway
MAYER FREDERICK, 63 Hanover
MOORE S. & R. G, 6 S Charles

Owens Wm. F., 160 W Baltimore
Peters George A., 214 W Baltimore
Raymond & Burton, 38 W Baltimore
Rea John H. & Co., N E c South and Pratt
ROSE B., Agt., 92 S Eutaw
Schiff Meyer, 123 N Howard
Schofield B., 459 W Baltimore
SEIBERT E., 35 W Baltimore, Wholesale and Retail Dealer in Undershirts and Drawers, Hosiery, Yarns, Gloves, Small Wares, &c.
SHIPLEY, ROANE & CO., 303 W Baltimore
Shipley Mrs. Sarah Jane, 110 W Lexington
SONNEBORN HENRY, 315 W Baltimore
STINE B., 73 W Baltimore
THANHOUSER JACOB, 124 W Pratt
Towles Wm. P. & Bro., 145 W Baltimore
WINCHESTER & CO., 157 W Baltimore. (See advertisement p. 4 front.)
Zirckel William, 56 W Pratt

Gilders.

(*See* CARVERS.)

Glass Cutters.

Wolf E. A., Uhler's al n S Charles

Glass Manufacturers.

Chapman J. J., 3 S Charles
Edwards R, jr., 24 S Charles
George Andrew J., 41 S Charles
Reitz & Eberhardt, 37 Hughes

Glass Stainers.

GERNHARDT H. T., Holiday c Fayette

Glass, Window.

BAKER BROTHERS & CO., 32 and 34 S Charles. (See advertisement p. 5 back.)

., Jn , 50 North.
it op. Druggists.)

1facturer.

l W Pratt

aters.

l, 22 N Frederick

Pencil Case
rs.

l E c Second and
AL GOLD PEN
REPOINTED and
actorily, other-

l., 96 W Balti-

tractor.

wly's whf

Polishers.

l, GRINDER &
Uhler's al, bet
)ver

Retail.

inde, 255 Alice

Hollins
ow
Mulberry
Eutaw
Light
llen
6 & 188 S Broad-

ght
iv c Eager
'ayette
c Fayette
H., Caroline c

Lexington
ombard c Spring
)eth, 75 S Dallas
Montgomery
I, 38 N Paca

Bartholmai Conrad, Central av c
  Gough
Barton Wm., 139 Hollins
Batzer John, 225 Eager
Baumeister Wm., 218 Alice Anna
Beahan John S., New Church
BEAN R. M., 130 Dugan's whf
Becker G. W., 112 S Eutaw
Beier B., 266 Alice Anna
Bell John, 168 Franklin
Bender Christian, 10 Union
Bennett John, 218 W Lexington
Berry Wm. H., 65 Camden
Beyer Mrs. Catharine, 56 E Lom-
  bard
Bingham Owen, 43 Bethel
Bitter Christian, Wolf c Gough
Boehine A., 128 Hanover
Bogue James, 11 Mercer
Bond John, Caroline c Jefferson
Born Mrs. Ellen L., 208 Cross
Bothmann C., 210 Hanover
Bouldin J. P., Bond c Lombard
Bourman Henry, 755 Light
Bower Conrad, 35 S Oregon
Bowers Mrs. R., 7 Park
Boyd John, 117 Fremont
Boyd John J., Fayette c Arch
Bradley P. E., 168 E Pratt
Brady Hannah, 282 Montgomery
Brinkman C. H., 138 S Howard
BROADERS H. R , 74 Hanover
Brockmeyer Mrs. T., Eager c Stir-
  ling
Broderick Wm., 33 Greenmount av
Brooks A., 6 Greenmount av
Broom George, Wolf c Bank
Brown Philip, 21 Brown
Brown R., 48 N Eutaw
Brundige William, 109 N Eutaw
Bruning Henry, 9 Warner
Buchheimer John, President c
  Eastern av
Bucksti Wm., 26 Second
Bufter John, 22 New
Burgess C. W. & Son, 166 N Gay
Buschman Frederick, 317 Hanover
Byrnes P. W., Ross c Jasper
Cadow Jas. E. & Co., 16 Penn av

Caffery Thomas, 360 W Pratt
Callahan James, 51 Tyson
Campbell Catharine, 26 S Poppleton
Campsen John, 264 Light
Carroll John, 103 N Calvert
Carter John W., 61 Camden
Cassidy B., Greenmount av, c Monument
Cassidy F., 2 Greenmount av
Cassidy Luke, 49 Britton
Cassidy Martin, Exeter c Hillen
Cassidy Mrs. M., 82 Greenmount av
Cassidy Patrick, 4 Valley
Cassidy Samuel, 576 N Gay
Caughy Benjamin & Co., 9 Pennsylvania av
Chrystal John, N E c Gay and Forrest
Chum Sol., 612 N Gay
Clark A., 191 Gough
Clarke John 237 Gough
Clark Patrick, 392 S Charles
Clark R. A., 30 E Lombard
Cobb J. & Son, 31 N Liberty
Cole John R., 50 N Eutaw
Colton John, 68 Mulberry
Cook Wm.. Caroline c Pratt
Cook H. W. & Co., 15 Commerce
Corcoran Stephen, 95 McElderry's wbf
Cornelius N., 165 Forrest
Corn William, Dallas, c Pratt
Correll C. E., agent, Lombard c Poppleton
Cosgrove J. H., 82 Richmond
Crammer N. J., 76 Hillen
Crawford John, Ann c Pratt
Crossman J. H., 118 W Lexington
Crowley Mrs. Honora, Caroline c Lombard
Custy John, 364 S Charles
Custy John, 88 S Howard
Cuff P., 38 Block
Davis George, Biddle c Ross
Dawson D., 74 Hillen
Decker Wm., 246 Columbia
Deigan Thomas, Bethel c Lombard
Delaney Charles, 29 Scott
Denoe Thomas, 666 W Baltimore

Derhan Mrs. R., 15 New
Devlin Felix, 24 Ensor
Dickerson A. A., 221 E Pratt
Dietz R., 115 N Eutaw
Distler Conrad, 227 Canton av
Dittman John H., 113½ McElderry's whf
Dixon Patrick, 29 S Paca
Donat M., 201 S Charles
Donert Mary, 199 S Charles
Dorritee James, 56 Raburg
Dowling Catharine, 65 Harrison
Downs W. H., 225 Light
Doyle James, 432 W Lombard
Doyle Mrs. B., Valley c Webster al
Doyle Thomas, 191 S Charles
Draine Richard, 33 Forrest
Drane James, 2 E Monument
Dressell G., Ross c Orchard
Driscoll Dennis, 217 Chesnut
Drohan Thomas, 79 Franklin
Dudley Miss Mary, 303 Light
Dun Margaret, 100 S Fremont
Duncan Eliza, 47 W Lombard
Dunlap Charles, Howard c Lexington
Dunn Edward, 580 W Lombard
DURDING JOHN T., 464 Light
Dyer Benjamin, 487 W Baltimore
Eberhart Joseph A., Aisquith c Sterling
ECKELMANN H. S., DEALER IN GROCERIES, WINES, LIQUORS, GERMAN PRODUCE, &c., 45 Marsh mkt space
Eckhardt Conrad, 5 Pine
EDMONDS SAMUEL & BROS., N W c Lexington and Pearl
Eggemann Henry, N E c Spring and Gay
Ehlers Louis, 378 Light
Ehrman Frederick, 338 S Caroline
Ehrman George, Mulberry c State
Eiehauer Frank, 218 Central av
Elkman H., Boston c Winsor
Ellis Isabella, 615 Light
Engelsmaur Daniel, 190 Biddle
Engleheardt Mrs. M., 89 Gough

Eversman J. G., 309 S Charles
Faber B., German c Liberty
Fachs Mary, 140 Cross
Fagan R , 235 Columbia
Fambach F., 63 Bank
FANGMEYER JOHN, S E c Baltimore and Gilmore
Farber J. M., 97 North
Farley Catharine, 131 S Fremont
Farlow John T., N W c Baltimore and Ann
Farnen Peter, 108 Bank
Fendall & Co., N E c Gay and Chew
Fenneman D., Lombard c Poppleton
Fenniman F., 272 Canton av
FINNAN B., 104 N Calvert
Finnen P., 31 Britton
Firoved David, Franklin c Chatsworth
Firoved John, 53 S Schroeder
Fisher A. & Son, 25 Penn av
Flamm Mrs. M., Holland c Lewis
Foster Sarah, 36 Gough
Foulk Casper W., 348 S Charles
Fowler Thomas, 175 and 177 E Baltimore
Fox James, Douglas c Forrest
Frank C. L., 33 Brown
Frank Henry II., 56 Clay
FRYER T., N E c Exeter and Fayette
Fullmenkamp John H., 573 W Lombard
Galben William, 213 Henrietta
GALLOWAY ELIZABETH, 681 W Baltimore
Gamble Mrs., N Caroline c Hampstead
Gates F., 85 N Paca
Gaule Michael, 92 Franklin
Geagan M., 297 W Pratt
Gerglein John, 107 N Eutaw
Gerkin Wm., Boyd c Amity
Germershausen Lewis, 1 Vine
GESSNER JOHN N., 44 Greenmount av
Getz Christian, Henrietta o S Eutaw

Glanser Chas. F., 832 W Baltimore
Gleninger J. R. & Co., 7 N Charles
Glennan John, 34 Ross
Gluck Henry, Caroline c Chew
Goldhammer Peter, 229 S Sharp
Goldheimer Mrs. Elizabeth, Sharp c Henrietta
Goldman Mrs. S., 56 Ensor
Gorman B., 79 Richmond
Gornell R., 53 North
Goullard John, 178 Hanover
Graham Edward, 138 Harford av
Gray Bernard, E Monument c Beuren
Greb Peter, 170 N Howard
Green Charles B., N W c Gay and High
Greenabaum N.. Orleans c Spring
Greyton C. T., 329 Aisquith
Griffin Mrs. Mary, Caroline c Madison
Gude Justus C., 67 German and Lombard c Eutaw
Gunther Wm., 109 S Dallas
Guyton C. T., 37 Ensor
Hall John, Caroline c McElderry
Hamill Mrs. Ann, Caroline c Hammond al
Hamilton Robert, 68 Camden
Hammel Mrs. Caroline, 80 Henrietta
Hammond Lloyd, 410 S Charles
Hampson A. J., 81 Charles
Haneman R., N E c Gay & Edward
Hannibal Mrs. A., 118½ E Lombard
Hart Samuel, 59 North
Harvey Ann C., 214 and 216 Hollins
Hasseur Andrew, 70 McElderry
Haulman Joseph, 407 W Pratt
Healy John, 26 E Pratt
Hebebrand Peter, 360 S Sharp
Heckmann Frederick, 16 Park
Heider Henry, 273 Hanover
Heine W., Wolfe c Lombard
Hellwig George, 154 S Fremont
Heman Mrs. E., Albemarle o Style
Herbert Daniel, 87 Henrietta
Henry Daniel, 88 Britton

10

Henry Jane, 238 Hollins
Heser George, 464 Canton av
Hiellees M., Aisquith c Cornet
Hilderbrand A., 29 S Poppleton
Hill Lewis H., 223 Hanover
Hill Wm., 237 E Baltimore
Hinternight Conrad, S Eden c Stiles
Hiner Mrs. E., 84 Hamburgh
Hipsley E. G., 184 N Gay
Hoffman Wm., 29 E Pratt
Hogan John F., S E c German and
  Fremont
Holden Patrick, 130 Ensor
Holdfelder John, Central av c East-
  ern av
Hollander Mrs. L. S., 33 N Fremont
Holle Julien, 67 N Schroeder
Hollins George, Fayette c Charles
Hollman Henry, 16 Raburg
Holmes Richard, 171 Penn av
Hook Charles, Ensor c Monument
Hoopper James I., 650 W Baltimore
Horigan Peter, 168 Columbia
HORN JOSEPH, N E c Paca and
  Lexington
Howe E., 2 Josephine
Hubbard Bridget, 42 Williamson
Hughes J., Jefferson c Spring
Hughes Philip, 479 W Pratt
Hulsmann Henry, 90 Cross
Humenler H., Park c Clay
Hunt J. W., Exeter c Fayette
HUTCHINS L. H., 233 N Gay
Hutton Mrs. C., 68 Penn av
Ijams Clever, 38 S Republican
Ijams & Hutchins, 108 N Gay
Ingram Wm., Hanover c Hill
Izinsky John, 58 Thames
Jackson James M., Baltimore c
  Spring
Jacobs M., 77 Harrison
Johnson C. J., 89 Chesnut
Johnson John, East c Hillen
Kaetzenberg S., 311 Canton av
Kaiser George, 500 N Gay
Kalavelage J. W., 307 S Charles
Kalkman H. F., 29 N Poppleton ·
Kaste Ernst, 1 Leadenhall
Kaufmann Joseph, 362 Light

Kavanaugh D., Front c Hillen
Kelly Mrs. Ellen, Forrest c Hull's
  la
Kemp Harmon, 88 Central av
Kennard G. J., 235 N Gay
Kernan Michael, 481 W Pratt
Kernan Thomas, 90 Britton
Kessler John, 37 Pine
Keyley Richard, 409 W Pratt
Keyting Patrick, 89 Britton
Kideger Lewis, S Schroeder
Kimball George, 400 S Sharp
Kircher John, 261 Hanover
Kirkwood Mrs. Ann, 135 Cross
Kirwan B., 124 Ross
Kisendorfe George, N E c Caroline
  and Gay
Knatz Philip, 865 W Baltimore
Knawss Louis, 74 Pollard
Knefely Henry, 5 Harrison
Korte William, 396 Canton av
Kraft Mrs. M., S E c Lexington
  and Liberty
Kratz John, Howard, c Montgom-
  ery
Kraumer & Goldsborough, 161 For-
  rest
Krauk Frederick, 309 Canton av
Krenen John, Eagen c Aisquith
Kretz Henry, 332 Canton av
Kroger Clement J., 78 Henrietta
Kriete George, 33 S Oregon
Kuhn George 10 Eden
Laessig John H., N W c Fayette
  and Poppleton
Lalor Lawrence, 34 East
Lathen William, Caroline c Jeffer-
  son
Lawrence F. L., N E c Lexington
  and Green
Leber J. H., 46 N Fremont
Lindsay A. B., Forrest c Hillen
List Mrs. M., 948 W Baltimore
Lovell S. G., N W c Baltimore
  and High
Lower C., 143 Hollins
Lowenthal Simon, Harrison, c Fay-
  ette
Ludwig John, 426 Hanover

McAdam Mary, Exeter, c Front
McAllister Mrs. M., Albemarle, c Fawn
McConkey Martha, 16 Chesnut
McCoy Daniel, 114 W Fayette
McCrath John, 195 S Charles
McCurdy D., 160 S Wolf
McCURLEY FELIX, 733 W Baltimore
McCurley John 723 W Baltimore
McDermitt John, 799 W Baltimore
McEvoy Sarah, 188 Hollins
McGan Patrick, 147 Eager
McGee Patrick, 173 S Chester
McGreevy H., 132 Harford av
McGreevy Wm., 171 Eager
McKenna Bernard, 127 Holiday
McKenna F., Neighbor c Argyle al
McLane Edward, 827 W Baltimore
McLean Wm. H., 52 N Charles
McMahon Joseph, Exeter c Front
McMann S., 171 N Eutaw
McNeill James, 63 Boston
McNEILL & CO., N E c Gay and High, BEST FAMILY GROCERIES
McNorton M., 48 Forrest
Maier John G., N E c Gay and Frederick
Mally A., 2 McHenry
Mankin J. W., 66 N Howard
Manly Mary Jane, 267 Hollins
Manning M., 10 L Paca
March Washington, 101 Hanover
March Wm. G., 143 W Lexington
Mares George, Ann c Alice Anna
Martin George W., Essex c Alice Anna
Mathias Ament, Jefferson c Eden
Matthai C. E., Ann c Baltimore
Matthews John N., 25 Centre mkt Space
Mauler Conrad, 193 Eastern av
Mayer John H., 264 S Howard
Mediuger & Co., 158 and 160 Forrest
Meehan P., N E c Gay and Madison
Meier L. G., 134 Franklin
Menack Joseph, 50 N Register

Middendorf Henry C., 46 Leadenhall
Miller Henry, 46 President
Miller Mary, S Republican c Lombard
Millhenry G., Ross c Tasker
Mishavein Mrs. E., 552 W Pratt
Mitchell Elisha, Caroline c McElderry
Mitten Henry, West c Washington
Momberger George, Gist c Essex
Montgomery John, East c Hillen
Mooney Patrick, 63 Gough
Moore Jacob, 314 Allice Anna
Moore Wm., 154 N Calvert
Morris James, 72 Pine
Morton Robert, Aisquith c Madison
Moser Wm. W., 314 S Sharp
Muller Charles, 294 S Charles
Muller Charles F., 2 Ewing
Mullett Mrs. Margaret, Caroline o Orleans
Murphy Wm., 98 Bank
Murray Margaret, East c Douglas
Muse Henry, 6 S Poppleton
Myer D. W. & C. M., 14 W Baltimore
Nebe Charles, 54 Raburg
Neibough S., 215 Light
Newbaur Mrs. Margarette, 220 S Sharp
Newcomer Samuel, 14 N Stricker
Newman Christopher, West c Hanover
Noel Samuel H., 52 Gough
Nolan C., High c Front
Nolan Mrs. M., 57 Arch
Nugent John, 129 North
O'Neal John, 242 German
Ortman Mrs. S., 42 Douglas
Otto Frederick, High c Style
Owens James, 482 N Gay
Parrish E. S., 1 Columbia
Paul K. L., 124 S Howard
Peach G., 305 Aisquith
Penn Mrs. S., Ann c Lombard
Peters J. J., Portland c Emery
PETERS MRS. C., 93 W Lexington

Pfau Henry, 614 Light
Pfister F., 253 S Charles
PITT J. C., Garden c Biddle
Plitt Theodore, 650 Light
Polk Robert M., 30 Ensor
Printy John. 216 Light
PRUETT JAMES, 487 N Gay
Pryor Mrs. Ann S , 213 Gough
QUINEY DANIEL, 120 N Exeter
Ragen Mrs. Catharine, 37 York
Rebstoch Charles, 367 S Eutaw
Redding John, 123 N Exeter
Reed Francis, 36 Warner
Reese Charles & Co., c Eutaw, Madison, and Garden
REESE EDWARD, 366 W Baltimore
Reiger Jacob, 394 S Charles
Reiley Philip, 8 Tyson
Reitz H. L. & Sons, 93 Hanover
Rennart Henry, 254 S Eutaw
Ressell Carl, 151 N Register
Rexter Jane, Warren c Montgomery
RICHERS HENRY N., 231 S Charles
Rienhardt B., 123 W Madison
Riepe L., 25 Pine
Rixse George, 8 Scott
Rock M. A., 85 North
Roesenburg John, 64 Sommerset
Rogers John, Baltimore c Schroeder
Ross E. C., 15 W Baltimore
Ross George, 310 S Eutaw
Roth Christian, 52 President
Roth George, 25 Brown
Roth Henry, 258 Canton av
Rouseman Henry, 12 Warner
Rudel John, Central av c Bank
Rudolph Mrs. R. M., 406 S Charles
Russell Patrick, Caroline c Chew
Ryan C., N Front c Hillen
Ryan H., 26 S Schroeder
Ryan J. F., 48 Centre
Sach Ameila, 126 S Front
Sachtleben H., Mulberry c Chatsworth
Salom Francis, Exeter c Necessity al
Sandneh Julis F., 201 S Charles

Savage Wm. H., 102 Richmond
Schaeffer Frederick, 268 Alice Anna
Schaeffer George, 76 N Gay
Schaffer -Mrs. Catharine, 231 Henrietta
Schieve B., 13 New
Schimer Mrs. E., 36 Albey's al
Schlarman Henry, 224 Columbia
Schleifer Wm., 39 S Liberty
SCHMENNER J. H., Franklin c Chatsworth
Schnibbe D., 190 S Eutaw
Schoanhres John, 393 Canton av
Schriner Conrad, 60 Penn. av
SCHRŒDER A. J., 211 Gough
Schroder Mrs. H., 132 Hanover
Schulz A. H., 516 Alice Anna
Schulz Louis, 72 S Fremont
Schwab J. & A., 220 S Broadway
Schwehi F., S Fremont c Dover
Scotti H. E., 85 McElderry's whf
Scroder Louis, 50 Hamburg
Shaw Mathew, High c Hillen
Shear Charles, 140 S Howard
Sheckell Richard M., 740 W Baltimore
Shoemaker J., 43 N Eutaw
Shot Mrs. Ann, German c Penn
Shriver Martin, Forrest c Hull's la
Sills Edward P., N Green c Saratago
Singerfeather F. H., 301 Light
Slaven Michael, 236 Light
Sling Conrad, 83 Spring
Sliver Albert, 210 S Charles
Smith A., Carlton c Fayette
Smithson Mrs. Anna, Lombard c Lloyd
Smith Mrs. E., Caroline c Madison
Snooks John, 4 Mosher
Spamer Mrs., N Caroline c Hampstead
Sparklin B. J., 112 N High
Spicer Hiram, 430 W Lombard
Stafford Laurence, N Caroline c E Fayette
Stahm S., 110 Spring
STANSBURY DARIUS, 115 and 117 N High

Stansbury John S., 12 and 14 Penn av

STANSBURY J. T., 857 W Baltimore c Calhoun

Stanton Thomas, 33 York

Steibel Jacob, Aisquith c Jefferson

Stein Mrs. M., 87 Greenmount av

Stewart E. H., 13 Market space

Stevens Joseph, 215 E Baltimore

Stidman Mrs. C., 31 Fremont

Stiebel Conrad, 262 Washington

Stiebel S., 222 S Broadway

Stradmeyer John, 191 Eager

Straus H. & Bro., 268, 270, and 247 S Broadway

Strauss Joseph, 255 N Gay

Stromenger John, Aisquith c Madison

Stump G. M., Fremont c Conway

Sullivan D., S W c Lexington and Pine

Sullivan James, 285 S Eutaw

Sutherland Thomas, Caroline c Mulliken

Sweeny F., 43 Henrietta

Tapman Samuel, 296 Light

Theily Frederick, 43 Marion

Thiele Louis, 248 S Charles

Thomas E., 189 Eastern av

Thomas John, 341 S Howard

Thomans J. H., Arch c Josephine

Tiemeyer Chas., 55 S Eutaw

Torney Carston, 260 Light

Tracey Jefferson, 353 Canton av

Trainer Bernard, 47 Park

Treanor Arthur, Washington c Cross

Troe George, 98 S Dallas

Tucker & Bro., Mulberry c Chatsworth

Ueman Henry, 74 Mulberry

Ullrich E. W., 233 Hollins

Ullrich William, 42 Columbia

Umstad Jacob, 598 W Lombard

Valter Daniel, 35 Brown

Van Drehle J. H., 53 S Charles

Veedtry Anthony, 97 Low

Vonderhost J., 38 Second

Vogelgesang Jacob, Johnston c Cross

Walker Henry, 63 Market space

Walker Mrs. M., 104 Jefferson

Watson Joseph, S Caroline c Eastern av

Warnken Lewis, 135 S Front

Warrenburger Catharine, Hanover c Henrietta

Webb A. P., 36 N Paca

Weber Charles, 372 Light

Wehage Caroline, 381 S Charles

Weiend Henry, 286 S Charles

Weinig Casper, Burk c Alice Anna

WEITSELL HENRY, 82 Lancaster

Weiller Charles, 219 E Pratt

WEIR JOHN, 127 Greenmount av

Weller Henry, 192 S Howard

Wess B., Bond c Mulliken

Westly Hiram, 9 Mercer

Wested Louis, 202 S Fremont

Wessinger Charles, Bank c Bond

Wheeler J. C., 159 Forrest

Whelan William W., 142 W Baltimore

White Arthur, c Front and High

White M., 683 W Baltimore

White Sarah, High c Low

White Thomas, Tessier c Biddle

Wienek Frederick, 114 Henrietta

Wigchyram Aaron, 314 Canton av

Wilen John, 22 E Lombard

Williams Peter, 55 Gough

Williams Mrs. R., 26 New

Winfelder John, 227 Eastern av

Wingate John H., Henrietta c Warner

Winn John, Aisquith c Hull's la

WODE ANN MARIA, 273 S Charles

Wood W. H., 105 S Charles

Wooters Mrs. Sarah, 268 Light

Wurzbacher John, 194 Cross

Yerscheid John, 339 S Bond

Zellard William, 159 German

Zorbeck Mrs. C., 33 Bank

10*

Grocers, Wholesale.

(*See also* PRODUCE COMMISSION MERCHANTS; *also* PRODUCE DEALERS; *also* PROVISION DEALERS.)

ADAMS & DAVIDSON, 7 Commerce, GROCERS & COMMISSION MERCHANTS

AYRES & COULTER, 1 Ellicot, first door ab Pratt and rear of 55 Light, Grocers and Commission Merchants, Dealers in Foreign and Domestic Liquors, Cigars, &c.

Bansemer W. G. & Co., 108 W Lombard

Barnes Winston, 55 W Pratt

Blackburn & Bro., Franklin c Eutaw

Boswell & Dorsett, 147 W Pratt

Brinkley Joseph B. & Co., 59 S Calvert

Brown V. J. & Co., 66 Exchange pl

BURNS & CO., 96 Light st whf

CHESNUT WILLIAM & CO., N W c South and Pratt

Cochran James E., 84 Light st whf

Coleman & Bailey, 105 & 107 Thames

CONN WILLIAM, 101 Franklin

Coslin W. S., 55 South

DE LA MAR C. M. & CO., 96 W Lombard

Deetjen T., 74 and 76 Thames

DINSMORE & KYLE, 156 Pratt st whf

DOWELL JOHN, 55 S Calvert, GROCER AND COMMISSION MERCHANT

Duvall & Iglehart, 128 Light st whf

Edmonds W. E. & S., S W c Lexington and Green

Edmondson Jos. A., 29 Cheapside

ENSEY LOT & SON, S W c Baltimore and Eutaw, WHOLESALE GROCERS and COMMISSION MERCHANTS

FERGUSSON & TYSON, 121 W Lombard

Fink & Bro., S W c Franklin and Eutaw

FOLEY D. J. & BROTHER, 50 South

FREELAND, HALL & CO., Wholesale Grocers and Dealers in Wines and Liquors, 143 W Pratt

GARDINER, STUART & CO., GROCERS, 37 CHEAPSIDE.

Gregg Andrew & Co., 109 Franklin

GROVE FRANCIS & CO., 19 Commerce, WHOLESALE GROCERS & COMMISSION MERCHANTS

HABERSHAM & BARRETT, 53 Exchange pl

Haslett G, 133 N Howard

HOFFMAN H. K. & CO., 45 S Howard. (See advertisement.)

HOOPER GEO. W., c South & Pratt

Hopkins T. & G. T., S W c Pratt and Light

HUMRICHOUSE C. W., 20 COMMERCE, WHOLESALE GROCER.

Hyatt & Stump, 56 South

Jackson Ch's M. & Co., c Smith's whf and Pratt

KING W. W., 40 Ellicott

Leatherbury John E., 6 W Pratt

LEVERING & CO., 2 & 3 Commerce

LUMSDEN ROBERT, GROCERY & COMMISSION MERCHANT, 41 Cheapside

MARKELL CHARLES, S E c Calvert and Lombard

Merritt W. K. & Co., 53 S Calvert and 57 Cheapside

MITCHELL EDWARD & SON, 90 W Pratt, GROCERS & COMMISSION MERCHANTS, and Dealers in FOREIGN and DOMESTIC LIQUORS, TOBACCO, CIGARS, &c.

MITCHELL JOHN T. & CO., 13 & 17 Mercer

MITCHELL M. A., 2 Spear's whf

Miles & Hopkins, 68 S Calvert

MORTON A. B. & SONS, 103 Smith's whf

MYER JAS. & CO., 39 Cheapside n Pratt, GROCERS and COMMISSION MERCHANTS

Needham A. & Sons, 142 Light st whf

OVENDORF & BEAM,

325 W BALTIMORE,

S E c Howard,

DEALERS IN

Groceries, Wines, Liquors, and Teas.

Produce Commission Merchants.

SAMUEL OVENDORF. GEO. F. BEAM.

PADGETT W. A. & W. W., 17 Commerce
Pardoe & White, 105 South
Pearson George, 5 N Liberty
RAMSAY JAS. G., 13 Thames, F P
RAU JOHN C. & CO., Howard c Franklin
Reynolds William & Son, 40 N Howard
Schwab H. & M., 210 Lexington
Segerman Wm. H., 8 & 10 Penn. av
SIMMS & TYSON, 64 S Gay, one door from Pratt, GROCERS and COMMISSION MERCHANTS.
SLATER GEORGE, 10 and 12 Commerce
Slingluff C. D. & Son, 13 N Howard
SMITH J. & SON, 35 Cheapside, GROCERS AND COMMISSION MERCHANTS, and dealers in Liquors, Tobacco, Cigars, &c.
TUBMAN B. G. & CO., 102 Light st whf
TURNER JOHN T., 40 Ellicott
Townshend, French & Co., 80 Light st whf
UHRIG JOHN, Howard c Franklin
VICKERY & MUIR, W Falls av (City Block), near Havre de Grace Steamboats. GROCERS AND COMMISSION MER-

CHANTS. DEALERS IN SALT, FISH, FLUID, TOW LINES, CORDAGE, &c.
WOODS, BRIDGES & CO., 6 and 8 Commerce
Young & Carson, 77 Exchange pl

Grocers, Wholesale and Retail.

BOSWELL & DORSETT,
147 W. Pratt,
GROCERS AND COMMISSION MERCHANTS,
FOR THE SALE OF
TOBACCO, GRAIN, FLOUR,
BACON, &c.

COOK & SPEDDEN, 165 Light st whf, Grocers and Commission Merchants
Coward Thomas R., 114 Light st whf
Cox Geo. A. & Son, 103 Hanover
Denison & Brother, 219 W Pratt, and 51 W Baltimore
DOWNEY JOHN & SON, Wholesale Dealers in GROCERIES, WINES, AND LIQUORS; Also, FLOUR AND COUNTRY PRODUCE GENERALLY, 133 Franklin bet Paca and Eutaw
DUNLAP C. LEWIS, 13 W Baltimore
Goubart J. & Co., 205 W Pratt
Green & Yoe, 88 W Baltimore
Hengst S. & R., N E c Franklin & Paca
KELLY CALEB & CO., 402 W Pratt
Knowles James W., 90 Dugan's whf
Lawrence E. G. & Bro., 422 W Baltimore
McCready & Phillips, 7 W Falls av block
McKANNA P., 325 W Pratt
Mister Abraham, 98 Light st whf

Pattison & Woolford, 102 Dugan's whf

REESE EDWARD, FAMILY GRO-CER, 366 W Baltimore adjoining Eutaw House

REESE G. H. & BROTHERS, 207 and 209 W Pratt, Wholesale and Retail Tea Dealers and Family Grocers. Importers of fine groceries. Gerhard H. Reese, Thomas M. Reese, Henry Reese.

Sewell C. A. & Co., S E c Pratt & Hanover

Shields R. D., 20 Penn. av

Stephens John A. & Co., 92 Light st whf

TIERNAN P. & SON, 12 N Charles

Torney Otto, 103 McElderry's whf

Wilkinson James, 122 Dugan's whf

Wilson & Burns, 30 S Howard

Guano.

(See also FERTILIZERS.)

Barret Brothers, 29½ South

Cooper E. K., South c Water

RHODES B. M. & Co., 82 South st, Bowly's whf. (See advertisement front cover.)

WHITELOCK W. & Co., 44 South

Gunpowder.

BEATTY CHARLES W., agent, 153 W Pratt

WEBB A. L. & BRO., c Pratt & Commerce, agents for Dupont's Powder and Safety Fuse.

Gun and Pistol Makers.

McCOMAS A.,

51 S Calvert,

MAKER AND IMPORTER

OF

Guns, Rifles, and Pistols.

Merrill, Thomas & Co., 239 W Baltimore. (See advertisement.)

MILNOR JOHN P., JR , & CO., 117 W Baltimore. (See advertisement opposite Military Goods.)

POULTNEY & TRIMBLE, 200 Baltimore

Gunsmiths.

Cromwell L., 271 S Ann

Cromwell Levi, 118 Thames

Escherich Anton, 477 W Baltimore

Harris William, 116 W Pratt

Pipins J. C., 20 Ensor

SCHUMAKER C., 58 W Pratt, Manufacturer and Dealer in Guns, Rifles, and Pistols, fishing-tackle, &c. SPORTING APPARATUS GENE-RALLY

* Hair Cloth, Damask, &c.

WILKENS WILLIAM & CO., Pratt c Charles

Hair Dressers, "Ladies."

BASTIEN MM'E E., LADIES' HAIR DRESSER, AND CHIL-DREN'S HAIR CUTTER, 96 W Lexington bet Liberty and Charles. HAIR BRAIDS, BANDEAUX, CURLS, WIGS, &c., Toilet Articles, Fancy Goods, Combs, Brushes, &c.

Fagret Madam Lucelle G., 40 N Charles

PAINI MADAME FRANCES, LA-DIES' SHAMPOOING AND HAIR DRESSING; also Children's Hair Cut. Keep constantly on hand a large assortment of Hair, Braid, Curls and Perfumery of the best quality, 17 N Calvert

TUSTIN MRS. M. J., LADIES' HAIR DRESSER, AND CHIL-DREN'S HAIR CUTTER, 120 W Lexington bet Howard and Park. BRAIDS, BANDEAUX, CURLS, WIGS, &c. constantly on hand and made to order; also *Perfumeries and Fancy Goods*

Hair Dressers.

ADAMS JAMES P., 2 Harrison
Albieght F. W., 147 W Madison
ANDERSON JAMES, 42 E Fayette
Andrae Ch., 356 W Pratt
Bader H., 191 W Lexington
Bailey David G., 152 N Gay
Barck John, 201½ W Lexington
Barsch Philip, 217 Canton av
Bishop Wm. H., 198 W Pratt
Blum George, 96 Richmond
BOECKNER CHARLES, 4 N Eutaw
Boninger John, 236 E Lombard
Briscoe Louis, 134 N Howard
Brice Philip, 73 Thames
Brown Louis M., 32 W Fayette
Chambers Alfred, 49 W Fayette
Chase Joseph, 67 W Pratt
Collins Isaac, Bond c Pratt
CONKLIN JOHN A., 167 Forrest
CONKLIN WILLIAM, 14 S Howard
Cotten J. A., 1 S Eutaw
Davis A. G., 6 N Calvert
Davis L., 807 W Baltimore
Eastlow Alexander, 297 Alice Anna
Ehilgey Andrew, 78 Greenmount av
Ernstberger Frank, 191 W Pratt
Fernandis John A., 128 S Broadway
Ferrandini Cipriano, 4 N Calvert
Fisher H. & O., 60 S Eutaw
Fowler J. M., 199 Light
Frey George, 114 Mulberry
Fridgel John, 187 S Sharp
Frisby James, 122 N High
Funk A., 91 N Calvert
Gatto Dominico, 11 S Gay
Georgius F. G., 17 Holiday
GERKE JOHN H., 119 N Calvert
Getz Conrad, 96 Bank
GREEN C., 31 W Pratt
Green H. C., 8 Eden
Gremm E., 46 Ensor
Griffin John T., 272 Montgomery
Hanfman L., 264 S Broadway
Harvey T., 70½ Hanover
Haschert George, 378 Saratoga
Helluing A., 268 Canton av

Hildebrand Henry, 32 E Lombard
Hill Wm. S., 824 W Baltimore
Hoffman Peter C., 361 Canton av
Hudson Levi, 116 N Eutaw
Hurse John, 64 W Fayette
Jaeckel Wm., 66 Thames
Janette E. F., 21 E Pratt
Jarboe John W., 238 W Lexington
JOHNSON JAMES H. A., 37½ German
Johnson Walter L., 4 N Gay
Jones John A., 23 E Baltimore
Kelly Geo. M., 16 N Eutaw
Kiener K., 7 W Pratt
Kramer Casper, 132 Eastern av
Krauss Wm., 65 N Gay
Krebs John, 15½ W Baltimore
Kroh Harmon, 216 S Sharp
Laws B., 41 Market space
Lebark Charles, 217 E Baltimore
Leonhardt C. B., Ann c Pratt
Lohman A., 13 Frederick
Lohman L., 177 Franklin
Mann James, 103 N Howard
Marsh Wm., 71 Market space
May Isadore, 174 E Baltimore
Meyer Abraham, 203 S Charles
McCabe S., 178 W Pratt
Montgomery James, 106 Light st whf
Moxley C. H., 12 North
Murray Wm. H., 4½ McClellan's al
Nickolas Casper, 257 Hanover
Nicols J. W., 61 E Baltimore
Nolte Bernard, 351 N Gay
Nolte F., 36 Ensor
Oldham Wm., 96 N Gay
Paini Joseph, 17 N Calvert
Parraway Wm. E., 78 S Eutaw
Pfaezgraf Henry, 90 N Gay
Pfeiffer Edward, 399 W Baltimore
Phelan J., 144 Forrest
Plyman John, 48 Camden
Pohnert E., 63 S Howard
Powell John 127 North
Powell J. D. & R., 212 E Pratt
Quandt Charles, 40 N Green
Rauft Charles Q., 533 W Baltimore
Reese T. H., 220 Light

Reese Andrew, 41 York
Reider John, 348 Canton av
Reiman Galthelf, 120 Thames
Rermberg Charles, 105 N Paca
Roberts Augustus, 4 Light
Rossler Christian, 121½ Franklin
Ruppeart John A., 352 S Charles
Rust August, 439 W Baltimore
Scheeler Henry, 667 W Baltimore
Schellenberger George J., 53 E
   Baltimore
Schleringer George, 65 President
Schillenberger, Joseph, 50 N Caro-
   line
Schimpf Christian, 247 S Broad-
   way
Seippel Conrad, 116 S Ann
Slipper George, 409 Light
Smith J. W., 4 Bank la
SPRIGG JAMES F., 119 S Fre-
   mont
Stengel John, 37 Market space
Stipe Lewis, 46 S Wolf
Stoffregen Charles, 18 Penn av
Stryer Peter, 117 E Pratt
Susman S., 244 Canton av
Tailor Henry, 8 Park
Toomey J., 13 S Calvert
Tydings Charles, 104 Franklin
Varley Thomas P., 4 St. Paul
WILLIAMS JOHN J., 247 Light
Wright Charles, 22 E Baltimore
ZIMMERMANN CHAS., BARBER,
   HAIR-DRESSER, AND HAIR DYER,
   61 Hanover

Hair—Ornamental.
Kauffman J., 4 Fayette

Hair Restoratives.
JONES JOHN A., perfumer, in-
   ventor, and manufacturer of
   Hair Dye, 23 E Baltimore

Hair Seating and Curled Hair.
Merryman O. P. & Co., 151 W Fay-
   ette
WILKENS WILLIAM & CO.,
   Pratt c Charles

Harbor Master.
Landin Thomas S., 93 McElderry's
   whf

Hardware Commission Merchants.
Cole Wm. H., 35 S Charles
Dugan, Jenkins & Co., 33 S Charles
KEITH M., JR., & SON, 23 S
   Charles. (See advertisement.)
SPEAR BROTHERS, 41 S Charles.
   (See advertisement)

Hardware Importers.

Buck E. D. & Brother, 86 and 88 W Pratt
Duer John, 8 Hanover
Hopkins, Harden & Kemp, 336 W Baltimore

JESSOP & FULTON,

IMPORTERS AND DEALERS

IN

FOREIGN AND DOMESTIC

HARDWARE & CUTLERY,

4 Hanover Street.

KANN SOLOMON J., Importer and Dealer in ENGLISH, GERMAN AND AMERICAN BUILDING AND CABINET HARDWARE, Cutlery, Tools, and House Furnishing Articles, 43 and 45 Harrison
King & Huppman, 307 W Baltimore

LONEY F. B. & CO.,

IMPORTERS AND DEALERS IN

HARDWARE, CUTLERY,

CHAINS, &c.,

3 Hanover st., n Baltimore st.

Francis B. Loney, Wm. R. Barry, Robert S. Finley, Irvin Neale, Joseph P. Elliott.

Magruder, Taylor & Roberts, 272 W Baltimore

NORRIS C. SIDNEY,

Importer and Dealer in

Cabinet, Builders' & Machinists'

HARDWARE,

Also, J. Moss & Gamble Bros. Files, Steel, &c.,

36 HANOVER ST.

Penniman & Bro., 10 N Howard
Porter R. B. & Son, 78 and 80 W Pratt
Proctor & Brother, 166 W Pratt
Reuter A. & Sons, 56 W Baltimore
WAESCHE F. R. & CO., Importer and Dealer in Foreign and Domestic Hardware, 232 W Baltimore
Wagner Lewis, 435 W Baltimore
WARD BROTHERS, 9 S Calvert
WATERS CHARLES E., 15 S Charles
Whiting James & Co., 130 W Pratt

Hardware and Cutlery, Retail.

Black John, 160 N Gay
Brian John G., 136 N Gay
CORTLAN & CO., 216 and 218 W Baltimore
Daiger Frederick, 324 W Pratt
Davidson F. H., 160 Franklin
Easton Charles P., 767 W Baltimore
Gorsuch Jehu, N W c Gay & Front
Greenfield Caleb W., 236 W Lexington
Henderson D., 146 Forrest
Herzog John, N E c Lexington and Park
Holmes R. S., President c Pratt
Hopkins J. A., 15 N Howard
Kann Jacob, 104 N Gay
Kirkley John W., 104 Pennsylvania av

Kleppish H. M., 110 W Lombard
McMILLAN WILLIAM D., dealer in HARDWARE, CUTLERY, TIN WARE, GLASS, PUTTY, &c., 333 W Pratt bet Paca and Green, a few doors above the Columbia House or Three Tun Tavern, respectfully informs the public that he will keep constantly on hand a general assortment of the above articles, and invites them to call and examine his stock. Goods delivered to any part of the city.
Reddish John H., 187 S Broadway
Reuter Andrew, 46 Harrison
Shriner Peter, 123 Franklin
Smull David B., 82 W Pratt
Staylor Henry, 95 Harrison
Stewart C. J., 3 S Liberty
Wilcox Henry, 142 N Gay
Wilcox T. J. & Co., 170 Forrest

Hardware and Cutlery, Wholesale.

ANDERSON BROTHERS, N W c Pratt and Light
Baker & Brown, 10 W Pratt
Bradford G. W., 102 Franklin
CORTLAN & CO., 216 and 218 W Baltimore
Curley James W., 17 N Howard
Foy James, 64 S Calvert
Glenn Samuel & Bro., 16 S Charles
HICKLEY R. & BRO., 8 N Howard
Hopkins J. A., 15 N Howard
JESSOP & FULTON, 4 Hanover
KEEN & HAGERTY, 37 and 39 S Calvert
KLEPPISH H. M., wholesale dealer in HARDWARE AND CUTLERY, 110 W Lombard, up stairs
LONEY F. B. & CO., 3 Hanover
Porter R. B. & Son, 78 and 80 W Pratt
WEBB H. W., N W c Pratt and Calvert

Harness Makers.

(See SADDLE & HARNESS MAKERS.)

Hat and Cap Manufacturers.

(See also CAP MAKERS.)

BERNHARD J., 208 W Pratt, MILITARY AND FANCY HAT AND CAP MANUFACTURER. Particular attention paid to orders.
Coupland Richard, 60 S Charles
Craft W. G. & Co., Breidebaugh al
Eaverson & McCord, 47 S Charles
Greenwood Wm. S., agt., 2 Light
ROSENSWIG E., 344 W Baltimore
White J. D., Fayette c Frederick

Hat Trimmings.

CONNOLLY EDWARD, 311 W Baltimore. Importer of Hatters' Furs, Plushes, &c., and dealer in Hat Trimmings. The highest price in cash always paid for Shipping Furs.

Hats and Caps, Retail.

ARTHUR W. W.,

1 W Baltimore, ad'g the Bridge,

Fashionable

HAT AND CAP

MANUFACTURER.

Dealer in Ladies' Furs, &c.

Austrian B., 213 S Broadway
Banchardt W., 45 N Eutaw
Bert Peter, 298 W Pratt
Besel S., 230 N Gay
Boston & Price, 82 W Baltimore
Burns Edward, 40 Centre mkt space
Cari James E., 119 N Howard
Charles Thomas J., 205 S Broadway
Church Mary, 332 W Pratt
Cox & Co., 190 W Baltimore
Crozier Chas., 198 S Broadway
De Goey William, 212 W Pratt

Dittrich & Bro., 178 N Gay
Frost II., 140 N Gay
Grant Xenophon, 494 W Baltimore
GRASSER CH., 334 W Pratt
Hammer J. A., 99 N Howard
Hampson E., 193 W Baltimore
Hellmann Joseph, 180 N Gay
Hindes S. & Son, 100 N Gay
Hobbs W. P. T., 66 W Baltimore
Hurtt H. N., 224 W Pratt
    HURTT W. T., 38 N Green,
FASHIONABLE HAT AND CAP MANUFACTORY
Kerschner B. F., 426 W Baltimore
Kersting Mrs. C., 332 S Charles
Livingston Francis, 232 Light
Lotz L., 44 W Baltimore
Lynch Joshua & Co., 49 W Baltimore
McPhails James L., 132 W Baltimore
Marsh Henry C., 118 Franklin
Miller Henry, 241 Light
Minnighausen H., 352 W Pratt
Nicely Harry C., 34 W Baltimore
Quail G. K., 238 W Pratt
Quigley W. S., 24 Pennsylvania av
Raymo Charles M., 82 N Gay

Raymo Lewis, 117 N Gay
Ruben Jacob, 225 W Lexington
Ruben J., 675 W Baltimore
Saphor J., 266 S Charles
Silverstine, F., 193 Pratt
Singewald T. H., 223 S Broadway
TAYLOR R. Q., 5 N Calvert
Terrick Mrs. H., 46 Centre mkt space
Towson Charles, 33 N Eutaw
Trott James E., 82 and 86 Mkt space
Vansant Joshua & Son, 109 W Baltimore
Vorsteg Hermann, 256 N Gay
Wahl Jacob, 225 S Broadway
Wiel A. & Brothers, 28 W Pratt
Wiel S., 14 Centre mkt space
Winter Henry, 578 W Baltimore
Zink A., 221 S Charles

Hats and Caps, Wholesale.

BURNS GEO. W., 338 W Baltimore
Cole Wm. R. & Co., 274 W Baltimore
DIXON WM. T. & BRO., 306 W Baltimore, Wholesale Dealers and Commission Merchants in Hats and Caps, Boots and Shoes—Wm. T. Dixon, James Dixon, Jr.
GRINNELL & JENKINS, 275 W Baltimore
Hickley R. I., 44 N Howard
ROSENSWIG E., 344 W Baltimore
Warder & Barrett, 266 W Baltimore
White & Rosenberg, 76 and 78 S Charles

Hay Packer.

McDonnell E., 75 N Calvert

*Hermetically Sealed Canned Goods.

(See also OYSTER PACKERS.)

ESTABLISHED IN 1847, MUMSEN, CARROLL & CO., 18 Light. (See advertisement opp. Oyster Packers.)

11

A. FIELD,

STEAMED FRESH COVE

OYSTERS,

Put up by A. FIELD, at his old established stand,

309 *W. LOMBARD.*

These Oysters retain all their original flavor and toughness. Warranted to keep twelve months in any climate. (See advertisement opposite Oyster Packers.)

THOMAS KENSETT & CO.,

HERMETICALLY SEALED

OYSTERS, FRUITS, &C.

WEST FALLS AVENUE.

JOHN T. MITCHELL & CO.,

MANUFACTURERS OF

PRESERVES, JELLIES,

PICKLES, AND

HERMETICALLY SEALED

FRUITS, OYSTERS, &c.,

Nos. 13 *and* 17 *Mercer St.,*

Bet. Light and Calvert Streets,

BALTIMORE, MD.

MUMSEN, CARROLL & CO., 18 Light. (See advertisement opposite Oyster Packers.)

Shriver James & Co., 375 S Sharp

SHRIVER JOHN L. & BROS., HERMETICALLY SEALED OYSTERS, FRUITS, MEATS, Vegetables, POULTRY, Pickles, Preserves, Jellies, Catsups, and SCHRIVER'S BALTIMORE OYSTER KETCHUP, 307 W Pratt,—William Shriver Jr., Jno. L. Shriver, Albert Shriver.

THOMAS E. C. & SONS, Lexington c Arch

THOMAS S. W. & E. C., JR., 143 German. (See advertisement opposite Oyster Packers.)

THOMAS WM. H., 184 York n Howard

Hides and Leather Dealers.

(*See also* LEATHER DEALERS.)

APPOLD GEORGE & SONS, 8 and 10 Water

BALTIMORE UNITED BUTCHERS' ASSOCIATION, Incorporated Feb. 10th, 1858. Have always on hand HORNS, HIDES and TALLOW of the first quality, which they offer to the trade at the lowest prices. All orders addressed to the Clerk, at the Hide and Tallow House, corner of McKim and Neighbor Sts. will be promptly attended to.

BARTON WILLIAM J. & SON, 7 and 9 Cheapside c Lombard, Dealers in Hides, Oils, &c.

Crane W. & Son, c Cheapside and Water

Deford B. & Sons, c Calvert and Lombard

Dyrnforth M., 169 Light st whf

GRUPY FRANCIS H., 42 S Calvert, *dwelling* c Chase and Eden

Hewlett J. Q. & Son, 96 Lombard and 6 Water

Hoffman & Deford, 84 W Lombard

JENKINS EDWARD, 13 Cheapside, Hide, Oil, and Leather Dealer. Leather bought and sold on commission, Agent for Norton & Owen's Double Grinding Bark Mills
Poland, Jenkins & Co., 12 Water

Horse Shoers.

(*See also* BLACKSMITHS.)

Anderson David, 104 German
Beatty William, 16 Barre
Carey J. H., 3 Marion
Daley John, 188 Columbia
Fulton John W., 221 Biddle
HEAGERTY M., 761 W Baltimore
KEENAN JAMES, 86 Holiday
Pumphrey J., 316 Montgomery
Sheedy Michael, 138 German
Skirmer James, 314 Montgomery
Spence George, 3 W Falls av
Tumoney John, 126 Ensor

Hose Makers—Leather.

DUKEHART R. W.,

MANUFACTURER

OF

FIRE,

GARDEN, and

BATH HOUSE

HOSE;

FIRE, ARMY, and NAVY BUCKETS;

Torches, Wrenches, Suction-hose, Elastic Tubes, Hose Pipes and Screws, Rivets, Burrs, &c. ;

Stretched Leather Belts of superior quality,

18 Water Street.

HASKELL J. H., 33 S Eutaw. (See advertisement op. Leather.)
HORTON H. P., 41 N Frederick

Hosiery Importers, Jobbers, and Wholesale Dealers.

DIETZ L. D. & CO., 308 W Baltimore. (See advertisement inside back cover.)

DROST & SUTRO,

IMPORTERS

and

WHOLESALE DEALERS

in

HOSIERY,

ZEPHYR WORSTED,

EUROPEAN and AMERICAN

FANCY GOODS,

DRESS TRIMMINGS, &C.,

253 W Baltimore.

G. A. DROST.   E. SUTRO.

Felber & Adams, 251 W Baltimore
HILGENBERG CHARLES, importer and dealer in HOSIERY, GLOVES, MITTS ; German and Domestic Yarn, Trimmings, Notions, &c., 35 N Eutaw.
HODGES BROTHER, 23 Hanover
Luitz & Flack, 18 Hanover
Mann E., 63 W Baltimore
Meyer Ferdinand, 139 W Baltimore
RINGGOLD J. P. & BRO., 175 W Baltimore, six doors below Light
SEIBERT E., 35 W Baltimore

STELLMANN, HINRICHS & CO.,

IMPORTERS

OF

HOSIERY AND SMALL WARES

and

COMMISSION MERCHANTS,

21 Hanover Street.

JNO. STELLMANN.
CHRISTOPHER HINRICHS.
HENRY J. FARBER.

Hosiery Manufacturers.

DIETZ L. D. & CO., 308 W Baltimore. (See advertisement inside back cover.)

FELBER EDWARD, 193 S Broadway

Hosiery and Gloves— Retail.

(*See also* GENTS' FURNISHING STORES.)

Colton Henry, 10 Ensor
Colton John, 235 W Pratt
Gude H. P., 359 W Baltimore and 151 Madison
Heisler S., 19 W Baltimore
Hempel J. C., 268 N Gay
Hilgenberg Charles, 35 N Eutaw
Hinse William A., 134 W Lexington
Jordan Francis, 94 W Pratt
JORDAN & ROSE, 1 N Howard, one door north of Baltimore
KNIPP JACOB, JR., 33 N Howard (Lovejoy's old stand), dealer in Undershirts and Drawers, Hosiery, Yarns, Gloves, Small Wares, &c.
SMITH VICTOR, dealer in Hosiery, Gloves, Undershirts, and Drawers, 87 Hanover, bet Camden and Conway

VOGELER C. H., 103 W Baltimore
Young Mrs., 203 and 205 Hanover mkt

Hotels.

(*See also* RESTAURANTS ; *also*, TAVERNS.)

BARNUM'S CITY HOTEL, Z. BARNUM, proprietor, N Calvert and Fayette sts
BAUGHER J. L., 158 Franklin
Black Horse, James Grover, Prop'r, High c Low
Brown Louis, 119 N High
Carling M., 63 Penn. av
CHARLESTON HOUSE, T. Bond & Co., Proprietors, 76 W Pratt. Good accommodation for permanent and transient boarders. Terms moderate.
COLEMAN'S EUTAW HOUSE, Eutaw c Baltimore. (See advertisement outside back cover.)
EASTERN HOTEL, Mrs. B. SHANNON, Prop'rs, 43 Centre Market. PERMANENT & TRANSIENT BOARDERS ACCOMMODATED ON REASONABLE TERMS.
ELTERMAN HOUSE, Wm. Koors, Prop'r, 36 W Fayette
EUTAW HOUSE, Baltimore c Eutaw. (See advertisement outside back cover.)
FOUNTAIN HOTEL, Light st. WILLIAM H. CLABAUGH, PROPRIETOR. Omnibuses and Baggage Wagons in attendance to all the Steamboat Landings and Depots.
FULTON HOUSE, Geo. W. Buck, Prop'r, 34 W Pratt
GEN. WAYNE HOTEL, HENRY FAIRBANKS, Prop'r, Baltimore c Paca
GREEN HOUSE, J. & B. L. Wagner, Prop'rs, 190 W Pratt
Hanway Sam'l, 132 Hillen
Holcombe's Hotel, 124 W Baltimore

Kassell John, 228 S Charles
LEISENRING G., Franklin c Howard
LLOYD'S UNITED STATES HOTEL, President st, op the Philadelphia Depot. MEALS TO SUIT THE TRAINS.
McGEE JOSEPH H. & BRO., Paca c German. (See advertisement inside front cover.)
McGEE'S MILLER'S HOTEL and DROVE STABLES, Paca c German. (See advertisement inside front cover.)
Maltby House, L. U. Maltby, Prop'r, 180, 182, and 184 W Pratt
MANSION HOUSE, ISAAC ALBERTSON, Prop'r, c Fayette and St Paul. Board $1.00 per day.
Marsh John, Franklin c Eutaw
Myers & Kemp, 92 W Baltimore
Peabody House, Edward Lloyd, Proprietor, St Paul c Centre
Phillips Finn, Fremont
RINN'S HOTEL, J. S. Rinn, Proprietor, 40 W Pratt. Good accommodation for permanent and transient Boarders. Meals from 6 A. M. to 12 P. M.
RISING SUN, S. H. Magness, Proprietor, 74 N High. Stanford Stage Line leaves at 8 o'clock.
Schilling M. F., S E c Franklin and Eutaw
SHERWOOD RICHARD P., Fayette c Harrison

SLADE WM. A., High c Hillen
STANSBURY W., 37 Penn. av
Starr Joseph, N Front c Low
Street D. & C., 150 Forrest
SUSQUEHANNA, John C. Voshell, Prop'r, op Calvert st Station
Three Tuns, Pratt c Paca
Tracy & Stansbury, 130 N Front
Union, J. B. Stephenson, Prop'r, Thames c Bond
UNION, Wm. J. Lloyd, Prop'r, S W c Pratt and Charles
UNITED STATES HOTEL, President op Philadelphia Depot
WASHINGTON, JOHN BARR, Prop'r, Eutaw c Camden. (See advertisement op. Insurances.)
Western, D. T. Shaw, Howard c Saratoga
Whitehall, G. W. Hughes, Prop'r, 92 Bank
White House, C. P. Stuart, Prop'r, 186 W Pratt
William Tell House, 1 W Pratt

*House Cleaner.

Peck F. J., 87 North

House Furnishing Warehouses.

Armiger Richard, 87 Harrison
CORTLAN & CO., 216 and 218 W BALTIMORE, IMPORTERS OF HOUSEKEEPING GOODS, TABLE CUTLERY, FANCY and FAMILY HARDWARE.
Daws Henry, 464 W Baltimore
DIGGS JOHN R., 219 W Baltimore

per, Tin, and Sheet Iron Ware,
Britannia and Silver Plated
Ware, Cutlery, &c. A general
assortment of House Furnishing
Goods.

Stoves repaired at short notice.

Forney H. S., 11 N Howard
Greenfield A. H., 167 W Lexington
Harrington & Mills, 140 W Balti-
more
JARDEN SAMUEL, 89 Harrison.
(See advertisement opposite Oil.)
KANN SOL. J., 43 and 45 Harri-
son
Reip J. Henry, 335 W Baltimore
ROBINSON JOSHUA, 333 W Bal-
timore, first Tin Store above
Howard : TIN AND SHEET
IRON WARES, BLOCK TIN,
BRITANNIA METAL.
SCHAEPPERLE   CHRISTIAN,
255 S Charles
SHANAMAN JOHN, 30 and 32 N
Eutaw
Stewart John M., 246 N Gay

SYLVESTER & HOPKINS,

182 W Baltimore opposite Light,

dealers in

HOUSE FURNISHING GOODS,

Family Hardware, Silver Plated
and Britannia Ware, Block Tin
Ware, Japanned and Plain Tin
Ware, Wooden Ware, Mats, Baskets, Brushes, Water Coolers, Re-
frigerators, &c.

WARD EDWARD J., 218 W Pratt,
dwelling 382 W Fayette

Hucksters.

Adams Edward, Centre mkt and
Hanover mkt
Affing Christina, Hanover mkt
Agnes N. Chandler, Hanover mkt
Aichell John, Hanover mkt
Airey James, Hanover mkt

Airey Tobias, 12 Richmond mkt
Ambold John, Lexington mkt
Ames Catharine, 65 Centre mkt
Amick Sarah, Hanover mkt
Amos James H., Richmond mkt
Anderson Mrs., Hanover mkt and
Bell Air mkt
Andrews Samuel J. W., 22 Fell's
Point mkt
Ara Catharine, Hanover mkt and
Lexington mkt
Bakeman Mrs., Hanover mkt
Baker Benard, Fell's Point mkt
Baker Conrad, Fell's Point mkt
Baker George, Hanover mkt
Baker M., Fell's Point mkt
Baker William, Hanover mkt and
Hollins mkt
Baldwin Thomas, Lexington mkt
Barbanks & Cross, Lexington mkt
Barney Mrs. M., 3 Richmond mkt
Barren John, Hanover mkt, Lex-
ington mkt and Centre mkt
Barringer Mrs., Hanover mkt
Bateman William, 35 Centre mkt
Bayley Mrs. L., 51 Hollins mkt
Beal Lee, 3 Hollins mkt
Beard Mrs. Catharine, Lexington
mkt
Bennet L. M., Hanover mkt
Beuhoff C., Centre mkt
Biden George, Lexington mkt, and
26 Richmond mkt
Biggin Francis, 10 Hollins mkt
Bill Mary, Centre mkt
Blacenps Mr., 380 Bell Air mkt
Bond Alexander, Lexington mkt
Bond B., 105 and 107 Centre mkt
Bond George, Centre mkt
Bond James, Lexington mkt and
Bell Air mkt
Bond Josiah, 8 Richmond mkt
Bond Thomas, Fell's Point mkt and
Centre mkt
Bond William, Hanover mkt and
Centre mkt
Bopp Mary, 58 Centre mkt
Borden Catharine, 57 Centre mkt
Borge Miss, Bell Air mkt

Born Barney, Lexington mkt
Bradley William, Bell Air mkt
Brien John G., 215 Bell Air mkt
Brinkman Mr., Bell Air mkt
Britton .John, 16 Richmond mkt and Lexington mkt
Brode Alexander, Lexington mkt
Brodie John, Lexington mkt
Brosus Jacob, 9 Richmond mkt
Brotan Joseph, Centre mkt
Broughton Joseph, Hanover mkt
Brown Charles, Hanover mkt
Brown Eliza, Centre mkt and Bell Air mkt
Brown James, 92 Centre mkt
Brown Reuben, 1 Hollins mkt
Brown Samuel R., Hanover mkt
Bruhn Jacob, Hanover mkt
Bruin Mrs., 144 Centre mkt
Bruner Hamilton, Lexington mkt
Buch Rosinna, Fell's Point mkt
Buchtould F., Fell's Point mkt
Buckman George, Centre mkt
Bunting G., Bell Air mkt
Buoy Mrs., Centre mkt
Butler Rebecca, Hollins mkt
Byer George, Hanover mkt
Calloway George F., Hanover mkt
Cambell Mrs., Centre mkt
Carlisle W. H., 229 Bell Air mkt
Carr Mrs., Centre mkt
Carr Mr., Centre mkt
Cassidy Patrick, Lexington mkt
Chandler B. Centre mkt
Chandler Mrs. Nancy, Lexington mkt
Chester George, Lexington mkt
Chester Michael, Lexington mkt and Centre mkt
Chester William, 364 Bell Air mkt
Clark William A., Centre mkt
Clawson Joseph, Centre mkt
Clodice Henry, Bell Air mkt
Cloris Francis, Lexington mkt and 109 and 111 Centre mkt
Colburn Mrs. H., Lexington mkt
Cole Miss, 185 Bell Air mkt
Coleman Mrs., 223 and 225 Hanover mkt

Collins Mary & Son, Fell's Point mkt
Commil Mrs., Centre mkt
Conner Ann, Fell's Point mkt
Connoly Timothy, Hanover mkt
Conrey Mrs Mary, Lexington mkt
Constein Mrs. C., Lexington mkt
Conuff F., Fell's Point mkt
Cook Catharine, 236 Bell Air mkt
Cook George, Bell Air mkt
Copeland Robert, Hanover mkt
Corrigan Michael, 191 Bell Air mkt
Cosgrove Patrick, 32 Hollins mkt
Cosgrove Sophia, Fell's Point mkt
Coth John, Lexington mkt
Counsellman John B., Lexington mkt
Craig John, 315 Bell Air mkt
Craig Thos. W., Hanover mkt
Crawford Robert, Bell Air mkt
Crisell Jacob, 19 Richmond mkt
Crist Wm., Fell's Point mkt
Cristman Jacob, Bell Air mkt
Crocker E., 193 Centre mkt
Crocket Eliza, Hanover mkt
Cromwell Richard, Lexington mkt
Cross John, 40 Hollins mkt
Cross John W. T., Lexington mkt
Crow Mrs. Sarah, 13 Richmond mkt
Cullan John, Lexington mkt
Daley Patrick, Bell Air mkt
Dalsher H., 19 and 21 Centre mkt
Danes C., Hanover mkt
Dannmer G., Lexington mkt
Davis Richard, Lexington mkt
Davis Thomas P. & Co., 78 Fell's Point mkt
Deal Mrs., 25 Fell's Point mkt
Dean Christopher, 27 Fell's Point mkt
Deanhar Caspar, Hanover mkt
Deans Mary, Hanover mkt
Decker Joseph, Centre mkt
Deckman Caroline, Hanover mkt
Delcher Henry, Hanover mkt
Delcher James A. & George B., Lexington mkt
Delcher Thomas, 29 Centre mkt

Delcher Thómas B., Centre mkt and Hanover mkt
Denn Caroline, 35 Fell's Point mkt
Devine Julius, Lexington mkt and Hollins mkt
Dhleis Miss, Bell Air mkt
Dieger John, Fell's Point mkt
Dillehunt J. T., Bell Air mkt
Ditus J., 87 Centre mkt
Doff William, Bell Air mkt
Dougherty Mary, Centre mkt
Dorch George, Hanover mkt
Dorret T. H., Centre mkt
Drachsler Thomas, 263 Bell Air mkt
Dresden Catharine, Bell Air mkt
Drexter Mrs., 297 Bell Air mkt
Driebank Ann, Lexington mkt
Drupan Anne, 192 Centre mkt
Dughter M., Bell Air mkt
Dukehart Adam, Fell's Point mkt
Dulcher T., Lexington mkt
Duncan Charles, Lexington mkt
Duncan, Stewart & Co., Hollins mkt
Dunkin Charles, 53 Hollins mkt
Dunn G. W., Hanover mkt
Dunphy Mrs. M., Lexington mkt
Eagan Mrs., Bell Air mkt
Edell Samuel, 12 Richmond mkt
Edward Escott, 100 Centre mkt
Effick Miss Olinda, Centre mkt, 24 Bell Air mkt, and Hanover mkt
Eickeman Mrs., 18 Hollins mkt
Eidman David, Hanover mkt
Eidman John, 53 Hollins mkt
Eisle George, Centre mkt
Eistler Catharine, Fell's Point
Elias Mrs. C., 2 Richmond mkt
Elliott Thos., Lexington mkt
Emlook Agnes, Hanover mkt
Emmichs Mr., Centre mkt and Bell Air mkt
Engel Miss Mary, Lexington mkt
Erdman Frank, Centre mkt
Erdman Susan, Centre mkt
Erkine Charles, Bell Air mkt
Eryll Mrs. Margt., Hanover mkt
Etter Henry, Fell's Point mkt

Ever Wm., Lexington mkt
Everby P., Centre mkt
Ewell John, Lexington mkt
Faulkner Adam, Fell's Point mkt
Faulner Kelly, Fell's Point mkt
Fefel & Fowler, Lexington mkt
Fell A. Lewis, Lexington mkt
Fell Mrs. Mary, Hanover mkt
Fell Peter, Centre mkt and Hanover mkt
Felter Elizabeth, Fell's Point mkt
Fetel John, 61 Centre mkt
Fisher Charles, Hanover mkt
Fisher John, 3 Hollins mkt and Lexington mkt
Fisher William H., 12 and 10 Fell's Point mkt
Fitzpatrick Peter, 311 Bell Air mkt
Fogoting Mr., 376 Bell Air mkt
Fork F. A., 33 Centre mkt
Forkus Mrs., 267 Bell Air mkt
Fowler George, Fell's Point mkt-
Fowler Isaac, Hanover mkt
Fowler Mr., 223 Bell Air mkt
Frank Jacob, Hanover mkt
Frederic Henry, 166 Bell Air mkt
Fryer Margt., Hollins mkt
Gaafner G., Lexington mkt
Galloway George F., Centre mkt
Galloway Mrs. Isabella, Richmond mkt and Lexington mkt
Games Mary, Centre mkt
Games Wm., Centre mkt
Ganent Samuel, Bell Air mkt
Gardner Mrs., 20 Fell's Point mkt
Gare Adam, Hanover mkt
Gary P. M., 301 Bell Air mkt
Geigher John, 122 Centre mkt
German Thomas E., 99 Centre mkt
Gibson James A., Bell Air mkt
Gibson Margt., 125 Centre mkt
Giles Lewis, Lexington mkt
Gillan Michael, Lexington mkt
Gillin Michael, Centre mkt
Gimple Mr., 188 Bell Air mkt
Goble Rachael, 246 Bell Air mkt
Goodimer G., Hanover mkt
Goodrich Elizabeth, Lexington mkt
Gordon Mrs. Anna, 346 Bell Air mkt

Grar S., Bell Air mkt
Gray John, 163 Bell Air mkt
Green Mrs. Anna, Hanover mkt
Green L. & Son, Lexington mkt
Greeneb Anna, Bell Air mkt
Greenewalt Mr., Fell's Point mkt
Gretz John, Hanover mkt
Greur L., Centre mkt
Greyt Hammond, Hanover mkt
Gribb Catharine, Fell's Point mkt
Gripps Rebecca, Bell Air mkt
GRISTILLE JACOB, Lexington
  mkt
Groesens Joseph, Bell Air mkt
Grooms E., 45 Centre mkt
Guise Margaret, Hanover mkt
Gumbert Mary, Lexington mkt and
  Hanover mkt
Gunder Mary, 108 Centre mkt
Gyner Poll, Hanover mkt
Hademan Mrs. A., Lexington mkt
Haden William, 158 Centre mkt
Haer L., Hanover mkt
HAGEN MRS. ANNA, Lexington
  mkt
Hahn L., Hanover mkt
Hakjesley C. C., Bell Air mkt
Hambleton Mrs., Hanover mkt
Hamill Mrs. J., Hollins mkt
Hamilton James, Bell Air mkt
Haminie John, Hanover mkt
Hardnot James, 4 Richmond mkt
Hardy Henry, Hollins mkt
Hargest J., Centre mkt
Harkess Thomas, Bell Air mkt
Harmine & Son, Fell's Point mkt
Harper John H., Centre mkt
Harriman J., 90 Bell Air mkt
Hart John, Lexington mkt
Hart Mrs., 370 Bell Air mkt
Hart William, Lexington mkt
Hartman Anna, Hanover mkt
Haverconn John, Fell's Point mkt
Hawkins William, 2 and 4 Hollins
  mkt
Hawkins William H., Lexington
  mkt
Hayner George, Hanover mkt
Hazlett D., 3 Hollins mkt

Heffner Michael, Hanover mkt
Heffner S., Bell Air mkt
Heffs M., Fell's Point mkt
Hellwing H., Bell Air mkt
Hemmett Philip, 170 Centre mkt
Henry Mrs. Mary, Hanover mkt
Hershfelt Mr., 100 Fell's Point mkt
Hesler Catharine, Centre mkt
Hessenbury Catharine, Lexington
  mkt
Hettrick Henry, Hollins mkt
Hewell J. H., Lexington mkt
Hickman C. T., 6 Hollins mkt
Hickman E., Bell Air mkt
Hickman E. C., Lexington mkt
Hillmer Wm., 5 Richmond mkt
Himen Chas., Fell's Point mkt and
  8 Hollins mkt
Hinnaman Emma, Hanover mkt
Hitts Mrs., Centre mkt
Hoff Wm., Fell's Point mkt
Hoffastead George, Hanover mkt
Hoffman Charles E , 101 Centre mkt
Hoffman Fred., Lexington mkt
Hoffman Mrs., 39 Fell's Point mkt
Hoffman Mrs. M., 172 Bell Air mkt
Hoffman & Bro., Hanover mkt, and
  51 Centre mkt
Hoffstader Joseph, Hanover mkt
Holiday William, Fell's Point mkt
  and Centre mkt
Holt Isaac C., Hanover mkt
Holts J. P., Centre mkt
Hoskell Catharine, Hanover mkt
Howard Patrick, Lexington mkt
Huddock James, 9 Hollins mkt
Hughes Josey, Centre mkt
Hughes Mary, Lexington mkt
Hughes R., 14 Richmond mkt
Hulse Mary, 200 Bell Air mkt
Hummel Mrs., Fell's Point mkt
Hummell Jacob, 238 Bell Air mkt
Hurst A., 16 Fell's Point mkt
Hurst Geo. H., Centre mkt.
Hutchings Robert, Lexington mkt
Hutton Andrew, Centre mkt
Ingland Adam, Hanover mkt
Irvin S., Centre mkt
Jackson Andrew, Lexington mkt

Jefferson Henry, 49 Centre mkt
Jefferson James, 71 Centre mkt
Jefferson N., Fell's Point mkt
Jefferts John, Centre mkt
Jeffries John, Lexington mkt
Jenkins Michael, Bell Air mkt
Jennings Michael, Bell Air mkt
Jockel Martin, Hanover mkt
Johnson Mrs., Centre mkt
Johnson Miss Mary, Hanover mkt
Johnson Paul, Lexington mkt
Johnston Charles J., Bell Air mkt
Jones Caroline, 41 Fell's Point mkt
Jones John, Bell Air mkt
Jones Mrs. R., Hanover mkt and
  Lexington mkt
Jones Rebecca, Centre mkt
Jones William B., Fell's Point mkt
Jones William H., Hanover mkt
Jubb Charles E., Centre mkt
Judold William, Centre mkt
Kaagen John, Hanover mkt
Kaan Matthew, Centre mkt
Kain Margaret, 37 Hollins mkt
Kalte Mrs. Catharine, Hanover mkt
Kane Lewis, Fell's Point mkt
Kane Levi, Hanover mkt
Kane Matthew, 24 Fell's Point mkt
Kaufman Gotter F., Centre mkt
Kayton T., 6 Richmond mkt
Keel Eliza, Hanover mkt
Keen Austin, Lexington mkt
Keen George, W Lexington mkt
Keen Samuel, Lexington mkt
Keenfelder C., 8 Richmond mkt
Keisner M., Centre mkt
Keller Jonah, Lexington mkt
Kelly Jane, Bell Air mkt
Kelly Julia, Bell Air mkt
Kelly Mrs., Hanover mkt and 203
  Bell Air mkt
Kemby William, Hanover mkt
Kenny C., Hanover mkt
Kerbz John, Hanover mkt
Kerchner M. C., Richmond mkt
Kimmet Catharine, Hanover mkt
Kine Mrs. Mary, 11 Richmond mkt
King Alexander, Centre mkt
King Elizabeth, Hanover mkt

King H., 8 Hollins mkt
King M., Lexington mkt
King Wm., 285 Bell Air mkt
Kittrick John, Centre mkt
Kittrick Peter, Bell Air mkt
Kittring Catharine, 12 Hollins mkt
Klindfelter Mrs. E., Richmond mkt
Knight Clare, Lexington mkt
Krieger George W., Hanover mkt
Krite Mrs. H., Hollins mkt
Kroll Mary, Centre mkt
Kruser Leonard, 6 Hollins mkt
Lambden Elizabeth, Hanover mkt
Lamville James, Lexington mkt
Lander S. M., 49 Centre mkt
Landey Henry, Hanover mkt
Landress Mary, Hanover mkt
Langwell Mrs. E., Lexington mkt
  and 1 Centre mkt
Lanster J. H., 178 Bell Air mkt
Lawrence Henry, Hollins st mkt
Laymon Bernard, Centre mkt
Leach Mrs. E., 15 Richmond mkt
Le Bond Mrs. J., Lexington mkt
Lee Joseph, Lexington mkt
Leeman Charles, Hanover mkt
Lefler Henry, Fell's Point mkt
Lemon Ann, Bell Air mkt
Leonard Mrs. B., Lexington mkt
Leonard John, Bell Air mkt
Leonard Richard, Lexington mkt
Lenz H., Hollins st mkt
Lesley Wm., Lexington mkt
Lesseller John, 368 Bell Air mkt
Lester George W., Lexington mkt
Levering John, Lexington mkt
Leving Susanna, Centre mkt
Lewis M., Lexington mkt
Lidard Mrs., Fell's Point mkt
Linakamber Mrs., 252 Bell Air mk
Liner Mary, Centre mkt
Linthicum & Co., Hanover mkt
Lippscheinder G., Hollins mkt
List John, 22 Richmond mkt
Listter Conrad, Bell Air mkt
Little Patrick, Hanover mkt
Lober John, Lexington mkt
Lomack Thomas, Centre mkt
Lomax Thomas, Lexington mkt

Long Mary A., Bell Air mkt
Long Michael, Lexington mkt and
Hanover mkt
Lott Mrs., 77 Centre mkt
Loux Mrs., Hanover mkt
Lowery John, Fell's Point mkt
Lusby D. K., Lexington mkt
Lusby Wm., 33 Richmond mkt
Lutz Wm., Centre mkt
Lyerock Mrs., 287 Bell Air mkt
McCann Dennis, Bell Air mkt
McCarthy Miss, Bell Air mkt
McCarty Martin, Hollins mkt and
Lexington mkt
McCarty Michael, 8 Hollins mkt
McCarty Patrick, Lexington mkt
and Hollins mkt
McClaskey Mrs. S., 1 Richmond
mkt
McCoaly & Smith, 243 Bell Air mkt
McConnell E., 2 Richmond mkt
McConnell Hugh, 2 Richmond mkt
McConnell William, 31 and 33 Hol-
lins mkt
McConville M. A., 8 Hollins mkt
McCoon Miss, Bell Air mkt
McCormick Alexander, Lexington
mkt
McCormick John, 3 Richmond mkt
McCory William F., 313 Bell Air
mkt
McCue M., Hanover mkt
McElroy Samuel, 34 Hollins mkt
McEvoy Samuel, Lexington mkt
McGreay Thomas, Bell Air mkt
McGuire J., 177 Bell Air mkt
McHugh Thomas, 112½ Light st
mkt
McKeldine D. W., Centre mkt
McLachlin Francis, 31 Centre mkt
and Lexington mkt
McTagger Mrs., 210 Bell Air mkt
Mack Samuel, Lexington mkt
Maggat Mrs., Centre mkt
Maidlow C., 20 Richmond mkt
Maidlow Charles C., Lexington mkt
Maidlow & Kane, Centre mkt
Maisch F. J., 11 Hollins mkt
Mames Susan, 39 Centre mkt

Marker M., Lexington mkt
Martin Mrs , 289 Bell Air mkt
Mason Geo. E., Centre mkt and
Hanover mkt
Matthew Mr., Centre mkt
Matthews Isaac, Lexington mkt
Matthews John, Lexington mkt
May Miss A. J., Lexington mkt
Maylie Jacob, Hanover mkt
Mayne Jacob, Centre mkt
Maynus Mrs. Susan, 235 Bell Air
mkt
Meeke Wm., Fell's Point mkt
Melcher Charles, Lexington mkt
Meller A. W., Hanover mkt
Meltzcher K., Hanover mkt
Merchline Caroline, Hanover mkt
Meredith Wm. B., 97 Centre mkt
Merrette T. H., Lexington mkt
Merryman W., 17 Richmond mkt
Meurer E. Nicholas, Fell's Point
mkt
Midlin Martha, Fell's Point mkt
Miller Annie, Hanover mkt
Miller Catharine, Hanover mkt
Miller Frederick, Fell's Point mkt
Miller John, Hanover mkt
Miller Miss, 190 Bell Air mkt
Miller Mrs., 172 Centre mkt, Fell's
Point mkt, and Bell Air mkt
Milroy Mrs., Centre mkt
Mitchell Henry, Bell Air mkt
Mitchell John, Lexington mkt
Mitchell John S., Lexington mkt
Mitchell Mrs. S., Lexington
Mitchell Mrs., Hanover mkt
Mitchell S., Centre mkt
Moore John, Fell's Point mkt
Morton Dixon, 12 Richmond mkt
Mulligan Mrs., 17 Richmond mkt
Murr Jacob, 209 and 211 Hanover
mkt
Murray Mrs. Anna, Lexington mkt
Murray Mrs. C., Lexington mkt
Murray Mrs., Hanover mkt and
Centre mkt
Murray Peter, Fell's Point mkt
Murray Sarah, 61 Centre mkt
Muser Geo., Fell's Point

Myer Mrs., Hanover mkt
Myers Patrick, Hanover mkt
Myser Mrs. M., 11 Richmond mkt
Nelson Martha, Fell's Point mkt
Newell J. D , Lexington mkt
Nicoll Wm. D., 21 Richmond mkt,
    Lexington mkt and Centre mkt
Nicolas John, 278 Bell Air mkt
Nicols Caspar, 79 Centre mkt
Nichols Mrs., Bell Air mkt
Nightbart Geo., Bell Air mkt
Nixon John, Hanover mkt
O'Brien James, 107 Bell Air mkt
O'Connor Mrs. Margaret, Hanover
    mkt and Centre mkt
Oddo John, Lexington mkt
Ogden M. J., Bell Air mkt
Ogier Nicholas, Lexington mkt
O'Glaughlin Francis, Hanover mkt
Orste George, Fell's Point mkt
Owings Mrs. S., 12 Richmond mkt
Padeset R., 87 Centre mkt
Padgett Wm. H., 3 Hollins mkt
Page E. M., 10 Richmond mkt
Paine James, Centre mkt
Parker Miss Mary, 219 Bell Air
    mkt and Fell's Point mkt
Partner & Law, Fell's Point mkt
Patterson Mrs. M., 3 and 4 Hollins
    mkt
Pauden Mary, Lexington mkt
Peacock Mrs., 239 Bell Air mkt
Peed Robert, 23 Richmond mkt and
    Centre mkt
Peel Robert, 253 Bell Air mkt
Peence Louisa, 10 Hollins mkt
Pendergrast Thos., Lexington mkt,
    Hanover mkt and Centre mkt
Perkins Anna, 249 Bell Air mkt
Perkins William H. H., Centre mkt
    and 273 Bell Air mkt
Phelps Austin, Lexington mkt
Phelps Charles, Lexington mkt
Phillips Mr., Bell Air mkt
Pilsch Jacob, Centre mkt
Pierce John R., Lexington mkt
Piece Michael, Hanover mkt
Plum Sarah, Hanover mkt
Plumhoff H. G., 94 Fell's Point mkt

Porn Catharine, 21 Richmond mkt
Pout M. R., Bell Air mkt
Preston Henry, 35 Richmond mkt
    and Lexington mkt
Price Mrs. S., 7 Richmond mkt
Pugey Ann J., Lexington mkt
Pullar Patrick, Hanover mkt
Purmyer Mrs., 221 and 223 Hanover
    mkt
Pusf John, Lexington mkt
Quick Peter, Hanover mkt
Quinlin & Co., Hanover mkt
Quinn Mrs. B., 9 Richmond mkt
Quinn James, Hanover mkt
Quinn Peter, Centre mkt
Raband Mr., 211 Bell Air mkt
Rafing, Mrs., Hanover mkt
Rainer Joseph D., Hanover mkt
Ramsey Eliza, Hollins mkt
Reburger Mrs., 22 Fell's Point mkt
Redwin Adam, Centre mkt
Reed Mrs. S., 7 Richmond mkt
Reed Wm., 42 and 44 Hollins mkt
Reed Wm. C., 326 Bell Air mkt
Reel Conradt, Hanover mkt
Refferty Henry, Centre mkt
Regan Mrs. M. A., Lexington mkt
Reuter Fred., 104 Centre mkt
Rice Caroline, Fell's Point mkt
Rich Mrs. Anna, 42 Hollins mkt
Richardson F., Lexington mkt
Richter William, Lexington mkt
Richmond Mary Ann, Lexington
    mkt and 113 and 115 Centre mkt
Richmond Mrs. M., 14 Richmond
    mkt
Richmond Samuel, 13 Richmond
    mkt
Rickus G. W., Fell's Point mkt
Rickert Mary, Centre mkt
Ridge Mary, Bell Air mkt
Ridgeway Ann, Bell Air mkt
Riggins Mrs., Hanover mkt
Riley Mary, Hollins mkt
Riley Thomas, Hanover mkt
Rineck Mary, 57 Hollins mkt
Rineck Thomas, Lexington mkt
Ring Edmund, Hollins mkt
Rite Edward M., Hanover mkt

Rite James, 331 Bell Air mkt
Rite Joseph, Centre mkt
Robinson D. N., Lexington mkt and Hanover mkt
Robertson William, 270 Bell Air mkt and 99 Centre mkt
Robinson Mrs., Centre mkt
Rodewick C., 17 Hollins mkt
Rodewig Mrs. C., Hanover mkt
Roloson Hugh, Hanover mkt
Rose Jacob, 21 and 23 Hollins mkt
Ross James D. H., Bell Air mkt
Rose Mary, Hanover mkt
Rose Thomas, 81 Centre mkt
Rost Louis, Centre mkt
Rott Mrs., 186 Bell Air mkt
Rudas Joseph, Hanover mkt
Ruley Samuel, 37 Fell's Point mkt
Ruppf Louis, Hollins mkt
Rupert Dietrich, Hanover mkt
Russell Fred., 12 Hollins mkt
Russell Margaret, Lexington mkt, Hanover mkt and 71 Centre mkt
Ryan William, Hanover mkt and 25 Centre mkt
Ryett Peter, 48 Hollins mkt
Sahiller C., Bell Air mkt
Sallemon Mrs., 14 Fell's Point mkt
Sanders Mrs., 292 Bell Air mkt
Sangway E., 99 Centre mkt
Sapp John W., 309 Bell Air mkt
Sarnacher Mrs., 234 Bell Air mkt
Scarb Robert, Lexington mkt
Schaeffer Mrs. E., 20, 22 and 26 Hollins mkt
Schaible C. F., Hanover mkt and 2 Hollins mkt
Schmidt Barbara, Hanover mkt
Schmidt Christian, Fell's Point mkt
Schmidt Henry, Centre mkt
Schmidt Mary, Centre mkt
Schroeder H., 32 Richmond mkt
Schroeder Mrs., Centre mkt
Schular Martin, Hanover mkt
Schumaker Thomas, Hanover mkt and 110 Centre mkt
Schawartz John, Hanover mkt
Scibly Mary, Fell's Point mkt
Seaman Christina, Hanover mkt

Seibert Catharine, Bell Air mkt
Seifert Christopher Hanover mkt
Selby Peter, Centre mkt
Seymour H. C., 40 Hollins mkt
Shaefer William, Hanover mkt
Share Charles, Bell Air mkt
Sheeler A. H., Bell Air mkt
Shepperd Mary, Hanover mkt
Shipperd Miss C., 13 Richmond mkt
Shore Christian, Fell's Point mkt
Shott D., 14 Hollins mkt
Shumit George, Lexington mkt
Sladen James, Centre mkt
Slaisman M., 25 Richmond mkt
Slater John, Fell's Point mkt
Slaven P., 9 Centre mkt
Slaysman Mrs., Centre mkt
Slewhouse Eliza, Lexington mkt
Smercher Henry, Centre mkt
Smerst Mrs., 230 Bell Air mkt
Smith Andrew C., Bell Air mkt
Smith Ann, Hanover mkt and 92 Centre mkt
Smith Eliza, Hanover mkt
Smith E. H., 191 Centre mkt
Smith Geo., W Lexington mkt
Smith Henry, Hanover mkt and Centre mkt and Lexington mkt
Smith James, Centre mkt
Smith John, 8 Hollins mkt, Fell's Point mkt, and Lexington mkt
Smith Mary, Hanover mkt
Smith N., 87 Centre mkt
Snider Jacob C., 208 Bell Air mkt
Snyder & Frush, 16 Richmond mkt and Centre mkt
Spillman Martin, 9 Hollins mkt
Spoke C., 18 Richmond mkt
Spungenberg Mrs. M., Hanover mkt
Sput Christian, Bell Air mkt
St. John James, 250 Bell Air mkt
Stakeman John, Hanover mkt
Stanley Maria, Fell's Point mkt
Stephenson J. B., Fell's Point mkt
Stevens E., 11 and 13 Centre mkt
Stewart James, 12 Richmond mkt
Stewart P., Centre mkt

12

Stewart Duncan & Co., Hanover mkt
Storm G. N., Hanover mkt
Straus Mrs., 228 Bell Air mkt
Strong J. E., 1 Richmond mkt
Sturgeon Fred'k 335 Bell Air mkt
Sungstram Rachael, Hanover mkt
Swan Ann, 22 Centre mkt
Swansburg Mrs. M., 35 Hollins mkt
Sweakenodekloren George, Hanover mkt
Sweeny Owen, Lexington mkt
Tabull G., Lexington mkt
Taggert Mrs., 24 Richmond mkt
Talbot E. G., Centre mkt
Taylor Wm., Bell Air mkt and Fell's Point mkt
Teller Mrs. S., Lexington mkt
Telly A. G., Centre mkt
Theal Mrs. P., Lexington mkt
Thompson Mrs. Mary, E Lexington mkt
Thornton John, Lexington mkt
Thorp Cath., Centre mkt
Tighe John, Bell Air mkt
Tile Mrs., Bell Air mkt
Tisner Amos, Fell's Point mkt
Toft John, 19 Richmond mkt
Torsbeek John, Lexington mkt
Townsend Charlotte, Centre mkt
Townsend William, Hanover mkt
Tracey Mrs. Ruth, Lexington mkt
Tracey S. S., Hollins mkt
Tracey Thos., Lexington mkt
Tratel Henry, Lexington mkt
Trayson Mrs. Ruth, Hanover mkt
Tubbs John, Hollins st mkt
Tuffman Leonard, 295 Hanover mkt
Turner M., Lexington mkt
Tuskin E., Centre mkt
Tuston Mrs., 233 Bell Air mkt
Van Collom Miss, Hanover mkt
Vandolph Richard, Bell Air mkt
Varney M. J., Bell Air mkt
Vincent James, Hanover mkt
Vinhiller Gottfred, 294 Bell Air mkt
Vondergreen M., Bell Air mkt
Von Hagel Mrs., Fell's Point mkt
Wagner Catharine, Bell Air mkt

Wagner George, Bell Air mkt
Walker Mrs., Centre mkt
Walker Samuel, Lexington mkt
Wallace Martin, Lexington mkt
Ward James E., Bell Air mkt
Warfield Caleb, Hanover mkt
Warfield D. & C., Lexington mkt
Warfield E. & C., Centre mkt
Warfield John, Centre mkt and Lexington mkt
Warner Mary, 33 Fell's Point mkt
Warrington John E., 31 and 33 Fell's Point mkt
Watts Mrs. C., Bell Air mkt
Way George W., Hanover mkt
Wayson Mrs., Bell Air mkt
Weaver Francis, Hanover mkt
Wedekine Eliza, Centre mkt
Wegard Elizabeth, Hanover mkt
Welden George, 116, 118 Centre mkt
Welk Michael, Hanover mkt
Wheeler A., 95 Centre mkt
Wheeler Charles, Hollins mkt
White T. W., Lexington mkt
Whitfield Eliza, Bell Air mkt
Whitestone Julia, Lexington mkt
Wienholt Christopher, Centre mkt
Wigond Elizabeth, Centre mkt
Wilkison James, Hanover mkt
Willoustub Mary, Hollins mkt
Wilson James, Lexington mkt
Wilt Anna, Bell Air mkt
Wingerder Mary, 89 Fell's Point mkt
Winn Miss H., 2 Richmond mkt
Wolf Mrs. A., Lexington mkt
Wolf Frederick, Lexington mkt
Wood B., Fell's Point mkt
Wood Mrs., 225 Bell Air mkt
Wooden James, 4 Richmond mkt
Woodfield John, 75 Fell's Point mkt
Wright Edward M., Lexington mkt
Wright Luther, Bell Air mkt
Young Mrs. C., 10 Richmond mkt
Youngman Wm., Hanover mkt
Zaro Catharine, 25 Centre mkt
Zell Lewis A., Hollins mkt

*Hydrant Manufacturer.

Clark L. P., 44 Holiday

*Hydrometers.

SHARP & DOHME, Importers of HYDROMETERS for ALCOHOL, LYES, SUGAR, &c., CHEMICAL APPARATUS, BAROMETERS, &c., Howard and Pratt sts

Ice Dealers.

Cochran T. J. & Co., W Fall's av
Kephart Peter, 16 Dover
Oler W. H., 176 W Fall's av
SUMWALT DAVID, Mulberry c Howard

India Rubber Goods.

Corbitt Isaac, 93 W Baltimore
MAXWELL W. G., 166 W Baltimore

Infirmaries.

Baltimore, S W c Green and Lombard
Union Protestant, Division bel Mosher and McMechin

Ink Makers.

DIETZ L. D. & CO., 308 W Baltimore. (See advertisement inside back cover.)

Insurance Agents.

Boggs Wm. & Co., 12 S Gay
Carey George, Second adj Post Office
Didier Henry A., Commercial bdg, 45 S Gay
ENGLER ADOLPH, 18 Second, AGENT FOR GERMANIA FIRE INSURANCE CO. OF NEW YORK
HOPPER'S S. W. T., 69 Second, op Town Clock, old established Insurance Agency. Fire, Life, and Marine Insurance.

JOHNSON'S

INSURANCE ROOMS,

73 & 75 Second Street,

BALTIMORE.

Luckett R. C., 83 Second
MACKENZIE COLIN, 79 Second
MONTAGUE CHAS. P.,
77 Second,
MARINE, FIRE, and LIFE
INSURANCE CO.
PROUD J. G. & SONS, 63 Second
RICHARDSON E. J. & SONS, 9
North. (See advertisement inter-
leaved.)
SPEAR WILLIAM, 65 Second
Thompson S. G., 24 Second
Trump C. N., 59 Second
Webb Wm. P., 89 Second
Wilson H. P. C., 5 North

Insurance Companies, Fire.

Associated Fire, 4 South
ÆTNA INSURANCE OF HART-
FORD. J. G. PROUD & SONS,
AGENTS, 63 SECOND
Baltimore, S W c South and Water
Baltimore Equitable Society, 19
South
Firemen's South c Second
Howard, South c Second
LIVERPOOL AND LONDON, 58
Exchange pl
Maryland Fire Insurance Co., N W
c Baltimore and North
National, 30 South
Peabody (The), Second adj Post
Office

Insurance Companies, Life.

Baltimore, 7 South
LIVERPOOL AND LONDON, 58
Exchange pl
Mutual, Geo. Carey, agt., Second
adj P O

Insurance Comp'ies, Marine.

Baltimore (The) Marine Insurance Company,

Corner of South and Water Sts.
JAMES HOOPER, Jr., President.
WM. L. MONTAGUE, Jr.
Vice-President.

MARYLAND MUTUAL (MA-
RINE) INSURANCE CO., 58
EXCHANGE PLACE, ADJOINING
THE POST OFFICE. WILLIAM
KREBS. SECRETARY. WM. W.
SPENCER, PRESIDENT.

MERCHANTS' MUTUAL INSURANCE CO., MARINE, 45 and 47 SOUTH GAY STREET. RICHARD D. FISHER, Pres't. GEORGE B. COALE, Sec'y.

Inspectors.

Dutton John, North (Lime)
Flour Inspector's Office, N W c German and Howard

Intelligence Offices.

Clancy Mrs. M., 202 N Eutaw
McELMOYLE, A., 8 N Frederick

Iron Fencing, Railings, Doors, Shutters, &c.

Dufur & Co., Uhler's al n S Charles
SMITH J. A., 182 Columbia, bet
Fremont and Scott, Manufacturer
of Wrought and Cast Iron Rail-
ings for Cemeteries, Public and
Private Buildings, &c. Orders
respectfully solicited.
Treulieb John, 17 Ensor

Iron Founders.

ASHLAND IRON WORKS, GEO.
SMALL, President, opposite 64
North
Bates James, President c Stiles
Benson B. S., 52 E Monument
Blake Joel N., North c Franklin
Deumead A. & W. & Son, North c
Monument
HAYWARD, BARTLETT & CO.,
24 Light and Scott c Pratt
HAZLEHURST & CO., William c
Hughes
HEATH F. W., 2 Gillingham al, r
44 S Howard, IRON FOUNDER
and PLOUGH MANUFACTU-
RER. CASTINGS MADE TO
ORDER.
Keener John H., 46 Thames
KILGOUR DAVID, Manufacturer
of all kinds of NUTS and WASH-
ERS, Punching Iron Railing,
&c., Armstead lane, and Iron
Foundry, York street.
Larrabee H. C., Plowman c Front
POOLE & HUNT, 161 North
RUSSELL JAS., 132 Thames
Sexton S., 158 Conway
WEISKITTEL A., Nos. 302, 304,
306 and 308 Alice Anna bet Wash-
ington and Chester, Fell's Point.
Always on hand, all kinds of
Stoves and Hollow Ware Castings.
All orders will be attended to
12*

with dispatch, and on accommodating terms.

Iron Gas Tubes.

BASSHOR THOMAS C. & CO., 26
Light. (See advertisement op.
Brass.)

Iron Manufacturers.

PATTERSON J. W. & E., 24 South
STICKNEY & CO., Dealers in
NAILS, PIG IRON, and CUM-
BERLAND COAL, and Manu-
facturers of BALTIMORE
PIG IRON, Office 57 Exchange pl
TYSON JAMES W., 7 South "Elba
Furnace."

Iron Merchants.

Hartshorne Joshua, 92 W Lombard
KEYSER, TROXELL & CO., 19 S
Calvert
Oudesluys Charles L., 57 S Gay

E. PRATT & BRO.,

27 and 29 S. Charles.

IRON, CUT NAILS, SPIKES,
HORSE AND MULE SHOES, TIN
PLATE, LEAD, ZINC, COPPER,
&c., &c., TAUNTON YELLOW
METAL AND CUMBERLAND
COAL.

ROGERS & BROOKE, 53 Exchange
pl, AVALON NAILS AND BOIL-
ER PLATES, C H A R C O A L,
WHEEL AND FORGE PIG
IRON, ANTHRACITE PIG
IRON, CHARCOAL BLOOMS,
WESTMINSTER IRON ORE.
Stein E. A., 99 W Lombard
STICKNEY & CO., 57 Exchange pl
WETHERALL W. G., 16 Water

Iron and Steel.

KEYSER, TROXELL & CO., 19 S Calvert

WETHERALL W. G., 16 Water, IMPORTER, DEALER AND AGENT FOR ALL DESCRIPTIONS OF IRON AND STEEL

Wyeth & Brother, 25 S Charles

Ivory Work.

Filler Frederick, 3 Park

Japanned Ware and Japanners.

Hanling P. M., 21 Grant
Walker W. F., 48 German

Jewellers.

(*See also* WATCHES AND JEWELLERS.)

Adams Samuel, 20 E Pratt
Behrens Jacob, 93 N Gay
Bein Charles, 81 W Lexington
BLAKE CHAS., 217 W Baltimore
Brackland B., 8 E Pratt
Brown James, 62 Ensor
Busch L., 279 N Gay
Crawford Wm., 7 Frederick
Ebaugh H., 111 N Gay
Fettings J., 205 E Baltimore
Franklin George, 25 Harrison
Freinsheim Chas., 153 W Madison
Friederich John, 183 E Baltimore
GEHRING J. G., 194 N Gay
Groneberg Edw., 70 E Baltimore
Heitner J., 2 S Charles
HOFFMEISTER JOHN, Manufacturer of Fine GOLD JEWELRY, Dealer in GOLD AND SILVER WATCHES, 78 N Pearl bet Lexington and Saratoga. *Watches and Jewelry Repaired with care.*
Hubers H., 215 S Broadway
Hybbeneth A., Eutaw c Marion
JANOWITZ S., 137 W Baltimore
JATHO HENRY, c Baltimore and High, Repairs Watches, Clocks, and Jewelry, on the most reasonable terms.

Kellner Michael, 273 N Gay
Kerlinger J. Chas., 131½ N Gay
Kesmodel Martin, Bank la
Klueber Chas. J., 29 W Fayette
Kramer F., 319 N Gay
Kummer Wolf, 79 Thames
Price R., 1 Grant c Baltimore
Raine Albert, 109 E Pratt
Raith Charles, 69 Penn av
Riefner John G., 243 Alice Anna
Rietsch Otto, 171 Franklin
Rupp Conrad, 270 Canton av
SAVILLE JAMES H., 110½ W Baltimore
Schaumloeffel W., 46 Ross
Sommer Jacob, 285 S Bond
Sommer John Philip, 231½ S Broadway
WEBB GEO. W., S E c Baltimore and Light

Job Printers.

(*See* PRINTERS.)

Junk Dealers.

(*See also* RAG DEALERS ; *also* PAPER STOCK.)

ASH GEORGE T., 128 Dugan's whf
Ayler John, 292 S Caroline
BAER LEWIS & BRO., pay the highest cash prices for WOOL, HIDES, SHEEP SKINS, RAGS, FEATHERS, COPPER, BRASS, PEWTER, LEAD, IRON, BEESWAX, WOOL AND FURS of all kinds, 3 and 5 Camden bet Charles and Light
Barrett William, 264 S Charles
Bolte Simon, 91 Chesnut
Bohager Francis, 11 Bank
Broderick John T., 86 Greenmount av
Brown & Short, 186 Light st whf
Bourdon Frank, 52 Chesnut
BOWMAN WILLIAM, dealer in WROUGHT AND CAST SCRAP IRON, OLD COPPER, BRASS, LEAD, PEWTER, ZINC, &c. All

kinds of PAPER STOCK, such as RAGS, CANVAS, OLD ROBE, BAGGING, &c., which he is prepared to purchase in large or small quantities, at the highest market prices, CASH. A large assortment of SECOND HAND COTTON, LINEN, AND GUNNY BAGS constantly on hand, for sale low, suitable for Bark, Feed, Grain, &c., second hand BLACKSMITH'S GOODS, such as ANVILS, BELLOWS, VICES, HAMMERS, &c. MACHINERY such as PULLEYS, SHAFTING, AND LEATHER BELTING. A general assortment of the above articles always on hand. N. B. Old Iron suitable for Blacksmiths, &c., Iron Yard c Eden and Eastern av

CHURCH & BROWN, 4 Dugan

Coleman & Cleaveland, 48 Thames

Deal Frederick, 292 Alice Anna

Dooley Thomas, 10 Central av

FRANK GEORGE M., 51 Thames

GARDNER ROBERT, Chesnut c Hillen

Gordon Mrs. A., 34 President

Grober Jacob, 200 S Sharp

Haines Henry, 157 Henrietta

Holmes Charles, 287 S Charles

Hulseman Henry, 128 Thames

Kernan Thos., 15 McKim

Kettler Frederick A., 305 S Bond

Lancaster Mrs. R., 66 Penn av

LEDDON GEORGE, 128 Dugan's whf, dealer in second hand Standing and Running Rigging, Anchors, Hooks, Thimbles, Oakum, Rope, Tar, &c.

Loos Peter, 22 Spring

Lowey P., 345 S Charles

McConnell P., 730 W Baltimore

McTeer Simon, 85 Chesnut

Riddle & Johnson, 1 W Fall's av block

SAVAGE CHARLES E., 34 and 36 Lee, Wholesale and Retail dealer in COTTON RAGS, SOFT WOOL-

LENS, CLOTH, ROPE AND PAPER STOCK, OLD IRON, COPPER, BRASS, LEAD, PEWTER, ZINC, GLASS, OLD RUBBER, &c.

Schmitt Conrad, 68 N Fremont

Sparenberg Henry, 19 Leadenhall

Steigerwald H., 255 Hollins

Stone Robert, 265 E Lombard

Taylor & Brothers, 170 Light st whf

Whitner Frank, 82 Lancaster

Winternik Chas., 79 S Howard

Winternitz Sam'l G., 26 Penna av

Wise John, 2 Castel av

Zorn Adam T., 12 Spring

Justice of the Peace.

(See also MAGISTRATES.)

Forrester Allen E., 28 St Paul

Hayward Wm. H., N W c St Paul and Fayette

Hiss Chas. D., 34 South

Irving Ambrose M., 47 N Eutaw

Johnson Joseph, 58 Camden

Logan Jos. T., 411 W Baltimore

PETERS EDWARD J., 12 Law bdg's, 36 St Paul

Reid Wm. H., 101 N Paca

Ritter Geo. W., 28 St Paul

Shipley Jos., 520 W Baltimore

Showacke John, 58 S Eutaw

Wilson P. T., 26 St Paul

Kindling Wood.

(See also WOOD.)

Johnson James H., 3 North

McCULLOUGH JOHN, Yard and Office, Pratt and Fremont and Park and Fayette. Wharf, Eutaw. (See advertisement.)

Knitted Goods.

(See also HOSIERY.)

DIETZ L. D. & CO., 308 W Baltimore. (See advertisement inside back cover.)

Laces and Embroideries.

(*See also* Hosiery; *also* Trimmings.)

BAMBERGER BROTHERS, 147 W Lexington
BONNEY E., 147 W Baltimore
BRUNT MRS. THOS., 189 Baltimore op St Paul
BRYAN SAMUEL L: & CO., 221 W Baltimore
FOUDRIAT MADAME, 64 W Lexington
GOLDENBERG & WEINBERG, 163 W Baltimore, Millinery Goods, Kid Gloves, &c.
HAMMERSLOUGH LEWIS, 155 W Lexington
HUTZLER M. & SON, Dealers in Embroideries, Laces, Hoop Skirts, Notions, &c., 71 N Howard c Clay
Linden E. C., 143 W Baltimore
TOLDRIDGE MRS. E., 191 W Baltimore

Ladies' Dress Patterns.

Mitchell Mrs. C. W., 63 E Baltimore
MULLER MRS. LOUIS, 110 W Baltimore. (See advertisement.)

Ladies' Dress Trimmings, Retail.

(*See also* Trimmings.)
Beck Mrs. M. E., 115 N Gay
O'Leary Miss A. O., Charles c Pleasant
Schultze Miss H., 38 N Charles

Ladies' Dress Trimmings, Wholesale.

BAMBERGER E., 274 W Baltimore
BRYAN SAMUEL L. & CO., 221 W Baltimore, 4 doors bel Charles, Manufacturers and Dealers in LADIES' DRESS TRIMMINGS, Hoop Skirts, Embroideries, Laces, White Goods and Sun Umbrellas.
DROST & SUTRO, 253 W Baltimore

Novelty, Ruffle & Co., 7 N Liberty
SISCO BROTHERS, 95 W Baltimore

TRIBLE JOHN E.,

223 W. BALTIMORE,

Manufacturer of

LADIES' DRESS

AND

Mantilla Trimmings,

HEAD NETS, &c.

---

*Ladies' Hair Dressers.

(*See* Hair Dressers, Ladies'.)

Ladies' Head Dresses.

BROWN M. & S., 243 W Baltimore, up stairs

BRUNT MRS. THOS.,

189 W. Baltimore, op. St. Paul,

Rich Embroideries

AND

LACE GOODS,

FANCY PINS, MOURNING

GOODS, ILLUSIONS, CAPES,

CAPS AND HEAD DRESSES

In Great Variety.

Sim Mrs. J., 495½ W Baltimore
TOLDRIDGE MRS. E., 191 W Baltimore bet Charles and Light, · dealer in Dress Caps, Head Dresses, Laces, Embroideries, French Flowers, &c., wholesale and retail.
TRIBLE JOHN E., 223 E Baltimore

Lager Beer Saloons.

(*See also* BREWERS, LAGER BEER ;
also RESTAURANTS ; *also* TA-
VERNS.)

Albers Siebelt, 290 S Ann
Albert J. G., 33 N Paca
Alles Philip, 52 Harrison
AMAN FREDERICK G., 53 S Li-
berty, LAGER BEER SALOON.
MEALS AT ALL HOURS.
Amass W. Y., 504 N Gay
AUER JACOB, Mulberry c How-
ard
BACHMAN FREDERICK, 215 S
Eutaw
Bailey William T., 240 E Lombard
Bartell C., 6 E Lombard
BAUMGARTNER A.,45 Albemarle
Becht James H., Thames c Anna
BEERE PATRICK, 63 President
Bellevue Garden, Henry Myers,
Proprietor, W Baltimore, op.
Stuart's Hospital
Ben Charles, 99 N Paca
Benner Otto, 100 Pennsylvania av
Betsel George, 68 Lancaster
Bitter L., 5 W Pratt
Black Mrs., 242 Canton av
Blanck John, 471 W Baltimore
BOBART THOMAS, 242 S Broad-
way
Boehm Constine, 50 S Wolf
BOLLER WM., 639 W Baltimore
BOTHMAN GUSTAVE, S Eutaw
c Lee
Bowman Philip, 43 N Frederick
Brandau Frederick, 59 President
Braul W., 45 E Pratt
BREMMER C. H., 243 Hanover
Brock John M., 6 E Pratt
Bucksbaum J., Central av c Lom-
bard
Bushman C. A., 201 W Lexington
Campbell James 55 N Frederick
Cella John, 66 President
Christ & Koltz, 8 E Monument
Clark Mrs., 7 Clay
Clum Chas., 23 Cross

Cook Henry, 241 Alice Anna
Cooper John, 7 Fish market space
Cooper Mrs. G., 107 E Pratt
Daiker John, 34 N Liberty
Daseball John F., 271 N Gay
Dash John P., 189 Hollins
Doerneg Henry, 20 Park
Duffy Simon, 178 Harford av
Eckhardt Conrad, 85 Harrison
Eickhoff T., 43 North
Eigenbrot Chas., 277 S Sharp
Eilbecher John V., 16 Lee
Engel Henry, 17 Harrison
Erpenbeck Henry, 219 S Broadway
Eveland John, 311 Fall's av
block
Eyes Charles, 167 Penn av
Faber T., 272 S Broadway
FEIGE A. H., 49 N Frederick
Fisher Chr., 20 Frederick
Fisher Eliza, 79 Chesnut
Flock Andrew, 253 S Bond
Frank A., Gilmor c Townsend
Freckmann Joseph, 68 S Eutaw
Freeberger Wolf, 32 S Paca
Fulling John, 211 W Pratt
Fuss John, 530 W Baltimore
GARDNER FR., importer of Rhine
wines and lager beer saloon, 8 N
High
Gaueatry C., 114 Thames
Grub L., 100 Light st whf
Gruss Wm , 179 W Lexington
Gumbern Michael, 75 Columbia
Haacke C. W., 82 S Dallas
Haffey Mrs. M. D., 64 President
Hagger Henry, 178 E Baltimore
Hahn Herman, Frederick c Fay-
ette
Hains Thomas S., Central av c
Jefferson
Hause Conrad, 256 S Caroline
Hause Michl., Broadway c Thames
Heck George, Caroline c Jefferson
Heid John, 23 N Frederick
Heil Herman, 280 S Broadway
Helwig August, 44 Leadenhall
Hendrick Henry, 17 S Liberty
Henkal Martin, 254 Central av

Herford Julius, 240 S Broadway
Herman Leer, 14 Park
Hesch J., 463 W Baltimore
Hett Henry, 141 W Lombard
HIELLER JOHN, RESTAURANT and LAGER BEER SALOON, 17 N Liberty
Hildebrand Charles F., 93 Thames
Hoffman George, 145 W Lombard
Hoffman Joseph H., 552 W Baltimore
Hogan John, 26 N Gay
Holler John, 60 Camden
Hoopes R., 244 Washington
Horr John, 158 S Broadway
Horr Wm., 253 Canton av
Huber Wm., 295 N Gay
Johannes Henry, 74 N Pearl
JONES MRS. BERTHA, Lombard c Marsh mkt space
Jordan C., 195 S Sharp
Jouffret M., 25 N Frederick
Jung Theodore, 446 W Baltimore
Jungen Geo. P., 65 Mkt space
Jerger John, 67 Mkt space
Kaiser Charles, 16 E Lombard
Kalle Henry, 21 N Frederick
Kauckf J., 266 S Broadway
Kaufmann Chas., 187 Montgomery
Kaylor Wm., 3 Camden la
KIELMEIER MAX, 42 Clay
KINZER JOHN, 172 E Madison
Kirsch Louis, 473 N Gay
Klages Frederick, Pratt c President
Klein E., 151 S Charles
Kleish John, 269 S Ann
Kloch F., 671 W Baltimore
Knapp Paul, Mount st
Kneictstedt Henry, 126 W Lombard
Knipschild John, 80 S Eutaw
Kohlas John, 60 S Wolfe
Kohler John, 44 Lee
Kolb John, 259 W Pratt
Kopp Ferdinand, 108 Hughes
Kraft Charles, Penn av c Orchard
Krantz Geo., 13 E Pratt
Krause John H., 35 N Frederick
Kremer Jacob, 319 S Bond
KRIEG PETER, 247 Alice Anna

Kroder John, 45 German
Kuhn Adam, 497 N Gay
Lagge J. T., 47 N Frederick
Le Brow T. C., 223 E Lombard
Leffer Chas., 33 Ensor
Letter Henry, 341 S Charles
Liedz Henry, 58½ Mulberry
Linder B., N Front c Gay
Link Conrad, 225 Alice Anna
Litzner John, Ann c Eastern av
Loengi Albert, 648 W Baltimore
Loos Henry, 12 N Frederick
MATTHAS PETER, 231 S Broadway
Menger H., 262 Canton av
Metz John F., Cross c Hanover
Metzman Louis, 42 N Caroline
MEYER GEO., 125 Franklin
MEYER MRS. K., 44 N Frederick
Meyer Peter, 60 Mkt space
Meyers John, 39 German
Miller Frederick, 1 Dover
MINTERLEIN FRED., 131 W Lexington
Mitchel Jos. C., Baltimore c Frederick av
Mormann Nicholas, 122 N Howard
Muhl Conrad 249 Alice Anna
Muller Christian, 244 Alice Anna
Neuberger Samuel, Broadway c Thames
Ochs Daniel, Bell Air av
Ochs Thomas, Central av c Pratt
Odenwalds Philip, 147 W Lombard
O'Hara Peter, 12 Fish mkt space
Ostertag B., 156 Franklin
Otto Charles, Spring c Gough
Otto Theodore, 41 Harrison
Perkins Frederick, 251 Canton av
Pfaff Conrad, 53 Bank
Pfeil August, 11 Brown
Pohr H. S., 11 W Fayette
Popp John, 43 Ensor
Pregel Matthias, 57 N Frederick
Randft Joseph, 356 W Pratt
REDFIELD MRS. ANGELINE, S Caroline c Fleet
Rehmert G., 223 Alice Anna
REICHERT CONRAD, 267 N Gay

Reik L. F., 697 W Baltimore
Reitz Martin, 245 S Broadway
Reynolds John, 556 W Baltimore
Rhine Louis, 250 S Broadway
Richter A., 7 Clay
Richter Lawrence, 224 S Broadway
Richter Louis, Alice Anna c Ann
Ringler George, 244 Canton av
Roese Henry, 302 Montgomery
Roesninck F. W., 117 Thames
Rogdes Amos C., 788 W Baltimore
Rose Henry, 302 Montgomery
Rosenthal Simon, 6 Central av
ROTH GEORGE, 737 W Baltimore
ROTHHAAS JOHN, 26 E Lombard
Rowe John, 93 Low
Ruppert Joseph, 215 Eastern av
Schaeffer Charles W., Canton c
  Washington
SCHALLHAS WM., 35 N Paca
Schauer George, 199 E Pratt
Scheffer John, 39 S Paca
Scherer John, 582 W Baltimore
SCHIERBAUM AUGUSTUS, 74 S
  Charles
Schieve Mrs. B., 13 New
SCHMEIMG A., 98 Thames
SCHMITH JOHN, 241 Eastern av
Schmitz T., 645 W Baltimore
Schnapp R., Paca c Ross
Schreiber E., 286 S Ann
Schuckle Charles F., 112 Ross
Schueszler Lorenz, 38 S Wolf
Schuh Charles, 385 Canton av
Schultheiss J., 267 S Ann
Schultz Andrew, 103 E Pratt
Schuncke John, 28 Albemarle
Schutze August, 302 S Caroline
Schutze J., 58 Ensor
Schwab Conrad, 72 N Fremont
Schwartzhaupt Conrad, Albemarle
  c Plowman
Schwick Reuben, 601 N Gay
Schwing George, 98 Central av
Schwinn H., 114 Franklin
Schwinn Jacob, S E c Concord and
  Pratt

SENFT HENRY,

IMPORTER
and
WHOLESALE DEALER IN
RHINE WINE,
Paca c Baltimore.

Shillinger Mrs. J., Washington c
  Warren
Siebold T., 351 Saratoga
Sittig Henry, 255 S Bond
Silverstine Philip, 213 Central av
Sinsz Nicholas, 42 Hughes
Skorl Carl, 113 Hollins
Smith C., Penn. av c Biddle
Smith Joseph, 163 Franklin
Smith Lewis, 54 German
Smith Peter, 292 S Ann
Snyder Stephen, 27 W Fayette
Speidel Jacob F., 14 President
STINNER JOHN, 83 Mulberry
Straus G. W., 61 S Charles
Strifer Jacob, 186 E Baltimore
Strohmaier B., 171 Franklin
Stureen George, 79 Bank
SULTAN HENRY, TURNER AS-
  SOCIATION (MEALS AT ALL
  HOURS OF THE DAY), 300 W
  Pratt
Sykes Charles, 42 E Pratt
TEEPE WM., 13 Frederick
Theuerjuhe W. F., 57 Hanover
Triess John F., 94 Thames
Vieneg Henry, 264 Canton av
Voight Wm. A., 348 Light
Vogle Henry, 104 N Howard
Vonheine John H., 67 S Howard
Walter Philip, 247 Central av
Weaver Elizabeth, 260 S Broad-
  way
Weil M. H., 19 Frederick
Weiss John, 56 Park
Wessells A., 282 S Ann
Wetschky Charles, Thames c Ann
Weyhing Albert, 796 W Baltimore
Wiegand Henry C., S E c Camden
  and Howard

Wiegand John, Broadway c Lancaster
Winchester John, 33 Thames
Wode Louis, 292 S Charles
Wolflong Henry, Concord c Lombard
Young Allen, 27 Ensor
Zuel Conrad, 219 Light

Lamps and Chandeliers.

(*See also* GAS FIXTURES.)
AMMIDON & CROMBIE, 337 W Baltimore and 52 German. (See advertisement interleaved op Oil.)
BOOZ JAMES, 66 S Caroline, DEALER IN LAMPS, WICKS, CHIMNEYS, BURNERS, &c. Also COAL OIL.
Chappell Mrs. L., 185 Mulberry
COOK & HERRING, 7 S Charles. (See advertisement op. China.)
GARDNER WM. G. & CO., 1 S Liberty. (See advertisement op Oils.)
Hamill R. W. & Co., 64 Hanover
HAMILL & CO., 125 N Gay
Hardester Thomas, 250 Light
HARDESTER & BOKEE, 321 W Baltimore n Howard
Horton Wm., 434 W Baltimore
Lenz Henry, 665 W Baltimore
Massicot Robert, 338 N Gay
Merrick Conrad, 841 W Baltimore
Merz Henry, 254 W Pratt
NEWBOLD J. F., 2 E Baltimore
Schaeffer Wm. H., 128 Penna av
Schle Mrs. E., 153 Franklin
Spilcker W. & H., 136 W Baltimore
Treusch P., 236 S Broadway
WAGNER AUGUST, 36 Harrison. (See advertisement interleaved op Brass Founders.)
Waidner Mrs. Caroline, 742 W Baltimore

Land Companies.

The Brooklyn Building and Aid Union. The Brooklyn Land Company. The Patapsco Land Company. R. W. Templeman, Sec'y, 48 Lexington.

Last Manufacturers.

Marchell J. L., Lombard c Grant
Merriken J. S., 118 W Lombard

Laundry.

Search C., 1 E Baltimore

Lawyers.

Alexander William, 76 W Fayette
Atkinson Joseph T., 36 St Paul
Baldwin R. W., 29 St Paul
Bannon M., 32 St Paul
Barry Lewellyn L., 80 W Fayette
Battee R R., 24 St Paul
Benzinger Fred. F., 19 Law Bdgs
BERRY THOMAS W.,
ATTORNEY AT LAW,
82 W Fayette
Blackburn John C., 34 St Paul
BLANCHARD E. WYATT, 38 St Paul
Bond Geo. M., 33 St Paul
Bond Wm. B., 32 St Paul
BOULDIN R. J., 6 St Paul
Brent Robert J., 31 W Lexington
Brice Geo. H., 46 St Paul
Brickenstein L. C., 43 N Charles
BROWNING WARFIELD T., 59 W Fayette
Brune Fred. W., 40 St Paul
Brune F. W., jr., 9 N Calvert
Brown Geo. Wm., 40 St Paul
Brown Stewart, 40 St Paul
Brown & Brune, 40 St Paul
Bryan W. S., 36 St Paul
Byrd Alfred H., 17 St Paul
Campbell J. M., 29 W Lexington
Carroll James, 31 St Paul
Carter Bernard, 29 W Lexington
CINNAMOND GEORGE R., 59 W Fayette
CINNAMOND & BROWNING, 59 W Fayette
Cochran & Stockbridge, Law bdgs, 36 St Paul
Cole Wm. J., 70 W Fayette
Collins Wm. H., 34 St Paul
Cook W. W. L., 48 W Lexington

Courtney David, Jr., 3 Spurrier's ct
CROSS E. J. D., 31 W Lexington
Cummiskey Eugene, 43 St Paul
DANELS- BOLIVAR D., 57 W Fayette
Daniel Wm., 67 W Fayette
Davis Henry Winter, 56 St Paul
Dobbin Geo. W., 42 St Paul
DONALDSON THOS., 38 St Paul, *residence* Howard County
Duffy Edward, 28 St Paul
Dulany H. R., 36 St Paul
Emory D. C. H., 47 St Paul
Farerandis Walter, 2 Spurrier's ct
Findlay John & L., 22 Law bdgs
FISCHER LEWIS C., 31 Lexington
FISHER WM. A., 43 St Paul
Fowler David, 31 Lexington
Frazier J. M., 74 Courtland
Friese Philip C., 61 W Fayette
Frick Wm. F., 82 W Fayette
Gale Levin, 34 St Paul
Garey Henry F., 85 W Fayette
Gill George M., 36 St Paul
Gill N. R., 32 St Paul
Gilmor Robert, Jr., 20 Law bdgs
Gittings R. J., 47 St Paul
GLOCKER THEODORE, 63 W Fayette, ATTORNEY AT LAW and SOLICITOR IN CHANCERY
Griffith J Howard, 33 St Paul
Gwinn Charles J. M., 41 St Paul
HACK OLIVER F., 7 Counsellor's Hall, Lexington n Charles
Hambleton J. D., 43 St Paul
Hanan J. S., 31 St Paul
Hardester R. C., 67 W Fayette
HARRIS J. MORRISON, 5 Spurrier's ct, Lexington
Henderson T. F., 34 St Paul
Heuisler Joseph S., 24 Law bdgs
Hill Wm. B., 70 W Fayette
HINKLEY & MORRIS, 43 N Charles
Hobbs A. H., 32 St Paul
Horwitz Benj. F., 26 N Charles
Horwitz Orville, 38 St Paul
Ing John H., 59½ W Fayette
Israel Edward, 34 St Paul
13

Johnson H. Edgar, 35 N Charles
Johnson John, 29 St Paul
Johnson Reverdy, 41 St Paul
Johnson Reverdy, Jr., 26 N Charles
JONES & MYLES, 53 W Fayette, Johnson's Buildings, bet Calvert and St Paul, ATTORNEYS AT LAW, SOLICITORS IN CHANCERY AND CONVEYANCERS. Morris J. Jones. James Myles.
Kalkman V. H., 13 Lexington
Keene John H., jr., 15 St Paul
Kerr Charles G., 31 St. Paul
Keerl Thomas M., 37 N Charles
Kilbourn E. G., 32 St Paul
Knott A. Leo, 26 Law bdgs
LATIMER JAS. B., S W c Fayette and St Paul
LANAHAN THOS. M., 31 W Lexington
Latrobe F. C., St Paul c Lexington
Leakin Sheppard A., 11 Law bdgs, 36 St Paul
Latrobe John H. B., St Paul c Lexington
McALLISTER R. A., 72 Bank
McFarland C. Dodd, 7 Counsellors' Hall, Lexington
McLane James L., 43 St Paul
McLaughlin Patrick, 80 W Fayette
Machen Arthur W., 47 St Paul
MAGRUDER J. H., ATTORNEY AT LAW, 72 W Fayette. *Collections promptly attended to.*
MALCOLM JAMES, 27 W Lexington
MATHEWS R. STOCKETT, 46 Lexington
MATHEWS & LONEY, 46 Lexington
Maund Geo. C., 80 W Fayette
May Henry, 31 W Lexington
Moale Randall H., 70 W Fayette
Morrison Robert D., 28 St Paul
MUSSELMAN AMOS F., 21 W Lexington
Nelson A. B., 15 St Paul
Nicholson James M., 38 St Paul

LAW / LEA

O'Brien Wm. J., 49 W Fayette
Pennington H. B., 51 W Fayette
Pennington J., 82 W Fayette
Pinkney Fred., 46 St Paul
Pitts Chas. H., 47 St Paul
POE JOHN P., 25 W Lexington
Poe Neilson, 25 W Lexington
Presstman Benj. C., 30 St Paul
Preston J. A., 31 St Paul
Preston Wm. P., 65 W Fayette
Price Wm., 29 St Paul
QUINN J. R., 24 St Paul
Reynolds Luther M., 74 W Fayette
Reynolds Wm J., 38 St Paul
RICHARDSON M. L., 32 St Paul
RIDGELY ANDREW STERETT, 41 St Paul
RIDGELY CHARLES W., 34 St Paul
RITCHIE ALBERT, 21 Lexington
Robinson L. H., 38 St Paul
ROBINSON N., 32 St Paul
ROGERS ROBERT LYON, 2 Spurrier's ct Lexington
Root H. R., 5 St Paul
Salmon E. W., 26 N Calvert
SCOTT T. PARKIN, 16 St Paul
Scott W. Parkin, 16 St Paul
Small John, Jr., 1 W Lexington
SMITH J. DEAN, 35 N Charles
Snyder John J., 53 W Fayette
SPRAGUE E. R., 5 St Paul
Steele Nevett J., 82 W Fayette
STEEL & TAGART, 82 W Fayette
Sterling A. Jr., 26 N Calvert
Steuart W. J., 31 St Paul
Stevens F. P., 48 W Lexington
Stewart John, 33 St Paul
Stockett J. Shaff, 45 St Paul
Swann Edward, 40 St Paul
SWINNEY EPAPHRODITUS, Attorney and Counsellor at Law, Office 53 W Fayette op Barnum's
Tagart S. H., 82 W Fayette
Thayer N. J., 29 St Paul, Assistant District Attorney
THOMAS DANIEL M., 29 W Lexington
THOMAS JOHN H., 37 St Paul

Thomas John J., Jr., 6 St Paul
Thompson Henry F., 31 W Lexington
Tiernan Chas. B., 45 St Paul
TORMEY FRANCIS D., 21 W Lexington
Tyson John S., Jr., 29 St Paul
Wallis S. Teackle, 37 St Paul
Walsh T. Yates, 26 N Calvert
Ward Wm. J., 26 N Calvert
Warfield O. C., 13 St Paul
Warner J. G., 61 W Fayette
Warrington T. J., Charles o Fayette
WATERMAN W. J., ATTORNEY AND COUNSELLOR AT LAW, 83 W Fayette n Charles
Waters Andrew G., 34 St Paul
Waters William S., 17 St Paul
WEBSTER HENRY, 9 N Calvert
Whelan Thomas Jr., 16 St Paul
WHYTE WM. PINKNEY, 21 Lexington
Wilcox A., 28 N Calvert
Williams George H., 13 North
Williams Loyd W., 6 St Paul
Wilson & Lipscomb, 14 Law bdg, 36 St Paul
Wolf A., 17 W Lexington
Wyatt Chas. H., 48 St Paul

Leather Belting

CHASE WELLS & GEHRMANN, 6 S Howard. (See advertisement op Yarns, Batts, Wicks, &c.)
DUKEHART R. W., 18 Water
HASKELL J. H., 33 S Eutaw. (See advertisement interleaved.)

Leather Dealers.

(See also HIDES AND LEATHER; also CURRIERS; also MOROCCO.)

ACHEY FREDERICK & SON, 22 S Liberty. (See advertisement interleaved.)
ANDERSON JAMES G., 5 Balderston n Light. (See advertisement interleaved.)
Bartlett & Co., 134 W Fayette

BARTON WILLIAM J. & SON, 7 and 9 Cheapside c Lombard, LEATHER DEALERS, KEEP CONSTANTLY ON HAND A LARGE ASSORTMENT OF ALL KINDS OF UPPER AND SOLE LEATHER; ALSO, MOROCCO LININGS AND BINDINGS.
Brooks Robert, 257 W Baltimore
COAKLEY BROS., 18 S Calvert, importers of LEATHER AND SHOE TRIMMINGS, English and French Calf and Kid Skins, Boot Webbs, Lastings, Galloons, Laces, Buttons, Fitters' Twist, Hemp. Flax, Machine Silk, Gaiter Uppers, &c.
Darraugh D., 16 S Calvert
GRUPY FRANCIS H., 42 S Calvert, *dwelling* Chase c Eden dealer in HIDES AND LEATHER, OIL AND TALLOW, TANNERS AND CURRIERS' TOOLS AND SHOE FINDINGS.
Hewitt Elmer, Jr., 50 S Calvert
Hoffman M., Jr., 560 W Baltimore
JENKINS EDWARD, 13 Cheapside
Klees Henry & Sons, 15, 17 and 19 Saratoga
ARRABEE E. & SONS, 20 S Calvert, LEATHER AND SHOE FINDING HOUSE.
Mason Charles, 166 Forrest
MAYNARD, ELY & ROSE, 46 S Calvert
SCHLARB P. & H., 61 S Sharp n Pratt
SELWAY ROBERT, 14 S Calvert
Startzman David, 44 S Calvert
Startzman J. & L., 54 S Calvert
Sullevan Thomas H., 36 S Calvert
Trautman A., 467 W Baltimore
TRAUTMAN G. C., 104 N Pearl

Leather and Findings.

(*See also* BOOT AND SHOE FINDINGS.)
COAKLEY BROTHERS, Leather and Shoe Trimmings, 18 S Calvert

GRUPY FRANCIS H., 42 S Calvert, dwelling c Chase and Eden
LARRABEE E. & SONS, 20 S Calvert
MAYNARD, ELY & ROSE, 46 S Calvert
SCHMIDT JACOB, 312 W Pratt

Libraries.

(*See also* READING ROOMS.)
Maryland Institute, Centre market space c Baltimore
Mercantile Library Association.— *President*—Geo. B. Cole. *Librarian*—B. P. Waters. 19,000 Volumes. Athenæum Building, Saratoga c St Paul.

Lime and Hair.

(*See also* CEMENT.)
Dorsey Michael, 112 Light st whf
GREEN JACOB, 44 Buren

McALLISTER JAMES,

Successor to

ELIJAH STANSBURY,

Albemarle c Fawn.

LIME, HAIR, CALCINED PLASTER,

AND

Hydraulic Cement.

The undersigned has on hand the above Articles, which he offers for Sale on accommodating Terms at his Old Stand,
Corner of Albemarle and Fawn Sts., Old Town,
(Near the depot of the Phil. and Balt. R. R. Co., President St.)
ORDERS will be thankfully received and promptly attended to.

SCHARF WM. JAMES, 825 W Baltimore
Slothower J., 27 N Green
Streets John S., 4 Hollingsworth
Trotton Thomas, 33 Cheapside

.Linens.

BROWN ROBT. D. & CO., 2 German, Importers of Irish Linen

MILLIKEN R. H.,
No. 195 W. BALTIMORE ST.,
Importer and Dealer in

LINEN GOODS
EXCLUSIVELY.

Lithographers.

BROSS EDWARD, 149 W Lombard. (See advertisement.)
HOEN A. & CO., 73 and 75 Second, PRACTICAL LITHOGRAPHERS
Thunckel & Co., Baltimore c Sharp

SACHSE E. & CO.,
104 S. CHARLES,

LITHOGRAPHIC ESTABLISHMENT,
Publishers of the Camps of the U. S. Army around

WASHINGTON, BALTIMORE,
FORTRESS MONROE,
And Other Places; and also of Views of Cities.

Livery and Sale Stables.

ANDERSON JOHN, 131 W Madison
Blades John R., 301 E Lombard
Brogan Phillip, 100 S Howard
Brutsche F., 58 Clay
CENTRAL STABLES, 111 W Lexington bet Park and Liberty, JOHN D. STEWART, *Proprietor.* Coaches for Shopping, Weddings, &c. Horses on Livery by the Day or Month.
Cook David, 122 Ensor
Cowen Thos., 24 S Poppleton
Cox E., Bank c Bethel
Delphy George & Bro., Howard c Franklin
Dobbins John, 34 N High

Gaither Washington, 9 Columbia
Garvey James, 154 N Calvert
GEN. WAYNE LIVERY & SALE STABLES, JOHN THOMAS, PROPRIETOR, Baltimore c Paca
Gordon James, 100 German
Hartzell L., 95 N Paca
Hartzell & Clark, 80 German
Humphreys T. W., 34 Lancaster
Johnson A., 93 Holiday
Kearneys Edward, Centre c St Paul
Kemp Henry, 72 German
LANE & KRAGER, 1 N Paca
McConnell George W., 74 N Calvert
McGEE JOSEPH H. & BROTHER, Paca c German. (See advertisement.)
McGlennon J. H., 184 German
McGowan George, 2 Mulberry
Mann & Brother, 167 N Howard
Meyers George, Fremont c Ramsey
Miller Wm. C., 86 German
Moffatt R., 161 N Howard
O'NEAL PATRICK, 175 German
Oppenheimer Samuel, 8 S Paca
Phillips F., Fremont c Ramsay
Quinn Michael, 80 Central av
Reilly George, 25 W Lombard
Rider Peter, 47 S Caroline
Ritzriefner John, 176 Alice Anna
Roney & Landers, 36 North
Shipley Joseph P., 3 Orchard
STEWART'S (A. E.) Calvert Stables, op City Springs, 63 N Calvert, near Saratoga. (See advertisement.)
STEWART JOHN D., 111 W Lexington
Sherlock Wm., 88 W Fayette
Spangler M., 30 W Lombard
Talbot B., 42 North
THOMAS JOHN, Baltimore c Paca
WAMBACH A., 102 S Eutaw
Wheat & Scott 405 W Baltimore
Wheeler A. C., Hanover c Conway

Wilkinson James. Bond c Bank
Wollet John P., 12 Temple
Woodward N. R., 31 North

Loan Office.

(*See also* PAWNBROKERS.)

Ulman Jacob & Benjamin F., 22 N Gay

Locksmiths and Bell-hangers.

Berger M. R., 710 W Baltimore
Brudu C., 173 Columbia
Clark James, 147 W Fayette
Debiring B., 338 W Pratt
Distelbard George, 584 W Baltimore
Evat E., 55 Light
Fitzberger H., 102 W Lexington
Gibson & Bohannan, 1 Cheapside
Hentz Adam, 174 Alice Anna
Hoffman Henry, 59 German
Joh Jacob, 47 Penn. av
Jung Frederick, 30 N Gay
Kirk Samuel E. & Bro., c Calvert and Lombard
Lees Wm., 14 S. Schroeder
May F. L., 125 W. Madison
Phillips Charles, 73 N Front
Thorniz Andrew, 50 Light
Voigt Thos. W., 263 E Lombard
Warren Samuel, 90 N Calvert

Locomotive Builders.

(*See* STEAM ENGINE BUILDERS.)

Looking-Glass and Picture-Frame Makers.

(*See also* CARVERS.)

Barrett M. & Bro., 82 N Howard
Barrett & Debeet, 71 W Baltimore
BUTLER, PERRIGO & WAY, 168 W Baltimore (Tracy Building), MIRRORS, GILT WORK, ENGRAVINGS, PASSEPOURTOUTS, &c.
BYRNE JOSEPH, 32 N Calvert n Lexington, Picture-Frame Maker, Carver, and Gilder.

13*

Eckhardt Wm., 58 N Gay
Fryer James, 206 W Baltimore
Harrington & Mills, 140 W Baltimore
HEWITT GEO. W., 9 N Gay
Lossman J., 521 W Baltimore
McGrew William, 92 N Howard

MANN JOHN,

Wholesale Dealer in all kinds of

American Clocks,

And Manufacturer of

Mahogany, Rosewood, and Gilt Frame

LOOKING-GLASSES,

A large and varied assortment of Toilet Boxes, Work Boxes, Portable Desks and Clock Trimmings always on hand.

N E c Charles and Lombard Sts.

BALTIMORE.

Myers Wm. P., 33 W Baltimore
OLIVER & REMINGTON. LOOKING-GLASS and PICTURE-FRAME MANUFACTURERS, and Dealers in French and German Looking-Glass Plates, Engravings, &c., 50½ N Howard
SEAGER THOMAS, 17 S Sharp, LOOKING-GLASS and PICTURE FRAME MANUFACTURER, and Dealer in FRENCH and GERMAN LOOKING-GLASS PLATES, PRINTS, &c.
Vickers Clement, 25 W Baltimore

Lumber Commission Merchants.

(*See also* LUMBER DEALERS.)

BURNS F. H., 56 W Falls av
Cockey & Co., E Falls av and Canton av

Cross Wm. S. & Bro., E Falls av c
Eastern av
McDougall & Clarke, 158 W Falls av
THOMAS & HUGG, 56 E Falls av

Lumber Dealers.

(*See also* LUMBER COMMISSION
MERCHANTS.)

ALLEN ALEXANDER & CO., 56
W Falls av
Boyd Joseph H., 12 S Caroline
BURNS & SLOAN, LUMBER
DEALERS, c of Eutaw and Ger-
man, and 132 Light st whf.
S. Burns.   G. F. Sloan.
CARSON C. H. & CO., LUMBER
DEALERS, W side Union dock,
adjoining Norfolk Steamboat whf.
Carvill H. Carson, David Carson.
CATE A., E Falls av and Fawn
Church E. J., Monument c Aisquith
Coates John, 355 W Pratt
Coates & Glenn, ft of S Howard
Eareckson V. O., Falls av bel Pratt
George S. & Son, 37 N Green
Gollibert Simon M., 140 Thames

GRAFFLIN J. W.,

E Falls av c Canton av.,

Lumber, Ship Plank, and Locust Treenails.

HELFRICH & HAY, S W c Concord and Bowly, and 762 W Baltimore op Oregon, Lumber Dealers. All kinds of Building, Cabinet, and Wheelwright Lumber
constantly on hand.
Herring Henry & Son, E Falls av
and Canton av
KIRBY JOHN & SONS, Mill c
Bowly
Mathews Thos. & Son, 100 N High
Merryman Charles, Green c Pratt

Mottus Theodore, Penn. av c Pres-
ton
Page Washington A., 182 Light st
whf
Readys Samuel, 69 President
Scharf Thos. G., W Baltimore bet
Calhoun and Streker
Thomas John & Son, 296 S Eutaw
Thomas Jos. & Son, Pratt c Green
Thomas & Price, 56 E Falls av
TURNER JOHN C., 140 Light st
whf
WEST W. & W. H., Lumber deal-
ers, N E c Mill and Bowly sts,
McElderry's whf; constantly on
hand all kinds of White and Yel-
low Pine Lumber, Laths, Shin-
gles, Pickets, &c. *Dwelling* N
W c Pratt and Exeter.
WILLIAMS J. & J. & CO., 130 S
Charles
WILLIS S., c E Falls av and
Eastern av, Lumber Yard, dealer
in all kinds of Lumber, Shingles,
and Laths, which will sell cheap
for cash.

Machine Card Manufacturer.

HASKELL J. H., 33 S Eutaw.
(See advertisement.)

Machinists.

(*See also* IRON FOUNDERS ; *also*
STEAM ENGINES.)

BASSHOR THOMAS C. & CO., 26
Light. (See advertisement.)
CHASE WELLS & GEHRMANN,
6 S Howard. (See advertisement
opposite Yarns, &c.)
Clarkson Jos. & Sons, 75 N Front
Codd Edward J., 259 S Caroline
HAZLEHURST & CO., William c
Hughes
Holtzmann George, 287 W Pratt
Miller Wm. H. & Bro., President c
Fawn
Murray James & Co., 42 York
MURRAY WM., 192 N Exeter

MURRAY, CLARK. THORNTÒN & CO., 42 and 44 York n Light. (See advertisement.)
Nason James S., 26 N Howard
Norwood & Taylor, 4 E Falls av

POOLE & HUNT,

FOUNDERS AND MACHINISTS.

Office.—161 North.

Works at Woodberry, Northern Central Railroad.

Schiller Charles, 11 Swan
Wells J. & Sons, 136 Eastern av
Witney Geo. H., Uhler's al bet Charles and Hanover

Machinists' Tools.

CHASE WELLS & GEHRMANN, 6 S Howard. (See advertisement opposite Yarns, Batts, Wicks, &c.)

Magazines.

(*See* BOOKSELLERS AND PUBLISHERS ; *also* NEWSPAPERS.)

Magistrates.

(*See also* JUSTICES OF THE PEACE.)

Duncan James W., 289 S Bond *dead*
Hayward Wm. H., Fayette c St Paul *dead*
Hebden Wm. H., 176 S Broadway *dead*
Nalls B. F., 64 W Fayette
Spicer Samuel G., 72 W Fayette *dead*
Whalen Stephen, Broadway c Lancaster *dead*

Mahogany.

(*See also* LUMBER DEALERS.)

WILLIAMS J. & J. & CO.,

IMPORTERS

. AND

DEALERS

IN

MAHOGANY AND ROSEWOOD PLANK AND VENEERS,

And every description of Lumber used by Cabinetmakers, Coachmakers, Wheelwrights, &c. Also, Cabinet Hardware of all kinds.

130 S CHARLES, n CONWAY.

J. A. WILLIAMS,
W. W. KENNEDY.

Maltsters.

(*See also* BREWERS.)

DENMEAD FRANCIS, Block c W Falls av

Mantillas and Cloaks.

J. BICKERTON & CO,

183 W. BALTIMORE,

(Two doors from Light.)

IMPORTERS AND MANUFACTURERS OF CLOAKS, MANTILLAS, AND SHAWLS.

COHEN MOSES, 269 W Baltimore
Hybbeneth Mrs. M., Eutaw c Marion

E. W. JOY,

107 W. BALTIMORE.

IMPORTER AND MANUFAC-
TURER OF LADIES' CLOAKS,
SHAWLS, MANTILLAS, AND
PARASOLS.

(SENER) SCHEER M. A., 165 N
Lexington, Importer and Manufacturer of CLOAKS and MAN
TILLAS, Respectfully solicits the
attention of the Ladies and Merchants to call and examine the
Stock before purchasing elsewhere. Ladies', Children's, and
Infant's ready-made linen. All
orders promptly attended to.
Wilson Mrs. E. A., 74 Lexington.

Manufacturers' Findings.

CHASE WELLS & GEHRMANN,
6 S Howard. (See advertisement
op. Yarns, Batts, Wicks, &c.)
HASKELL J. H., 33 S Eutaw.
(See advertisement op. Leather
Dealers.)
Towner Darius F., 332 W Baltimore
Towner John F. & Co., 342 W Bal-
timore

*Masonic Jewels.

SISCO BROTHERS, 95 W Baltimore. (See advertisement.)

Marble Dealers and Work-
ers.

Gaddess Alex., Sharp c German
Henderson Wm., 33 E Pratt
LYETH ANDREW H., 562 and 564
W Baltimore
McGrane P., 120 N High
Maxwell David, Eutaw c Saratoga
Maxwell John W., 140 N Calvert.
(See advertisement.)
Morgan John C., 2 N Green

Mullan John P., 148 N Eutaw
Packie Alexander, W Lombard
Sisson Hugh, North c Monument
Steuart Jos. L. & Bro., 18 W Pratt
Vinson S. J., 106 W Lombard

JOHN WHITELAW,

STEAM STONE

AND

MARBLE WORKS,

Whf ft Washington.

All kinds of CUT STONE WORK
furnished promptly. The trade supplied with Stone in the block, or
sawed to dimensions.

Winternight H., N E c Gay and Frederick

Mathematical, Nautical, and
Philosophical Instrument
Makers.

HAGGER & BRO., 72 W Pratt
WALTHER PETER, 70 W Pratt

Merchants, Commission.

(*See also* DRY GOODS, COMMISSION;
also GROCERS, WHOLESALE; *also*
MERCHANTS, GENERAL; *also*
MERCHANTS, SHIPPING AND COM-
MISSION; *also* MERCHANTS, IM-
PORTING AND COMMISSION.)
ADAMS & DAVIDSON, 7 Com-
merce
Applegarth Wm. & Son, 37 W Pratt
BALDERSTON, WARD & CO., 14
and 16 German
Barnes Winston, 35 W Pratt
Berry N. E., 63 W Pratt
BEVAN, PHILLIPS & CO., 14
Bowly's whf
Bigham M. M., N W c Franklin and
Eutaw

BOND THOS., N W c Calvert and Pratt
BOSWELL & DORSETT, 147 W Pratt
Boyle John P. & Co., 4 Exchange pl
Brown J. F., 12 S Eutaw
Brown M. J. & W. A., 11 W Pratt
BROWNE & RONEY, 67 S Gay
BROWN ROBERT D. & CO., 2 German
BRUNE F. W. & SONS, 89 and 91 Smith's whf
BURNS & CO., 96 Light st whf
BUZBY DAVID T., 6 Exchange pl
CAMERON C. C., 50 S Howard
CAMP & SUTHERLAND, 22 Second
Carr R. H. & Bro., 69 S Charles
CASSARD F. W., 61 South
CHESNUT WM. & CO., N W c South and Pratt, WHOLESALE GROCERS and COMMISSION MERCHANTS. Wm. Chesnut, S. P. Townsend.
CHILDS, J. W., 92 Light st whf
CLARK LEWIS & CO., 184 W Baltimore
Conner James 174 W Pratt
Conway John R. & Son, 31 Cheapside
Cooke William & Sons, 82 Light st whf
COOK & SPEDDEN, 165 Light st whf, Grocers and Commission merchants
Corner James & Sons, ft Buchanan whf
Coulbourn S. D., 79 South
Cox & Brown, 10 Corn Exchange bdg
Cox and Pope, S W c Howard and Fayette
Crichton Wm. & Son, Wood Bowly's whf
DIETZ L. D. & CO., 308 W Baltimore. (See advertisement inside back cover.)
DINSMORE & KYLE, 156 Pratt st whf, GROCERS AND COMMIS-

SION MERCHANTS, dealers in Liquors, Tobacco and Cigars.
DIXON WM. T. & BRO., 306 W Baltimore
DOWELL JOHN, 55 S Calvert
DRAKELEY & FENTON, 387 W Baltimore
EASTMAN I. B. & CO., 70 Exchange pl
ELLICOTT WM. M. & SONS, 3 Spear's whf
ELLICOTT & HEWES, 67 Exchange pl
Emory Wm. H., 6 Wood
ENSEY LOT & SON, S W c Baltimore and Eutaw, COMMISSION MERCHANTS AND WHOLESALE GROCERS.
FERGUSSON & TYSON, 121 W Lombard
Gale R. W., 92 Light st whf
GARMENDIA C. G. DE, 13 Commerce
GIBNEY, HALL & CO., 90 Spear's whf
GIESE J. HENRY, 21 Spear's whf
GRANT & BRO., 30 Light st Baltimore, EDWD. B. GRANT, 16 Broadway, New York. JAMES B. GRANT, 39 Walnut st, Cincinnati, Commission Merchants for the purchase and sale of merchandise generally.
Griest Moses, 88 Light st whf
Hall C. A. & T. H., 4 Camden
Hall Thomas J. & Co., 143 Pratt
Hall & Loney, 56 Buchanan's whf
Harrison George L., 6 O'Donnell's whf
Heslen R. M., N W c Pratt and Gay
HOFFMAN H. K. & CO., 45 S Howard. (See advertisement.)
Hopkins T. & G. T., S W c Pratt and Light
HUMPHREYS & CO., 4 Light st whf
HUMRICHOUSE C. W., 20 Commerce
Hunt M. & CO., 119 Smith's whf

HYATT C. C. & R. H. & CO., 147 W Pratt (up stairs), Commission Merchants and Agents for the sale of Tobacco, Grain and Country Produce generally.

Jackson Chas. M. & Co., Smith's whf c Pratt

Jenkins & Williams, 116 Light st whf

KEENE E. A. & CO., 59½ S Charles

KELSEY & GRAY, Buchanan's whf c Pratt

Kenly & Tilghman, 18 Bowly's whf

KIDDER C., 16 Bowly's whf

KOEHLER H. & CO., 128 W Lombard

Larus J. R., 6 Spear's whf

Leatherbury John E., 6 W Pratt

LEE STEPHEN S., 50 S Gay

Levering Laurason, 3 Commerce

Levering T. W. & Sons, 55 Commerce

LEVERING & CO., 2 and 3 Commerce

Lippincott J. B., 58 Exchange pl

LUMSDEN ROBERT, 41 Cheapside

Lyles William, 84 Light st whf

McConky & Parr, 91 and 93 Bowly's whf

McDONNELL JAMES, 47 Calvert and 47 Cheapside

MACY W. D., 129 McElderry's whf

MARTIN WM. R. & CO., 72 S Calvert

MATTHEWS THOS. R. & SONS, 18 Bowly's whf

Meixsel & Grafton, 149 W Pratt

MITCHELL EDW'D & SON, 90 W Pratt

MITCHELL M. A., 2 Spear's whf

Mitchell Oliver & Co., 53 W Pratt

Murguiondo P. De, 59 S Gay

MYER JAMES & CO., 39 Cheapside

Myers John, 62 Buchanan's whf

NEALE, HARRIS & CO., 26 Commerce

Needham A. & Sons, 142 Light st whf

NYCE B. BROOKE, 1 Guilford

ORENDORF & BEAM, 325 W Baltimore c Howard

OWENS J. S. & CO., 55 W Pratt

OWENS W. H., FARMERS' and PLANTERS' AGENT, 7 Corn Exchange bdg, Wood st

PADGETT W. A. & W. W., 17 Commerce

Pawson & Bowdoin, 95 Smith's whf

Pearce Thomas, 20 Bowly's whf

Pearce & Gray, 66 Buchanan's whf

Pearson Joseph, 102 Light st whf·

PENN & DYER, Exchange pl c Commerce

Perot W. H., N W c Gray and Pratt

Perry A. A., Gray c Lombard

Phillips Samuel & Co., 97 South

PHILLIPS SAMUEL & CO.,
COMMISSION MERCHANTS,
Bowly's whf.

PICKRELL JOHN F., COMMISSION MERCHANT, 73 Smith's whf

PITT CHARLES F., 116 W Lombard

POPE F. F., 85 South

POULTNEY & MOALE, Commission merchants, 44 W Lombard

Price John S., 63 W Pratt

Purington Z. S., 39 and 41 W Pratt

Reynolds J. W. & E. & Co., 90 Light st whf

RHOADS W. & SON, c Smith's whf and Pratt

Rieman & Sons, Fayette c Howard

Ridgely David, N E c Pratt and Howard

Robertson & Briscoe, 149 W Pratt

Robins T. V. B., 5 Wood

Ross J. W. & Co., 6 Spear's whf

Sellman Alexander, 156 W Pratt and 2 Ellicott

SEEVERS A. F. & W. R., 44 South

SIMMS & TYSON, 64 S Gay, one door from Pratt, GROCERS AND COMMISSION MERCHANTS.

Slingluff C. D. & Son, 13 N Howard

SOPER SAML. J. & CO., 42 and 44 S Charles

SPALDING B. R. & CO.,

TOBACCO AND GRAIN,

18 Commerce.

STELLMANN, HINRICHS & CO., 21 Hanover

Street James B., 16 Bowly's whf

Sullivan John & Son, 2 Camden

TAYLOR JACOB H., 134 Dugan's whf

TAYLOR & GARDNER, 8 German

Townshend, French & Co., 80 Light st whf

TUBMAN B. G. & CO., 102 Light st whf

TUDOR & TOWNSEND, 110 W Lombard

Tull T. J. & Co., 6 Bowly's whf

Turner John T., 40 Ellicott

VICKERY & MUIR, W Falls av (City Block).

Warfield Henry M., 16 Spear's whf

WHEATLEY, DORSEY & CO., 88 Spear's whf

Whedbee & Dickinson, 107 South and Bowly's whf

WHITE THOMAS & CO., 112 Spear's whf

WHITEFORD JAMES, COMMISSION MERCHANT, 7 Spear's whf. Receives and Sells Flour, Whiskey, and all kinds of Country Produce. Cars full loaded come to Warehouse door, dwelling 21 N Front

Williams John S. & Bro., 52 Commerce

Wittman Wm. W., 92 Light st whf

WOODS, BRIDGES & CO., 6 and 8 Commerce

Wright Maxwell & Co., 18 Second

Merchants, General.

BELT TRUEMAN & SONS, 1 Ellicott

Dade & Dorsey, 128 S Charles

DARE, SPROSTON & CO., 95 S Charles, FLOUR, GRAIN, TOBACCO, AND GENERAL COMMISSION MERCHANTS

Delamar C. M. & Co., 96 W Lombard

Denson & Buck, 100 Light st whf

Henderson John & Co., S E c Commerce and Pratt

HUNT, CLARK & CO., MERCHANTS, 53 W Pratt. W. H. Hunt, S. R. Clark, C. W. Hunt.

Laurping Wm. & Co., 89 S Charles

Martin & Co., 101 W Lombard

Meredith Gilmor, 49 Exchange pl

PARKHURST J., Jr., & CO., 78 Bowly's whf

PARKHURST S., 76 S Bowly's whf

Payne Wm. S., 63 Pratt

PEARSON & COLEMAN, 106 W Lombard

PICKRELL JOHN F., COMMISSION MERCHANT, 73 Smith's whf

Rosenberger & Co., 68 South

SCHAEFER ADOLPHUS C., 50 South

STUART J. D. & CO., 27 Cheapside

Turner Jonathan, 25 W Pratt

Wambersie E. C., 63 S Gay

WEBB A. L. & BRO, S W c Pratt and Commerce, Rail Road Track in front of Warehouse, GENERAL COMMISSION MERCHANTS and agents for the sale of DUPONT'S POWDER AND SAFETY FUSE.

Williams John & Son, 99 Smith's whf

Merchants, Forwarding and Transportation.

FRICK E. A., 165 North
MATHEWS & FITZHUGH, 128 N Howard

Merchants, Importing and Commission.

DIETZ L. D. & CO., 308 W Baltimore. (See advertisement inside back cover.)

Merchants, Shipping and Commission.

BEVAN, PHILLIPS & CO.

SHIPPING

AND

Commission Merchants,

No. 14 Bowly's Wharf,

BALTIMORE.

Boninger Brothers, 29 S Charles
Brauns F. L. & Co., 11 Cheapside
Cheston James & Son, Cable c Patterson
FISHER RICHARD D. & CO., 54 S Gay
FITZGERALD, BOOTH & CO., 6 S Gay
FOARD & ROGERS, Shipping and Commission Merchants and agents for Baltimore and Liverpool Packets, 16 Bowly's whf.
JOSEPH O. FOARD.
C. HOWARD ROGERS.
FRANKLIN LEWIS A., 59 S Gay, GENERAL SHIPPING AND COMMISSION MERCHANTS.
GERDES, BULLING & WEHRHAME, 143 W Lombard
GEYER & WILKENS, 122 W Lombard
Gittings, Lambert & Co., 58 Buchanan's whf
Hand S. G., 101 Smith's whf
Hand Thomas J. & Co., 56 S Gay

Hodges B. M., jr., Gay c Lombard
HOWELL WM. & SON, 60 S Gay
Huffington W. W., 81 Smith's whf
HUGHES JOHN, 2 Corn Exchange. South
HURLBURT SAMUEL, 44 South

KIDDER C.,

Shipping and Commission

MERCHANT,

No. 16 Bowly's Wharf,

BALTIMORE, MD.

Kirkland, Chase & Co., 83 and 85 Smith's whf
Knox & Co., 125 Smith'a whf
LESLIE ROBERT & SON, 61 S Gay
LURMAN & CO., 31 S Charles

MATTHEWS THOMAS R. & SONS,

SHIPPING

AND

Commission Merchants,

No. 18 Bowly's Wharf,

THOMAS R. MATTHEWS.
THOMAS R. MATTHEWS, JR.
WILLIAM P. DAWSON.

MURGUIONDO P. DE, 59 S Gay
PENDERGAST CHA'S, 77 Smith's whf
Pendergast Jerome A., 77 Smith's whf
Pendergast Brothers, 77 Smith's whf
SCHUMACHER A. & CO., 9 S Charles
Small Wm. & Edward, 93 Smith's whf
Spence & Reid, 5 Spear's whf
STEWART C. MORTON, 52 S Gay

Stirling & Ahrens, 54 Buchanan's
wbf
Tesdorpf & Siebert, 63 Exchange pl
TUCKER R. & II. R., 52 S Gay
Von Kapff & Arens, 22 German
Whitridge Thomas & Co., 22 and
24 Bowly's whf
YATES J. C. & CO., N W c Gay
and Pratt

Metal Dealers.

KEEN & HAGERTY, *TIN AND
JAPAN WARE MANUFAC-
TURERS*, and DEALERS in
TIN PLATE, SHEET IRON,
&c., 37 and 39 S Calvert, c Water
and Cheapside
LISSBERGER D. & RROTHER, 8
Camden
Millar Frank H., 29 Light
Oudesluys Charles L., 57 N Gay
PARKER E. L. & CO., 83 S Charles.
(See advertisement.)
POPE GEORGE A., 75 Smith's whf.
(See advertisement.)
PRATT E. & BRO., 27 and 29 S
Charles
Schoemperg E. & Co., 126 Forrest

Military Goods.

ARMY AND NAVY GOODS COM-
MISSION HOUSE. A LARGE
ASSORTMENT at NEW YORK
PRICES. A. STOWELL, AG'T,
178 W Baltimore, bet Calvert and
St. Paul
CANFIELD, BRO. & CO., 229 W
Baltimore c Charles. (See ad-
vertisement interleaved.)
GMINDER JACOB, 10½ S Calvert,
MANUFACTURER OF MILI-
TARY ORNAMENTS, such as
SHOULDER STRAPS, BUGLES,
EAGLES, SABRES, CANNONS,
LETTERS, FIGURES, &c.; also
dealer in Military Goods gene-
rally.
McCORMICK THOS., 149 W Bal-
timore c Calvert
14

MERRILL, THOMAS & CO., 239
W Baltimore. (See advertise-
ment interleaved.)
MILNOR JOHN P., JR., & CO.,
117 W Baltimore. (See adver-
tisement interleaved.)
Rosenswig E., 344 W Baltimore
RUSSELL BENJAMIN, 293 W
Baltimore
SAUTER P. & BRO., MANUFAC-
TURERS of MILITARY ORNA-
MENTS, 20 Sharp st n German.
Constantly on hand Wreaths,
Bugles, Cross Cannon, Letters,
Figures, Straps, &c. &c.
SEEGER JACOB, 23 German
SISCO BROTHERS, 95 W Balti-
more. (See advertisement inter-
leaved.)
STOWELL A., 178 W Baltimore

Milliners.

(*See also* STRAW GOODS; *also*,
DRESSMAKERS.)

Aldridge Barbara, 861 W Balti-
more
Anderson Mrs. A., 160 Hanover
Andreae Charles, 189 S Charles
Ashe Mrs. Susan, 176 Hanover
Atkinson Mrs. M., 294 N Gay
Ballard Mrs. C., 90 Richmond
Bean Mrs. C. T. A., 66 N Pearl
Beech Mrs. Jane, 63 N Liberty
Benterwald Mrs. C., 53 Pearl
Bialla M., 47 N Howard
Bona Elizabeth, 33 Brown
Boyd R., 741 W Baltimore
Bradford Mrs. Mary, 155 W Madi-
son
Brian Mrs. M., 276 N Gay
Bright Mrs. E., 462 W Baltimore
Butler Mrs. M. A., 4 S Poppleton
Campers Mrs. M., 123 W Lexington
Caples A. M., 71 N Eutaw
Chappel A. E., 185 Hanover
Clendenen Mrs., 110 W Lexington
Coale Misses, 41 N Gay
Correll Mrs. Ann, 566 W Baltimore

Daeplitz Solomon, 114 W Lexington
Davis Mrs. L. A., 68 N Pearl
Delahays Mrs. A. E., 59 E Balti-
more
Dierker Miss E., 194 S Charles
Dobler Mrs. A. C., 163 E Baltimore
Dosch Virginia, 240 Washington
Ellender Mrs. G., 73 Forrest
Fink Mrs. E., 71 Ross
Fredrich Mary, 381 W Pratt
Gauss Mrs. R., 275 N Gay
Gardneco E. A., 161 W Lexington
Gibbons Mrs. S. A., 48 E Baltimore
Golden Miss, 76 W Lexington
Gunby C. L., 2 S Poppleton
Guyton Miss E. F., 80 N Howard
Hahn S. & E., 57 N Liberty
Hamilton Mrs. M. A., 61 N Charles
Hammer S. C., 103 N Eutaw
Harvey Miss K., 98 W Lexington
Headington Mrs. C., 187 Biddle
Henderson David, 282 N Gay
Herring Mrs. O., 80 W Baltimore
Hess Louis, 35 N Howard
Hilderbrandt Margaret, 555 W Bal-
timore
Hohlbein Mrs. Jacob, 70 N Pearl
Howard R., 41 E Baltimore
Hutchson Mrs. M. J., 38 N Schroe-
der
Ireland Mrs. E. P., 32 N Green
Jenkins Mrs. Elizabeth, 480 W Bal-
timore
Johnson Mrs. K., 269 N Gay
Jonson Miss Fanny, 82 W Lexing-
ton
Kadden Emanuel, 232 S Broadway
Kellner Miss Maria, 231 Canton av
Kennard Mrs. Susan, 223 N Gay
Kerchner Mrs. L. C., 160 W Lex-
ington
Kessler Miss Lizzie, 108 W Lexing-
ton
Kinsey Mrs. S., 171 E Baltimore
Koehlert H.. 449 W Baltimore
Korn Mrs. C., 468 W Baltimore
Kraut Hannah, 314 N Gay
Lallemand Mrs., 45 E Baltimore

Lebranthwait Miss M. A., 179 E
Baltimore
Lee Mrs. L. T., 56 W Lexington
Leonard Mrs. M., 63 N Charles
Levy Mrs. J., 199 N Gay
Lind Miss Fanny, 49 N Howard
Lipper W. B., 201 N Gay
Lisner Abraham, 83 N Gay
Lochary Mary, 3 W Baltimore
McKiragan M. A., 105 N Eutaw
McPherson Mrs. M. E., 108 W Lex-
ington
Mitchell Mrs. C. W., 63 E Baltimore
MULLER MRS. LOUIS, 110 W
Baltimore. (See advertisement of
newspapers.)
Newman Benj., 54 Centre mkt space
Noyes Mrs. J. H., 508 W Baltimore
Odendhall Madame S., 75 W Lex
ington
Oppenheim J., 249 N Gay
Owen Mrs. E. J., 47 N Howard
Parsons Mrs. R., 149 W Madison
Patrick Mrs. C., 271 E Baltimore
Pepleer Mrs. Louisa, 250 Hanover
Raith Mrs. Eliza, 69 Penna. av
Reynolds Mrs. C., 100 Pearl
Robinson Mrs. E., 98 S Broadway
Rose Mrs., 148 W Lexington
Rosenbaum J., 168 W Lexington
Sank R., 72 N Eutaw
Sarlouis Mrs. A., S E c Lexington
and Eutaw
Saville Mrs. A. J., 36 W Pratt
Schlersnei Mrs. M., 183 E Pratt
Schoenberg S. E., 183 and 219 N
Gay
Smith Mrs. L., 58 N Eutaw
Solze C. C., 68 S Sharp
Sprigg Mrs. Jane, 69 S Sharp
Stern Mrs. D., 29½ N Howard
Stork & Hamilton, 278 N Gay
SUTOR MISS S., 101 E Baltimor
Thomas Miss M. & R., 186 Madiso
avenue
Thompson Mrs. Mary, 103 W Lex
ington
Thursby Mrs. L., 130 N Gay
Timson & Allen, 47 E Baltimore

Turner Miss Mary D., 17 E Baltimore
Tyte Mrs. Ann, 57 E Baltimore
Ullman Bertha, 154 S Broadway
Wahl Mrs. A. R., 95 N Gay
Walter Mrs. Mary A., 714 W Baltimore
Wiedly Mrs. W., 336 S Charles
Williams M. A., 93 N Exeter
Winfelder Mary, 227 Eastern av
Young Mrs. L. P. Steward, 74 N Charles

Millinery Goods.

(*See also* SILK AND FANCY GOODS; *also* STRAW GOODS.)

Armstrong, Cator & Co., 237 W Baltimore

BAMBERGER E.,

247 W Baltimore bet Hanover and Charles,

Dealer in

Ribbons, Millinery Goods,

DRESS TRIMMINGS,

Hoop Skirts, Fancy Goods and General Auction Bargains.

BROWN M. & S., 243 W Baltimore bet Charles and Hanover (up stairs, IMPORTERS AND MANUFACTURERS OF PARIS FLOWERS, FEATHER HEAD ORNAMENTS AND MILLINERY GOODS.
Coburn Mrs. J., 19 N Gay
Crane Benjamin & Co., 249 W Baltimore
Goldenberg H. & Co., 51 N Howard
GOLDENBERG & WEINBERG, 163 W Baltimore, Laces and Embroideries.

Goldman Edward, 490½ W Baltimore
Grinsfelder & Bro., 25 N Howard
JORDAN & ROSE, 1 N Howard, one door North of Baltimore, Jobbers in MILLINERY GOODS, HOSIERY, HOOP SKIRTS, NOTIONS &c. *Job lots from New York Auctions received daily.*
KEYSER MOSES, Sharp c Pratt
Loewenthal Mrs. J., 27 N Howard
Mimmi Mrs., 53 Hanover
Munroe Mrs., 53 Hanover

OBERNDORF & LAUER,

243 W Baltimore, bet Charles and Hanover,

Importers and Jobbers of

RIBBONS, MILLINERY and WHITE GOODS,

Notions, Trimmings, and General Auction Bargains, and Manufacturers of

HOOP SKIRTS.

Seldner S. W., N W c Howard and Fayette
STRAUSS BROTHERS, 54 Hanover and 649 W Baltimore
Thompson Miss Maria T., 84 Hanover
Weingarten A., 166 W Lexington
Young George W., N E c Charles and Lexington

Mill Pick and Hammer Manufacturer.

Green J. J., North c Centre

Mill Stones.

Morris & Trimble, Falls av n Pratt
STARR B. F. & CO., S E c North and Centre

Millwrights.

MURRAY, CLARK, THORNTON & CO., 42 and 44 York. (See advertisement.)
Valentine & Thompson, Falls av c Lombard

Millers, Merchant.

(*See also* FLOUR AND FEED ;. *also* FLOUR MILLS.)

DYER SAMUEL, 38 Commerce, Manufacturer of Reservoir Family. Extra and Superfine Flour.
GAMBRILL C. A. & CO., 32 and 34 Commerce, Manufacturers PATAPSCO AND CHESAPEAKE FLOUR. C. A. Gambrill, R. G. Macgill, P. H. Macgill.
Price Joseph, 50 Commerce
TYSON & BROTHER, 40 Commerce, Manufacturer of Extra Super Flour and kiln-dried Corn Meal.
Wright & Canby, Commerce c Cable

Milk Dealers.

(*See also* BUTTER DEALERS.)

Burns Wm., 114 N Caroline
Mescaslin Robert, 141½ Central av
Norris Eliza, 19 Central av
Stockdale B. C., 28 N Eutaw

Mineral Waters.

(*See also* BOTTLERS.)

Egerton A. B., 99 W Baltimore
Pier G. W. & Co., Hanover c Baltimore
Randall D. A., S W c Calvert and Fayette
Thomas John, Bell Air mkt
WALSH EDMOND, 29 S Frederick

Mining Companies.

Coulter G. T., Second adj P. O.
Garden Hill Mining Co., 34 Second
Guilford, 34 Second
Lough Jos., 34 Second

North State Copper and Gold, 34 Second
Silver Hill, 34 Second
TYSON ISAAC JR. & SONS, 7 South, General Mining

Morocco Manufacturers.

(*See also* LEATHER DEALERS ; *also* HIDES AND LEATHER; *also* CURRIERS.)

Ballauf Augustus, 69 Harrison
Brandt H. & Bro., 29 Saratoga
Carrigan D., 168 N Front
Kalbfus & Locher, 8 S Calvert
Klees Henry & Sons, 15, 17 and 19 Saratoga
RAABE CHARLES, LININGS AND MOROCCO MANUFACTORY, 31 Saratoga.

Music Stores.

McCAFFREY HENRY,

Music Publisher,

205 *W Baltimore bet Charles and Light*

The largest assortment of Music in the City can be found at this Establishment.

Miller & Beacham, 10 N Charles
Schmidt T. A., 34 N Charles
Willig George, 1 N Charles (publisher)

Musical Instrument Makers.

(*See also* PIANOS.)

Boucher W., Jr., 38 E Baltimore
Eisenbrandt C. H., 78 W Baltimore
HILDEBRANDT C. H., MUSICAL INSTRUMENT MANUFACTU-

Fashionable Milliner,

110 W. Baltimore St.,

BALTIMORE.

Bonnets made and trimmed to order,

IN THE

Most Fashionable Style.

RER, 19 N Liberty op. the Liberty Engine House. Clarionets, Flutes, Fifes, &c., made to order. Repairing done at the shortest notice, and warranted in all cases.
Kreiner Geo., 267 Montgomery
Kummer August, 47 Harrison
Kummer & Schetetich, 81 N Front
SAUER FRANCIS, 98 W Baltimore and 29 Holiday (drums)
Schreiber John G., 39 Albemarle

Mustard Manufacturer.

MARKELL CHARLES, S E c Calvert and Lombard

Nail Makers.

(*See also* HARDWARE.)

AVALON NAIL WORKS, 53 Exchange pl
KEITH M. JR. & SON, 23 S Charles. (See advertisement.)
PRATT E. & BRO., 27 and 29 S Charles
Wyeth & Bro., 25 S Charles

*Nautical Instrument Manufacturers.

(*See also* MATHEMATICAL, NAUTICAL, AND PHILOSOPHICAL INSTRUMENT MAKERS.)

HAGGER & BRO., 72 W Pratt, Manufacturers and Importers of NAUTICAL AND MATHEMATICAL Instruments, *Chronometers for sale or hire. Chronometers rated by transit observations. The oldest establishment in the city.*

WALTHER PETER,

70 W Pratt c Gay.

All kinds of Nautical Goods manufactured and warranted equal to best imported, wholesale and retail.

Naval Stores.

SMITH C. HART, Agent for Geo. S. Page & Bro., 111 Smith's whf. (See advertisement.)

*Needles.

DIETZ L. D. & CO., 308 W Baltimore. (See advertisement inside back cover.)

News Agents.

(*See also* BOOKSELLERS AND PUBLISHERS.)

Crowley James, 116 W Baltimore
Reid Mrs. E., 686 W Baltimore
Taylor Henry, 111 W Baltimore

Newspapers.

American Farmer, N. B. Worthington, editor, 2 Carroll Hall
Baltimore American and Commercial Daily Advertiser, Dobbin & Fulton, proprietors, 128 W Baltimore
Baltimore Clipper, Bull & Tuttle, proprietors, 134 W Baltimore
Baltimore Price Current, Geo. U. Porter, publisher, Merchants' Exchange Reading Rooms, Second
Baltimore Republican, B. H. Richardson & Co., proprietors, 72 W Baltimore
BALTIMORE WECKER, William Schnauffer, publisher, 3 N Frederick. (See advertisement interleaved.)
Catholic Mirror, Kelly, Hedian & Piet, proprietors, 174 W Baltimore
GAZETTE, Carter & Co., publishers, 112 W Baltimore. (See advertisement interleaved.)
GERMAN CATHOLIC PEOPLE'S GAZETTE, J. & C. KREUGER, publishers, *office* 114 W Baltimore, *residence* 56 W Baltimore n Gay

German Correspondent, Frederick Raine, editor and publisher, 3 S Gay

Lutheran Observer, Storck & Neil, 160 W Baltimore

Methodist Protestant, S. W. Ewing, 12 N Gay

Rural Register, S. Sands, proprietor, 134 W Baltimore

SUN (THE), A. S. ABELL & CO., proprietors, S E c South and Baltimore. (See advertisement interleaved.)

SUNDAY TELEGRAM, Cole & Norris, publishers and proprietors, 122 W Baltimore. (See advertisement interleaved.)

Night Work.
Streib K., 141 S Wolf

Notaries Public.
(*See also* CONVEYANCERS; *also* LAWYERS.)

LATIMER JAS. B., S W c Fayette and St Paul

Murdoch Wm. F., Commercial Bdgs, 45 Gay

NORRIS THOMAS M., S W c Gay and Lombard

RICH THOMAS R., 81 SECOND (2D FLOOR), NOTARY PUBLIC

WARREN LEANDER, 61 Second, Notary Public and Marine Business attended to.

Notions.
(*See also* YANKEE NOTIONS.)

Dietz L., 151 Franklin

DIETZ L. D. & CO., 308 W Baltimore. (See advertisement inside back cover.)

HOBLITZELL JAS. H., 273 W Baltimore

JORDAN & ROSE, 1 N Howard

Levy A., 59 W Baltimore

MAYER & BROTHER, 4 N Howard

Oberndorfe, J., 288 W Baltimore

OBERNDORF & LUNER, 243 W Baltimore

TORNEY JOHN H.,
WHOLESALE AND RETAIL
Notion and Variety Store,
192 W Pratt.

Oars, Sweeps, Sculls, &c.
Delano W. H., 45½ W Pratt
Neily R. W. & Son, 115 Thames

Oil Machine.
HARDESTER & BOKEE, 321 W Baltimore n Howard. (See advertisement interleaved.)

Oil Manufacturers.
(*See also* PAINTS, OILS, &c.)

BOLTON HUGH & CO., 81 McElderry's whf

BURNS & CO., 96 Light st whf, COMMISSION MERCHANTS and Dealers in OILS, PAINTS, GROCERIES. FLOUR, LIQUORS, &c.

CAPRON & CO., 79 South

CRESCENT COAL OIL CO., of Baltimore, 62 S Gay. (See advertisement interleaved.)

Curran Charles, 210 N Gay

RICHARDSON & CO., 26 S Calvert c Mercer. (See advertisement interleaved.)

West C. & Sons, 306 W Pratt

Oil Merchants.
AMMIDON & CROMBIE, 337 W Baltimore and 52 German. (See advertisement interleaved.)

GARDNER WM. G. & CO., 1 S Liberty. (See advertisement interleaved.)

Hall A. C., 81 Smith's whf

PARKHURST J., Jr., & CO., 78 Bowly's whf, GENERAL COMMISSION MERCHANTS, and DEALERS IN OILS AND CANDLES. OILS—Sperm, Whale,

RICHARDSON & Co.
26
S, Calvert St. Cor. Mercer,
BALTIMORE.

MANUFACTURER'S OF NON PAREIL

THE PAREIL Co. 26 COAL OIL AXLE GREASE

BURNING & MACHINERY OIL'S SOAP'S & CANDLE'S

NONPAREIL

REFINED BURNING OIL,
LUBRICATING OILS,
JAPAN VARNISH,
PARAFFINE VARNISH,
AXLE AND WAGON GREASE,
CANDLES AND SOAP,
SPERM, WHALE, AND
LARD OILS.

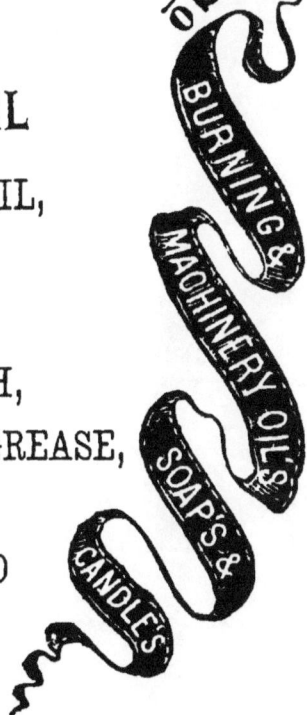

Patent, Elephant, Polar, Solar, Lard, Cod, Straits, Bank, Rosin. CANDLES — Sperm, Chemical, Imperial, Adamantine.

Oil, Coal.

AMMIDON & CROMBIE, 337 W Baltimore and 52 German. (See advertisement interleaved.)
BELVIDERE COAL OIL WORKS, CAPRON & CO., 79 South, op Corn Exchange. CRUDE PETROLEUM, REFINED PETROLEUM, DEODORIZED BENZINE, LUBRICATING OILS.
Bolton Wm. H. & Brother, 84 W Pratt
BOLTON W. B. & CO., 35 S Calvert and 26 Cheapside
BOOZ JAMES, 66 S Caroline, DEALER IN COAL OIL, COAL OIL LAMPS, WICKS, CHIMNEYS, BURNERS, &c.
Bowen & Mercer, 3 Exchange pl
CAPRON & CO., 79 South
COOK & HERRING, 7 S Charles. (See advertisement op China.)
CRESCENT COAL OIL CO. OF BALTIMORE, 62 S Gay. (See advertisement interleaved.)
Dubreuil & Co., Fremont c Lee
Ford C. W., 32 Light
GARDNER WM. G. & CO., 1 S Liberty. (See advertisement interleaved.)
Graham Wm., 379 W Pratt
HAMILL A. & W. J., 182 S Eden. (See advertisement interleaved.)
HAMILL R. W. & CO., 64 Hanover, Dealers in Carbon, Kerosene, and Coal Oils, Benzine, Machine Oil, and Axle Grease.
HAMILL & CO., 125 N Gay, Manufacturers and Dealers in Carbon, Kerosene and Coal Oils, with a large assortment of Coal and Ethereal Oil Lamps.
HARDESTER & BOKEE, 321 W

Baltimore n Howard. (See advertisement interleaved.)
JARDEN, SAMUEL, 89 Hanover. (See advertisement interleaved.)

McNEAL & JONES,

34 S Calvert,

DEALERS IN COAL OIL,

GREASING, LUBRICATING OILS,

ALCOHOL, &c.

MERRITT JOS. C. & BROS., 125 and 127 Eastern av. (See advertisement interleaved.)
NEWBOLD J. F., 2 E Baltimore, Wholesale and Retail Dealer in Kerosene and Coal Oil, and Lamps, &c.
Poultney Eugene, 136 W Pratt
RICHARDSON & CO., 26 S Calvert c Mercer. (See advertisement interleaved.)
Smith Robert M., 13 S Sharp
WALTHAM C. S., 62 N Eutaw, Dealer in Oil and Lamps of every description, Chimneys, Wicks, Shades, &c., all at the lowest prices. Lamps altered and repaired
West C. & Sons, 306 W Pratt

Oil, Coal, Retail.

Conradt Geo., High c Fayette
GRIMES CHARLES E., 63 W Lexington
Hamill J. H., S E c Franklin & Paca
Harteveld R. T., 59 Fremont
Kitner S., 227 S Broadway
Massicot Robert, 338 N Gay
Treusch Charles, 119 S Broadway
Treusch Philipiana, 236 S Broadway

Oil, Lard.

AMMIDON & CROMBIE, 337 W Baltimore and 52 German. (See advertisement interleaved.)

CHASE WELLS & GEHRMANN, 6 S Howard. (See advertisement op Yarns, Batts, Wicks, &c.)

GARDNER WM. G. & CO., 1 S Liberty. (See advertisement interleaved.)

· Oil, Linseed.

AMMIDON & CROMBIE, 337 W Baltimore, and 52 German. (See advertisement interleaved.)

GARDNER WM. G. & CO., 1 S Liberty. (See advertisement interleaved.)

RICHARDSON & CO., 26 S Calvert c Mercer. (See advertisement interleaved.)

Smith Thomas and J. M., 21 and 23 Smith's whf

Oil, Lubricating.

CRESCENT COAL OIL CO. of Baltimore, 62 S Gay. (See advertisement.)

Oil, Sperm.

CHASE WELLS & GEHRMANN, 6 S Howard. (See advertisement of Yarns, Batts, Wicks, &c.)

Oil and Candle Manufacturers.

(*See also* SOAP AND CANDLE MAKERS.)

AMMIDON & CROMBIE, 337 W Baltimore, and 52 German. (See advertisement interleaved.)

PARKHURST J., Jr., & CO., 78 Bowly's whf

RICHARDSON & CO., 26 S Calvert c Mercer. (See advertisement interleaved.)

Opticians.

(*See also* SPECTACLES.)

King. F. W. & R., 226 W Baltimore

SADTLER P. B & SONS, 212 W Baltimore, Opticians, and Importers and Dealers in Watches, Jewelry, Silver Ware, &c

Organ Builders.

Erben Henry, 7 S Eutaw

Tulley B., 7 S Eutaw

*Oyster Packers.

(*See also* HERMETICALLY SEALED CANS AND JARS.)

Baldwin Myer & Co., 90 W Falls av

Buckley & Smith, 121 Hillen

Callahan T. & D., ft Mill

FIELD A., 309 W Lombard. (See advertisement interleaved.)

Hatch C. B. & Co., 111 McElderry's whf

KENSETT THOS., 122 W Falls av and Central av c Bank

KING F. & CO., 247 W Pratt, OYSTER PACKERS. All orders for SHUCKED, SHELL, and CAN OYSTERS will be promptly attended to.

Maltby C. S., City Block n Falls av

MANN A. & CO., 38 York

NUMSEN, CARROLL & CO., 18 Light. (See advertisement interleaved.)

Pattinson T. S., 144 N Calvert

Price, Lansdale & Co., 91 and 93 McElderry's whf

Seth Robert L., 9 Albemarle

SHRIVER JOHN L. & BROS., 307 W Pratt

THOMAS S. W. & E. C., JR., 143 German. (See advertisement interleaved.)

Wentz Wm. A. & Co., S E c Pratt and Emory

Oyster Saloons.

(*See also* RESTAURANTS.)

Carter David, 853 W Baltimore

Kendall & McCart, 98 W Baltimore

Stone Edward, 1 Spring

Talbott E. K., 367 W Baltimore

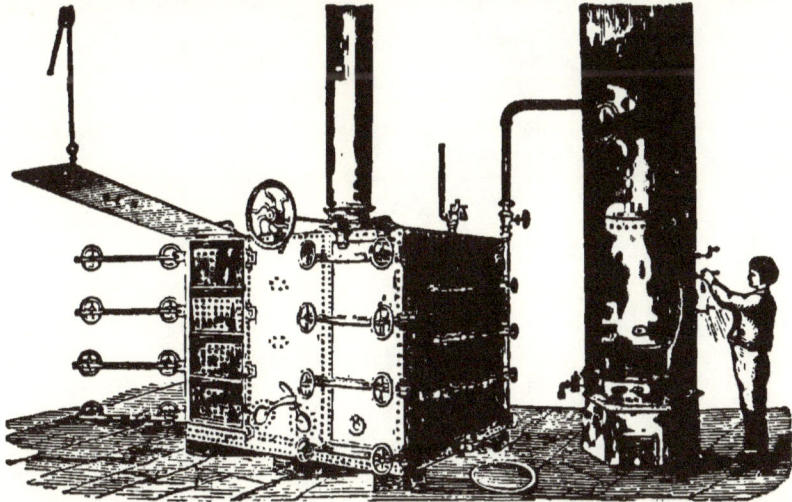

Oysters, Wholesale.

BARNES & DEBOW, WHOLE-
SALE DEALERS IN OYSTERS,
PRATT ST. WHARF.

Packets.

Australia Pioneer Line of Packets,
from New York to Melbourne
and Sidney. Thomas J. Hand
& Co., agents, 56 S Gay, up
stairs.
BALTIMORE AND LIVERPOOL.
FOARD & ROGERS, 16 Bowly's
whf
Boston Packets (Express Lines).
Thomas Whitridge & Co., 22 and
24 Bowly's whf
Boston (Regular Commercial Line).
T. R. Matthews & Son, agents, 18
Bowly's whf (Weekly).
Merchants' Line, Wilmington, N.
C., Packets. Weekly, from 117
Smith's whf. Dunnock & Weath-
erly, agents.
New Dispatch Line, from Baltimore
to Providence. Sail weekly. S.
Phillips & Co., agents, 95 South.
New Orleans (Henderson & Co. Re-
gular Line) leave twice every
month. *Office*, Pratt c Com-
merce.
New York. Semi-weekly, Wednes-
day and Saturday. Ross & Lyon,
agents, c O'Donnell's whf and
Pratt
Philadelphia Packets (Brown's
Line). Tuesday, Thursday, and
Saturday, via Canal, from 81
Smith's whf. J. W. Brown &
Son.
TAPSCOTT BROS. & CO., 68 South
Street, New York. JOHN Q. A.
HERRING, agent, 293 Baltimore
Sharp

ιcking-box Makers.

(*See* BOXMAKERS ; *also*,
CARPENTERS.)

Packing Houses.

(*See also* PROVISION DEALERS.)

Bankard & Krebs, 52 N Caroline
CASSARD G. & SON, PORK
PACKERS and HAM CURERS,
407 and 409 W Baltimore
Kimberly Brothers, 29 McKim

*Painters of Banners, Signs, and Show Cards.

EMMART & QUARTLEY, late of
SHRIVER & EMMART, at the old
sign depot, 276 W Baltimore,
nearly op Hanover

Painters—House, Sign, and Ornamental.

Anderson Wm., 2 L Sharp
ANDREWS P. F., 36 South,
HOUSE, SIGN, and ORNAMENTAL
PAINTER.
Baughman J. K., 46 N Schroeder
Benson William, 150 N Howard
Black L. W., 188 Biddle,
Blackstone W., 34 Mosher
Booth Samuel E., 72 S Eden
Bowen Thomas H., 23 German
Carr F. A., 524 W Baltimore
Christopher Milton, 3 W Pratt
Coates Robert E., 5 L Sharp
Conner R. R., 174 W Pratt
Costello Wm., 78 N Register
Crisp Elijah, 89 N Green
Dorwees E., 70 Ensor
EMMART & QUARTLEY, 276 W
Baltimore
Fonder Richard, Harrison c Gay
Frist John, 48 Marion
Gardner John M., Holiday c Fay-
ette
Georgius F., 50 N Pearl
Gillingham Sol., 69 N Fremont
GREEN GEORGE T., 51 South
House, Sign, and Ornamental
Painter.
Hall J. R., 297 S Charles
Heinz Charles, 83 N Schroeder
Hoffman E. R., 266 W Pratt

Hook Fred., 52 Clay
Howser Jacob R., Harrison c Baltimore
Huggins W., 16 N Oregon
Hulse & Davidson, 58 W Fayette
Hurst Thomas A., 91 N Schroeder
Jackell Fred., 7 New Church
Jeffreys T. R , Fayette c North
Jenkins Joseph B., 13 S Caroline
Jones Thomas, 219 W Fayette
Keams A., 88 St Paul
Keilholtz C., 11 L Sharp
Koch Henry, 145 S Wolf
Kone Andrew, 8 St Paul
Lacy M , 9 Camden la
Lambright C., 14 N High
McLean A., 2 Harrison
Maccubbin T. C., 42 North
Madden Wm. T., 142 N Calvert
Martino W., 129 Cross
Meakin Samuel, 87 Mulberry
Mohr & Landbreck, 133 Mulberry
O'Laughlin M., St Paul c Lexington
Plumber S., 200 S Charles
Redifer C. A., 24 L Sharp
Rice H. D., 13 S Caroline
Ross W. C., 6 Henrietta
Shriver & Co., 234 W Baltimore
Smith H. M. 24 S Liberty
Steidel H., 64 Penn. av

TURNER THOMAS K.,

HOUSE AND SIGN
PAINTER,

11 SOUTH STREET.

Vocke F. F., 266 Hanover
Weaver D. C., 124 N Eutaw
Weaver James, 418 W Baltimore
Welch John & Son, 146 Thames
Whelan Thos., 16 L Sharp
Wuchner G. A., 78 Albemarle
Zimmerman A., 263 Canton av

Paint Manufacturers.

MEYER AUG. G., 100 W Lombard
POPPLEIN G. & N. jr., 50 North.
(See advertisement on. Druggists.)
YOUNG GEO. W., 172 Light st whf,
Manuf tures CHROME YELLOW,
PRUSSIAN BLUES, CHINESE
BLUE, LAUNDRY and LOANGO
WASHING BLUES, WASHING
BLUES OF ALL KINDS. Colors of
all kinds, dry and ground in oil,
constantly on hand at wholesale
and retail.

Paints, Oils, &c.

BAKER, BRO. & CO., 32 and 34 S
Charles. (See advertisement.)
Ball Walter jr. & Co., 177 W Pratt
Barrett James, 89 Richmond and
240 W Lexington
BOLTON HUGH & CO., 81 McElderry's whf, have always on hand,
at their manufactory, Ethereal,
Camphene and Pine Oil, Kerosene
and Coal Oil, Copal, Japan,
B r i g h t, Black, Hatters' and
Headle Varnish, Rosin, Pitch,
Spirits of Turpentine, Paints and
Oil, Window Glass and Paint
Brushes of all kinds and sizes,
together with a variety of other
articles in their line, all of which
they offer for sale at the lowest
prices.

W. B. BOLTON & CO.,

55 S. Calvert, and 26 Cheapside,

Manufacturers and

DEALERS IN

Camphene, Ethereal and Coal Oil,
Window Glass, Paints,
Varnishes, &c.

Bolton Wm. H. & Bro., 84 W Pratt
BURNS & CO., 96 Light st whf
CANBY, GILPIN & CO., N W c
  Light and Lombard
CLOTWORTHY & FLINT, 339 W
  Baltimore
CURLEY HENRY R., 2 S Howard

WILLIAM DAVISON & CO.,

104 Lombard,

MANUFACTURERS OF

CHEMICALS,
  VARNISHES.
    PAINTS,
      WHITE LEAD, &c.

DODGE GEO. R. & CO.'S Artists'
  and Painters' Wholesale and Re-
  tail Supply Store, 42 W Baltimore
Fusselbaugh, W. H. B., 168 N Gay
HAMILL A. & W. J., 182 S Eden.
  (See advertisement op Oils.)
Harrison Mrs. D. E., 194 E Balti-
  more
Hays John, 313 N Gay
Hirshberg Henry, 31 Ensor
Holloway George, 183 Broadway
Holthaus Francis T., 10 W Balti-
  more
Holthaus & Bro., S E c Broadway
  and Thames
Hulls John, 128 N Gay
Keilholtz Otis, S E c Franklin and
  Green
King John & Son, Howard c Lex-
  ington
Loane George J., ft Cross
MEYER AUG. G., 100 W Lombard
POPPLEIN G. & N. JR., 50 North.
  (See advertisement op Druggists.)
RICHARDSON & CO., 26 S Calvert
  c Mercer. (See advertisement
  op Oil.)
RODENMAYER JOHN, 51 N Paca
SMITH J. IRWIN, 152 Pratt st
  whf

TOWNSEND T. J., 489 W Balti-
  more
VOGELER A. & CO., 5 S Libery
Watson Alexander D, 173 W Pratt
YOUNG GEO. W., 172 Light st whf

Paper Box Makers.

Bruehl & Hartel, 219 W Baltimore
Hill William, 76½ Dover
Martin William, 24 New Church
SEIDENNITZ F. W., 107 W Lom-
  bard c Light, Manufacturer of
  PLAIN AND FANCY PAPER
  BOXES, manufactures to order
  BOXES for Druggists, Perfumers,
  Hardware, Hosiery, Parasol,
  Shoe, Cord, Ink, and every other
  description of Paper Boxes
Stein I., 397 W Pratt

WEAVER LEVI,

Wholesale and Retail

PAPER BOX

MANUFACTURER,

17½ S Sharp st c German (up
  stairs), Baltimore.

L. W. has constantly on hand
and makes to order, all kinds of
Paper Boxes.

Paper Hangers.

Hallock Z., 264 N Gay
HOLLAND WILLIAM, 72 N How-
  ard
Holtz David A., 203 E Baltimore
MULLER LOUIS, 110 W Balti-
  more. (See advertisement op
  Upholsterers.)
Orth George P., 231 Eager
Thomas Philip J., 709 W Balti-
  more
Weber John, 246 Canton av
Willson Joseph E., 163 Madison av

Paper Hangings.

Albert A. & H. J., 26 N Eutaw
Apler Orlando, 608 W Baltimore
Batchellor Wallace, 167 Hanover
Beckley William, 202 N Gay
CROOK WALTER, Jr., 220 W Baltimore
DIETER & JOHNSON, 28 N Howard, one door ab Fayette, Importers and Manufacturers of Wall Papers, Gilt Shades and Venetian Blinds
Golder & Unduch, 33 Hanover
Griffith William H., 13 Gay
Hamilton Caleb, 66 N Eutaw
Happensett & Lindenberg, 2 Front
Head Washington, 702 W Baltimore
Herring O., 80 W Baltimore
Holtz Emanuel, 107 N Howard
HOWELL & BROTHERS, MANUFACTURERS and IMPORTERS OF PAPER HANGINGS, CURTAIN PAPER, WINDOW SHADES, &c., 260 W Baltimore, op Hanover
Hynson B. T., 54 N Howard
Mann Brothers, 121 Hanover
Mettee Albert R., 150 S Broadway
METTEE MILTON D., 41 N Eutaw n Lexington mkt (marble building), Dealer in Paper Hangings and Window Shades.
Moore George, 790 W Baltimore
MULLER LOUIS, 110 W Baltimore. (See advertisement op Upholsterers.)
Myers John W., 42 N Howard
Robinson John, 30 W Baltimore
Tumbleison C. H., 121 S Broadway

Paper Stock.

(*See also* JUNK DEALERS.)
Roby & Co., 118 Light st whf
SAVAGE CHARLES E., 34 and 36 Lee

Paper Warehouses.

BAKER & McCRACKEN, 120 W Lombard, Wholesale and Retail Dealers in Paper and Rags.

DUSHANE J. A.,

Commission Paper Dealer,

40 SOUTH CHARLES.

P. S. The highest Cash Price paid for Rags.

Fisher & O'Conner, 123 Hillen
Knight & Johnson, 21 S Charles

RUDOLPH WM.,

Paper and Paper Box Board

MANUFACTURER,

No. 31 S Hanover St., Baltimore,

And Dealer in Printing, Manilla, Wrapping, Straw, and all other kinds of Paper, Boards, &c.

Highest Cash Price paid for Paper, Rags, Rope, Bagging, &c.

Orders for Paper filled at short notice.

ROBINSON JAMES S.,

PAPER WAREHOUSE,

No. 5 S Charles Street,

A few doors below Baltimore St.,

BALTIMORE.

Keeps on hand and has made to order all kinds of Paper.

Purchases Rags, Ropes, Canvass, and other Mill Stock.

Wheelwright J. Mudge & Co., 14 Hanover
WILLIS & ADAMS, 12 S Charles

Patent Medicines.

Cox Mrs. M., 158 E Baltimore
DIETZ L. D. & CO., 308 W Baltimore. (See advertisement inside back cover.)

Gouley Louis, jr., 60 W Baltimore
Hance Seth S., 108 W Baltimore
LARRABEE E. & SONS, 20 S Calvert
Leonard Wm. T. & Co., 10 North
Lynch Wm., Falls Road n tollgate
Reinhardts Chas., 160 E Baltimore
Schoolfield & Co., 20 N Gay
SMITH HENRY R., 7 Mercer

Pawn Brokers.

(*See also* LOAN OFFICES.)

Dewolf S., 10 Harrison
Labe Isaac, 15 S Gay
Ulman Jacob & Benjamin F. 22 N
Gay

*Perfumers.

DIETZ L. D. & CO., 308 W Baltimore. (See advertisement inside front cover.)

Photographers.

(*See also* ARTISTS.)

BENDANN BROTHERS, 207 W
Baltimore
BRADY'S GALLERY, 159 W Baltimore. AMBROTYPES and
CARTE DE VISITES.
D'Almine George, 91 W Baltimore
Davis W., 63 E Baltimore
Dellafrank Francis, 300 N Gay
Enkle J. S., 25 W Baltimore
FISCHER & BRO., CENTRAL
PHOTOGRAPHIC GALLERY,
103 W Baltimore
Fulds S., 163 N Gay
Hinkle A., 357 W Baltimore
HOHLWEG'S VINCENT, Cards de
Visit, AMBROTYPE and PHOTOGRAPH GALLERY, 531 W
Baltimore, bet Pine and Fremont
ISRAEL & CO., 125 W Baltimore
Johnson Joseph, 73 W Baltimore
Korn Charles, 472 W Baltimore
Leach & Damp, 127 W Baltimore
McCarriar Jas., 9 W Baltimore
Massicott Wm., 234 W Lexington
Miller W. J., 256 W Pratt

15

Mottz Henry, 217 W Baltimore
Munder T., 131 W Baltimore
Perkins J. W., 211 W Baltimore
PERKINS P. LENFIELD, 99 and
207 W Baltimore. (See advertisement interleaved.)

PERRY & BRO.,

PHOTOGRAPH GALLERY,

121 W Baltimore n South

EUGENE A. PERRY, JAMES B. E.
PERRY.

Politzer I., 427 W. Baltimore
Pollock H., 155 W Baltimore
Ridgely R. D., N E c Eutaw and Lexington
Salgues & Co., 105 W Baltimore
Schaefer Henry, 671 W Baltimore
Shorey Wm. F., 87 W Baltimore
Stahn Matthew, 91 N Gay
TAYLOR G. W. H., 147 W Lexington
Troppmann H , 61 Hanover
Tucker Joseph, 466 W Baltimore
Varden & Lansdale, 220 W Baltimore
Volkmar Charles, 8 N Frederick

F. WAGNER'S

GALLERY OF

PHOTOGRAPHY,

No. 63 S W c Baltimore and Gay.

Wagner Henry, 220 Light
WALZL J. H., 213 W Baltimore n
Charles
Walzl Louis, 65 W Baltimore

WALZL'S RICHARD. GALLERY
OF PHOTOGRAPHY, 77 W
BALTIMORE

WEAVER J. W.,

AMBROTYPE & PHOTOGRAPH

Skylight Gallery,

85 W Baltimore n Tripolett's al.

Weaver Wm. H., 147 E Baltimore
Weilepp A., 19 E Baltimore
Wheedons M., 135 S Broadway
Whitehill Louis, 282 N Gay
WHITEHURST J. H., 123 W Baltimore. (See advertisement interleaved.)
Wilson Charles, 93 W Baltimore
Wunder G , 333 W Baltimore
Young J. H., 205 and 231 W Baltimore

Photographic Materials.
King Wm. & Bro.. 2 N Liberty
WALZL J. H., 213 W Baltimore n Charles, Photographic Materials of all descriptions.

Phrenologist.
Setchell J. W., 84 W Baltimore

Physicians.
(*See also* DRUGGISTS.)
Adkisson W. H. H., N E c Eutaw and Saratoga
Albers H., 237 W Pratt
Andre John R. D., 71 Aisquith
Armitage James, c Paca and Fayette
Baldwin Edwin, 124 N Exeter
Bantz Edward, 22 Columbia
Bartscher R Dr., 36 Watson
Baxley H. Willis, 185 W Fayette
Beatty George D., 116 St Paul
Benson Geo. W., 199 Hanover
Bode W., 159 W Lombard

Borck E., jr., 429 W Baltimore
Brewer G. G., 76 N Green
Brooks J. D., 163 Aisquith
Brown S., 501 W Baltimore
Buckler Thomas, 41 W Lexington
Bull B. H. D., 260 W Pratt
Butler J. H., 8 N Green
Busk Thomas M. Albemarle, dwg N E c Broadway and Pratt, one door from Lombard
Chatard F. E., Lexington c Charles
Chew S. C., 68 N Paca
Chunn J. T., 181 Madison av
Cockey E., S E c Watson and Exeter
Cox E. Gover, 92 N Paca
Creek J. W., 99 North
Cunningham C. T., Central av c Pratt
Dalrymple Wm. D., 143 N Eutaw
Damman John, 76 N Fremont
Darre Geo. H., 29 S Eutaw
Dashiell J. N., Broadway c Alice Anna
Davis W. H., 43 W Lexington
DAVIDSON DR. SAMUEL A:, 67 S Charles bet Pratt and Lombard
Dorsey E. G., 102 S Eden
Doyle J. A., 21 S Gay
Dunbar John, 151 W Lombard
Dwinelle James E., 117 S Broadway
Emory A. Walsh, 65 E Baltimore
Erich Augustus, 114 S Broadway
EVANS DR. THOS. B., OFFICE, c Ann and Alice Anna; RESIDENCE, 18 Jackson square
Fay George, 12 Eden
Fleming J. P., 122 N Green
Friese B., 220 Alice Anna
Fulton R. K., 53 S Sharp
Garch James, 70 S Sharp
Gill William F., 214 Biddle
Goldsborough Dr., 90 Pearl
Hartman John, 165 Aisquith
Hammond Milton, 284 W Lexington
Haynel A., 90 N Eutaw
HELDMANN DR. J. A., 120 N Pearl

Henkle Wm., 168 S Anna
Hess Dr. F., 61 N Front
Hillegist Edmond, 72 Ensor
Hintze F. E. B., 21 S Gay
Hoffman Daniel P., 279 W Fayette
Huet Dr. A., S E c Frederick and Fayette
Hungerford H., 639 W Lombard
Inloes Dr. H. A., 92 S Broadway
Jenkins Felix, 145 W Fayette
Johnston C., 34 Mulberry
Jones Buckler, Broadway c Gough
Keck Dr., 76 E Lombard
Kemp William M., 55 N Green
Kerstenbrock A., 192 Hanover
Keyser C. C., 170 German
Kinnemon Dr. P. S., N E c Pratt and Gough
Knight S. T., 112 N Green
Knowles Wm. G., 55 S Sharp
KROZER JOHN J. R., 273 W Lexington
Larkin W. D. F., 729 W Baltimore
Lee R. C., 260 W Pratt
Lemon A. H., 107 Gough
Liebman Augusta, 47 N Front
Linthicum J. G., 824 N Baltimore
Littell N. W., N Green c Mulberry
Lockwood Mrs. E., 236 W Lexington
McCullough J. Haines, 107 N Paca
McKew D. L., 154 S Sharp
McManus F. A., 15 N Eutaw
Mackenzie J. P., St Paul c Lexington
Mackenzie J. S., St Paul c Lexington
Mahon O. S., 138 N Exeter
Maris E. A., 68 St Paul
Martin Samuel B., 131 E Pratt
Martin Samuel H., 131 E Pratt
Merryman M., 134 W Fayette
MIDDLETON JOHN D., Homœopathic Physician, 137 W Fayette
Miller Edward A., 194 Biddle
Monmonier John F., 225 E Baltimore
Monmonier Louis, 225 E Baltimore
Montgomery J., 134 N Eutaw

Morgan G. E., 66 N Charles
Murdock T. F., 107 St Paul
Mittenberger G. W., 152 W Lombard
O'Donnell D. A., 39 N Gay
Owens Henry W., 103 W Fayette
Owens Thomas, 103 W Fayette
Painter Dr., Chiropodist, 20 E Baltimore
Panetti Jacob, 245 S Bond
PAPE E., 55 N Eutaw
Patterson J. H., 80 St Paul
Patrick Thomas L., 114 S Bond
Piek Charles, 16 Eden
Powell J. F., Pratt c Exeter
Prince Edward, 90 Thames
Reed James A., 73 E Baltimore
Rich Arthur, 39 W Lexington
Richardson C. C., 95 Columbia
Richardson S. S., 315 W Fayette
RIDER DR. WM. G., 90 Mulberry
Rieley Wm., 47 W Lexington
Roberts G. C. M., 135 and 114 Hanover
Rose John, 57 S Sharp
Sappington Thomas, 207 Franklin
Schmidt J., 94 N Eutaw
Starr H., 16 N Liberty
Stevenson James S., 134 N Exeter
Surrell W. G., 191 W Lombard
Tarr Wm. H., 63 N Front
Thomas James C., 37 S Sharp
Thomas Richard, 37 S Sharp
Thomas E. S., 172 N Exeter
Titcomb Mrs. S., 51 E Baltimore
VERDI C. S., 43 N Calvert
Wagganer A., 101 W Lexington
Wagner Chas. W., 235 S Eutaw
Waters E. G., 21 Hollins
Webster H. W., 128 S Sharp
Webster Dr. H., 179 S Charles
White J., 727 W Baltimore
Whitridge J., 49 N Charles
Whitridge Wm., 49 N Charles
Williams Wm. J., Temple c Baltimore
Wilson Dr. P. H., 72 N Green
Yeates H. P. P., 117 N Exeter

Piano Fortes.

(*See also* MUSIC STORES ; *also* MUSICAL INSTRUMENTS; *also* ORGAN BUILDERS.)

BALTIMORE PIANO FORTE MANUFACTORY, J. J. WISE & BROTHER, 31 Hanover
Benteen Fred. D., 80 W Fayette
Gaehle & Co., N E c Eutaw and Fayette
HEINEKAMP WM., PIANO MANUFACTURER, 511 W Baltimore n Pine
KNABE WM. & CO., 1, 3, 5, and 7 N Eutaw. *Warehouse*, W Baltimore. (See advertisement inside back cover.)
Newman Brother & Sons, W Lombard c S Oregon
Stieff Charles M., 7 N Liberty
THIEDE WM. F., 132 W Lexington

Picture Dealer.

(*See also* LOOKING-GLASS & PICTURE-FRAME MAKERS.)

Cooke Warren E., 278 W Baltimore

Pipes, Smoking.

Dickenson, Bowen & Co., Grandby and E Falls av
DIETZ L. D. & CO., 308 W Baltimore. (See advertisement inside back cover.)

Plane Maker.

(*See also* EDGE TOOLS.)

Ross W. C., 44 Light

Planing Mills.

(*See also* SASH, BLINDS and DOORS.)

EHRMAN & BERSCH, 210 S Howard. (See advertisement op. Box Makers.)
Maughglin & Johnson, 55 W Pratt and E Falls av, n Pratt st bridge
Robinson E. W., Caroline c Alice Anna

TURNER JOHN C., 140 Light st whf
Wilson J. W. Jr., S Eutaw c Cross

Plaster Mills.

Dunnington J. A., ft Hughes

Plaster Paris and Plaster Workers.

ROMM NICOLAS, 433 W Baltimore, Fancy Plastering and Ornaments ; also Rough Casting done to stand the weather.
Russell William, 34 S Eutaw

Plumbers.

(*See also* GAS FITTTERS.)

Brawders & Cary, 7 Eutaw House
Broderick D., 88 St Paul
Brooks E. F., 13 N Eutaw
Calaghan P. & Co., 30 N Calvert
CHAISTY EDWARD J., JR., 49 N Calvert one door from Saratoga, CALVERT PLUMBING WORKS.
Clark L. P., 44 Holiday
Connelly J. C., 85 Mulberry
Conway John W., 175 German
CONWAY JOHN W. & CO., 3 S Green
Dorry E. G., Broadway, c Pratt
Dunnett Wm., Eutaw c Madison
Fleming S. B., 148 N Eutaw
Grattan Thomas L.,78 North
Hibbitts Thomas, 519 W Baltimore
Hughes Robert, 46 St Paul
Hurder Frederick, 115 St Paul
Hunter S., 136 W Fayette
Knipp G., 131 Henrietta
Lee John W., 784 W Baltimore
Loney & Brother, 156 N Gay
Lyons A. J. & Co., 8 & 10 Holiday
McCahan Daniel, 2 Null
McCahan & Co., 161 E Pratt
McCall P. A., 326 W Pratt
McCart John, 90 St Paul
McLaughlin P., 55 E Baltimore
McLaughlin & Irwin, 202 E Pratt

E. HUBBALL,

6 and 8 N Liberty,

PLUMBER,

and dealer in

HYDRAULIC RAMS,

Double and Single Action Lift and Forcing Pumps, Water Wheels, Pen Stocks, Fire Plugs, Slide Valves, Horse Powers, Ornamental Fountains, Bath Tubs, Water Closets, Iron & Copper Boilers, Cooking Ranges, Leather Hose, Iron Pipe, Lead Pipe, Sheet Lead, Pig and Bar Lead, Block and Bar Tin, Zinc, &c. &c.

Mallalien Edward, 62 N Howard
Mannis & McAllister, Paca c Saratoga
Newton Wm. M., 64 Thames
Osler E P., 6 S Paca
Potter C. W., 34 Second
Ratican Thomas J., 1 Frederick
Reilly J. & Son, 142 N Calvert
Rock James P., Holliday c Saratoga
SINDALL & SHOREY, 2 W Pratt
Vandiker William, 323 W Fayette
Ward John, 13½ N Frederick

Pocket Book and Portmonnaie Manufacturers.

(*See also* MOROCCO CASES.)

DIETZ L. D. & CO., 308 W Baltimore. (See advertisement inside back cover.)
- Husgen James, 178½ W Baltimore
Koehlert H., 449 W Baltimore
MORITZ ALB., 541 W Baltimore, Manufacturer and Dealer in Pocket-Books, Portmonnaies, Satchels, &c.

Potteries.

Greble B., 76 Ensor
HERMAN J., 765 Light, Earthenware Pottery
Linton Wm. & Co., N W c Lexington and Pine

PERINE M. & SONS, POTTERIES AND SALESROOM 711 and 713 W Baltimore, MANUFACTURERS OF STONE and EARTHENWARE, also CIRCULAR FIRE BRICKS for Coal Stoves.

Powder.

(*See* GUNPOWDER.)

*Preserved Fruits.

(*See also* HERMETICALLY SEALED CANNED GOODS; *also* OYSTER PACKERS.)

ESTABLISHED IN 1847.

NUMSEN, CARROLL & CO.,

PRESERVERS, PICKLERS, OYSTER PACKERS, &c.,

No. 18 Light Street,

BALTIMORE.

MITCHELL JOHN T. & CO., 13 and 17 Mercer
THOMAS WM. H., 184 York n Howard

Printers.

Beach Brothers, 82 W Baltimore
BROSS EDWARD, 149 W Lombard. (See advertisement.)
Bull & Tuttle, 134 W Baltimore
Hanzsche F. A., 234 W Baltimore
Hanzsche & Co., Light c Baltimore
Hartmann Charles, 29 Holiday
Huber Henry E., 6 N Charles
Innes W. M., 164 W Baltimore
Kelly, Hedian & Piet, 174 W Baltimore
King & Bro., 162 W Baltimore
Kroth Theodore, 20 Second

15*

JAS. LUCAS & SON,

13 AND 15 S. CALVERT,

STEAM JOB

PRINTERS.

Murphy & Co., 182 W Baltimore
Polmyer Wm., S E c Gay and Baltimore
Robinson Henry A., 106 W Baltimore
ROSE J. B. & CO., 5 S Calvert n Baltimore, BOOK AND JOB PRINTERS at CASH PRICES.
Schneidereith C. W., 67 S Sharp
Sherwood & Co., 6 N Gay
Slater John Y., N W c Charles and Baltimore
SUN (THE) PRINTING OFFICE, Baltimore c South. (See advertisement op Newspapers.)
THE PRINTING JOB OFFICE, Sun Iron Building, Baltimore c South. (See advertisement op Newspapers.)
Toy J. D., 2½ St Paul c Baltimore
WANDS, W. W., CARD AND JOB PRINTER, 166 W Baltimore, next door to Adams' Express Co. Printing of all kinds executed with neatness, dispatch, and at the lowest possible rates.
Warner Wm. G., N E c Gay and Pratt
Watts W. W., 2 S Calvert
Woods John W., 202 W Baltimore
Woody W. & Son, 158 W Baltimore
Young James Sr., 114 W Baltimore

Printers, Plate.

ANDERSON JAMES M. & SON, 148 W Baltimore
Sandys Edwin, 62½ W Baltimore

Produce Commission Merchants.

(*See also* GROCERS; *also* MERCHANTS, COMMISSION.)

ARMSTRONG & MILLER, (Successors to Armstrong & Reese,) PROVISION and PRODUCE COMMISSION MERCHANTS, 4 Commerce
BAER & BRO., 143 N Howard, Produce, Provision and General Commission Merchants. Geo. H. Baer, C. W. Baer.
BERRY J. THOS., 28 S Howard, Flour, Grain and General Produce Commission Merchant
BLACKBURN C. & BRO., Eutaw c Franklin
BOND JAS. JR., 6 Hollingsworth, Fruit and Produce Dealer, and Commission Merchant
BOND THOMAS, N W c Calvert and Pratt, PRODUCE DEALER and COMMISSION MERCHANT. All consignments promptly remitted for and personally attended to.
Bond Wm., 1½ Hollingsworth
Boggs A. L. Jr., 141 N Howard
Bosley James, 203 North

BROWN & TOY,

PRODUCE

AND

GENERAL COMMISSION

MERCHANTS,

124 North.

BUZBY DAVID T.,

6 Exchange place,

COMMISSION MERCHANT

For the sale of

BUTTER, CHEESE, AND WEST-
ERN PRODUCE.

Agent for

/

Kingsford's Oswego Starch,

STICKNEY & POOR'S MUSTARD,

OAKLEY'S SOAP.

CAMERON C. C.,

50 S Howard n Pratt,

GENERAL PRODUCE

AND

Commission Merchants.

CAPRON & CO., 79 South, GEN-
ERAL PRODUCE AND PRO-
VISION COMMISSION MER-
CHANTS. F. B. Capron, Ed-
ward Snowden.

Carson Joseph & Co., 43 and 45
Light

CHESNUT WM. & Co., N W c
South and Pratt

Clark & Bro., 378 W Baltimore

Clautice Francis, 69 W Pratt

Coleman & Co., S W c Paca and
Franklin, Wholesale and Retail
Dealers in Eggs, Butter, Lard,
Tallow, Dried Fruit, Seeds, and
Country produce generally.

CORNELL & SON, 70 South

CORNER WM. H., 54 South

COX JOHN R. & POPE. S W c
Howard and Fayette, PRODUCE
AND GENERAL COMMISSION
MERCHANTS, FLOUR, GRAIN,
BUTTER, DRIED FRUITS, &c.

Crossley J. P., 31 N Green

DELCHER WM. J., Wholesale and
Retail PRODUCE DEALER IN
APPLES. POTATOES, ONIONS,
DRIED FRUITS AND CRAN-
BERRIES, and all kinds of
COUNTRY PRODUCE, 154 W
Pratt.

Dippell George, 105 Franklin

Dixon R. W. K., 116 Light st whf

DORSEY WM. A., 68 South, Commission Merchant for the sale of
Flour, Grain, Seeds, and Produce
generally.

DRAKELEY & FENTON, 387 W
Baltimore

Ebert O. A. & Co., 10 Spear's whf

EHRMAN GEO. M.,

FLOUR & PRODUCE

COMMISSION MERCHANTS,

And Dealer in

CORN MEAL, GRAIN, MILL
FEED, BALED HAY, &c.,

N W c Howard and Pratt sts.,

BALTIMORE.

ELDER SAMUEL & CO. (formerly
Thos. Black & Co.), FLOUR, PRO-
DUCE AND GENERAL COMMISSION
MERCHANTS, 32 N Howard

ELLICOTT & HEWES, 67 Ex-
change pl, COMMISSION MER-
CHANTS AND DEALERS IN
BUTTER, CHEESE, &c.

Evans Thos. H., 80 and 82 Light st
whf

FRICK E. A.,

PRODUCE AND GENERAL

COMMISSION MERCHANT,

165 North.

Gardner E. N., 149 N Howard
GIESE J. HENRY, 21 Spear's whf, Commission Merchant. Flour, Grain, &c.
Girvin J. M., 23 Spear's whf
GIST & WELLS, 126 and 128 S Eutaw op Baltimore and Ohio R. R. Depot, Railroad track in front, GENERAL PRODUCE COMMISSION MERCHANTS. John Gist, John M. Wells.
GOVER & GARDNER, 13 Commerce n Exchange pl. FLOUR, GRAIN, AND PRODUCE DEALERS AND COMMISSION MERCHANTS FOR SALE OF PRODUCE GENERALLY.
GRIFFITH R. R. Jr., 14 Commerce
GROVE FRANCIS & CO., 19 Commerce
HENGST S. & R., N E c Franklin and Paca, PRODUCE COMMISSION MERCHANTS and dealers in GROCERIES AND LIQUORS. Samuel Hengst, Reuben Hengst
Hewes John G., 366 and 368 W Pratt
HINKS C. D & CO., 257 W Lombard
HOFFMAN H. K. & CO., 45 S Howard. (See advertisement.)
Hopkins & Janney, 124 S Eutaw
HYATT C. C. & R. H. & CO., 147 W Pratt
Jones, Lewis & Co., 70 Light st whf
KAHLER ADAM, 2 S Eutaw, Flour and Produce Commission Merchant, also dealer in Corn Meal, Grain, Mill Feed, Baled Hay, &c.

Kauffelt & Buchanan, 130 North
KILBURN URI, 45 South, Produce Commission Merchant and dealer in Butter, Cheese, &c. Butter packed for exportation.
Kraft John W. & Co., 3 Cheapside
Lester James M., 165 N Howard

McCLERNAN JOHN,

PRODUCE

And

Commission Merchant,

201 North op Calvert Station.

McDANIEL JAMES L., 27 Light c Water. (See advertisement.)
McPherson John H. T., 79 South
MATHEWS & FITZHUGH, 128 N Howard, Forwarding and Commission Merchants. *References:* Jesse Slingluff, President of the Commercial & Farmers' Bank of Baltimore; Robert Y. Stokes, President of the Central Bank, Frederick, Md.
Mathews & Leitch, 4 Spear's whf
Mathiot & Co., 6 Bowly's whf
MALTBY O. E. & CO., 25 Cheapside, PRODUCE and GENERAL COMMISSION MERCHANT. BUTTER, CHEESE, DRIED SUGAR CURED HAMS, &c.
Meixsel & Grafton 149 W Pratt
Miller J. F. & Co., 83 South
Norris William E. & Co., 114 S Eutaw
NYCE B. BROOKE, 1 Guilford
ORENDORF & BEAM, 325 W Baltimore c Howard
Payne Wm. S., 63 W Pratt
Pendleton Philip P., 171 and 173 N Howard
Penrose E. G. & Co., 153 N Howard

POUMAIRAT & McCULLY, 47 and 49 Light, *COMMISSION MERCHANTS*, FOR THE SALE OF *PROVISIONS, FLOUR, GRAIN,* AND OTHER *WESTERN PRODUCE*.

QUINCY JOHN D., 61 S Gay, *PRODUCE* and *COMMISSION MERCHANT*, FOR THE SALE OF *FLOUR, HAMS,* and *WESTERN PRODUCE*. Cash advances made on Consignments.

Randolph & Latimer, 66 South

Reiman Henry & Sons, 24 N Howard

Roddy J. D. & Co., 21 Cheapside

RUFF B. F., 120 North

Sauerwein P. & Son, 101 N Howard

SHRIVER BROTHERS, *PRODUCE COMMISSION MERCHANTS*, 376 W Baltimore

SHURTZ W. D. & CO., 11 Commerce

SLAGLE C. W. & CO.,

PRODUCE

AND GENERAL

COMMISSION MERCHANTS,

118 and 133 North.

Small George, 64 and 66 North

SNIVELY ADAM, 5 Commerce, Commission Merchant and Wholesale Dealer in Cheese, Butter, Lard, Fish, and Produce generally. Butter packed for exportation.

Stine J. R. & Co., 126 North

STONEBRAKER & CO., 53 and 55 S Howard, FLOUR, PRODUCE, AND COMMISSION MERCHANTS. LIBERAL CASH ADVANCES MADE ON CONSIGNMENTS.

Thomas & Moon, 5 S Eutaw

TREGO, MORGAN & CO., 22 Commerce

TUDOR & TOWNSEND, 110 W Lombard, Produce and Commission Merchants in Flour, Grain, Seeds, Lard, Butter, Cheese, Country Produce generally.

Welsh J. B. & Son, 64 South

WHITE FRANCIS,

PRODUCE AND GENERAL

COMMISSION MERCHANT,

163 North Street.

White James & Co., 22 Commerce

White J. R. & Co., 90 Light st whf

WHITEFORD JAMES, 7 Spear's whf

WILKINS GEO. T., 55 Light, second door north of Pratt, Dealer in Flour, Grain, Mill Feed, Corn Meal, Beans, Peas, Clover and Timothy Seed, Bailed Hay and Straw.

Winchester Isaac, 124 Light st whf

Wilson James, 121 North

Woods Wm. & Co., 110 W Lombard

YOUNG GEORGE & CO.,

COMMISSION MERCHANTS,

199 North Street.

Zell P. & Sons, 147 and 149 N Howard

*Produce, Foreign.

(*See also* FRUITS, WHOLESALE ; *also*, PRODUCE COMMISSION MERCHANTS.)

BLOCK AUGUSTUS, 96 W Lombard
BLOCK EDW'D, 114 W Lombard
NOEDEL & WILHELMY, 379 W Baltimore
NORDLINGER & CO., 102 W Lombard
VOCKEY THEODORE, 132 W Lombard

Produce Dealers.

(*See also* GROCERS.)

Bond Thomas, N W c Calvert and Pratt
Bond William, 1½ Hollingsworth
Burnes Catharine, 46 Hollins mkt
CLAUTICE FRANCIS, 69 W Pratt, Wholesale and Retail Produce Dealer. Consignments promptly attended to. Shipping Orders carefully put up.
Cook Catharine, 149 Centre mkt
DOWNEY JOHN & SON, 133 Franklin
Effelk C., 139 Centre mkt
Ehrman George M., N W c Howard and Pratt
Fink & Bro., 112 N Eutaw
Friteman Selina. Bell Air mkt
Garnel George W., 158 W Pratt
GOSNELL GEORGE W., 158 W Pratt n Light op Philadelphia steamboat whf
Herron Catharine, Fell's Point mkt
HIEATZMAN J. M., 43 Hollins mkt and Lexington mkt
Hinds Elizabeth, Bell Air mkt
Hoffman Ellen, 3 Centre mkt
Ilgenfritz M S., 56 N Eutaw
JEBB HENRY, 52 St Charles
Lycock Mrs., Centre mkt
McCune A., 40 Centre mkt
Marr John G., 53 & 55 Hollins mkt
Roberts W. H., 172 Forrest

Ross James Centre mkt
Shewbrooks William & Co., 174 Light st whf
Tracy ——, Centre mkt
TRUETT OLIVER, S W c Pratt and South and N E c Pratt and Cheapside
VONEIFF G. L., 444 W Baltimore, German and French Produce.
Wallach Eliza, Bell Air mkt
Wardell S., N W c Pratt and Cheapside

Provision Dealers.

Adams J. C., 28 Second
Adams J. C. & Son. 40 Second
ARMSTRONG & MILLER, 4 Commerce
Austin T. S., 61 W Lexington
Ayers James H., Baltimore c Bond
Balz Richart, N E c Fremont and Fayette
Bankard & Krebs, 52 N Caroline
Barnes William, 498 N Gay
Basley Eliza, Centre mkt
Baverhoven Lewis, 87 Fell's Point mkt
Beech William, Centre mkt
Belts William E., 123 N Calvert
Bennett L. H., 2 Hollins mkt
Bersick M., S Poppleton c Lombard
Billman George, 1 S Poppleton
Bishop Mr., Bell Air mkt
Blacklars, Central av c Pratt
Blaney Mrs S., Lexington mkt
BUTLER & OAKFORD, PROVISION MERCHANTS AND CURERS OF THE CELEBRATED "EAGLE" BRAND FAMILY HAMS, BACON, SIDES, SHOULDERS, FAMILY HAMS, LARD, BEEF, PORK, &c., 14 Water bet Calvert and South.
Byer C., 9 S Poppleton
CAPRON & CO., 79 South, GENERAL PRODUCE AND PROVISION COMMISSION MERCHANTS. F. B. Capron, Edward Snowden.

CASSARD GEORGE. DEALER IN PROVISIONS, 46 South.
CASSARD G. & SON, 407 and 409 W Baltimore, PORK PACKERS, HAM CURERS AND DEALERS IN PROVISIONS.
CASSARD F. W., 61 South
Clark Mrs R., Mulberry c Paca
Clement A. D., 44 N Calvert
Cole John E., 859 W Baltimore
Cohen Isaac, 65 Fell's Point mkt

CORNELL & SON,

70 South, next door to the new Corn and Flour Exchange,

Commission Merchants

and Wholesale dealers in

Butter, Cheese, Lard, Grain, Seeds, Provisions & Produce of all kinds.

Wm. C. Cornell,   Noah J. Cornell.

Cost Mrs. A., 64 Fell's Point mkt
Cost Mrs. B., 148 Centre mkt
COULTER & CO., 53 and 55 Light, Commissson Merchants and Dealers in Bacon, Pork, Lard, Butter, Cheese, Fish, Salt, Provisions, and Western Produce generally.
Covert A. H., 117 Smith's whf
Crawford George C., Bell Air mkt
Doyer Ellen, 227, 229 Hanover mkt
Dryden Edward, Hanover mkt
Eaves Casper, 104 Fell's Point mkt
Eden Mark, Centre mkt
Essig Fred'k, Lexington mkt
Ferhimer Samuel, 242 Alice Anna

DRAKELEY & FENTON,

387 W Baltimore,

Corner of Paca,

Commission Merchants

For the Sale of

PROVISIONS

AND

PRODUCE.

Frankeberg E. F., 86 Fell's Point mkt
George & Jenkins, 43 South
Gill Noah, Bell Air mkt
Godman Wm. H., 61 Penn. av
Goforth G. W., Bell Air mkt
Goodbread Geo., 41 Hollins mkt
Gordon Mrs. C., Lexington mkt
Gottlieb P., 106 Jefferson
Grape J., 119 Hillen
Hack F. A., 376 W Baltimore
Haines Mrs. C., Lexington mkt
Hanson Wm. E., N W c Eager and Aisquith
Hassieg Fred., 30 and 32 Hollins mkt
Harvey J. G. & Co., 75 Exchange pl
Hessey F., 231 Centre mkt
Hewell L., 13 Brown
Hill Mrs., Fell's Point mkt
Hoffman Charles, 377 W Baltimore
Hoffman A. & Bro, Lexington mkt
Hogg Edmund, Mulberry c Charles
Homer C., Fell's Point mkt
Hughes Robert, Centre mkt
Isler George, Lexington mkt
Ison Geo., 90 Fell's Point mkt
Keller A. J., 210 Madison av
Kimberly Brothers, 51 W Pratt
Kitterick Mrs., Bell Air mkt
Legg John, Bond c Orleans

LOVE, MARTIN & CO., 5 Exchange pl
McDANIEL JAMES L., 27 Light c Water. (See advertisement.)
McGinis J., Lexington mkt
Mahlil Jacob, Lexington mkt
MALTBY O. E. & CO., 25 Cheapside
Marshall L. W., Lexington mkt and Hollins mkt
MEGEE C. T., S Caroline c Pratt
Merrieidth Mrs. Harriet, 254 Light
Myers, L., 58 N Poppleton
Miller John, Lexington mkt., and 97 Centre mkt
Miller Sapphira, Fell's Point mkt
NYCE B. BROOKE, 1 Guildford, Commission Merchant for the sale of BUTTER, CHEESE, EGGS, &c.

PEARSON & COLEMAN,

106 W LOMBARD,

Between Light and Charles,

GENERAL

𝔓𝔯𝔬𝔳𝔦𝔰𝔦𝔬𝔫 & ℭ𝔬𝔪𝔪𝔦𝔰𝔰𝔦𝔬𝔫

MERCHANTS,

Bacon, Lard, Pork, Butter, Cheese, Candles, Soap, &c., constantly on hand.

Advances made on Consignments.

POUMAIRAT & McCULLY, 47 and 49 Light
Price Mrs. Sarah, 219 and 221 Hanover mkt
Pinus E., 99 Centre mkt
REYNOLD'S ISAAC SONS, PROVISION DEALERS, 12 Balderston
Rieman Wm. J. & Co., 371 W Baltimore
Rieman & Sons, Fayette c Howard
Rodgers Anna, Hanover mkt
Ruckle Geo. W., N E c Gay and Monument

Ruil Mrs. Anna, Lexington mkt
Schelplake Miss C., Lexington m ·
Schmitt John, Franklin c Pine
Scroggin & Turner, Centre mkt
Servering John R., Fell's Point m...
Shaney Margaret, Centre mkt
Shimever John, 71 Fell's Point mkt
Slater James, 79 Gough
Smith Margaret, Centre mkt
SMITH & NICODEMUS, PROVISION MERCHANTS, 381 W P timore. S. R. Smith, J. C. Nicdemus.
Snyder J. H., Lexington mkt
Snyder John, 39 Fell's Point mkt
Snyder Mrs. M., Lexington mkt
Snyder Wm., Lexington mkt
Spangler F., 158 Orleans
Stevens H. H., Bell Air mkt
Streobel Charles, 284 Montgomery
SWEENEY & HARRIS, PROVISION DEALERS and PACKERS FOR HOME AND FOREIGN MARKETS, 205 W Lexington bet Paca and Green. HAMS, BACON, LARD, SMOKED BEEF, Tongues, &c. P. Sweeney, G. W. Harris.
Taylor E. J., 52 Centre
VOSBURGH & CO., 72 South and 8 Bowly's whf
White A. D., Hanover mkt
WIEST F. A., 903 W Baltimore
Wieneke John G., 43 Fell's Point mkt
Wust Henry, 61 Ross
Wust John P., 114 Ross

Publishers.

(See BOOKSELLERS AND PUBLISHERS.)

Pump Makers.

(See also BLOCK AND PUMP MAKERS.)

Aler & Sisselberger, 43 N Paca
HUBBALL E., 6 and 8 N Liberty
Sisselberger Andrew, 159 Penn. av

NORTHERN
1863. CENTRAL RAILWAY. 1864.

THE
SHORT ROUTE TO THE NORTH, WEST, NORTHWEST AND SOUTHWEST.

Equipments and facilities for the safe, speedy, and comfortable transportation of passengers unsurpassed by any route in the country.

TWO THROUGH TRAINS DAILY

for BUFFALO, NIAGARA FALLS, ROCHESTER, SYRACUSE, ELMIRA, and all points in Northern, Central, and Western New York. Mail Train in the A. M. and Express Train in the P. M. make close connections at Harrisburg with the Pennsylvania Central Railroad for all points in the Great West.

THROUGH TICKETS

to CLEVELAND, DETROIT, CHICAGO, ST. PAUL, COLUMBUS, INDIANAPOLIS, ST. LOUIS, DAYTON, CINCINNATI, CAIRO, LOUISVILLE, and all other principal points, and baggage checked through to destination.

COMMUTATION TICKETS,

good for thirty trips between any two points at about two cents per mile.

SEASON TICKETS,

good for three, six, nine, or twelve months, at very low rates, for the accommodation of persons living out of town, or located on or near the line of the road.

FREIGHT.

By this route freights of all description can be forwarded to and from any point on the Railroads of Ohio, Kentucky, Indiana, Illinois, Wisconsin, Iowa, and Missouri; also to Buffalo, Rochester, and all points in Central and Western New York. Merchants entrusting the transportation of freights to this Company can rely on its speedy transit.

For freight contracts or shipping directions apply to or address the Agents of the Company.

WM. BROWN, Agent for Western Freight,
80 North St., Baltimore, Md.

J. M. DRILL, Agent for Northern Freight,
Calvert Station, Baltimore.

ED. S. YOUNG,
General Freight and Passenger Agent.

PHILADELPHIA,
WILMINGTON, & BALTIMORE RAILROAD.
THE ONLY DIRECT ROUTE BETWEEN
WASHINGTON AND NEW YORK.

On and after Monday, April 27th, 1863, Passenger trains will leave as follows :—

TRAINS FOR PHILADELPHIA.

Leave Baltimore at 8.40 A. M. and 10.10 A. M. (Express), 1.10 P. M. (Express), 5.35 P. M., and 8 35 P. M. (Express).
Wilmington at 6.45 A. M., 9.00, and 12.08 P. M., 1.57, 4.10, 6.00, 9.10, and 11.30 P. M.
Salisbury at 2.15 P. M.
Milford at 4.55 P. M.
Dover at 6.30 A. M. and 6.10 P M.
New Castle at 8.30 A. M. and 8.30 P. M.
Chester at 7.40, 9.43 A. M., 12.46, 4.40, 6.46, and 9.58 P. M
Leave Baltimore for Salisbury and intermediate stations at 5.35 and 8.35 P. M.
Leave Baltimore for Dover and intermediate stations at 1.10 P. M.

TRAINS FOR BALTIMORE.

Leave Philadelphia at 4.00 A. M. (Express, Mondays excepted), 8.15 A. M., 11.35 A. M. (Express), and 3 P. M. and 12.00 M., night.
Chester at 8.15 A. M., 11.35 A. M., 1.15 P. M., 3, 4.30, and 11.00 P. M.
Wilmington at 4.00 A. M. (Mondays excepted). 8.15 A. M., 11.35 A. M., 1.15 P. M., 3, 4.30, and 11.00 P. M.
New Castle at 8.15 A. M. and 4.30 P. M.
Dover at 8.15 A. M. and 4.30 P. M.
Milford at 8.15 A. M.
Salisbury at 8.15 A. M.

TRAINS FOR BALTIMORE.

Leave Chester at 8.51 A. M., 12.08 and 3.36 P. M.
Wilmington at 5.00, 9.30 A. M., 12.35 P. M., 4.10 P. M., and 1.00 P. M.

Freight train, with Passenger Car attached, will run as follows :—
Leave Philadelphia for Perryville and intermediate places at 6.30 P. M.
Leave Wilmington for Perryville and intermediate places at 8.30 P. M.
Leave Wilmington for Philadelphia and intermediate places at 4 P. M.

SUNDAYS ONLY.

4 A. M. and 12 M., from Philadelphia to Baltimore.
11 A. M. and 12 M., from Philadelphia to Wilmington
7 P. M. and 11.30 P. M., from Wilmington to Philadelphia.

WILLIAM STEARNS, Superintendent.

Rag Dealers.

(See PAPER STOCK; also
JUNK DEALERS.)

Rail Road, City.

City Passenger R. R., Eutaw c Baltimore. Henry Tyson, *Pres.*;
Thos. S. Phillips, *Treas.*

Rail Road Companies.

Baltimore and Ohio R. R., Camden
st, station bet Howard and Eutaw.
Wm. P. Smith, Superintendent.
NORTHERN CENTRAL R.R., station Culvert st. E. S. YOUNG,
GENERAL FREIGHT AND PASSENGER AGENT (See advertisement
interleaved.)
PHILADELPHIA, WILMINGTON & BALTIMORE R. R., President st. (See advertisement
interleaved.)

Refrigerators.

Evans P., 494 W Pratt

Reading Rooms.

(*See also* LIBRARIES.)

Merchants' Exchange Reading
Rooms, New Exchange bdgs adj
Post Office, have on file papers
from all parts of the world. A
record is kept of all the marine
news of interest to Baltimore.
Subscription $10 per annum.
National Union, 131 W Baltimore.
A. Aitkin, *Supt.*

Regalia Manufacturers.

(*See* MASONIC JEWELS.)

Restaurants.

(*See also* DINING ROOMS; *also* TAVERNS; *also* LAGER BEER SALOONS; *also* HOTELS.)

Ackerman Peter, 94½ S Charles
Ameys Joseph H., 1 N Green
Anderson John, 23 Thames

16

Allen W. M., 8 Light
Ballauf A., 71 Harrison
Barker W. G., 3 Holiday
BARTZ DANIEL, RESTAURANT
AND DINING SALOON, 28 Light
Bauernschmidt G. & Co., 281 W
Pratt
BEACON LIGHT, Henry J. Luck,
Proprietor, 98 W Pratt
Becker Conrad, 310 W Pratt
Becker Henry, 102 N Gay
Beckers Nicholas, President c Eastern avenue
Berry E., 53 Thames
Biebl Joseph M., 24 Centre mkt
space
Blake John, 1 North
Blauch Jeremiah, 679 W Baltimore
Boylan Geo., 198 Hollins
Brandt Henry, Forrest c Monument
Brooks Christopher, 138 S Eutaw
Brown Andrew, 169 S Broadway
Brown J., 85 Thames
Bubert John D., 100 S Charles
Bucksti William, 26 Second
Bulack Jacob, 65 W Pratt
Bunch John, 36 President
Burgandy John, 13 Dover
Burris John, 7 Market space
Byrne Hugh, 70 President
Campbell Wm. H., 9 Frederick
Canavan James, 162 N Calvert
CARROLL P. H., 114 S Howard,
Restaurant and Dealer in Wines,
&c.
Cassiday P., 19 W Lombard
Childs Mrs. M. N., 67 President
Childes & Thompson, 17 E Pratt
Clackner M. T., 11 McClellan's al
Cloud Charles F., 415 W Baltimore
Coakley A. J., 122 N Gay
Coath John, 19 Fish market space
Collins Mrs. Jas. E., 75 Thames
Connelly J. C., 82 S Howard
Connelly M., 121 S Howard
Connolly Michael, Fulton c Frederick
Connolly Mrs. Ann, 9 Fish market
space

CHARLES STREET

GREEN HOUSE,

KEPT BY

PETER ARNOLD,

58 S. CHARLES STREET,

BALTIMORE, Md.

TRAVELLERS AND BOARDERS

Will always find

Good Meals and Refreshments, and the best Accomodations.

Connor John, 5 Cheapside
Conway Patrick, 3 Market space
Copperman J. E., 74 N Gay

COTTAGE SALOON,

HIGH STREET, bet BALTIMORE

and FAYETTE.

CHRIS. SHAW,

PROPRIETOR.

Creighton M., 39 Market space
Crone Edward, 75 N Gay
Crone Wm. C., 15 N High
Daily Eugene, 1 Wine
Daly James, 65 South
Dawson J., 104 S Howard
Diffenbaugh John, 866 W Baltimore
Doberer John, 199 W Lexington
Donahoo J. F., 42 W Fayette
Doyle J. M., S E c Charles and Lombard
Eich Henry, 89 N Gay

ELLINGER'S JOHN F., "HERE IT IS" RESTAURANT, S E c Lee and Light. OYSTERS AND REFRESHMENTS served in every style at the shortest notice. WINES AND LIQUORS of all kinds and choice CIGARS constantly on hand.
Ellinger William, 38 W Fayette
EXCHANGE RESTAURANT, adj Post Office, entrance on Second and Lombard
Fallon Peter, 216 W Lexington
Feffel Joseph jr., Baltimore c Republican
FICK WM. G., 57 Thames
Files Joseph, 2 Hawk
Fisher Charles T., 59 Spring
Fitzgerald John, 67 Thames
FITZPATRICK JOHN, Vauxhall Restaurant, 223 Light
Fleming Wm., 38 Centre market space
Flisehman John, 17 Dover
Foltz G. & H. Ehlen, 5 Lovely la
Frank C., 45 Brown
Gabrio Henry, 29 N Green
Garrett W. A., 245 S Broadway
Geekie Charles W., 123 W Baltimore
Germann Jacob K., 248 S Broadway
GILMOUR'S SALOON, 125 W Baltimore. (See advertisement.)
Greaf C., 95 Hanover
Green Captain William, 156 Light st whf
Green William P., 48 E Lombard
Green T., 56 Thames
Gublinghorst J. G., 66 Light
Haffecke Charles, 5 South
Hannibal Henry, 51 Harrison
Hannon Barney, 29 Market space
Harker J. V., 101 Greenmount av
Harrington Joshua, 21 Ensor
HEIKER GEORGE, 29 Brown
Helmlings Harry, 62 W Fayette

HEMPEL FREDERICK,
NATIONAL HALL RESTAURANT,
10 N Frederick.

Herzog Thomas, 308 W Pratt
Hesse Christian 267 W Pratt
HEWITT FRANKLIN W., 257 N
Gay
Hocet Andrews, W Pratt c Poppleton
Hofana William, Bond c Lancaster
Hoffman Michael, 152 Franklin
HOFFMANN MRS. J., 55 Market
space
Holdefer Henry, 32 E Pratt
Holliday Thomas, 136 E Lombard
Homberg Henry, 59 N Gay
Hooper Wm., 22 W Lombard
Houseman A. C., 413 W Baltimore
Houmhunsen ——, 211 Montgomery
HUMPHREY HENRY, N E c Sharp
and Camden
Hunter Alexander, 63 Thames
Hurra Albert J., N E c Gay and
Central av
Imhofe John, 40 Second
Johnson Edward, Falls av c Eastern
av
Johnson Richard, 215 W Lexington
Kaupp John, W Fayette
Keach Cyril W., 26 German
Keener J., 71 S Charles
Keilbar Henry, 323 S Bond
Kelly James, 7 Dover
KELLY & SHAW, "Ruby Saloon,"
2 South
Kernan U., 19 E Baltimore
Keyse George, Light c Baltimore
Kid Joshua, 128½ Forrest
KIERNEN B., "Shade's Restaurant," 31 South
Kinsley Barney, 181 W Lexington
KLMEFELTE JESSE, 37 W Fayette
Kooke Herman, 273 S Bond
Koors Wm., 36 W Fayette
Kreutzer George, 69 N Gay
Kunsman W. H., 126 Light st whf
Laib John, 208 W Lexington

Lamott N., 41 Penn. av
Langley Edward, 143 E Pratt
Lapsley Mrs., 78 Thames
Ledley Wm. M., 150 W Fayette
Lee Thomas, 31 W Fayette
Lenz Alexander, 84 S Howard
Leonard John, 33 Market space
Link Harmon, Bond c Pratt
LOTZ JACOB, 6 N Frederick
Love Margaret, Fell's Point mkt
Lowery John, 105 Fell's Point mkt
LUDWIG JOHN, 47 W Fayette
Lutts John F., 69 Market space
Lutz Michael, 335 S Bond
Lutzs Ellen, 13 Second
Lyons John, Centre c St Paul
Lyons T., 52 Thames
McAbee John T., 116 Franklin
McCabe James, 186 W Lexington
McCLASKEY ALFRED, 3 Powman
McCormick P., S W c Eutaw and
Mulberry
McDonald Donald, 47 N Paca
McDONALD'S L., TRAVELLER'S
HOME, 62 President, 1 door from
Eastern av, n Philadelphia Depot.
Is prepared to furnish persons
with Meals and Lodging. Board
ing by the Day or Week on reasonable Terms.
McDonell Jas., 54 S Howard
McDowell Thomas, 154 N Gay
McGurk James, 1 Bank la
McMah John, 59 Market space
McMann M. L., 93 W Lombard
McTange Peter, 10 W Water
Mann C. H., 50 W Fayette
Mann Fletcher John, Fayette c
Harrison
Mankin Henry, 65 Thames
Mason & Kelly, 10 S Sharp
Miles Charles, 5 Market space
Miles Charles A., 66 W Fayette
MINCE JOSEPH, 48 W Fayette
Montahenke Henry, 25 Light
MONTGOMERY MRS. H. C., 157
and 159 W Madison

Moon Adam, N W c Gay and Broadway

Morris William, 31 W Lombard

Morten Mary. 5 L Paca

MUHLS LEWIS B., 187 Lexington

MULLER FRANCIS, 33 W Fayette

MULLEY JOSHUA, 37 W Fayette

Mullin John, 188 W Lexington

Mullin T., 14 South

Murphy H., 3 N Calvert

Myers U. M., 258 S Broadway

Mysall John, Light c Lombard

Nevins John, 18 S Gay

NEW YORK EATING HOUSE, PATRICK BEERE, Proprietor, 63 President n Philadelphia Depot. BOARDING BY DAY OR WEEK.

Nicholson Andrew, 6 N Green

Oban Patrick, 211 Light

O'Day Mrs. B., 106 S Howard

O'Neal L., 107 W Lombard

Ott Louis, 8 Centre mkt space

OUR HOUSE, by BERTHA JONES, Restaurant and Eating Saloon, 47 Lombard c Marsh mkt space

Owen George, 16 W Lombard

PARKER J., 4 N Liberty

Paul C. L., 124 S Howard

PEIRSON J. T., N E c Holiday and Fayette. Best quality Wines and Liquors. Meals at all hours.

Perry E. W., 9 Camden

Peters P. F., 101 Thames

Pierson Joseph T., S W c Holiday and Fayette

PIQUETT JOHN T., 502 W Pratt

PRESTON PATRICK, 72 N Calvert c Pleasant

Purdy G. W., 136 and 138 N Calvert

Raab Emile, 59 Chesnut

Reilly P., 78 W Fayette

Rielly Joseph, 11 South

Rooney M. D., 29 W Pratt

Rose Wm. H., 24 N Gay

Rossdeusher John, 49 Columbia

Rowlett Richard, 5 N High

Russell Wm., 20 Mercer

RUTHEFORD JOSEPH, Proprietor, 128 W Baltimore. (See advertisement.)

SCHAPPERLES F., S W c Gay and Harrison

SCHAUB JOHN G., 259 S Broadway

Scheppach J. M., 171 W Pratt

Schoelfield P., 218 N Gay

SCHOFIELD & SALOM'S SOUTH STREET HOUSE, 58 South. The subscribers having taken this old and favorably known stand, are prepared to serve up the delicacies of the season to their friends. We have a few bottles left of those Old Wines (Sherry and Madeira) purchased at the sale of the effects of the late Solomon B. Davies, to which we call particular attention, as they are guaranteed genuine, and among the oldest Wines in the city. There is in connection with the House a SPLENDID BOWLING SALOON.

SCHIERBAUM AUGUSTUS, 74 S Charles

Schulten J. H., 99 Thames

Seymour Wm. H., 118 N Gay

Shaffer Joseph, S Green c Baltimore

SHAMBURG JOHN, 43 S Liberty, RESTAURANT AND OYSTER SALOON.

Shamburg Wm., 160 W Lombard

Shamburg Wm. & Co., 29 S Liberty

Shee Thos. F., 19 Pleasant

Sherman Chas., 21 E Monument

Shuckman Conrad, 254 Montgomery

Smith George, 74 S Eutaw

Smith Mrs. Henry, 54 Thames

Smith Thos. H., 355 S Bond

Snyder D., 41 German

Spangler Wm., 22 W Lombard

Spiegel Charles, 58 Centre mkt space

STAG HALL, 59 Hanover n Pratt, JOHN J. PETER, Proprietor.

STEHL HENRY, 193 W Lexingten

Strasberger Charles, 33 N Gay

Swearer Benj., 3 S Eden

Swearer Charles, 1 Grand

SWOPE JOHN C., 15 Dover
Tate Robert, Dover c Camden la
Thompson F. J., 341 S Bond
THOMPSON GEO. F., 11 Mkt space
Tibbels Thomas, 183 W Lexington
Torborg Mrs. Anna, Lexington c
Park
Towsend T., N E c Baltimore and
Eden
Uhlenburg George, 66 German
VAUXHALL RESTAURANT,
JOHN FITZPATRICK, PROPRI-
ETOR, 223 Light
Vine Mrs. Ann, 9 Neighbor
Wallenwein George, 59 Thames
Wallis A., 152 W Fayette
Walter John, 85 Harrison
Ward Laurence, Plowman c Front
Ward Owen, 16 Fish mkt space
Waters Ferdinand, 203 W Lexing-
ton
Webb D. C., 89 Thames
Weber Louis M., 20 Centre mkt
space
Weber Wm. G., 131 N Howard
Weller Philip, 23 Centre
Wickham John, 5 Dover
Wilhelm Wallice, 14 Fish mkt space
Windwart H., 127 W Fayette
Young Rob., 218 S Front
Zimmer Frederick, 211 W Lexington
ZOUAVE HOUSE, late OLIVE'S
HOTEL, John Olive, proprietor,
94 S Charles, bet Camden and
Pratt

Roofing.

GEISS NICHOLAS, 112 S Howard
(metallic)
LINDALL & SHOREY, 2 W Pratt
(metallic)
Rothrock & Peacock, 10 Eutaw
House (metallic)
SHANAMAN JOHN, 30 and 32 N
Eutaw (metallic)
SMITH C. HART, agent for George
S. Page & Brother, 111 Smith's
whf (cement). (See advertise-
ment.)

Saddle and Harness Ma-
kers.

(*See also* TRUNK MAKERS.)

ARMSTRONG & CRAIG, 118 W
Fayette
Beveridge John, 279 W Pratt
Boyd J. H., 48 German
Bregel Henry, 48 Greenmount av
Briding E. W., 183 W Pratt
Collmus Solomon, 123 N High
Creamer Alexander, 317 Aisquith
Daily Thomas, 41 South
Day Alfred G., 421 W Baltimore
Edeler George, 350 W Pratt
Eigenraug F., 142 Forrest
FARQUHARSON F. L., 17 S Cal-
vert
Gaither Greenbray, 175 W Pratt
Getz John, 176 N Gay
GILL LUTHER, 336 W Pratt
Goepfert Christian, 251 S Bond
HAMMOND JOHN D., *SADDLE,
HARNESS, TRUNK AND
COLLAR MANUFACTU-
RER*, WHOLESALE AND RETAIL,
348 W Baltimore, 3 doors below
the Eutaw House.
Herman William 392 W Pratt
Hoffman Joseph E., Fremont c Co-
lumbia
Hunt Samuel, 202 W Baltimore
Jacobs John F., 31 Market space
Jameson John W. & Co., 90 N How-
ard
Jenkins M. W. & Co., 10 South
Jurgens J. C., 45 N Paca
Klug Joseph A., 426 Light
Laporte Arnold, 576 W Baltimore
Lerch Augustus, agent, 155 and 157
W Pratt
Lowenstein George, 301 Alice Anna
Mackenzie Thomas and Sons, 222
W Baltimore
MERCER LUTHER O., MANUFAC-
TURER OF *SADDLES, HAR-
NESS, TRUNKS* AND *COL-
LARS*, WHOLESALE AND RE-
TAIL, 334 W Baltimore.

LAWSON ROBERT,

277 W Baltimore n Sharp,

SADDLE, TRUNK,

HARNESS AND COLLAR

MANUFACTORY,

Wholesale and Retail; Also

MILITARY WORK

of every description.

Miller Charles, 229 Alice Anna
O'BRIEN JAMES (successor to Richard Lilly), 7 S Calvert, Saddle, Harness and Trunk maker.
Platt William, 9 Light
Reister A. H., 131 Hillen
Rice John, 59 Ross
RICHARDS JOHN P. & CO., 55 German
Ruckle J. N., S E c Pratt and Howard
Sawl J. W., 265 W Baltimore
SCHULTZ GEO. J., 55 N German n Eutaw, manufacturer of Harness, Saddles and Collars. Repairing promptly attended to.
Sendelbach J., 27 W Lombard
Simson Isaac, 34 Harrison
Steinbach C., 344 W Pratt
Stevens Joseph, 36 North
Thumm J. F., 149 Franklin
Toner John, 127 Franklin
Wilkins B., 6 Light
Winterling John, 414 Canton av

Saddle Tree Maker.

Oyster Jacob, 113 S Caroline

Saddlery Hardware.

Campbell A., 13 Light
JENKINS EDW. & SONS, 180 W Baltimore, Importers of, and Dealers in SADDLERY AND COACH

MATERIALS. Austin Jenkins, Alfred Jenkins.
Keenan, McNally & Co., 18 S Charles

ALLEN PAINE,

IMPORTER

AND

DEALER IN

Saddlery, Hardware and Coach Trimmings.

2 S. Liberty.

Safes.

L. H. MILLER,

255 W. BALTIMORE,

FIRE AND BURGLAR PROOF SAFES, THE BEST IN USE.

SPEAR BROTHERS, Agent for the sale of Fire Proof Safes, 41 S Charles. (See advertisement.)

Sail Makers.

ADKISSON WM. & CO., SAIL MAKERS, S W c Camden and Light st whf and 98 Light st whf
BROWN J. C., SAIL MAKER, 107 (FOOT OF) SOUTH
Buck B. C., 85 Smith's whf
Carter Wm. H., 111 Smith's whf.
Clark Thomas & Son, 128 Dugan's whf
Farland John F., 81 Smith's whf

HAMBLETON THOS. B., 6 Bowly's whf, SAIL, AWNING AND TENT MAKER
LAMDIN & WADDY, SAIL MAKERS, S W c FREDERICK and PRATT
LOANE J. W., 2 Bowly's whf (next door to c of Pratt), PRACTICAL SAIL MAKER
Milbourne, Adams & McGee, 4 Light st whf
Miskiman Thos., 130 Dugan's whf
Mitchell & McAllister, 92 Light st whf
Shaw & Byrn, 123 McElderry's whf
Tall W., 73 Smith's whf
Travers J. H., 2 Spear's whf
Tregoe Geo. W., 77 Smith's whf
WAKE JOHN C., SAIL MAKER, 103 McELDERRY'S WHARF, East Side of new Dock

Sailing Packets.

(*See* PACKETS.)

Salt Dealer.

GREACEN JOHN, Salt Dealer, 83 Exchange

Sand and Emery Paper.

POPPLEIN G. & N. JR., 50 North. (See advertisement.)

Sash, Blind and Door Makers.

(*See also* CARPENTERS AND BUILDERS.)

Maughlin & Johnson, East Falls av n Pratt st and 55 W Pratt
Stevens Geo. O. & Co., 47 W Pratt

Saw Makers.

(*See also* FILE MAKERS.)

BROWN HENRY C. & CO., Uhler's al one door from Charles bet Lombard and Pratt. (See advertisement.)
Toland Wm., 85 N Front

Saw Mills.

EHRMAN & BERSCH, 210 S Hanover. (See advertisement.)
Ives Wm. H., 11 Frederick
SHORT JOHN H., Uhler's al bet Charles and Hanover
THOMAS JOSEPH & SON, Park c Clay
Tyler G. K. & Co., *office* Pratt c Patterson, *mills* Boston st, Harris Creek, Canton

Scale Makers.

Fairbanks & Co., 246 W Baltimore
Marden Jesse, S E c Charles and Balderston
Murdock Richard, 46 S Charles
SPEAR BROTHERS, agents for the sale of Platform .and Counter Scales, 41 S Charles. (See advertisement.)

Schools.

(*See* APPENDIX FOR PUBLIC SCHOOLS.)

Baltimore Female College, 53 St Paul
Fosters Misses, 56 N Green
Guinzburg Rev. Dr., 111 W Fayette
Knapp Frederick, 19 S Gay
Langs George A., N E c Lombard and Albemarle
McDermot Jane (Ladies'), 13 S Broadway
Morrison Horace, 144 W Fayette
Newton Academy, Thos. Lester, Principal, 798 W Baltimore
Parsons E. (Commercial), 14 N Paca
Stevenson Mrs. M., 29 Pine
Young Ladies' Collegiate Institute, Hamilton Terrace, 241 N Eutaw

Scourers.

(*See also* DYERS.)

Cowan A., 111½ W Lexington
Emory John, 203 Biddle
FISHER & BROTHER, FRENCH STEAM SCOURERS, *Offices*, 139 W Fayette and 55 W Baltimore

Herman Mrs. J., 64 N Eutaw
Keating John, 71 Richmond
Keller J., 95 W Lexington
Schroede S. & Co., 277 E Baltimore
STRASBURGER JOHN, 51 Harrison

Seamstresses.

(*See also* DRESS MAKERS.)

Brown Mrs. Hester, 205 Biddle
Sitler Miss Sarah, 87 N Green

Second-Hand Stores.

Bedgars August, 58 Penn. av
Birch Charles, East c Front
Bloxham John, 56 Harrison
Blum Daniel, 76 Harrison
Brhe Simon, 45 Penn. av
Clark James, 224 W Lexington
Cohens G., 6 and 8 Harrison
Collins Wm. C., 39 Harrison
Constam Aaron, 173 S Caroline
Cooper Wm., 14 Chesnut
Derna Israel, 295 S Bond
Dietrich Henry, 53 Harrison
Dietrich Leonhardt, 74½ Harrison
Ehrlich Jacob, 245 N Gay
Elias Joseph, 55 Penn. av
Eltzers Louis, 27 Harrison
Emerick Philip, 28 Harrison
Goldsmith J., 38 Douglas
Goodman Isaac, 62 Harrison
Haas Nathan, 43 Harrison
Hamburger Mrs. Matilda, 30 Harrison
Hamburger Moses, 10 Harrison
Hammond Wm., 71 Harrison
Hartogensis H. S., 36 Harrison
Hecht Simon, 279 Canton av
Hunt Edward, Chesnut c Hillen
Isaac John, 10 Bethel
Feckgerson John, 101 N Schroeder
John Isaac, 42 Harrison
Kann Julius, 61 Harrison
Leon Saml., 32 Harrison
Mauer Henry, 95 Low
Maun Richard, 11 Carlton
Meara Mrs. Hannah, 55 Harrison
Meeghan John, 107 N High

Morgan Mrs. Mary, 53 Forrest
Neigal Henry, 26 Harrison
Nickel Conrad, 23 Pine
Oppenheim D., 22 Harrison
Parr Henry, 293 N Gay
Pfstrr Bartona, 291 S Bond
Rosenberg Joseph, 22 President
Rosenheim B., 34 Holland
Rosenthal L., 34 Penn. av
Simon Elias, 44 Harrison
Slokett Simon, 33 Douglas
Smith A., 93 Harrison
Solomon Isaac, 56 Mosher
Stern Henry, 63 Ross
Strasburger G., 36 Penn. av
Weisler Mrs. Rebecca, 295 Alice Anna
Weiss H. & Co., 53 Penn. av
Wheatfield Miss S., 67 Penn. av

Seedsmen.

(*See also* AGRICULTURAL IMPLE-MENTS.)

Ault Samuel & Son, Calvert c Water
BRUSTER & GRIFFITH, 49 N Paca
CROMWELL RICHARD, 46 and 48 Light. (See advertisement.)
Desvarreux James, 164 N Gay
Feast John & Son, N E c Fayette and Calvert
Feast Samuel & Sons, N E c Charles and Saratoga
NORRIS THOMAS, 141 W Pratt
WHITELOCK W. & CO., 44 South
WHITMAN E. & SONS, 22 and 24 S Calvert

Sewing Machines.

GROVER & BAKER, SEWING MACHINE CO., 181 W Baltimore. (See advertisement interleaved)
HOLTZMANN GEORGE, 287 W Pratt
Lanpher A. M., 4 E Baltimore
McKENNEY J. F., 7 N Liberty.
SEWING MACHINE REPAIRING and RENTING.

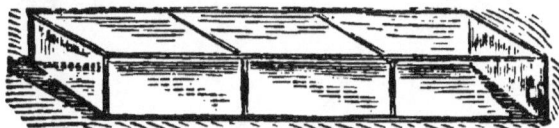

Shanks Thomas, 36 N Green
SINGER MANUFACTURING CO ,
  159 W Baltimore. (See advertisement interleaved.)
Walmsley Brothers, 205 W Baltimore
WHEELER & WILSON'S, W.
  Merrell, agent, 214 W Baltimore. (See advertisement interleaved.)

Sewing Machine Stitching.

GROVER & BAKER SEWING
  MACHINE CO., 181 W Baltimore. (See advertisement interleaved.)

Sewing Silks.

DIETZ L. D. & CO., 308 W Baltimore. (See advertisement inside
  back cover.)
GROVER & BAKER SEWING
  MACHINE CO., 181 W Baltimore. (See advertisement interleaved.)

Ship Builders and Ship-wrights.

Fardy John T. & Bro., 33 Hughes
  and south side of Basin
Robb John, 285 Washington
Uniack John J., Hughes c Covington

*Ship Cabooses.

Smull David B., 82 W Pratt

Ship Chandlers.

APPLEGARTH J. A. & CO., 109
  Smith's whf
Coleman & Bailey, 105 and 107
  Thames
Deetjen T., 74 and 76 Thames
DURAND JOHN H., 132 W Pratt,
  head of Bowly's whf: Factory,
  c John and Eden ; MANUFACTU-
  RER and WHOLESALE AND RE-
  TAIL DEALER in *PATENT*
  Cordage, Oars, Oakum, Blocks,
  Tar Twine, &c. &c,

HOOPER GEO. W., c South and
  Pratt, *SHIP CHANDLER &*
  GROCER. IMPORTER OF
  CHAIN   CABLES,   AN-
  CHORS,   WINDLASSES,
  BOLT ROPE, HEMP, PA-
  TENT CORDAGE, BUNT-
  ING, SPIKES, PAINTS,
  OILS, OAKUM, BLOCKS,
  SAIL DUCK, TWINE, &c.
Jackson Charles M. & Co., c Smith's
  whf and Pratt
Jones Levin, 166 and 168 Light st
  whf

JONES & WILEY,

SHIP CHANDLERS

AND

DEALERS IN MANILLA CORDAGE,

166 Light Street Wharf.

James Jones.   Alex. Wiley.

MITCHELL M. A., 2 Spear's whf
MORTON A. B. & SONS, 103
  Smith's whf, *GROCERS* and
  SHIP CHANDLERS. Con-
  stantly on hand a full assortment
  of MANILLA and HEMP CORDAGE,
  PAINTS, OILS, and Cabin Stores.
RAMSAY JAS. G., 13 Thames, F
  P, *SHIP CHANDLER, GRO-*
  CER, & CORDAGE MANU-
  FACTURER, keeps constantly
  on hand a general assortment of
  SHIP and CABIN STORES and
  SHIP CHANDLERY.
Torney Otto, 103 McElderry's whf
Waite R. C., Hughes c Covington

Ship Joiners.

Cruckshank   Charles,   Mill   bel
  Bowly
KING J., 115 Smith's whf
Mills John E., ft Henry

MORRIS CHARLES T.,

STEAMBOAT

AND

SHIP JOINER,

138 Thames Street.

Wagner Louis, Thames c Wolf
Worthen W. D., York c Johnson
Young Joshua A., ft Mill

*Ship Plumber.

BOOS HENRY,

SHIP PLUMBER,

109 Thames.

Shipsmiths.

Belbin Wm., 97 Mill
German & Lyle, 145 McElderry's whf
Lawson Henry S., 2 Fell
YEWELL JOHN, 188 Light st whf, Ship and Machine Smith. Orders promptly attended to.

Shipping Offices.

Fry G., 103 Thames
Kirby, Hooper & Price, 61 Thames
Peed John W. & Co., Pratt c Smith's dock

Shot.

Merchants' Shot Tower, Wm. P. Loman, Pres't; Richard Kemp, Sec'y; Fayette c Front.

Shovel and Spade Manufacturers.

(*See* AGRICULTURAL IMPLEMENTS.)

Shirt Manufacturers.

(*See also* GENTS' FURNISHING GOODS.)

Adams T. W., 146 and 171 W Baltimore

Belton T. W., 259 W Baltimore
Betton Thomas, 8 E Baltimore
Betz Mrs. S., 248 Canton av
Blimline II., 2 N Liberty
Dawkins & Co., 155 W Baltimore
Donohue R., 240 W Baltimore
Freidenrich Leon, 302 W Baltimore

LEWIS LAUER & CO.,

283 W BALTIMORE,

MANUFACTURERS OF

Shirts, Bosoms, Collars, Drawers, Overalls, &c.

Importers and Jobbers of Gents' Furnishing Goods.

Magee Wm. P., 60 N Eutaw
Towles Wm. P. & Bro., 145 W Baltimore
WINCHESTER & CO., 157 W Baltimore. (See advertisement.)

Show Cards.

Finegan J., 82 W. Baltimore

Show Case Makers.

RAU C. F. & CO., 20 McClellan's al. (See advertisement.)
SAUER FRANCIS, 98 W Baltimore and 29 Holiday, Manufacturer of Show Cases, in Silver-Plated Metal and Wooden Frames; also Military and Band Drums, with all the latest improvements, cheaper than any other manufacturer.

Silk and Fancy Dry Goods, Importers and Jobbers.

(*See also* DRY GOODS; *also* FANCY GOODS.)

BREHME O. & CO., 12 Hanover

Silver Platers.

BURGESS JOHN, c Fayette and Sharp
Churchill L., 19 Mercer
FEICHMAN S., 80 N Eutaw
GRESHOFF F. A., 2 S Charles, Gold and Silversmith, Electro Plater, and Fire Gilder.
Hawkins F. A., 24 S Liberty
Holmes Wm., Bank la
LANGE R., 91 W Lexington
Sturm Albert, 54 Camden
WAGNER AUGUST, 30 Harrison. (See advertisement interleaved op Brass.)

Silversmiths.

(*See also* JEWELLERS.)

Kirk Samuel & Sons, 172 W Baltimore
Thompson Richard, 143 W Fayette
WARNER A. E., 10 N Gay

Skirts, Hoop.

BAMBERGER E., 247 W Baltimore
BONNEY E., 147 W Baltimore, Wholesale and Retail Dealer in HOOP SKIRTS, CORSETS, RIBBONS, LACES, EMBROIDERY, FANCY & MILLINERY GOODS.
DIETZ L D. & CO., 308 W Baltimore. (See advertisement inside back cover.)
JORDAN & ROSE, 1 N Howard
Lederer Sam'l, 83 N Gay
Meierhof M., 37 N Howard
OBERNDORF & LAUER, 243 W Baltimore
Pohl A., 129 W Lexington
Smoot Miss Kate A., 466 W Baltimore
White M. A., 85 N Howard

Slate Dealers.

Schmick Philip, 32 W Falls av
Schmick Ph., 21 Watson
Stevens George O., 47 W Pratt

Slave Dealers.

Campbell B. M. & W. L., 282 W Pratt

Snuff Mills.

STARR ROBERT, 25 S Calvert, Snuff Manufacturer—RAPPEE, SCOTCH, MACABAU, CONGRESS, &c.

Soap and Candle Makers.

Armstrong James & Co., 31 Concord
FARINGER CHARLES, 14 Constitution and 5 Liberty al; MANUFACTURER OF SOAP AND CANDLES. Has always on hand and for sale, CANDLES; Brown, Yellow, White and Fancy SOAPS.
HUGHES JAMES, 57 and 59 Arch
Kimberly Harry, 27 and 29 Buren
McAdam Edward, 30 Buren

SMITH & CURLETT,

MANUFACTURERS OF

SOAPS,

Adamantine and Tallow

CANDLES,

CORNER OF

HOLIDAY AND PLEASANT.

Webb Charles & James, Ensor cor Chew

Soap Stone Manufacturers.

MARYLAND SOAP STONE COMPANY, ALBERT W. BERRY, *Treasurer*, 420 and 422 W Pratt, are prepared to furnish, for any part of the United States or Europe, their superior Stone, in BLOCKS, SLABS, REGISTER STOVE FUNNEL BLOCKS; Linings for Stoves, Furnaces, Cooking Ranges, Ovens, Grates, and Fire-places; also, Wood and Coal, Franklin and Air-tight Stoves and Fire-places.

Spectacle Makers.

(*See* OPTICIANS.)

Spice Mills.

(*See* COFFEE ROASTERS AND SPICE FACTORS.)

---

*Spice and Mustard Mills.

MARKELL CHARLES,

PROPRIETOR OF PACA MILLS,

Manufacturer and Dealer in

Whole and Ground Spices and Mustard.

AGENT FOR

Preston's Chocolates; Burdict & Bartlett's Oil Paste Blacking; Essence of Coffee; Yeast Powders; Indigo, &c.
Warehouse, S E c Calvert and Lombard, Baltimore.

Spool Cotton.

DIETZ L. D. & CO., 308 W Baltimore. (See advertisement inside back cover.)

*Stables, Drove, Sale, and Exchange.

McGEE JOSEPH & BRO., Paca c German. (See advertisement inside front cover.)

Stage Lines.

Emmittsburg, passing thro' Westminster. Leaves N E c Saratoga and Howard, at 7 A. M., except Sunday
Govanstown & Townstown. Leaves cor Holiday and Fayette, for Townstown, at 8 A. M. and 4½ P.M., and Sun Office c South and Baltimore, for Govanstown and Townstown, at 10 A. M. and 4 P. M.
Reisterstown. Leaves cor Howard and Saratoga daily (except Sunday), at 3 P. M.

Standeford's Line to Kellville.— Leaves Rising Sun Hotel, 74 N High, Tuesday, Thursday, and Saturday, at 8 A. M.

Stair Builders.

(*See* CARPENTERS AND BUILDERS.)

Stationers.

Bonsal Louis, Baltimore c Frederick
Bradford & Briggs, 62 W Baltimore
Caspari A. R., 129 N Howard
Chickering E. C., 226 W Pratt
Doyl A. J., 11 Pennsylvania av
Dutton T. W., 162½ E Baltimore
Harrison W. E. C., 86 Hanover
Hebden, Mrs. Sarah, 151 S Broadway
HENNIGHAUSEN L. & G., 28½ W Pratt
Kurty T. Newton, 151 W Pratt
Mason George, 74 W Baltimore
Minifie Wm., 114 W Baltimore
Neilson, Mrs. Mary A., 44 Thames
Ramesey J. A., 115 S Broadway
Rose H., 16 N Howard
Selby & McCauley, 32 W Baltimore
Taylor Henry, 111 W Baltimore
Turner Samuel C., 3 S Charles. (Wholesale.)
Walsh Catharine, 191 S Broadway
WEISHAMPEL J. F., Jr., 8 Eutaw House c Baltimore and Eutaw; also. 484 Baltimore n Pine
WHITNEY, CUSHING & CO., 6 N Howard
Williams John, 22 Water

Statuary.

Mattare J., 26 N Gay

Steamboat Companies.

Baltimore & Philadelphia (via Canal) Steamboat Co., Leaves Light st whf, daily (Sunday excepted) at 3 p. m.

Baltimore & Susquehanna Steam Co. Steamers leave daily at 5 for Havre de Grace, Port Deposit, and Tide Water Canal. J. J. Taylor, Agent, lower end W Falls av

Chester River, steamers Chester and Arrow leave every day (Sunday excepted) from Light st whf, at 7 a. m., stopping at all public landings. H. B. Slaughter, *Proprietor*, Capt. John Sheet, Agent

Fortress Monroe. The Baltimore Steam Packet Co.'s steamboats leave ft of Concord daily (Sunday excepted) at 4½ p. m. M. N. Falls, General Agent.

Groves A. Jr., Agent, 34 S Wharf

Individual Enterprise, Eastern and Western Shore Steamers Kent and Champion, Samuel J. Plenty, President, Eastern and Western Wharves and 98 Light st whf

New York & Baltimore (via Canal) Transportation Line, Steamer leaves Light st whf daily (Sunday excepted), J. Alexander Shaver, Agent, 3 Light st whf

Powhattan, for City Point and Richmond, Tuesday, Thursday and Saturday at 3 p. m., J. Brandt, Jr., *Pres.*, 5 Light st whf

Steam Engine Builders.

HAZLEHURST & CO., VULCAN WORKS, William c Hughes, Baltimore, BUILDERS OF IRON HULLS AND MARINE ENGINES, STATIONARY ENGINES, STEAM FIRE ENGINES, IRON BRIDGES, RAILWAY MACHINERY, SUGAR MILLS, SAW MILLS, ROLLING MILLS, FLOUR MILLS, AND ALL OTHER DESCRIPTION OF HEAVY MACHINERY. AMPLE WHARF ACCOMMODATION, WITH A POWERFUL CRANE, AFFORD GREAT FACILITIES FOR THE RE-

17

PAIRS OF STEAMERS.— PLANS, SPECIFICATIONS, AND ESTIMATES PREPARED AND FURNISHED.

REEDER CHAS., Hughes c Henry

Steamboat Ferry.

Locust Point Steam Ferry Co., ft Broadway

Steam Gauge Manufacturers.

BASSHOR THOS. C. & CO., 26 Light. (See advertisement op Brass Founders.)

McSHANE HENRY & CO., 157 North. (See advertisement op Brass Founders.)

Steam Heaters.

(*See also* FURNACES, HOT AIR.)

Hayward, Bartlett & Co., 24 Light

McAvoy H. L., 13 Light

Steam Pumps.

(*See also* BLOCK AND PUMP MAKERS; *also* PUMP MAKERS.)

BASSHOR THOMAS C. & CO., 26 Light. (See advertisement.)

Steamship Companies.

LIVERPOOL, NEW YORK & PHILADELPHIA STEAMSHIP CO., JOHN Q. A. HERRING, Agent, 293 Baltimore c Sharp

STEAMSHIP GREAT EASTERN, JNO. Q. A. HERRING, Agent, 293 Baltimore c Sharp

Steel Manufacturers,

KEITH M. JR. & SON, 23 S Charles, Agents for Naylor & Co. (See advertisement.)

Stencil Cutters.

Cesati A., 116 W Lombard

Conner R. R., 174 W Pratt

Esati A. C., 115½ W Lombard

GREEN GEO. T., 51 South, is prepared to cut COPPER STENCILS in a superior style, on moderate terms.

Stereotypers.

(*See* ELECTROTYPERS.)

Stevedores.

Dickerson Geo. & Son, Buchanan's whf

Stone Yards,

(*See also* MARBLE DEALERS AND WORKERS.)

Gault & Bro., 432 W Pratt
Oliver & Fleming, 10 President
Packie Alex., Davis c Monument
Silverwood & Sheckells, 372 W Pratt
Stechele Peter, 94 Central av
Wright A., W Pratt c Penn

Storage.

Baylies James L., 22 Spear's whf
Middleton Richard, 119 Smith's whf
Willis H. N., O'Donnell's whf

Stove Manufacturers.

(*See also* STOVES AND RANGES.)

Bibb & Co., 39 Light
Bryan C., 53 S Calvert
Collins, Heath & Co., 22 Light
Hayward, Bartlett & Co., 24 Light
Lohmuller Henry, 237 Alice Anna
Norris Thomas, 49 S Calvert
Parker Albert, 227 Alice Anna
SEXTON S. B. & CO., 111 W Lombard
Stewart Joseph W., 369 W Baltimore
Swan Wm. H., S E c Light and Lombard
Weatherby J. & Sons, 40 and 42 Light
WOLF EDMUND (Successor to WOLF, STANLEY & Co.), NA-TIONAL STOVE WORKS, WHOLESALE STOVE MANUFACTURER, N E c Light and Lombard

Stoves and Ranges.

(*See also* FURNACES, HOT AIR; *also* TIN AND SHEET IRON WORKERS.)

Baurn Philip, 66 S Sharp
Bechtel John W., 93 N Eutaw
Chasterfield Robert, 604 N Gay
Collins, Heath & Co., 22 Light
FEICHTMAN S., 80 N Eutaw
Fisher Charles, 92 N Gay
Fisher F. M., 14 W Lombard
GEIGER E. L. H., 88 N Howard
GLUCK WM., 79 and 81 N Gay
Harig J. & B. L., Hanover c Hill
Helm John F., 52 S Calvert
Herrlich Charles, 17 and 19 Second
Hoffman Benjamin, 237 S Charles
Hutchinson Brothers, 14 Light
Kann Jacob, 104 N Gay
Koch Jacob, 241 Hanover
Masenberg Geo., 28 S Poppleton
Meyer G. & Co., 505 W Baltimore
Oldershaw J. B., 217 W Pratt
Lawton Jervis, 752 W Baltimore
Letmate F., 46 Penn. av
Richards J. H., 442 W Baltimore
Rosenthall M., 30 and 32 Penn. av
SEXTON S. B. & CO., 111 W Lombard, MANUFACTURERS OF STOVES, PATENT PARLOR HEATERS, Patent Iron Bedsteads, Furnaces, C o o k i n g Ranges, Parlor Grates, &c.
Schaffer Allen G., 114 N Gay
SINDALL & SHOREY, 2 W Pratt
Thaler Lawrence, 371 N Gay
WARD EDW. J., 218 W Pratt, *dwelling* 382 W Fayette
WEATHERBY J. & SONS, 40 and 42 Light, HOT AIR FURNACES AND STOVE DEALERS
Wollrah George, Pratt c Fremont

Straw Goods.

(MARKED THUS * WHOLESALE;
See also MILLINERS.)

Carroll Thos. G., 101 W Baltimore
Frye J., 19 S Charles
*Griffin R. B. & Sons, 17 S Charles
*GRINNELL & JENKINS, 275 W
Baltimore
RASIN I. F., 39 N Charles
Ringrose M. M., 29 N Howard
TIRALLA J. F., 105 W Baltimore

Sugar Refiners.

BALTIMORE STEAM SUGAR RE-
FINERY, DOUGHERY, WOODS
& CO., Lombard and Concord sts
and Jones' Falls.
C. M. Dougherty. H. Woods, jr.
John L. Weeks.
Maryland Co., F. W. Brune & Sons,
Agents, O'Donnell's whf

Surgical Instruments.

(See also DENTAL INSTRUMENTS.)
ARNOLD FRANCIS, 15 S Sharp
Daily W. F., 11 Light
Hesse John, 233 S Charles
REINHARDT CHARLES C. (late
firm of Chas. C. Reinhardt & Co.),
7 N Gay n Baltimore, Cutler and
Surgical Instrument Manufactu-
rer. Keeps constantly on hand,
a large assortment of Surgical and
Dental Instruments, at the lowest
Cash Prices. Also, Patentee and
Manufacturer of the latest and
most approved GLASS PAD TRUSS,
Double and Single, patented Oc-
tober 7th, 1856.—Also, Patents
received from England & France.
Reinhardt H. D., 206 W Pratt

Surveyors.

Bouldin A., 9 North
Bouldin O. & R. J., 9 North (City)
Dawson Wm., 61 W Fayette
Lumley D. T., 63 Second
MARTENET S. J., 6 South ·

Office Surveyor of Baltimore Coun-
ty, Wm. H. Shipley, Deputy, 48
Lexington
SHIPLEY WM. H., DEPUTY
SURVEYOR OF BALTIMORE
COUNTY, 48 Lexington.
TEMPLEMAN R. W., 48 Lexington
TEMPLEMAN R. W. & WM. H.
SHIPLEY, 48 Lexington

Surveyors, Marine.

Binney Joshua, S W c Gay & Lom-
bard
Clackner Joseph,   do   do
Cole Joseph B.   do   do

Suspender Maker.

Klotz Adam F., 251 W Pratt

*Sutler's Supplies.

MERCHANT J. & SON, 174 W
Pratt. (See advertisement.)

Syrups.

SMITH HENRY R., 7 Mercer st,
Baltimore, Refiner of Syrups, Ho-
ney, and Manufacturer of Essence
of Jamaica Ginger, Peppermint,
American Pain Killer, &c., for
Sutler's trade.

Tailors.

(See also CLOTHIERS.)
Alexander James, 9¹ N Eutaw
Bacheiner Henry, 376 S Charles
Bauer C., 15 Ensor
Bauer G. L., 259 N Gay
Bayer A., 36 E Baltimore
Bayer George, 447 W Baltimore
Beamshle Fred'k H., 284 S Charles
Beauchamp R. S., 189 W Pratt
Bernheimer S., 704 W Baltimore
Bonhagen Henry, 44 E Pratt
Bomtsch E., 245 S Charles
BOPP L., 154 Light st whf
BOYD WILLIAM, 3 N Charles
Bichy Herman, 13 N Liberty
Browne Thomas, 213 E Baltimore
Buchheimer P., 2 E Pratt

Bunting & Ridgely, 3 North
Burgess Wm. & Son, 5 S Sharp
BUSCHMAN & ELLERMEYER,
  MERCHANT TAILORS, 9 N
  Liberty
Buschmann C. A., 220 W Lexington
Buschmann H., 135 W Lexington
Christopher Wm., 502 W Baltimore
Cohen M., 221 Light
Collison Wm., 7 S Sharp
Cox Wm. H., 606 W Baltimore
Cronaw Edward, 123 S Broadway
DEPKIN HENRY, 89 W Lombard,
  FASHIONABLE TAILOR.
  "THE FASHIONS RECEIVED
  MONTHLY."
Distler Conrad, 146 Central av
Dowling George, 48 S Wolf
Doulongr Conrad, 309 S Bond
Driscol R. J., 58 S Howard
Eickenbaugh Henry, 26 Ensor
Engelmyer Sol. L., 66 Park
Fedon F., 107 N Calvert
FELGNER F. W., 14 St Paul
Fetter Martin, 61 Gough
Fisher Alexander, 74 Harrison
FONTAINE J. L., 215 W Pratt
Ford Joseph Y., 15 S Gay
Ford Wm. H., 31 N Howard
Frederick Chn., 13 N Gay
Frederick Fred., 13 Holiday
Fries F. L., 1 St Paul
Fuhr M., 127 W Lombard
Goodman Henry, 66 Market space
Granger J., Bank la
Greeabaum Isaac, 216 S Broadway
Green Wm. F., 222 W Pratt
GRIFFITHS J. A. & J. B., 2 Light,
  Merchant Tailors. Always on
  hand a full assortment of Cloths,
  Cassimeres, and Vestings.
Grote John, 89 N Front
Grothaus George F., 11 W Balti-
  more
GROTHOUS C., 14 W Pratt
Hahn F., 123 Lombard
Hain Christian, 179 W Pratt
Hamburger Philip, 212 S Broad-
  way

Hamburger & Bro., 203 S Broad-
  way
Hammer C., 65 S Eutaw
Harig Henry, 288 S Ann
Harzinger Jacob, 185 Broadway
Harris Joseph, 52 N Howard
Hartman Isaac, 4 S Gay
Hartman J. P., 197 W Baltimore
Helsby Samuel, Liberty c German
HENKELMAN & HINDS, 129 W
  Baltimore op American Office.
Hexter George, 182 Broadway
HEYN MARTIN, 16 North
Hilberg Frederick, 24 Second
Hilberg F. L. & Co., 8 South
Hirsh B. D., 106 W Pratt
Hodge Wm., 243 S Charles
Hopkins & Eichman, 230 W Balti-
  more
Hoxley John, 55 N Gay
Jacobs John, 29 Harrison
Johnson James, 44½ E Baltimore
JOHNSON ROBERT, 357 W Balti-
  more
Jones James, 28 South
Jordan Ed., 157 S Broadway
Jordan Ed. & Co., 153 Broadway
Justus Adam, 47 Bank
Kahnn Joseph, 120 S Dallas
Kathan John, 32 German
Kauffman Warner, 109 S Broadway
Keibn S. J., 226 W Lexington
Kelly T. & Son, 3 N Liberty
Keyworth C. B., 276 W Baltimore
King Samuel, 670 W Baltimore
Kirsch Frederick, 372 N Gay
KLOMAN LOUIS, JR., 9 S Gay,
  French Tailor. On hand a good
  assortment of French stuffs for
  Gentlemen after the newest style,
  which I will dispose of on the
  most reasonable terms. All or-
  ders thankfully received and
  promptly executed.
KNEEN THOMAS, 291 W Pratt
Koeler C. F., 108 Light st whf
Koestner T., 57 Forrest
Kontner Henry, 590 W Baltimore
Kornmann John, 430 W Baltimore

KRONHEIMER M., 61 S Howard, bet Pratt and Camden, Merchant Tailor and Clothing Establishment. A superior assortment of Ready Made Clothing always on hand.

Kues Charles, 260 Canton av

Kunkel Michael, 31 S Wolf

Larsson S., 137 W Lombard

Lautenberger Wm., 21 S Liberty

Leonard Patrick, 268 S Charles

Lewis R., 153 W Lombard

Lindeborn Henry, 46 Henrietta

LINTHICUM & CO., 6 N Calvert

LONG & TANNEBAUM, 162 & 164 Light st whf

Lowekamp John H., 64 Park

LOWENBERG HENRY, 19 Light

Ludwig J. A., 109 N Paca

McCORMICK THOMAS, MILITARY TAILOR, Baltimore c Calvert, Military Goods of all descriptions furnished.

McDOWELL FRANCIS 236 W Pratt

McKuin Ed., 510 W Pratt

McPherson Duncan, Charles c Barnet

Manaca Joseph R., 227 W Lexington

Mathers Irvin, 224 W Baltimore

MAYER FREDERICK, 63 Hanover, Merchant Tailor and Gentlemen's Furnishing Store.

Mecke Adam, 12 President

MEHLGARTEN A., 137 Franklin

MEINETSBERGER STEPHEN, 24 S Sharp

Menke F., 433 W Pratt

Mengellack Christian, 90 S Dallas

Merluzzi N. A., 12 W Baltimore

Meyer Christian, 49 Albemarle

Miller P., 437 W Baltimore

Moser Henry, 92 S Dallas

Munkewitz John A., 330 S Charles

Nall John, 20 Carlton

Neuman Benjamin, 56 Centre market space

Nicklas George M., 106 Pearl

Ochs Frederick, 7 Warner

Oehm C. N., 150 Light st whf

Oehm Frederick William, 243 W Pratt

Orenh Simon, 16 Bethel

OSSE CHARLES, 294 W Pratt

Ostendorf & Hamman, 60 N Howard

PATTERSON & FIELDS, 81 Thames op Broadway, F. P., Merchant Tailors and Clothing Establishment

Perry & Bro., 192 N Gay

Peter George, 7 S Gay

Pfeifer M., 32 N Paca

Pfister J. F.. 38 Ross

Phillips James, 43 N Liberty

Pinning Charles, 19S N Gay

Pollock M., 18 Harrison

Price B., 64 N Howard

Purnell Charles B., 246 W Pratt

Rau George D., 244 N Gay

REILLEY P., 93 N Howard

Reinach Isaac, 750 W Baltimore

Reinheimer Fr., 209 S Eutaw

Richardson J. W., 12 N Gay

Rob E., 50 S Charles

Roberts David, 22 Bethel

ROBERTS H. T., 6 St Paul

Roessler Edward, 37 German

Rosenburgh Henry, 38 Harrison

Rothschild S., 230 S Broadway

SANDERS GEO. W., 51 Hanover

Schauer M., agent, 3 Water

Schmidt & Ebel, 304 W Pratt

Schmith C., 10 Chesnut

Schulheis William, 672 W Baltimore

Schultz Peter, 12 W Baltimore

Shane Mrs. H., 34 Camden

Shoemaker William, 191 Henrietta

Simon Theo. & Brother, 317 W Pratt

Sinclair Francis H., 776 W Baltimore

Smith M. N., 35 N Gay

Sondheimer Samuel, c Exeter and Low

17*

Sonnaman Henry, 498 W Baltimore
Spicer J., 165 Franklin
STAUF HENRY, *MERCHANT TAILOR*, 45 W Baltimore bet Frederick and Gay
Steinbach Gottlieb, 259 S Bond
Steinbach Jacob, 240 Alice Anna
Stewart Alexander, 75 Richmond
Stern P., 148 Forrest
Stine Joseph, 144 W Baltimore
Story John T., 491½ W Baltimore
Street M. L., 20 Second
Strohmeyer George, 8 N Gay
Tacuber John F., 54 Ensor
Taylor L. D., 15 S Calvert
Teals Geo. McKendree, N E c Frederick and Baltimore
Tracy M. & Sons, 166 W Baltimore
Traut Louis, 513 W Baltimore
Trego W. C., 98 S Bond
Vanoisdell H., 152½ N Eutaw
Viaene J., 219 W Baltimore
Walter John, 147 S Wolf
Weber Casper, 315 W Pratt
Weber Philip, 654 W Baltimore
WEIKEL PETER, 7 Light, adj Fountain Hotel. Always on hand a good selection of Cloths, Cassimeres, and Vestings.
Weyfforth B., 40 N Paca
Wiegman John, 209 S Broadway
Wieseman John, 343 S Bond
Willfing Henry, 66 Ross
Williams B., 71 S Schroeder
Winkelman Casper, 56 Greenmount av
Wustard H., 42 S Republican

Tailors' Trimmings.

Buschmann Victor H., 2 Hanover
FOCKE EDW. L., 252 W Baltimore
Harrington & Bogue, Baltimore c Charles
LAUER LEWIS & CO., 283 W Baltimore
MOORE S. & R. G., 6 S Charles, Importers, Dealers and Manufac-turers of CLOTHIERS' AND TAILORS' TRIMMINGS, SHIRTS, COLLARS, and FURNISHING GOODS GENERALLY.
Wise L. E., 253 W Pratt

Tanners.

APPOLD GEORGE & SONS, North ab Madison
Bayfield & Gregg, 2 Centre
Klees Henry & Sons, 15, 17 and 19 Saratoga
Heald John H. & Co., North c Madison

MAYNARD, ELY & ROSE,

TANNERS AND CURRIERS,

AND

DEALERS IN

All Kinds of Shoe Manufacturers' Goods,

Would call attention, especially of the trade, to our celebrated Calf and Kip Skins, now almost entirely used in place of imported Skins.

MAYNARD, ELY & ROSE, Store, 46 S. Calvert.

SELWAY ROBERT, Tanner and Currier, 14 S Calvert, TANNERY c Saratoga and Carey. Full assortment of sole and finished leather, which will be sold low for cash, at No. 14 S. Calvert St.
STARTZMAN A., Central av bet Pratt and Gough

Taverns.

(*See also* HOTELS; *also* RESTAURANTS; *also* LAGER BEER SALOONS.)
Bell Ellen, 152 S Eutaw
Black John, 164 Harford av
Bleiker Julius, 42 S Howard
BUTLER MISS BLANCH, 155 Eastern av

Calder Mrs. Rosanna, 157 Eastern av
Campbell Peter, 73 Chesnut
Cunningham John, 413 S Charles
Corcoran Patrick, 62 Lancaster
Davis J. V., 163 Eastern av
Dickinson Wm., 161 Eastern av
Diver John, 151 Eastern av
Enelbach M., 75 Hanover
Everhardt, Geo. G., 42 N Paca
Everline Michael, 200 W Lexington
Flagerty W., 259 Hanover
Ferris B., 154½ W Pratt
Giles Mary Ann, 149 Eastern av
Hallworth Allen, 165 Eastern av
Hawks Curtis, 14 Cross
Hering Mrs. H., 60 Lancaster
Horn John, 19 Dover
Hoyt Starr, 159 Eastern av
Imhofe Henry, 23 W Pratt
Jackson Mrs. Susan, 133 Eastern av
KEEGAN PATRICK, c Front and Bath
Keerle Mrs. Nancy, 137 Eastern av
Knowles Henry, East c Half Moon al
McCail Ellen, 508 W Pratt
McLane Samuel, 518 W Pratt
Mailley James, 38 President
Manley James, 145 Eastern av
Marren Terrance, 195 E Lombard
Nugent T., 204 W Lexington
Rochfort J. F., 39 President
Schenermann C., 71 Hanover
Schmidt Robert, 273 S Sharp
Silk Mary, Charles c Henrietta
Smith Mrs. E., 57 South
Stapleton Timothy, 49 President
Wehage H. H., 221 Hanover
Welsh Mary, 39 W Lombard
Welsh Thos., 213 Light
WELTNER ADAM, 77 Hanover
White Isabella, 167 Eastern av
Wilson Henry, 822 W Baltimore
Wolbaun —, 5 W Lombard

Taxidermists.

Wolle Alexander, 30 Second

Tea Dealers.

(*See also* GROCERS.)

(*Marked thus * are Wholesale.*)

*GILLET GEO. M. & Co.,

TEAS,

56 S Gay St.

G. M. GILLET, HENRY MOALE.

---

*HABERSHAM & BARRETT, 53 Exchange pl, IMPORTERS AND DEALERS IN TEAS AND EAST INDIA GOODS.

KUHN & TYSON,

DEALERS IN TEA,

c Eutaw and Fayette.

FRANKLIN KUHN, W. J. TYSON.

---

*Martin, Gillet & Co., Lombard c Frederick
*REESE G. H. & BROTHERS, 207 and 209 W Pratt
Robertson Thomas, 436 W Baltimore
*SANDERS GEORGE & CO., 65 Exchange pl

Teachers, Dancing.

(*See* ACADEMIES, DANCING.)

Teachers, Languages.

Dantziger J. C., 100 Hanover
Gravier Leon, 97 St Paul
KOCH GEORGE, 104 East

Teachers, Music.

Fry Charles, 20 N Liberty
Polk E., 10 N Green
Weaver Miss M. A., 165 N Eutaw

Telegraph Offices,

American Telegraph Co., Baltimore c South
INDEPENDENT TELEGRAPH CO., 21 SOUTH, AND BRANCH OFFICE, CORN EXCHANGE.

Thread Importers,

DIETZ L. D. & CO., 308 W Baltimore. (See advertisement inside back cover.)

Tin Can Manufacturers.

Campen John, 266 Light
EWALT SAMUEL A., 519½ W Baltimore, Manufacturer of every variety of FRUIT AND OYSTER CANS. All orders promptly attended to. Capping done at the shortest notice.
O'Ferrall John & Co., 169 S Howard
SHOTT PHILIP, 411 and 413 W Baltimore, Manufacturer of Oyster and Fruit Cans of all sizes.

Tin and Sheet Iron Workers.

(*See also* STOVES AND RANGES.)
Bateman B. M. G., 270 Light
Borgley Samuel, Barre c Warner
Campbell Henry J., 309 W Pratt
Dailey & Bro., 759 W Baltimore
Evans John, 18 W Baltimore
FEICHTMAN S., 80 N Eutaw
Fisher Charles, 92 N Gay
Fisher F., 36 N Liberty
GEISS NICHOLAS, 112 S Howard bel Conway. *TIN* and *SHEET IRON WORKER*. Metallic Roofing and Spouting done in the best manner and at the lowest prices. All kinds of tinware made to order. Orders for Stove and Jobbing Work promptly attended to,
GLUCK WILLIAM, 79 and 81 N Gay
Goetz August, 286 N Gay
Goetz John A. G., Brown c Elizabeth
Hetzell John J., 74 N Howard
KEEN & HAGERTY, 37 and 39 S Calvert c Water and Cheapside, WHOLESALE *TIN AND JAPANNED WARE MANUFACTURERS*, and dealers in *HARDWARE, IRON CASTINGS, &c.*
Kerns John F., 734 W Baltimore
Kines & Brother, Harden's ct and Williamson
Lawb Fred., 290 S Sharp
Loney & Brother, 156 N Gay
McMILLAN WILLIAM D., 333 W Pratt
Mills Ezekiel, 385 W Baltimore
Ness Alfred S. & Co., 30 S Calvert
Oldershaw J. B., 217 W Pratt
Reip A. H., 335 W Baltimore
ROBINSON JOSHUA, 333 W Baltimore

SHANAMAN JOHN,

30 and 32 N Eutaw,

Manufacturer

OF ALL KINDS OF

*TINWARE,
PAINT AND PRESERVE CANS, CANISTERS,*

and

DRUGGISTS' TINWARE.

Wholesale and Retail.

Roofing and Spouting,
House Furnishing Goods.

Smiley James, 517 W Baltimore
WARD EDWARD J., 218 W Pratt, *dwelling*, 382 W Fayette

Tinsmiths.

Bordley S. C., 56 Hollins mkt
Collins James, 14 W Fayette
Crout H., 48 Penn. av
Foss C. M., 10 N Eutaw
Fry Jacob, 271 S Sharp
Goetz Daniel, 52 Central av
Hand T. B., 33 E Baltimore
Hanson Peter, 32 E Baltimore
Hilderbrundt Frederick, 205 Hollins
Johns Casper, 18 Bethel
Knaus Ferdinand, 4 and 6 Ensor
Leine L., 258 S Ann
Lester Thomas, 28 President
Letmate A., 47 Ensor
Letmate W., 59 Penn. av
Lloyd R., 136 N Eutaw
Meyer Lawrence, 44 Park
Moxley Wm., 1 Dover
Myers Fred., 343 Light
Parkinson & Brown, 58 North
Reip L. J., 28 N Paca
Rosenbush Sampson, 19 Ensor
Roth Frederick, Bell Air mkt
Schim Adolph, 407 Canton av
Shebberley C., Lexington mkt
Shop Mrs. C., Lexington mkt
Snyder F., 65 E Pratt
Staudt Charles, 89 Orleans
Stoefield Henry, 164 S Fremont
Thaler Geo. & Bro., 106 Franklin
Theisz Conrad, 82 Pearl
Volk James, 11 Pine
Waltz John, Caroline c Orleans
White Henry, 175 Franklin
Willhelm Mrs. L., 71 Penn. av
Wolf Wm. N., Central av c Gough

Tobacco Commission Merchants.

Armistead, Riggs & Co., 33 S Gay
BELT TRUEMAN & SONS, 1 Ellicott, TOBACCO and GENERAL COMMISSION MERCHANTS.
Berry N. E., 63 W Pratt
BOYD W. A. & CO., 33 South
COURTNEY & SON, 65 S Gay

DARE, SPROSTON & CO., 95 S Charles
DE FORD CHARLES D. & Co., 37 S Gay, TOBACCO COMMISSION MERCHANTS and IMPORTERS OF HAVANA CIGARS & LEAF TOBACCO.
Etchison & Dorsey, 104 S Charles
FENDRICH BROTHERS, 49 South
Foster W. T., 70 Exchange pl
Frick & Ball, 57 Exchange pl
GUNTHER & RODEWALD, 90 W Lombard, 1 door west of Exchange pl, GENERAL COMMISSION MERCHANTS and TOBACCO FACTORS.
Heald Jacob & Co., 58 and 60 S Gay
HYATT C. C. & R. H. & Co., 147 Pratt
OWENS J. S. & CO., 55 W Pratt
PARLETT B. F. & CO., 92 Lombard and 5 Water n South, WHOLESALE DEALERS IN MANUFACTURED and LEAF TOBACCO, IMPORTED HAVANA and GERMAN CIGARS, and MANUFACTURERS OF FINE HAVANA AND OTHER CIGARS.
PLEASANTS JOHN P. & SONS, 52 South, Tobacco Commission Merchants.
Seemuller A. & Sons, 55 Exchange pl

Tobacco Manufacturers.

BECK & BACHMANN, TOBACCO MANUFACTURERS, PROPRIETORS of PIMLICO TOBACCO WORKS, BALTIMORE COUNTY. Office—113 W Lombard.
BONN ANTHONY S. & CO., 172 W Pratt
Cromer Thomas W., 341 W Baltimore
GAIL G. W. & AX, 28 Barre
HAMILTON GEO. W., 112 W Pratt
HUNCKEL PH., 24 S Charles

HUNTER WM., Agent, NAVY and NATURAL TOBACCO MANU-FACTORY, 152 W Pratt c Hollingsworth

---

MIDDLETON & DORSEY,

Manufacturers of all kinds of

CHEWING

TOBACCO,

Navy lbs. and ¼ lbs.,

Bright and Light Pressed 5s and 10s.

FACTORY—103 Charles.

WAREHOUSE—126 W Pratt.

Schultz Charles, 33 W Lombard
WATTS G. S. & CO., 21 S Calvert, MANUFACTURERS OF CIGARS, AND AGENTS FOR THE SALE OF MANUFACTURED TOBACCO, & Dealers in HAVANA CUBA, and SEED LEAF TOBACCO.
Garrard S. Watts.   James W. Wolvington.   John M. Holmes.

WEBB NATHAN & BROTHER,

No. 148 W Pratt,

Manufacturers of Navy lbs. & ¼ lbs.

5s and 10s,

NATURAL, SPUN, AND TWIST

TOBACCO'S,

DWELLING—326 W Saratoga.

WILKENS H. & CO.,

Manufacturers of

SMOKING AND FINE CUT

CHEWING

TOBACCO'S.

Also, Importers of Tobacco, Havana and Bremen Cigars,

181 W Pratt, bet Charles and Hanover.

---

*Tobacco Pipe Manufacturers,

DICKINSON, BOWEN & CO.,

TOBACCO PIPE

MANUFACTURERS,

Corner Granby St. and East Fall Avenue,

Opposite Pratt St. Bridge,

BALTIMORE, MD.

Also, sole Patentees and Manufacturers of

"The Patent Double Tube Tobacco Pipes,"

In Meerschaum, Bruyere Root, and other Materials.

Tobacco Warehouses.

BIRD E. CARRERE, 28 W Pratt, 3d door E of Centre Market space, Wholesale and Retail Manufacturer and Dealer in FOREIGN and DOMESTIC CIGARS, TOBACCO, SNUFF and PIPES, of all kinds, cheap for Cash.

BOLENIUS G. H., 202 W Pratt, c
  Charles, MANUFACTURER and IM-
  PORTER OF CIGARS, DEALER IN
  LEAF, MANUFACTURED and
  FINE CUT CHEWING & SMOK-
  ING TOBACCO, PIPES, &c.
BOYD WM. A. & Co., 33 South,
  WHOLESALE DEALERS IN LEAF
  and MANUFACTURED TOBAC-
  CO.
COFFROTH, MILLER & CO., 330
  W Baltimore
Dellevie Samuel, 20 W Pratt
DINSMORE & KYLE, 156 Pratt st
  whf
FENDRICH BROTHERS,49 South,
  Manufacturers of Chewing Tobac-
  co and Cigars, and Dealers in all
  kinds of Leaf Tobacco, Plain and
  Fancy Pipes, &c.
GAIL G. W. & AX, 28 Barre
Gephart John, jr., 320 W Baltimore
GUNTHER & RODEWALD, 90 W
  Lombard

HUNCKEL'S PH.

LEAF TOBACCO

and

CIGAR AGENCY.

Havana, Yara and Cuba Tobacco,
Connecticut, Pennsylvania and
Ohio Seed Leaf.

24 S. CHARLES.

Marriott & Gould, 35 South
Moorehead John & Brother 14 N
  Howard
MYERS W. H., 5 Water, MANU-
  FACTURER OF CIGARS and dea-
  ler in CHEWING, SMOKING AND
  LEAF TOBACCO. All goods
  guaranteed as represented, or no
  sale.

PARLETT B. F. & CO., 92 Lom-
  bard and 5 Water
Perkins James T., Inspector (No. 1,
  State), ft Dugan's whf
Requardt J. J., Lombard c Market
  space
ROSENFELD S. & CO., 20 S Gay.
  (See advertisement.)
SCHROEDER JOSEPH, Baltimore
  c Frederick
State No. 3, P Griffith, S W c Light
  st whf and Conway
State Tobacco Warehouse No. 4,
  Wm. Welsh, S Charles
State Tobacco Warehouse No. 5,
  John Morehead, Inspector, S
  Charles
TAYLOR I. H., 97 W Lombard
Turner James, Inspector (No. 2), ft
  O'Donnell's whf
WEBB THOMAS N., Manufactu-
  rer and dealer in choice imported
  Havana Cigars, Virginia Chewing
  Tobacco, &c., wholesale and re-
  tail, S E c Madison and Garden.

Tobacco and Cigar Dealers.

(See also CIGAR DEALERS.)

Abbott William, 238 S Broadway
AHLERS CHARLES, S E c Gay
  and Eden
ALEXANDER M., 242 W Pratt
Allderdice John, 11½ W Fayette
Austermuhle N., 180 Orleans
Barker W. K., 265 W Pratt
Bateman James S., 125 Hillen
BECK JACOB, Gay c Caroline
Bell T. B., 84 N Paca
Bendorf Augustus, S Caroline c
  Fleet
Berndt Charles, 138 Aisquith
Beziat John M., 656 W Baltimore
Birkins William, 220 Hollins
Bixler Louis A., 102 N Howard
Black Samuel, 188 W Pratt
Blessing John, 241 N Gay
Bohlmann John, 465 W Baltimore
Boon John, ½ Second
Booth Simon 234 E Lombard

Boring John T., Columbia c Emory
Bowers T. W., 74 W Pratt
Bremner John, 186 S Sharp
BRINGMANN WM., 18 S Sharp, bet German and Lombard, dealer in Cigars, Tobacco, Snuff and Pipes.
Brinckmeyer Charles, 41 W Balti-
Brown G. W., 9 W Baltimore
Burke Amos, 184 W Lexington
Bussa John V., 354 W Pratt
Byer Andrew, 207 S Charles
Cameron Hugh, 84 Ensor
Castine E. M., 22 Second
Cetlinger H., 57 W Baltimore
Chalmers Mrs. Ann, 65 Penn. av
Cheery Edward, 420 W Baltimore
Clark John, 104 W Pratt
Cohen Lewis C., 377 W Pratt
Coleman Wm. F., 72 Central av
Crisp Joseph, 42 Thames
Cropp Mrs. D., 24 President
Catsenstein M., 24 W Baltimore
Cumming Wm. A., 189 W Balti-more, 2d door W of Light
Cummings J. P., 22 N Paca
Decker B., 14 Ensor
DEMITZ H. F., 118½ Light st whf
DILLEHUNT JOHN G., 167 E Baltimore
Donelson James L., 141 N Gay
Doub D. M. & Co., Baltimore and Calhoun
Draper Garrison, 162 Forrest
Dreves Francis, 16 Pine
Dundon Michael, 267 Light
Ebbighusen Georgeanna, 256 Canton av
Eisemen & Bro., 54 Central av
Eisenhardt John, 114 N Eutaw
Einstein Samuel, 195 W Pratt
Fankhand Henry, 206 W Lexington
Fehsenfeldt Louis, 77 Thames
Feldhaus F. A., Fayette c High
Feldman Henry, 262 Hanover
Fendrick & Bros., 155 Forest
File A., Light c Brown
FINLEY F. H. & BRO., South c Lombard

Fisher Wm. H., 221 W Lexington
FOX CHARLES, 302 W Pratt
Fox Hiram E., 187 W Baltimore
Freeman Saml. B., 188 Madison av
Frese John F., Orleans c Jefferson
Friedel John Peter, 84 Pearl
Frisbil Wm., 172 S Broadway
Fritag Christman, 656 Light
Fuld Isaac, 34 Ensor
Gaspari P. G., 427 W Baltimore
Gehrmann August, 71 Thames
Gettier Wm. P., 257 W Pratt
Gieske & Niemann, 120 S Charles
Gonder Wm., 167 Franklin
Grahm Andrew, 337 N Gay
Granger M., 109 N Howard
Grauer Samuel, 646 W Baltimore
Grauer Samuel, 170 W Pratt
GREGORY J. H. D., Tobacco and Cigar Store, 201 Light. Snuff, Pipes, and Smoking Tobacco on hand.
Greifru C., 379 Canton av
Gross G. R., 722 W Baltimore
Grove F., 159 Franklin
Gudberlet August, 203½ W Lexington
Gump S. R., 14½ Centre mkt space
Hadaway Wm. H., 63 Camden
Hamilton Geo. W., 112 W Pratt and 280 W Baltimore
Heiship Catharine, 142 S Fremont
Henneman Jesse, 46 Albemarle
Henneman John T., 195 W Lexington
Henkel John T., 102 S Broadway
Herr Francis, 313 Alice Anna
Hewell Lewis, 79 Hanover
Hickman Wm. H., N Caroline c Fayette
HILD JOHN C., 214 Light
Hoffman Elizabeth, 192 S Eutaw
Holtz Arnold, 56 North
Homan Amos, 12 Ross
Huhn Mrs. M., 110 Greenmount av
Humfield Amelia, 12 W Lombard
IHDE HENRY, 159 E Baltimore
Isaacs C. C., 36 South
Jaeger Edward, 21 E Baltimore

Johnson E., 51 Ross
Johnson James, 135 North
Johnson W. H., 21 Market space
Jones Charles, 180 S Broadway
Jones W. B., 2 N Frederick
Kelley Henry W., 59 S Broadway
Kellner John, 229 Canton av
Kensler Mrs. E., 328 S Charles
Kerckhoff G., 99 W Lexington
Kerner J. F., E Baltimore c High
KLEMM C., 105 N Calvert
Kniss Wm., 391 W Baltimore
Knipschild A., Fayette c Harrison
Koerber Ch., 175 S Broadway
Koerber F., 255 Eastern av
Krumme J. A., 67 N Gay
Kuhlmann H. & Co., 822 W Baltimore
Kuhne Francis, 91 N Gay
Lambrecht Ch., Pratt c Albemarle
Lavin John, Ann c Baltimore
LENZBERG M, 56 S Howard
Leopold W., 548 W Baltimore
Liebman & Dellivie, 50 N Front
LINDSEY C. D., 106 W Baltimore, Dealer in Havana, Domestic, and German Cigars, Chewing Tobacco, Pipes, &c.
McCARTY & BRO., 9 St Paul
Mankin Chas., 121 Thames
Mantz Wm. H., 401 W Baltimore
Martin Edward, 121 S Sharp
Maydwell J. C., 21 Penn. av
Mergareth Joseph, 347 S Bond
Merfeld Joseph, 68 N Howard
Meyer F. G., 744 W Baltimore
Meyers Louis, 252 S Broadway
MICHEL WM., 117 N Calvert
Michelman H. E., 18 Park
Miller D., 22 E Pratt
Miller G., McElderry c Eden
Milus Frank, 212 Alice Anna
MORSE & MARTIN, 228 Baltimore, Cigars, Pipes, Tobacco, &c., Agents for Bowen's patent double tube. Pipes.
Moxley Walter, 243 S Broadway
MUELLER F., Manufacturer of and Dealer in CIGARS, TOBAC-
18

CO, SNUFF, &c., S E c German and Liberty
MUTHERT F. R., 76 S Eutaw, 4 doors N of Camden, Manufacturer and Dealer in CIGARS, TOBACCO, SNUFF, PIPES, &c.
Muthert J. R. A , 15 Penn. av
Myers Humphrey, 113 Franklin
Neideliss Louisa, 63 S Sharp
NEWELL PETER, 176 W Pratt
Norris & Dulany, 46 N Eutaw
Norris M., 96 Richmond
Oppelt Edmund J., 42 N Green
Parlett N. E., 88¹ Light st whf
Paul Wm., 451 W Baltimore
Pausch George, Britton c Madison
Pfeil Mrs. C. E., 354 Light
Poske H. F., 7 E Pratt
PRIDGEON JOHNSON, 301 W Baltimore, Cigar and Tobacco Emporium. On hand Smoking and Chewing Tobacco, Tobacco Pouches, Sweet Brier Pipes, &c.
Quentin C. H., 256 Alice Anna
Reckert Chas. A., 72 Columbia
Rein Henry, 419 Light
Requardt J. F., 152 W Baltimore
Requardt J. J., Market space c Lombard
Rest Mrs. Francis, 282 S Charles
Richardson John 30 W Pratt
Roberts Charles, 141 W Lexington
Rosenbaum H., 233 Light
Rouvenac C., 270 S Sharp
RUDOLPH JACOB, 55 Hanover
Rutter John, 411 Canton av
Sachman Margaret, 51 S Charles
Sanner John H., 64 S Howard
Sauer John, 27 Scott
Schaffer Mary, 437 W Pratt
Schagemann Bernard, 294 Aisquith
Schmidt Philip, 46 S Bond
Schnuck Harmon, 68 Park
Schull C., 268 S Ann
Siligmin Eliza, 773 W Baltimore
Simmons S., 1 E Baltimore
Smith Frederick, E Baltimore c Front
Smith Geo. A., 509 W Baltimore

Smith Henry, 770 W Baltimore
Smith J. C., 155½ W Baltimore
Southcomb A. L., 127 S Broadway
Spamer George, 14 E Pratt
Spreehe A., Baltimore c Fremont
Sprugman Julius, 39 S Oregon
Stegmann F. R., 232 Hanover
Stempee Julius, S E c Holiday and Fayette
Strobel Henry, 221 S Broadway
Sutro E., 123 W Baltimore
Tallarott Christian, 102 Thames
TAYLOR ELIAS, 50 W Pratt
Taylor Brothers, 136 W Pratt
Tepkeng Fred., 43 Thames
Thorner A. H., 6 Light st whf
Tiemann Louis, 184 E Pratt
Timbs John K., 249 E Baltimore
Tinger Ch. F., 801 W Baltimore
Tinken G. A. F., 78 Hanover
Tobetbush H. W., 65 Ross
Uhl Francis A., Market space c Hawk
Unckback Mary, Lombard c Light
Vieweg Frank, 259 Alice Anna
Voigt Louis, 4 Columbia
Von Duering F., 162 E Baltimore
Walger Louis, 450 W Baltimore
Wambach Charles, 108 Light st wf
WARTMAN'S J. C., EUTAW CIGAR STORE, under Eutaw House. Importer and Dealer in Genuine Havana Cigars, Chewing and Smoking Tobacco, Meerschaum and Bryer Pipes.
Wasserman J. L., 146 S Eutaw
Waterman A. S., 122 Forrest
Weaver Mary, 268 S Caroline
WEBB SAMUEL M., 9 N Liberty. Importer and Dealer in Fine Havana Cigars, Chewing and Smoking Tobacco, and Pipes.
WEINGARTEN SOLOMON, DEALER AND MANUFACTURER OF TOBACCO, CIGARS, SNUFFS, &c., 173 W Lexington, 2d door from Eutaw. Always on hand, a good assortment of IMPORTED HAVANA, PRINCIPE and DO-

MESTIC CIGARS, and all kinds of TOBACCO and SNUFF, Wholesale and Retail, cheap for cash.
WEITMYER JACOB, 51 N Gay
Weise Julius, 64 S Ann
Wheatley N. D., 570 W Baltimore
Wicks William, 161 Penn. av
WILKENS H. & CO., 181 W Pratt
Wise Mrs. Mary, Ann c Gough
Worwell Mrs. Mary, 113 E Pratt
Westrick Charles, 104 Franklin
Zeun George, 188 Cross

Toy Stores.

(*See also* FANCY GOODS.)

Habinghausen Wm., 532 N Gay
HARBAUGH MRS. A. M., 121 N Calvert
Pridgen Wm. R., 194 Hanover

Transportation Lines.

(*See* p. 103, FREIGHT LINES.)

Baltimore & Boston, A. L. Higgins, agt., ft Long Dock
Baltimore Steam Packet Co., M. N. Falls, agt., Union Dock
Baltimore & Susquehanna Steam Co., for Havre de Grace and Port Deposit, J. J. Taylor, agt., City Block W Falls av
McFARLAND, STEPHENSON & CO., FAST FREIGHT LINE BETWEEN BALTIMORE AND WASHINGTON, *offices* 114 S Eutaw op Camden station, B. & O. R. R., and at Baltimore and Washington Depot in Washington, Alexandria and Georgetown. Freight transported promptly at lowest rates.
New York & Baltimore, J. Alex. Shriver, agt., 3 Light st whf

Trimmings and Dry Goods.

(*See also* DRY GOODS, RETAIL ; *also* VARIETY STORES.)

Agan Mrs. Eliza, 17 Penn. av
Baum Miss Ellen, Pearl c Saratoga

Belm H. J. T., 77 N Howard
Burns Mrs. Julia, 64 Chew
Campbell Mrs. M., 250 N Gay
Clark Mary Ann, Aisquith c Chew
Cleary Mrs. Ellen, 53 Harrison
Colton Wm. H., 144 N Gay·
Conn Mrs. M. A., 88 N Poppleton
Cowman & Bro., 59 N Howard
Creny M. J., 135 N Eutaw
Despeaux Mrs. E., 197 E Pratt
Dieffenbach Miss C., 460 W Baltimore
Dryden Mrs. R., 116 W Lexington
Elton Mrs. Elizabeth, 1 S Ann
Fanning Mrs. M., 190 E Baltimore
Fry Mrs. M., 6 Carlton
Griffith Catharine, 33 Harrison
Gude II P., 151 W Madison
Gump Mrs. M., 176 E Baltimore
Guthlein N., 226 S Broadway
Hutzler M., 23 N Eutaw
John August, 90 W Lexington
Keer Thomas, 190 N Exeter
Kermode John, 91 N Eutaw
Koontz Frank, 31 Central av
Lansburgh J., 27 N Eutaw
Lauer F., 69 N Howard
Lewis Ellen, 682 W Baltimore
McCaddin Mrs. M., 1 Clay
McDonnell Misses, 65 N Howard
McGuirk Mrs. M., Biddle c Monument
McNaughon Miss R., 26 Russell
McRae J., 116 N Calvert
Mehler W., 89 W Lexington
Merryman, C. & F., 139 N Eutaw
Mewshaw Dennis, 554 W Baltimore
Moulton James F. Sr., 482 W Baltimore
Needles John & Son, 43 N Charles
Pindell Thomas, 264 E Baltimore
Pollock Mrs. L., 794 W Baltimore
Rickerd Mrs. S., 94 N Schroeder
Rogers Jason, N E c Lexington and Pearl
Schultheis Mrs. R., 133 Mulberry
Soran Mrs., Bond c Gough
Smith Fanny, 129 S Sharp
Storm Mrs. C. M., 109 N Gay

Vreeland Mrs. A., 92 W Lexington
Welch Mrs. F. A., 84 W Lexington
Wicke William, 57 Pearl
Wirth Mrs. Anne, 42 Penn. av

Trunk Makers.

(*See* also SADDLE AND HARNESS MAKERS.)

BRAUL WILLIAM,
286 W Pratt and 44 S Exeter,
Manufacturer of

TRUNKS
and
CARPET BAGS,
Wholesale and Retail.

FARQUHARSON F. L., 17 S Calvert
HUNT SAMUEL, 202 W Baltimore
LAWSON ROBERT, 277 W Baltimore
Lingelbach Charles, 293 S Bond
McGee John, Calvert c Baltimore, 1 S Charles and 35 W Fayette
Ruckle J. N., S E c Pratt and Howard
Schuchmann & Heim, 1 E side Centre market space

SCHUCHMANN & MARION

Trunks, Valises,

AND BONNET BOXES,

34 N Eutaw.

SCHULZE ERNEST, S E c Baltimore and Charles and 2 Cider al. (See advertisement op Box makers.)
Shoemaker George, 391 W Pratt
Van Nortwick J. V. D., 259 W Baltimore

Truss Makers.

Bruce Robert, 448 Baltimore

Turners.

Frazier J. B., 261 Bond
Ladenberger John, Eastern av
Lindemann William, 243 S Bond,
McLain William, 46 Holiday
ROMBACH P. (successor to E.
Kessmodel), UMBRELLA, PAR-
ASOL AND CANE MANUFAC-
TURER AND FANCY TURNER,
61 N Eutaw.
SHORT JOHN H., Uhler's al bet
Hanover and Charles, STEAM
SCROLL SAWING AND TURN-
ING. All orders for Cabinet
Makers', Carpenters', Piano and
Coach Makers' work, promptly
executed. N.B.—TEN PIN BALLS
furnished at short notice.

A. STORCK'S

Steam Turning and Sawing

ESTABLISHMENT.

NO. 152 EAST ST.,

bet Hillen and Ensor,

BALTIMORE,

Where he is prepared to execute
all kinds of *Sawing and Turning*,
such as Bench Screws, Hand Screws,
Bed Posts, Carriage Hubs, Cart
Hubs, Cedar Posts. Stair Banisters,
Stair Newels, Piano Legs, Colum
Table Legs, Ten Pin Balls, &c., also
all kinds of straight and Fancy Scroll
Sawing.

THOMAS JOSEPH & SON, Clay c
Park

Type Founder.

Lucas Henry A., Bank la

Umbrellas and Parasols.

Bauchardt Wm., 75 N Eutaw
BECK FREDERICK, 121 W Balti-
more, Whip, Umbrella, Parasol
and Cane Manufacturer.
BEEHLER FRANCIS, 235 W Bal-
timore, Whip, Umbrella, Parasol
and Cane Manufacturer.
Buxbaum Jacob, 602 W Baltimore
Baylis William, 33 Chesnut (Re-
pairer)
DIETZ L. D. & Co., 308 W Balti-
more. (See advertisement inside
back cover.)
Fay T. C., 87 Chesnut
Fink Augusta, 32 Spring
Frank Solomon, 6 Spring
French E. F., 6 E Baltimore
Hymes Barney, 193 E Pratt (re-
pairer)
Hymes Emanuel, 32 Ensor (repairer)
Irwin T., 36 Bethel
Kuhn C. F., 73 N Eutaw
MAXWELL W. G., 16 W Balti-
more
MILLIKIN JAS. H. & SON, 267
W Baltimore
Pick Charles F., 49 Harrison
Racsh John, 5 Bethel
ROMBACH P., 61 N Eutaw
Ross Simon O., 98 Spring (repairer)
St. John Mrs. E., 942 W Baltimore

Undertakers.

BYRNE JAMES P., 39 N Front
Chase Samuel W., 180 S Howard
Leonard Wm. M., 782 W Baltimore
Loane Joseph, 568 W Baltimore
MARTIN & BEVANS, 11 S Calvert
Shope Catharine, 70 Chesnut
Teufel John, 283 W Pratt
Troll Frederick, 90 S Howard
WEAVER JACOB, 21 Ross, Metal-
lic Coffins and Zinc Cases on hand,
ready made Coffins furnished at
the shortest notice.

Upholsterers.

BOSSON & RUBENS, 19 N Eutaw

CROOK WALTER Jr.,

LARGE WHOLESALE AND RETAIL
STOCK OF

UPHOLSTERY AND CURTAIN
G O O D S,
Paper Hangings, Window Shades and Hollands, &c.,

AT THE CURTAIN, DAMASK AND
UPHOLSTERY WAREHOUSE,

220 W Baltimore n Charles.

Hart John, 456 W Baltimore
HOLLAND WM., 72 N Howard
MULLER LOUIS, 110 W Baltimore.
  (See advertisement interleaved.)
Rogge Charles M., 58 Pearl
Sinclair and Purvis, 5 N Charles
Sturges Mrs. Julia, 87 W Fayette

Upholsterers' Materials and Trimmings.

HOLLAND WM., 72 N Howard

Variety Stores.

(See also TRIMMINGS; also FANCY
GOODS.)

Adam Elizabeth, Lexington mkt
Addy James, 159 S Sharp
Allen Catharine, 209 S Charles
Blackburn Mrs. M., 80 Richmond
Bloham Mrs. A. D., 308 S Eutaw
Bohen R., 84 Fell's Point mkt
Bramburg Louisa. 114 Hollins
Brotzel John, 2 Columbia
Browning O. A., 63 North
Bunting Mary, 331 Light
Byrne Mrs. Mary, 247 N Gay
Carter L., 94 Columbia
Cauter Mrs. R., 206 Light
Cline Mrs. Mary, 162 Centre mkt
Cohen Simon, 185 N Gay and 90
  Fell's Point mkt
Coleman Martha, 498 W Pratt

Coleman Mrs. Mary N., 12 W Pratt
Condit H., Centre mkt
Crawford Elizabeth, 42 Hanover
Crow G., 78 Centre mkt
Daily Mrs. Catharine, 183 S Caroline
Dannun E., Hollins mkt
Deea Morris, 58 Harrison
Dennis A., 333 S Charles
Dexter Adam, 520 N Gay
Docktermann Conrad, 203 Light
Egan Henry, 171 Centre mkt
Evereard Mrs. Jane, Lexington mkt
Everett Jane, 79 Centre mkt
Eytle Jacob, 26 Leadenhall
Felt Charles, 110 S Howard
Ford John D., 191 N Gay
Franck John, 352 Light
FULLER MISS E., 157 N Gay
Gill Mrs. Elizabeth R., 455 N Gay
Greff Cath., 141 Centre mkt
Gregory Mrs. M., 119 Gough
Gregory Thomas, 14 Henrietta
Grim Amelia, 267 Hanover
Grosz Catharine, 303 S Bond
Grotjalm H., 417 W Baltimore
Hammann Mrs. E., 240 Canton av
Harettner Jacob, 132 Columbia
Heff Frederick, Fell's Point mkt
Hexter Geo., 225 Eastern av
Hodg Mrs. Sarah, 774 W Baltimore
Hoffmann Henry, 48 Hollins mkt
Hollingsworth Francis A., 215 E
  Lombard
Holsten A., 687 W Baltimore
Hooker Catharine, Bell Air mkt
Hudersfield Caroline, 70 Fell's Point
  mkt
Hushbach A., 7 S Poppleton
Hynds Mary C., 222 Columbia
Johns Mrs. Henrietta, 311 Alice
  Anna
Johnson Joseph, 749 W Baltimore
Johnson Sarah, 67 Fell's Point mkt
Jones Wm., 108 N Calvert
Jordan Francis, 94 W Pratt
Kelly B., 161 Centre mkt
Kelly John, 33 S Schroeder
Kelly Mrs. Julia, 428 W Baltimore

18*

VEN

Kerker Henry, Fell's Point mkt
Kolb Jacob, 246 Canton av
KREISEL FRED., 261 N Gay
Levy Joseph, 138 Light st whf
Lloyd Joseph, 227 Light
Lohmeyer Mrs. E., 612 W· Baltimore
McDermutt Miss Mary E., 341 N Gay
McKinly Margaret, 601 W Lombard
Maher Conrad, 30 Cross
Mariner T. P., 5 W Falls av
Mercer C., 70 S Eutaw
Meurer E. N., 254 Canton av
Mitchell Mrs. Mary, 35 W Lombard
Murray Lucy A., 391 N Gay
Nahring Mrs. Caroline, 181 S Caroline
O'Neal Thomas, 178 S Howard
Pentner Catharine, Fell's Point mkt
Perrine Achsah, 63 Columbia
Pusey Mrs. Maria, 874 W Baltimore
Quatmann Constance, 240 Canton av
Radicke L. M., 785 W Baltimore
Remare Mrs. E., 12 New
Rerbert Mary, 837 W Baltimore
Rewlen Sophia, 118 Colombia
Rider Conrad, 12 E Monument
Roach Mary, 37 W Lombard
Robert Mrs. Sarah, 225 Hollins
Rogers Henry, 16 S Fremont
Rolman Mary, 156 Centre mkt
Ross Thos., 67 Camden
Roth F. W., 251 S Howard
Rousclat John, 739 W Baltimore
Schmitt Valentine, 174 Lexington
Schminke Ann, 395 W Baltimore
Seabolde Louis, 313 Light
Shultz A., 124 Hollins
Sieblie Mary, Centre mkt
Sloan Mrs. M., 178 Orleans
Slide Wm., 120 S Howard
Smith George H., 60 Thames
Spence John, 127 Gough
Spencer John M., 478 W Baltimore
Stansbury R., 206 Mulberry
Steel Mary Ann, 8 W Lombard
Stier Amelia, 29 Hollins mkt
Sullivan Mrs. M., 100 Richmond

Tannatz Mrs. J., 77 Richmond
Taylor H., 787 W Baltimore
Torney John H., 192 W Pratt
Trow Mary Ann, Bell Air mkt
Uneke Peter, 72 Warner
Valient Mrs. J. A., 364 N Gay
Vassal Henry, 75 Fell's Point mkt
Vihmayer D., 12 New
Viper Elizabeth, Lexington mkt
Wall George, 98 N Howard
Wankell Mrs. Maria, Lexington mkt
Wesse Henry, 266 Canton av
Whitebread A., 48 Centre mkt, and Bell Air mkt
Williams Mary, 67 Hanover
Wood Thomas H., 355 Light
Wren Henry, Bell Air mkt

Varnish Makers.

DAVISON WILLIAM & CO.,

104 Lombard,

Manufacturers of

Chemicals, Varnishes, Paints, White Lead, &c.

MEYER AUG. G., 100 W Lombard
POPPLEIN G. & N., JR., 50 South. (See advertisement.)
RICHARDSON & CO., 26 S Calvert c Mercer. (See advertisement op Oils.)
SMITH C. HART, Agent for Geo. S. Page & Brother, 111 Smith's whf. (See advertisement interleaved.)

Venetian Blinds.

(*See also* SASHES, DOORS, and BLINDS.)

Dieter & Johnson, 28 N Howard
MULLER LOUIS, 110 W Baltimore. (See advertisement op Upholsterers.)
Yost John, 486 W Baltimore

*Vermin Exterminator.

Edwards Thomas, 101 N Eutaw

Veterinary Surgeons.

Thorne John, 144 N Front

Vinegar Manufacturers.

Dorsey S. H., 9 President
Elmer Louis, 2 O'Donnell's whf
Jacobs George, 117 Britton

L'ALLEMAND'S CHAS.,

DEPOT OF

Clarified Cider Pickling,

AND

Triple Strong Wine Vinegar,

OR

SPIRITS OF VINEGAR,

Warranted to be perfectly free of deleterious or injurious substances.

62 South Gay, near Pratt, up stairs.

Matthews Joshua, 107 McElderry's whf

Wagon Makers.

White & Albaugh, 106 Penn. av

Watch Case Maker.

VAN TROMP J., 19 Light c Mercer, WATCH CASE MAKER. Particular attention given to repairing.

Watches, Importers of.

JOSEPH I., 44 W Baltimore
Koch Wm., 209 W Baltimore

MAY HENRY,

127 W Baltimore n South,

IMPORTER OF

WATCHES & JEWELRY,

WATCH MATERIALS, GLASSES, AND FANCY GOODS.

WEBB GEO. W., S E c Baltimore and Light

Watches and Jewelry, Importers and Dealers in.

Akers Edward, 65 S Charles
BISSING W. F., 96 W Baltimore
BLAKE CHARLES, 217 W Baltimore n Charles, IMPORTER and DEALER IN FINE WATCHES, JEWELRY, SILVER WARE, &c.
Blum Wm., 529 W Baltimore
Brown Robert, 158 W Baltimore
Brown Thomas J., 90 W Baltimore
Brown Wm. & Co., 227 W Baltimore
CANFIELD, BROTHER & CO., 229 W Baltimore c Charles. (See advertisement.)
Castleburg J., 126 N Gay
Clark Gabriel D., Calvert c Water
Cohen & Lyon, 70 W Baltimore
Conner Mrs. E., 46 W Baltimore
Cronhardt Chas., 88 and 206 N Gay
Drummond Levin J., 31 W Pratt
Fasbender Marion J., 255 W Pratt
Geary & Weale, 177 W Baltimore
Gehring J. G., 194 N Gay
Gould James, 169 W Baltimore
HOFFMEISTER JOHN, 78 N Pearl
JATHO HENRY, Baltimore c High
Joseph I., 44 W Baltimore
Justis W. S., 102 W Pratt

JANOWITZ S.,

(late with Canfield Bro. & Co.,)

Practical Watchmaker

And Dealer in

Watches, Clocks, Jewelry, Silver and Plated Ware.

137 W Baltimore n Calvert.

WATCHES—SPECIALITY. Practical experience in the best establishments in Europe enables me to WARRANT ALL WATCHES SOLD OR REPAIRED.

KAEMPFF G. A., 248 Light
KAYSER ALEX., 42 Hanover, JEWELLER AND WATCHMAKER.
Koch Wm.. 209 W Baltimore
Larmour & Co., 10 Light
Lemkul Charles, 419 W Baltimore
Lewitoch Jacob, 16 W Pratt
Lewyt S. H., 45 N Front
Macke J. H., 251 W Pratt
MAY HENRY, 127 W Baltimore
Messer John H., 651 W Baltimore
MUELLER JOHN G., 247 Canton av bet Bond and Broadway, LEVER WATCH MAKER AND JEWELLER.
Myers Charles H., 438 W Baltimore
Nicklas John, 393 W Baltimore
Ostendorf J. A., 13 Pennsylvania av
Peithmann C. D., 30 W Pratt
Pepar C. H., 814 W Baltimore
PLUMMER J. F., 87 N Gay, WATCHMAKER & JEWELLER.
Pohlmann Daniel, 676 W Baltimore
Rodberg S. I., 120 N Gay
SAVILLE JAMES H., 110½ W Baltimore
Schofield Wm., 604 W Baltimore
Seile S. B., 82 N Gay
Spear Alexander L., 47 W Baltimore
Tschudy J., 235 Light

Uhl Philip, 35 S Paca
Walter Joseph M., 58 N Howard
Watlenscheidt A., 475 W Baltimore
WEBB GEO. W., S E c Baltimore and Light, GOLDSMITH AND JEWELLER, IMPORTER AND DEALER IN FINE WATCHES, RICH JEWELRY, SILVER AND PLATED WARE. Hair braiding in all its varieties. Every attention paid to neatness and durability in the repair and manufacture of Jewelry. Orders attended to with despatch.
Wellmarshausen F., 54 N Paca
WINDSOR G. S. & CO., 174 W Pratt
Wiener A., 49 N Eutaw
Woodcock Wm., 187 W Pratt
Wynn J. Robert, 282 W Baltimore

Watch Makers.

Holloway Robt., 118 N High
JANOWITZ S., 137 W Baltimore. (See card under Watches and Jewelry.)
JEANNERET Z., 209 W Baltimore (up stairs), Swiss Watchmaker. Chronometers, Watches, Clocks, and Musical Boxes of every description, carefully repaired and warranted.
Justis W. S., 102 W Pratt
Juzek T., 422 W Lombard
KIEL JOHN H., 25 E Baltimore
Nicklas C., 470 W Baltimore
Owens Francis, 103 Britton
Price M. H., 56 S Calvert
Rapin G., 169 E Baltimore
Rieman A. H., 161 E Baltimore
Seurll Henry, 7 St Paul
Steibel George H., 227 W Pratt
Woestman Frank 127 W Baltimore
Wynn C., 228 W Pratt

Watch Tools and Materials.

MAY HENRY, 127 W Baltimore

Weighers.

Andrew Charles & Co., 5 Spear's whf
Judah David, 61 S Gay
Merceret Louis, 79 Smith's whf
Morton G. C., jr., 63 S Gay
Seth W. G. & Son, Corn Exchange, Wood st

Wharfinger.

Seddon George, 128 Dugan's whf, (State)
Taylor Jacob H., 134 Dugan's whf

Wheelwrights.

(*See also* CARRIAGE AND COACH MAKERS; *also* WAGON MAKERS; *also* BLACKSMITHS.)

Breitschwerd C., 247 Alice Anna
Carrish Charles & Co., 25 Leaden-hall
Eilbacher John V., 16 Lee
Eisman E., 39 S Oregon
Fields W. H., 138 S Fremont
Frederick John, 404 Canton av
Fuller Philip, 12 E Falls av
Good & McCall, 17 Concord
Henry Charles, 3 Chesnut
Hinzlemann Matthew, Ridgely c Sterritt
Marsh Philip, York
Mooz John, 283 Washington
Ritter John, 212 and 214 Henrietta
Roth John, 395 S Charles
Smith James, 41 S Caroline
SMITH J. A., 182 Columbia
Thompson Joseph, 27 Centre
Timmerman Henry, 509 Light
Weaver Jacob, 23 Balderston
Wickes Geo. W., 1 and 3 E Pratt

Whip Makers.

BECK FREDERICK, 121 W Baltimore
BEEHLER FRANCIS, 235 W Baltimore

White Lead Manufacturers.

DAVISON WILLIAM & CO.,

104 W Lombard,

Manufacturers of

Chemicals, Varnishes. White Lead, Paints, &c.

Holthaus & Bro., Broadway c Thames
MEYER AUGUST G., MANUFAC-TURER OF WHITE LEAD PAINTS, VARNISHES, LAMP BLACK, SALTPETRE, &c., 100 W Lombard.
POPPLEIN G. & N. JR., 50 North. (See advertisement.)

White Washers.

Hall & Loney, 248 E Lombard
Heller F., 8 New
Johnson Horace, 49 Dover
Rockel H., 18 New Church

Wig and Toupee Makers.

(*See also* HAIR DRESSERS.)

Croyeau Augustin, 171 W Baltimore
Deville & Bourguet, 141 W Baltimore

Window Shades.

HOWELL & BROTHERS, 260 W Baltimore
Michael & Brother, 122 W Baltimore
MULLER LOUIS, 110 W Baltimore. (See advertisement op Upholsterers.)

Wines and Liquors—Importers of.

(See also WINES AND LIQUORS, WHOLESALE.)

BARTH & EDMEADES,

22 S. Calvert, late 21 South,

IMPORTERS OF

Brandies, Gin, Scotch Whiskey, Wines, &c. Pure Rye and Bourbon Whiskey of Celebrated Brands, Choice and Old, on Commission, always in store.

BIGGAR JNO. & CO., 2 Exchange pl

AUGUSTUS BLOCK,

Importer of

WINES, LIQUORS, CIGARS, AND DEALER IN GERMAN PRODUCE, FRENCH MUSTARD, AND CONTINENTAL SAUCE.

96 W. LOMBARD.

EDWARD BLOCK,

IMPORTER

AND

DEALER IN

WINES, LIQUORS, GERMAN and FRENCH PRODUCE.
Corks in all their varieties.

114 W. LOMBARD ST.

Boggs, Cottmann & Co., 46 W Lombard

Born Herman, Hanover c Camden

Boyle J. P. & Co., 4 Exchange pl

J. B. CHARRON & CO.,

Cor. Hanover and Lombard, Balt.,

IMPORTERS

OF

Wines, Brandies, Liquors, and Havana Cigars. Sole agent in Baltimore & Washington for E. Clicquot's Champagne.

C. G. DE GARMENDIA,

18 COMMERCE,

COMMISSION MERCHANT,

AND

IMPORTER OF

Wines, Brandies and Havana Cigars, Cordials, Olive Oil, &c., &c., Sole agent for the Celebrated Chas. Farre Champagne.

DE LA MAR C. M. & CO., 96 W Lombard, Wholesale Dealers in Foreign and Domestic Groceries of every description, Choice Fruits, Wines, Champagnes, Cigars, Preserves, Fancy Goods, &c.

DOLIVEYRA, PERIDO & CO., 6
Water three doors from South,
Importers of B R A N D I E S,
WINES, GINS and SCOTCH
WHISKEY, also SCOTCH AND
ENGLISH ALE AND PORTER AND
HAVANA CIGARS.
EIGHLBERGER OTHO W., 1 S
Howard
Ferry J. & Co., 51 Light
GARDNER F., 8 N High, Importer
of Rhine Wine

JAS. HAZLITT & CO.,

IMPORTERS OF

BRANDIES, GINS, WHIS-KEYS, WINES, &c.

39 and 41 S. Gay Street,

BALTIMORE.

J. H. & Co. are sole proprietors
of various brands of choice Old
Monongahela Rye Whiskeys.

HEIM, NICODEMUS & CO., 383
W Baltimore, IMPORTERS AND
DEALERS IN FOREIGN and DO-
MESTIC LIQUORS.
Hollins George, 14 N Charles
HOUSE SAMUEL A., 94 Light st
whf, Importer and Dealer in
Whiskeys, Brandies, Wines, Gins,
Cigars, &c.
KEENE E. A. & CO., 59½ S Charles,
IMPORTERS OF WINES, LIQUORS
AND CIGARS, also dealers in
OLD RYE and MONONGAHELA
WHISKEYS, and COMMISSION
MERCHANTS.

PH. HUNCKEL,

24 S. CHARLES,

Bet. German and Lombard,

Importer of

WINES, LIQUORS, AND CIGARS,
COGNAC BRANDIES, HOLLAND GIN,
OLD RYE AND BOURBON WHIS-
KEYS, CHAMPAGNE, C L A R E T,
HOCK, PORT AND M A D E I R A
WINES.

KOEHLER H. & CO., 128 W Lom-
bard, IMPORTERS OF WINES,
LIQUORS and CIGARS, and
COMMISSION MERCHANTS.
KRAUS R. & CO., 63 S Calvert and
38 Cheapside, IMPORTERS OF
WINES, LIQUORS and CIGARS.

HENRY S. LANKFORD,

61 S. Calvert, and 36 Cheapside,

BALTIMORE.

Importer and Dealer in

BRANDIES, WINES, GINS, CIGARS, AND SCOTCH AND IRISH MALT WHIS-KEYS, FINE OLD MONON-GAHELA, RYE AND BOUR-BON WHISKEYS, AND DO-MESTIC LIQUORS OF ALL KINDS.

Constantly on hand, a full and com-
plete assortment of liquors of
every description.

LINDEMAN E. C. & CO., 59 S
Charles
Long Lewis J., 248 N Gay

MARTIN WM. R. & CO., 72 S Calvert, Importers and Dealers in WINES, LIQUORS, and GENERAL COMMISSION MERCHANTS.

MYERS CHAS. H. & BRO., 72 Exchange pl

NOEDEL & WILHELMY,

379 W. Baltimore, bet. Eutaw and Paca,

IMPORTERS AND DEALERS

IN

WINES, LIQUORS, GERMAN AND FRENCH PRODUCE.

NORDLINGER & CO., 102 W Lombard, IMPORTERS OF FOREIGN PRODUCE, BRANDIES, WINES, GINS, CIGARS, &c. I. Nordlinger, E. Eising.

Pollatsek Rudolph, 134 W Lombard

Ridgely David, N E c Pratt and Howard

ROCHE & CO., 373 W Baltimore op Eutaw House, IMPORTERS OF WINES, BRANDIES, GINS, &c., and DEALERS IN ALL KINDS OF DOMESTIC LIQUORS.

Ross Chas. H. & Co., 9 Commerce

Schlott & Petzold, 124 W Lombard

Schneider M. & Co., 46 S-Howard

SENFT HENRY, Paca c Baltimore, Importer and Wholesale dealer in Rhine Wine.

Shields Thomas & Co., 145 N Howard

Sloan & Calwell, 17 & 19 Cheapside

THOMPSON THOMAS, 29 S Gay. (See advertisement.)

THOMPSON WM., 21 South, Importer of Liquors

Thomsen Laurence & Co., 64 Exchange pl

SIERNAN P. & SON, 12 N Charles

ULMAN & CO., 48 W Lombard and 5 N Gay, IMPORTERS OF BRANDIES, WINES, GINS, AND DISTILLERS OF WHISKEYS, FRUIT BRANDIES AND BITTERS.

VOCKEY THEODORE, 132 W Lombard, IMPORTER OF WINES, BRANDIES, GINS, AND DEALER IN DOMESTIC WHISKEY.

VONEIFF G. L.,

Importer and Dealer in

WINES, LIQUORS,

German and French Produce.

444 W Baltimore bet Pine & Pearl.

Walters W. T. & Co., 68 Exchange pl

Wilson John E., agt., N W c Howard and Camden

Zuckschwerdt C & Co., 116 N Howard

Wines and Liquors, Retail.

(*See also* HOTELS; *also* RESTAURANTS; *also* TAVERNS; *also* LAGER BEER SALOONS.)

Ahrling Henry, 72 Buchanan's whf

Anderson T. M., 152 N Calvert

Bell Ellen, 152 S Eutaw

Bodenschatz John, 44 Camden

Brashear George, North c Madison

Bredkempt H., Hamburg c Sharp

Brooks & Turner, North c Fayette

Burke Thomas, 94 W Falls av

Burns Henry, 190 W Falls av

Cadwalader George, 12 Concord

Cape John C., North c Eagen

114 S Howard
159 N Gay
9 S Bond
North
Neighbor
0 President
L, c East and

cord
Falls av
42 N Eutaw
p, 228 Alice Anna
amden
108 Dugan's whf
'atterson
., 22 Concord
'8 Light
North
gan's whf
0 Block
an, Light c Wer-

N Calvert
'ark
arles c Lee
10 Light
H., 5 Saratoga
M F., 188 Pearl
Buren
1 N Eutaw
300 Montgomery
6 Dugan's whf
0 Light st whf ·
gan's whf
ger
4 Dugan's whf
7 Harrison
nion Dock
hard
t c Bath
n, 138 Columbia
8 N Howard
North
tre mkt
bames
Union
bames
Forrest

Keeghan Peter, L Sharp c New Church
Kelly Wm., 82 W Falls av
Kernan Mrs. C., 173 Eager
Killman G, 21 Hughes
Kleibacker B., 100 Dugan's whf
Laake H. B., 275 S Ann
Lacy Solomon, Spring c Eastern av
Leurs John, 92 N Calvert
Lorenz George, 344 S Charles
McCarthy T., 207 W Lexington
McColgan N, 159 N Front
McDermott John, 5 Camden
McGowan John, 14 N Paca
McGrath James, 242 Canton av
McNally James, 100 St Paul
Manning Mrs. B., 51 Union
Mechaw Christian, 318 S Charles
Mercer James E., 208 Lee
Meyer Charles, 199 Montgomery
Miller Henry, 96 S Eutaw
Miller Nicholas, 1 Hughes
Moffatt Mrs. Louisa, 142 Hughes
Moog Jacob, 264 Hanover
Mulese O'Neil, 114 North
Mullen Henry, Falls av c Eastern av
Murray M., Concord c Lombard
Mussman John, 256 Montgomery
O'Brien John, 141 N Eutaw
O'Hara Peter, 10 St Paul
Oliver John, 64 Union
Oliver & Gamble, 726 W Baltimore
O'Neil Wm., 2 L Monument
Osings Henry, 54 Ross
Patterson John, 145 McElderry's whf
Pilkey J. P., 21½ Ensor
Perver James & Son, 119 W Lombard
Pritchett James, 204 Light
REINHARDT C. F., 165 E Baltimore, bet Eden and Central av, Dealer in Imported and Domestic WINES, LIQUORS, CORDIALS, and Syrups of all kinds of Fruit.
Rider Henry, 376 Osten
Rolker Herman H., 1 Camden
Russell Patrick, 98 Holiday
SCHRODER A. J., 211 Gough

Schultz Henry, 4 S Paca
Schumacher C. H., 69 Camden
Schutze Charles, 66 Thames
Seipp Mrs., 148 Light st whf
Senft Henry, Paca c Baltimore, Importer of Rhine Wine
Sesson Margaret, 141 Columbia
Shiedy Thomas, 2 S Paca
Shehan Edward, 166 W Falls av
Siebert Charles F., 14 E Lombard
SPITZ H. P., COMMISSION MERCHANT, Importer and Dealer in Foreign and Domestic LIQUORS, WINES, and CIGARS, 212 W Lexington, bet Green and Paca. Pure old Rye Whiskey for medicinal purposes always on hand.
STEIN HENRY, 206 Hollins
Stornoni G., 108 Light st whf
Stratmyer Fred'k, Henry & Hughes
Stumpf Frederick, Holland c Eager
Sullivan D., 115 North
Tate James T., 2 North
THEILE GEORGE, 22 Patterson
Thrush Geo. R., 19 W Pratt
Torberg John, Chesnut c Front
Tresgel C., 349 Canton av
Vendrehle J. H., 110 Dugan's whf
Vesey J. P., 117 McElderry's whf
Volk P., 496 W Lombard
WALDNER FRANCIS, N W c North and Saratoga
Walker George, 52 Union
WALLIS EDWARD, 89 North
Warnefld J., 152 Light st whf
Weitsell Henry, 82 Lancaster
Welsh John, 36 Block
Welter Geo. H., 40 E Pratt
Wicks Mrs. E., 55 Union
Wielage Mrs. Catharine, 97 Conway
WILLIAMS J. C., 202 Light
Young C. J., 4 S Gay
Zurliene Henry, 148 S Eutaw

Wines and Liquors, Wholesale.

ALVATER JOHN, 112 Central av.
(Liquor Refiner.)

BARTH & EDMEADES, 22 S Calvert
Buckler & Shipley, 85 and 87 S Charles
CLABAUGH G. W., 372 W Baltimore
Cotter & Nunan, 8 W Pratt
Dickey Charles E. & Co., 108 N Howard
DINSMORE & KILE, 156 Pratt st whf
Ellis & Cairns, 14 S Gay
Flack's Thomas J. Sons, c Bowly's whf and Guilford
FOLEY & COOK, 144 Franklin
FREELAND, HALL & CO., 143 W Pratt, dealers in Wines and Liquors and Wholesale Grocers
GOODE WILLIAM F., 188 Pearl, importer of Brandies, Gins, Scotch Whiskeys, Wines &c., Whiskeys on consignment from the most celebrated distillers.
Griffith S. C., 57 S Calvert
HEIM, NICODEMUS & CO., 383 W Baltimore
HOMRIGHAUSEN GEORGE, 39 Brown
HUNCKEL PH., 24 S Charles
Keys James N. & Son, 93 Franklin
Koons T. H. & Co., 142 Franklin
McCalgan Charles, 8 Saratoga
McDONNELL JAMES, 47 Calvert and 47 Cheapside, COMMISSION MERCHANT IN FOREIGN AND DOMESTIC LIQUORS, BEST BRANDS of OLD RYE AND MALT WHISKEYS.
NOEDEL & WILHELMY, 379 W Baltimore
NORRIS, CALWELL & CO., 322 W Baltimore and 213 Pennsylvania av
Ridgeley David, N E c Pratt and Howard
ROCHE & CO., 373 W Baltimore
SAUERBERG J. D. & CO., 21 & 23 Light c Mercer, IMPORTERS OF WINES, BRANDIES, GINS &c.,

dealers in Old Rye, Bourbon and Monongahela Whiskeys, also in Fancy Brandies, Bitters, Cordials &c.

SLATER GEORGE, 10 and 12 Commerce

STUART J. D. & CO., 27 Cheapside GENERAL COMMISSION MERCHANTS, SOLE AGENTS for THOMAS MOORE'S COPPERDISTILLED PURE RYE WHISKEY.

TREGO, MORGAN & CO., 22 Commerce, Produce Commission Merchants and Dealers in Foreign and Domestic Liquors.

TUBMAN B. G. & CO., 102 Light st whf, Importers and Dealers in WHISKEYS, BRANDIES, WINES, GINS, CIGARS, &c. &c.

VONEIFF G. L., 444 W Baltimore

WILLIAMS J. C., Wholesale and Retail Dealer in FOREIGN AND DOMESTIC WINES AND LIQUORS, 202 Light

Wines and Liquors, Wholesale and Retail.

DOWNEY JOHN & SON, 133 Franklin

ECKELMANN H. S., 45 Marsh market space

GLONINGER J. R. & .CO., 7 N Charles

HENGST S. & R., N E c Franklin and Paca

Quinn P. M., c High and Hillen

Rost John, 196 Alice Anna

Tiernan P. & Son, 12 N Charles

Wire Cloth Manufacturers.

Fowler Francis, N W c Liberty and Fayette

Wire Workers.

Balderson H. & Son, 12 S Calvert

Wood Dealers.

Beuchamp John, Lee c William

CRUSSE JOHN JR., Boston c Leakin, Canton

Ehrman T. S., 258 Washington

FORSYTH W. H. & CO., 165 Light st whf

Giese J. Henry, 9 South

Houck A. V., 61½ N Eutaw

McCULLOUGH JOHN C., Fremont c Pratt (See advertisement.)

Meyer F. C., 304 S Caroline

Michael Wm. H., Union Dock

North John, 144 Light st whf

Roney P., Mill

Schaeffer John M., Caroline c Lancaster

Timanus John F., 65 Green

Wright Levin, 112 Light st whf

Wood and Willow Ware.

ATWOOD B., 62 S Calvert, Manufacturer and Dealer in BROOMS, BRUSHES, PAINTED BUCKETS, Wooden Ware, Oyster and Market Buckets, Mats, Matches, Twine, Rope, &c. &c.

BEEBE L M., 94 W Lombard bet Calvert and Exchange pl, Manufacturer and Wholesale dealer in WOODEN WARE, CORDAGE, BRUSHES, BROOMS, MATS, PAPER, SIEVES, TWINE, &c.

Boehm, Rice & Co., 32 S Calvert

CHIPMAN GEO.,

Wholesale Dealer in

Brooms, Painted Buckets, Cedar Ware, Baskets, Brushes,

Mats, Cordage, Twine, Wicks, Matches, Blacking, Willow Ware &c., and Manufacturers of Painted Buckets, Brooms, Cedar Ware, and Brushes, c Calvert and Lombard St., Baltimore.

JARDEN SAMUEL, 89 Hanover.
(See advertisement op Oil.)
JOHNS WM. H., 15 S Sharp, Brush
Manufacturer.
Kees Lawrence, 125 N High

LORD CHAS. W.,

Manufacturer and Wholesale
Dealer in

BROOMS, WOODEN WARE, CORD-AGE, MATCHES, &C.,

And Importer of

FANCY GOODS,

The largest stock and assortment in
the United States and at the lowest price, 88 and 90 W Lombard
St., Baltimore.

Magne H., 408 W Pratt
White Robert B., 162 W Lexington

Wool Dealers.

BAER LEWIS & BRO., 3 and 5
Camden
McKeldin Wm., 104 S Charles

Woollen Goods, Manufac-turers.

WETHERED BROS.,

Manufacturers of Fancy

Cassimeres, Doeskins, Mel-tons and Fulled Cloth,

20 GERMAN.

Yankee Notions.

(*See also* NOTIONS.)

DIETZ L. D., & CO., 308 W Baltimore.   (See advertisement inside
back cover.)

Yarns, Bats, Wicks.

CHASE WELLS & GEHRMANN,
6 S Howard.   (See advertisement
interleaved.)
DIETZ L. D. & CO., 308 W Baltimore.   (See advertisement inside
back cover.)
GARY JAS. S. & SON, Alberton
Mills, 24 German.

JOHNSON W. HENRY,
Dealer in

SEINE TWINE, COT-TON YARN, &C.,

66 S Calvert St., Baltimore, Md.

Gill Twine, Carpet Chain, Tie Yarn, Wicks,

Shoe Thread, Cotton Laps, Broom
and Bottling Twines, Cotton,
Russia and Manilla Cord-
age, Cedar Ware, Wil-
low Ware,
Brooms, Painted Buckets, Mats,
Blacking, Ink, Howard's Matches,
&c.
☞ Spinning Wheels made and repaired.   Seines knit and hung to
order.

SCHULTZ E. T., 4 S Howard n
Baltimore.   (See advertisement
interleaved.)

*Yeast Powders.

Auld H., 33 N Fremont

APPENDIX.

Compiled Expressly for Cross & Co.'s Baltimore City Business Directory.

CITY GOVERNMENT.

JOHN LEE CHAPMAN,	*Mayor.*
ALFRED MACE,	*Secretary to the Mayoralty.*
JOHN A. THOMPSON,	*Register.*
J. F. MEDLART,	*Deputy Register.*
H. W. HAYDEN,	*Clerk to Register.*
SAMUEL MACCUBBIN,	*Comptroller.*
J. R. BROMWELL,	*Clerk to Comptroller.*
JOHN L. THOMAS, JR.,	*City Counsellor.*
AUG. M. PRICE,	*City Collector.*

MEMBERS OF CITY COUNCIL.

FIRST BRANCH.

Stephen Whalen,	1st Ward.	S. F. Streeter,	11th Ward.
Fred. C. Meyer,	2d "	John T. Bishop,	12th "
Edw. S. Lamden,	3d "	Oliver Dennis,	13th "
Wm. McClymont,	4th "	John F. Towner,	14th "
James Young (Pres.),	5th "	T. H. Evans,	15th "
Jos. J. Robinson,	6th "	Oliver M. Disney,	16th "
Noah Gill,	7th "	Philip Kirkwood,	17th "
A. J. Burke,	8th "	Thomas W. Cromer,	18th "
John Dukehart,	9th "	Robt. M. Proud,	19th "
D. H. Hoopes,	10th "	Thos. H. Mules,	20th "

ANDREW J. BUNDEL,	*Chief Clerk.*
GEORGE W. BROOKS,	*Reading Clerk.*
JAMES MADDUX,	*Sergeant-at-Arms.*

19*

SECOND BRANCH.

	Wards.		Wards.
Dr. A. Schwartze,	1st & 2d	C. Sidney Norris,	11th & 12th
John G. Wilmot,	3d & 4th	Samuel Duer (Pres.),	13th & 14th
Geo. I. Kennard,	5th & 6th	John Barron,	15th & 16th
Wm. Brooks,	7th & 8th	Wm. Moody,	17th & 18th
Jas. H. Markland,	9th & 10th	Valentine Foreman,	19th & 20th

SAMUEL H. COCHRAN, *Clerk.*
GEORGE W. CUNNINGHAM, *Sergeant-at-Arms.*

WATER BOARD.

Office, 17 *North Street.*

SAMUEL HINES—*Registrar.*   JOHN LEE CHAPMAN—*Mayor, President.*
JAMES S. SUTER, *Engineer.*

TAX DEPARTMENT.

AUG. M. PRICE—*City Collector.*   SAMUEL GUEST—*Cashier.*

HEALTH DEPARTMENT.

SAMUEL T. KNIGHT, M. D., *Commissioner of Health.*
GERARD E. MORGAN, M. D., *Assistant Commissioner of Health.*
WM. E. CLENDINEN, M. D., *Physician to Marine Hospital.*

Vaccine Physicians.

	Wards.		Wards.
Geo. W. Fay, M. D.,	1st & 2d	John Dickson, M. D.,	11th & 12th
Jas. E. Healey, M. D.,	3d & 4th	J. P. Fleming, M. D.,	13th & 14th
S. F. Powell, M. D.,	5th & 6th	J. W. P. Bates, M. D.,	15th & 16th
Jos. D. Brooks, M. D.,	7th & 8th	John Neff, M. D.,	17th & 18th
T. F. Murdock, M.D.,	9th & 10th	E. R. Burnetson, M.D.,	19th & 20th

PORT WARDEN.

GEORGE J. LOANE—*Port Warden.*   EDWARD H. FOWLER—*Clerk.*

HARBOR MASTERS.

| Martin W. Mettee, | 1st District. | Capt. Wm. Zachary, | 3d District. |
| Thos. S. Lamdin, | 2d " | John Beard, | 4th " |

Edward Wilson, 5th District.

TIDE WATER CANAL OFFICE.

GEO. W. LEUFFER—*President.*   T. M. ABBETT—*Treasurer.*

COMMISSIONERS OF PUBLIC SCHOOLS.

Office, N. E. Corner of Holliday and Fayette Streets.

GEORGE N. EATON,   *President.*
JOHN N. M'JILTON,   *Treasurer.*
WILLIAM D. M'JILTON,   *Secretary.*

Wards.	Commissioners.	Residence, or Place of Business.
1.	Henry C. Larrabee,	316 E. Pratt, and c. Front and Plowman.
2.	Wm. H. Hebden,	151 and 178 S. Broadway.
3.	C. L. L. Leary,	39 S. Broadway, and Eastern Hall.
4.	Thomas I. Pitt,	High c. Pratt.
5.	John F. Plummer,	98 Aisquith, and 89 N. Gay.
6.	Jas. T. Randolph,	229 E. Baltimore c. Broadway.
7.	Samuel E. Wheeler,	190 Aisquith, and Aisquith c. Monument.
8.	Charles Farringer,	14 Constitution.
9.	Louis Muller,	110 W. Baltimore.
10.	Wm. Daniel,	67 W. Fayette, and 41 Sharp.
11.	George N. Eaton,	54 Mt. Vernon pl., and 13 S. Charles.
12.	F. A. Crook,	Madison av. c. Townsend.
13	James H. Cox,	58 N. Green.
14.	Dr. E. G. Waters,	21 Hollins.
15.	J. W. Loane,	89 Barre, and 2 Bowly's whf.
16.	Dr. A. W. Colburn,	166 S. Paca.
17.	Steptoe B. Taylor,	373 Light.
18.	E. R. Petherbridge,	Hollins c. Stricker.
19.	W. C. Arthur,	Lexington n. Mount.
20.	Richard Sewell,	247 Biddle.

LOCATION OF PUBLIC SCHOOLS.

Schools.	Location.	Principal.
Central High School,	NE c Fayette & Holliday,	Tho's D. Baird, Ph. D.
Eastern Fem. do do	NE c Aisquith and Mullikin,	Nathaniel H. Thayer, A. M.
Western do do do	Fayette west of Paca,	D. A. Hollingshead, A. M.
Floating School,	Ship Ontario, Harbor of Baltimore, n Drawb'ge,	George C. Hale.
Normal Class,	NWc Calvert & Saratoga,	W. R. Creery.
Male Grammar School No. 1,	NE c Fayette & Green,	M. A. Newell.
Female " No. 1,	" " ".	Henrietta C. Adams.
Male " No. 2,	SW c Broadway & Bank,	William Kerr.
Female " No. 2,	" "	Mary McDermott.
Male " No. 3,	Aisquith n Fayette,	George B. Loane.
Female " No. 3,	NE c Fayette & Front,	Margaret Snyder.
Male " No. 4,	NE c Hanover & Lee,	Henry Cragg.
Female " No. 4,	" " "	E. A. Cross.
Male " No. 5,	NW c Monum't&Forrest,	Andrew S. Kerr.
Female " No. 5,	" " "	Mary Rice.
Male " No. 6,	Ross n Biddle,	Thomas S. Bennett.
Female " No. 6,	" "	Eliza Adams.
Female " No. 7,	SE c Chesapeake & Hudson (Canton),	Rebecca E. Horton.
Male " No. 8,	NW c Fremont & Ridgely al	John Basil, jr.
Female " No. 8,	" " "	Adelaide L. Hall.
Male " No. 9,	NWc Calvert & Saratoga,	George S. Grape.
Female " No. 9,	" " "	Rachel Parker.
Male " No. 10,	SE c William & Warren,	A. Z. Hartman.
Female " No. 10,	" " "	Mary M. Wilson.
Male " No. 11,	NW c Bond & Jefferson,	Robert H. Peregoy.
Female " No. 11,	" " "	Nancy W. Smith
Male " No. 12,	Barre west of Eutaw,	Wm. R. Creery.
Female " No. 12,	" " "	Anna P. Wise.
Female " No. 13,	NE c Aisquith and Mullikin,	Margaret Poole.
Male " No. 14,	NE c Gough and Stiles,	Wm. A Rippey.
Female " No. 14,	" " "	S. L. Bassford.
Male " No. 15,	SE c Schroeder & Wagon al,	J. F. Arthur.
Female " No. 15,	" " "	Mary W. Storke.
Male Primary School, No. 1,	NE c Fayette & Green,	Catharine E. Small.

Schools.			Location.	Principal.
Fem. Primary, No.		1,	NE c Fayette & Green,	Elizabeth Kirk.
Male	"	No. 2,	Stiles n High,	Mary A. Slicer.
Female	"	No. 2,	" "	Ann J. Groscup.
Male	"	No. 3,	NE c Gough and Wolf,	Georgia A. Duvall.
Female	"	No. 3,	" " "	Rebecca A. Davington.
Male	"	No. 4,	Hill bet Hanover and Sharp,	Sallie A. E. Pattison.
Female	"	No. 4,	" " "	Mary H. Thomiz.
Male	"	No. 5,	Edward n Aisquith,	Amanda Harker.
Male	"	No. 6,	Ann n Canton av,	Elizabeth A. Abbot.
Female	"	No. 6,	" "	Agnes P. Folson.
Male	"	No. 7,	Mullikin n Aisquith,	Priscilla Owens.
Female	"	No. 7,	" " "	J. E. Hughes.
Male	"	No. 8,	Caroline n Lombard,	Sarah E. Smith.
Female	"	No. 8,	" " "	Ann E. Driscoll.
Male	"	No. 9,	NW c Calvert & Saratoga,	Marietta A. Barrickman.
Female	"	No. 9,	NE c Fayette and Front,	Olivia A. Shaw.
Male	"	No. 10,	Hollins n Schroeder,	M. L. Slapley.
Female	"	No. 10,	" " "	Elizabeth P. Martin.
Male	"	No. 11,	NE c Schroeder & Pierce,	M. C. Mullikin.
Female	"	No. 11,	" " "	Jane H. Allen.
Male	"	No. 12,	Barre n Eutaw,	Laura Wamalung.
Female	"	No. 12,	" "	Laura Brian.
Male	"	No. 13,	Jefferson n Caroline,	Sarah E. Day.
Female	"	No. 13,	" "	Mary A. Joiee.
Male	"	No. 14,	Eutaw n Preston,	Susan Crawford.
Female	"	No. 14,	" "	Emily Ellis.
Male	"	No. 15,	SE c Republican & Wagon al,	Susan Helsby.
Female	"	No. 15,	SE c Schroeder and Wagon al,	Annie J. Whitworth.
Male	"	No. 16,	Hilton n High,	Mary Jones.
Female	"	No. 16,	" "	Mary Harma.
Male	"	No. 17,	SW c Light & Poulteney,	Sarah A. Sewell.
Female	"	No 17,	" " "	E. Virginia Addison.
Male	"	No. 18,	Walsh n Lanvale	Annie Frederick.
Female	"	No. 18,	" "	Isabella Fall.
Male	"	No. 19,	Frederick n Lombard,	Susanna F. Cary.
Female	"	No. 19,	" " "	Esther Wheeler.
Male	"	No. 20,	NW c Caroline and Holland,	Laura A. Ball.
Female	"	No. 20,	" " "	Rosalie Barrett.
Female	"	No. 21,	SE c Green & Lombard,	Maria E. Walter.
Female	"	No. 22,	Scott c St Peter's,	Matil'a B. Richardson.
Female	"	No. 23,	Bond c Chew,	Mary A. Reilly.
Female	"	No. 24,	Hudson c Chesapeake (Canton),	Margaret A. Hand.

Schools.		Location.	Principal.
Fem. Primary,	No. 25,	Eastern av n High,	Caroline Ing.
Female "	No. 26,	Harford av n John,	Mary S. Salter.
Female "	No. 27,	Locust Point,	Anna M. Smith.
Female "	No. 28,	East n Douglass,	Anne M. German.
Female "	No. 29,	Gilmore and Baltimore,	Elizabeth J. Burns.
Female "	No. 30,	Lombard c Washington,	Elizabeth A. Colston.

Evening Schools.

No. 3,	Aisquith n Fayette,	Wm. Elliott.
No. 4,	Hanover c Lee,	Henry Craig.

Music Teachers.

S. S. Root, Eastern District.
A. J. Cleaveland, Western District.

FIRE DEPARTMENT.
BOARD OF FIRE COMMISSIONERS.
Office, New City Hall.

JOHN T. MORRIS, *President;* WILLIAM H. STRAN, CHARLES W. WALKER, ROBERT TYSON, JOHN H. BAYLIES.
> CHARLES T. HOLLOWAY, *Chief Engineer.*
> JAMES L. STEWART AND J. WESLEY SHAW, *Assistant Engineers.*
> HENRY FULTON, *Clerk to Fire Commissioners.*
> F. H. B. BOYD, *Fire Inspector.*

Engine Company No. 1.—Paca bet Fayette and Lexington ; George Keyser, *Foreman.*
Engine Company No. 2.—Barre bet Sharp and Hanover; N. B. Norris, Jr., *Foreman.*
Engine Company No. 3.—Lombard bet High and Exeter ; James H. Gravenstine, *Foreman.*
Engine Company No. 4.—North bet Fayette and Lexington ; George W. Fisher, *Foreman.*
Engine Company No. 5.—Ann bet Pratt and Gough ; Philip Sherwood, *Foreman.*
Engine Company No. 6.—Gay c Ensor ; Robert McCleary, *Foreman.*
Engine Company No. 7.—Orchard n Madison ; W. G. Gorsuch, *Foreman*
Hook and Ladder Company No. 1.—Harrison bet Fayette and Baltimore ; Wm. A. McGraw, *Foreman.*
Hook and Ladder Company No. 2.—Paca bet Fayette and Lexington ; George H. Houck, *Foreman.*
Hook and Ladder Company No. 3.—12 Harrison, Charles Holloway, *Foreman.*

Police and Fire Alarm Telegraph.

'D. Pinckney West, *Superintendent.*
George W. Key, Daniel W. Nules, Charles G. Boston, William Barrett, *Operators.*
James H. Hooper, *Lineman.*

The Bells will strike the Number of the Box thus :—
If the Alarm comes from Box 24, they will strike

2———4,   2———4,

If from 35, strike

3———5,   3———5, &c.

In cases of general alarm, requiring the services of the entire Department, the Bells will be rung INCESSANTLY in quick succession.

List of Telegraphic Fire Alarm Stations.

1. CENTRAL POLICE STATION, Holliday st.
2. Calvert and Lombard sts.
3. Baltimore and Hanover sts.
4. Pratt and Gay sts.
5. No. 1 Truck House, Harrison st.
6. Charles and Camden sts.
7. Howard and German sts.
8. Pratt st. Bridge.
9. Charles and Mulberry sts.
12. No. 3 Engine House, Lombard st.
13. No. 2 Engine House, Barre st.
14. No. 1 Engine House, Paca st.
15. No. 6 Engine House, Gay and Ensor sts.
16. Holland and Aisquith sts.
17. No. 7 Engine House, Eutaw and Ross sts.
18. WESTERN POLICE STATION, Green st.
19. Lombard and Penn sts.
21. Bank and Exeter sts.
23. William and Montgomery
24. Caroline and Lombard sts.
25. Bond and Jefferson sts.
26. Cross st. Market.
27. EASTERN POLICE STATION, Bank st.
28. St. Paul and Fayette sts.
31. Fremont and Columbia sts.
32. Franklin and Chatsworth sts.
34. Belair and Central avenues.
35. Richmond Market House.
36. SOUTHERN POLICE STATION.
37. Charles and Eager sts.
38. North and Monument sts.
41. Harford Avenue and Eager st.
42. Drawbridge.
43. Fremont and Lexington sts.
45. Pratt and Poppleton sts.
46. Front and Foundry sts.
49. Calverton road and Baltimore street.
51. No. 5 Engine House, Ann st.
52. Pennsylvania av and Dolphin st.
53. Baltimore and Republican sts.
54. Canton avenue and Chester st.
56. Pennsylvania avenue and Fremont st.
61. Saratoga and Schroeder sts.
62. Madison and Forrest sts.
63. Broadway and Thames st.
64. Lexington and Stricker sts.
71. Pratt and Eutaw sts.
72. Clay and Park sts.
73. Cathedral and Monument sts.
81. Eutaw place and Dolphin st.
82. Canton avenue and Caroline st.
83. Baltimore and Wolf sts.

POLICE DEPARTMENT.

Nicholas S. Wood, Samuel Hinds, *Police Commissioners.*
William S. Browning, *Secretary to Police Commissioners.*

Marshal's Office.

William A. Van Nostrand, *Marshal of Police.*
William B. Lyons, *Deputy Marshal of Police.*
John T. R. Joynes, *Secretary.*
Jesse Sumwalt, William Root, *Messengers.*
Detectives.—John S. Pontier, William P. Smith, Isadore Reynolds, Frank Gates, Geo. H. Houck.

Eastern District.

Bank Street, between Bond and Broadway.

Captain.—Thomas H. Carmichael,	No. 100 S. Hight st.
Lieutenants.—Edwin F. Morris,	Wolf st., 5 doors from Fayette.
John H. Lynch,	No. 97 N. Bond st.
Sergeants.—Thomas A. Waltham,	No. 210 E. Pratt st.
William J. Smith,	No. 162 S. Ann st.
John Cademore,	No. 171 S. Ann st.
William T. Taylor,	No. 125 Jefferson st.
James Love,	No. 327 Monument st.
Edward C. Ford,	No. 223 E. Orleans st.

Middle District.

Corner Saratoga and Holliday Streets.

Captain.—Joseph Mitchel,	No. 33 Constitution st.
Lieutenants.—Alexander Owens,	No. 348 N Gay st.
Solomon C. Wright,	No. 161 N. Caroline st.
Sergeants.—Joshua Robinson,	No. 119 E. Monument st.
Henry Mullen,	No. 207 N. Canal st.,
Horace R. Simpson,	No. 39 Orleans st.
Edward Hatton,	No. 219 Orleans st.
George D. Brooks,	No. 194 Aisquith st.
John Edelman,	No. 385 Harford avenue.

Southern District.

Corner Montgomery and Sharp Streets,

Captain.—John S. Manly.
Lieutenants.—John Pancoast,
　　　　Robert M. Chambers.
Sergeants.—Nicholas Pamphilion,
　　　　Thomas Shanks,
　　　　William Gardner,
　　　　Jesse L. Lippey,
　　　　George H. Cline,
　　　　George Short.

Western District.

Green Street, North of Baltimore.

Captain.—William M. Woods.
Lieutenants.—Robert D. Owen,
　　　　John H. Snavely.
Sergeants.—Charles C. Handy,
　　　　Washington A. Grubb,
　　　　Walter Stahl,
　　　　John Vansant,
　　　　Jesse H. Murray,
　　　　Arthur Walters.

CUSTOM HOUSE.

S E CORNER GAY AND LOMBARD STREETS.

Office Hours, from 9 till 2½ o'clock.

H. W. HOFFMAN, *Collector.*
F. S. Corkran, Naval Officer.
F. S. Evans, Dep. Naval Officer.
John F. McJilton, Surveyor.
Geo. W. McElroy, Auditor.
Wm. Smith, Gauger.
H. R. Reynolds, Sup. Warehouse.

WM. T VALLIANT, *Dep. Col.*
Jno. Meredith, Appraiser Gen.
J. F. Wagner and Wm. Nichols,
　Appraisers.
Henry McElderry, Weigher.
Wm. Counselman, Measurer.

POST OFFICE.

EXCHANGE BUILDING, CORNER GAY AND LOMBARD STS.

WM. H. PURNELL, *Postmaster.*　　　C. J. R. THORPE, *Ass't.*

The Office is open during the week—in winter, from 7½ A. M. to 9 P. M.;
in summer, from 7 A. M. to 9 P. M. On Sundays, from 9 till 10 A. M.
Stamps for prepayment of letters can be had at the Post Office.

20

COURTS.

UNITED STATES COURTS.

THE CIRCUIT COURT, *of the Fourth Circuit*, sits in the city of Baltimore on the first Monday in April and November.

DISTRICT COURT of the U. S. for Maryland District, sits in Baltimore 1st Tuesday in March, June, September, and December.

STATE COURTS.

COURT OF APPEALS, sits at Annapolis, on the first Monday in June and December.   Wm. A. Spencer, Clerk.

FIRST CIRCUIT.—The Circuit Court for St. Mary's County sits on the 3d Monday in March and 3d Monday in November.

Charles—1st Monday in May and December.

Prince George's—1st Monday in April and November.

SECOND CIRCUIT.—Anne Arundel—3d Monday in April and 4th Monday in October.

Calvert—2d Monday in May and October.

Howard—3d Monday in March and 1st Monday in September.

Montgomery—1st Monday in March and 2d Monday in November.

THIRD CIRCUIT.—Frederick—2d Monday in February and 3d Monday in October.

Carroll—1st Monday in April and September.

FOURTH CIRCUIT.—Washington—1st Monday in March, 4th Monday in July and November.

Alleghany—1st Monday in January, 2d Monday in April and October.

FIFTH CIRCUIT.—*Superior Court, Court of Common Pleas, and Criminal Court*, all sit on the 2d Monday in January, May, and September.

The Circuit Court for Baltimore City, sits on the 2d Monday in January, March, May, July, September, and November.

ORPHANS' COURT, *for Baltimore City*—Meets every day, except Sundays, at 11 o'clock, and closes at 1 P. M.   Isaac P. Cook, Register of Wills.

SIXTH CIRCUIT.—Cecil—2d Monday in February, 1st Monday in April, 3d Monday in July, 2d Monday in October.

Harford—4th Monday in February, 4th Monday in April, 1st Monday in August, and 2d Monday in November.

Baltimore County—1st Monday in March, 3d Monday in May, 4th Monday in August, 1st Monday in December, at Towsontown.

ORPHANS' COURT, *for Baltimore County*—Meets at Towsontown, 1st Tuesday in every month. James L. Ridgely, Register of Wills.

SEVENTH CIRCUIT.—Caroline—2d Monday in March and 1st Monday in October.

Kent—3d Monday in April and October.

Queen Anne's—1st Monday in May and November.

Talbot—3d Monday in May and November.

EIGHTH CIRCUIT.—Somerset—2d Monday in January and July, and 1st Monday in April and October.

Dorchester—4th Monday in January, July, and April, and 2d Monday in November.

Worcester—3d Monday in January, May, July, and October.

U. S. Clerk's Office of District and Circuit Courts.

Masonic Building, St. Paul Street.

Commissioner of Insolvent Debtors.

EDW. PALMER, Office, Record Building, St. Paul Street, basement.

United States Marshal.

WASHINGTON BONIFANT, corner of St. Paul Street and Court House Lane.

www.ingramcontent.com/pod-product-compliance
Lightning Source LLC
Chambersburg PA
CBHW020854270326
41928CB00006B/703